Also in the Variorum Collected Studies Series:

NELSON H. MINNICH
The Fifth Lateran Council (1512–17)

NELSON H. MINNICH
The Catholic Reformation: Council, Churchmen, Controversies

LOUIS-JACQUES BATAILLON
La prédication au XIIIe siècle en France et Italie

JEAN-PIERRE DEVROEY
Etudes sur le grand domain carolingien

MANUEL C. DÍAZ Y DÍAZ
Vie chrétienne et culture dans l'Espagne du VIIIe au Xe siècles

BENEDICTA WARD
Signs and Wonders: Saints Miracles and Prayer
from the 4th Century to the 14th

WILLIAM E. MONTER
Enforcing Morality in Early Modern Europe

BERNARD HAMILTON
Monastic Reform, Catharism and the Crusades

JEAN RICHARD
Croisades et Etats latins d'Orient

ALFRED SOMAN
Sorcellerie et justice criminelle:
Le parlement de Paris (16e–18e siècles)

PAUL GRENDLER
Culture and Censorship in Late Renaissance Italy and France

C.R. CHENEY
The English Church and its Laws, 12th–14th Centuries

C.R. CHENEY
The Papacy and England, 12th–14th Centuries

ANTOINE DONDAINE
Les hérésies et l'Inquisition, XIIe–XIIIe siècles

Religious Culture in the Sixteenth Century

For Mary

John W. O'Malley

Religious Culture in the Sixteenth Century

Preaching, Rhetoric, Spirituality, and Reform

VARIORUM

Published by VARIORUM
Ashgate Publishing Limited
Gower House, Croft Road,
Aldershot, Hampshire GU11 3HR
Great Britain

Ashgate Publishing Company
Old Post Road,
Brookfield, Vermont 05036
USA

ISBN 0-86078-369-3

A CIP catalogue record for this book is available from the British Library.

The paper used in this publication meets the minimum requirements of American National Standard for Information Sciences — Permanence of Paper for Printed Library Materials, ANSI Z39.48-1984.

Printed by Galliard (Printers) Ltd
Great Yarmouth, Norfolk
Great Britain

COLLECTED STUDIES SERIES CS404

CONTENTS

This volume contains x + 282 pages

PREFACE

This second collection of my articles in the *Variorum Collected Studies Series* takes up where *Rome and the Renaissance: Studies in Culture and Religion* left off. It reflects my interest in preaching and Renaissance rhetoric that was barely visible in *Rome and the Renaissance* and also reflects the preoccupation with the early Jesuits that has recently consumed most of my professional time and energy. But in a few themes continuity with the previous volume is strong—Erasmus, Aquinas in the Renaissance, the character of Renaissance Humanism, the problem of reform. Giles of Viterbo, the star of the earlier book, also makes an appearance here.

The deepest continuity lies, however, in what I see as the central issue that I have wrestled with over the past twenty-five years, the relationship between religion and culture. The issue is indicated in the title of both volumes and in some form surfaces in most of the articles.

The only article in the present collection that perhaps needs a word to justify its inclusion is the last one. It comes from that body of my writings that are to some extent tracts for the times, and it might therefore seem inappropriate in a strictly academic collection like this one. I include it for two reasons. Some of my colleagues in the historical profession have told me that, despite its ecclesiastical framework, the article taught them some things about an historical phenomenon they thought they had perfectly understood. Secondly, it is similar to the penultimate article in that it tries to construct more adequate categories for comprehending big historical realities, and the two are also related in other ways, as will be clear from reading them.

As I look over these pieces, I am of course reminded of all the people who have helped me along the way. I have tried to make appropriate acknowledgements in each of them, but there is no way to capture all those kindnesses that occur simply as part of our daily round as scholars and that make our enterprise possible and humane. I feel grateful—and much in debt. In quite specific ways, I am indebted to my two research assistants—Benjamin Westervelt, who obtained for me permission from publishers to reprint these articles, and Mary Frances Smith, who compiled the index.

Finally, I dedicate this book to my cousin Mary Burriss Yungkurth, who has helped me understand another kind of history, my own.

JOHN W. O'MALLEY

Weston School of Theology
Cambridge, Massachusetts
September 1992

ACKNOWLEDGEMENTS

Grateful acknowledgement is made to the following publishers, journals and editors, for kindly permitting the reproduction in this volume of articles originally published by them: the editors of *Rivista di Storia della Chiesa in Italia*, Rome (for study I); Analecta Augustiniana, Rome (II); the University of California Press, Berkeley, Calif. (III); the Centro di Studi Francescani, Assisi (IV); the editors of *Michigan Germanic Studies*, Ann Arbor, Mich. (V); Associated University Presses, New Jersey (VI); the editors of *Erasmus of Rotterdam Society Yearbook*, Fort Washington, Md. (VII); Duke University Press, Durham, N.C. (VIII); the Crossroad Publishing Company, New York (IX); the editors of the *Heythrop Journal*, London (X); the editors of *The Way*, London (XI); the editors of *The Catholic Historical Review*, Washington, D.C. (XII); the editors of *Theological Studies*, Cambridge, Mass. (XIII).

PUBLISHER'S NOTE

The articles in this volume, as in all others in the Collected Studies Series, have not been given a new, continuous pagination. In order to avoid confusion, and to facilitate their use where these same studies have been referred to elsewhere, the original pagination has been maintained wherever possible.

Each article has been given a Roman number in order of appearance, as listed in the Contents. This number is repeated on each page and quoted in the index entries.

THE FEAST OF THOMAS AQUINAS IN RENAISSANCE ROME A NEGLECTED DOCUMENT AND ITS IMPORT

Lorenzo Valla's panegyric of Saint Thomas Aquinas has been the object of a number of studies [1]. The oration, delivered at the Dominican church of S. Maria sopra Minerva in Rome on March 7, 1457, the year of Valla's death, brings into focus a number of the famous humanist's concerns. It indicates, moreover, the serious divergences between the renewal of theology advocated by Valla and the style of theology created by Aquinas and other scholastic authors. Studies of the oration have, for the most part, treated it under this aspect.

Relatively little attention has been paid to the context in which Valla delivered the oration. That is, little attention has been paid to the celebration at the Minerva and the general status of Aquinas in Renaissance Rome. Paul Oskar Kristeller was the first scholar to suggest that such an investigation might be fruitful and to supply some useful information with which to begin [2]. I have, meanwhile, touched upon the problem in two publications, but in neither instance

---

AFP = Archivum Fratrum Praedicatorum; *DBI* = Dizionario biografico degli Italiani; *RIS* = Rerum italicarum scriptores.

[1] The most thorough study is by S. I. CAMPOREALE, *Lorenzo Valla tra Medioevo e Rinascimento. Encomion s. Thomae - 1457*, « Memorie Domenicane », n.s. 7 (1976), p. 11-194. See also ID., *Umanesimo e teologia tra '400 e 500, ibid.*, n.s. 8-9 (1977-78), p. 411-36; ID., *Lorenzo Valla. Umanesimo e teologia*, Florence 1972, esp. p. 3-5, 141-42, 304-10; P. MESNARD, *Une application curieuse de l'humanisme critique à la théologie: l'Éloge de saint Thomas par Laurent Valla*, « Revue Thomiste », 55 (1955), p. 159-76; H. H. GRAY, *Valla's Encomium of St. Thomas Aquinas and the Humanist Conception of Christian Antiquity*, in *Essays in History and Literature Presented by Fellows of The Newberry Library to Stanley Pargellis*, ed. H. BLUM, Chicago 1965, p. 37-51; M. FOIS, *Il pensiero cristiano di Lorenzo Valla nel quadro storico-culturale del suo ambiente*, Rome 1969, p. 456-69, (Analecta Gregoriana, 174); G. DI NAPOLI, *Lorenzo Valla. Filosofia e religione nell'Umanesimo italiano*, Rome 1971, p. 110-22 (Uomini e dottrine, 17); H.-B. GERL, *Rhetorik als Philosophie. Lorenzo Valla*, Munich 1974, p. 115-16.

[2] P. O. KRISTELLER, *Le Thomisme et la pensée italienne de la Renaissance*, Paris 1967, esp. p. 72-79. This work has been translated into English, though without the Latin documents appended to the French edition: *Thomism and the Italian Thought of the Renaissance*, in *Medieval Aspects of Renaissance Learning*, ed. and trans. E. P. MAHONEY, Durham 1974, p. 29-91 (Duke Monographs in Medieval and Renaissance Studies, 1).

with the intention of dealing specifically with the fortune Thomas enjoyed in Rome during this period [3].

I recently came across a text, however, that until now has escaped the attention of scholars who have dealt with Valla. The text throws considerable light on his oration, but on many other topics as well, including the history of Thomism and of the papal liturgies. The text is a brief section of a long and neglected work by Paris de Grassis, the papal Master of Ceremonies from 1504 until his death in 1528. The work itself is a revision by de Grassis of the second book of the *Ceremonial* that Agostino Patrizi prepared for Pope Innocent VIII in 1488, the most important liturgical book produced at the papal court in the fifteenth century [4]. De Grassis entitles his own revision simply *Supplementum et additiones*, thereby accurately indicating his dependence upon Patrizi. Besides bringing Patrizi's text up to date in some particulars, de Grassis also supplemented it, as the title indicates, with some information on topics that Patrizi had failed to handle. One of these sections is entitled: « De missa et festo sancti Thomae de Aquino ». This is the section to which I wish to call attention and which I have transcribed as an appendix to this article.

Unlike the famous diary by de Grassis that survives in so many manuscript copies, the *Supplementum* exists in only a few versions. The Biblioteca Ambrosiana, Milan, contains the manuscript copy of Patrizi's *Ceremonial* to which de Grassis made his emendations and additions. In the Vatican Library there is a polished version in book hand [5]. This latter version, surely done under de Grassis'

---

[3] J. W. O'MALLEY, *Some Renaissance Panegyrics of Aquinas*, « Renaissance Quarterly », 27 (1974), p. 174-92, and *Praise and Blame in Renaissance Rome. Rhetoric, Doctrine, and Reform in the Sacred Orators of the Papal Court, ca. 1450-1521*, Durham 1979, passim (Duke Monographs in Medieval and Renaissance Studies, 3).

[4] On the *Ceremonial*, see J. NABUCO, *Le Cérémonial Apostolique avant Innocent VIII. Texte du Manuscrit Urbinate Latin 469 de la Bibliothèque Vaticane établi par Dom Filippo Tamburini*, Rome 1966, esp. p. 9*-38* (Biblioteca « Ephemerides Liturgicae », Sectio Historica, 30). Patrizi's text was published by C. MARCELLO, *Rituum eccelsiasticorum sive sacrarum cerimoniarum S. S. romanae ecclesiae libri tres*, Venice 1516. See also P. SALMON, *Les manuscrits liturgiques latins de la Bibliothèque Vaticane*. III. *Ordines romani pontificaux rituels cérémoniaux*, Città del Vaticano 1970 (Studi e Testi, 260), and the several works by M. DYKMANS, *Mabillon et les interpolations de son Ordo Romanus XIV*, « Gregorianum », 47 (1966), p. 316-42; ID., *Le cérémonial de Nicolas V*, « Revue d'Histoire Ecclésiastique », 63 (1968), p. 365-78, 785-825; ID., *Le cérémonial papal de la fin du Moyen Age à la Renaissance*. I. *Le cérémonial papal du XIIIe siècle*, Rome 1977 (Bibliothèque de l'Institut Belge de Rome, 24).

[5] Biblioteca Ambrosiana, cod. I 185 inf., and Biblioteca Vaticana, cod. Vat. lat. 5634bis. The Vatican manuscript was copied soon after de Grassis finished the original version, and the scribe seems to have been a certain Petrus Borgolochus Bononiensis, f. 103^r. I am indebted to Father Marc Dykmans of the

supervision, is the presentation copy for Cardinal Petrus Isvalies, as the dedicatory letter shows, May 18, 1505. It is from these versions that I have made my transcription. The variants between them, indicated in the transcription, are minor.

This section on Thomas Aquinas does two things that are important. First, it supplies some firm information that has been lacking until now. This information concerns the origin of the feast and the degree of solemnity it was accorded at the papal court. Secondly, it provides a foundation from which to view the more general problem of the cultural and theological importance of Aquinas in Rome during the Renaissance, 1447-1521.

The text itself is unprepossessing. After stating that Pope Nicholas V established that the feast be celebrated annually in the church of the Minerva and that it be observed as a holiday in the Apostolic Palace, it notes that the entire Sacred College habitually assisted at the Mass. A brief mention is then made of the role of the cardinal protector, Oliviero Carafa. Next are described certain provisions for the Mass itself (« Ordo missae »), celebrated at the main altar of the church. These rubrics indicate the participation of the papal choir, the singing of the Creed, a sermon, a plenary indulgence, and similar matters. The text then describes how the cardinals were invited after the Mass to visit the chapel in the Minerva dedicated to the Virgin and to Saint Thomas. Typically detailed rubrics about the order of precedence among the cardinals are here spelled out. Finally, the circumstances under which the feast was to be transferred to another day are mentioned; some examples from the recent past of such transferals are given. The text contains other details, of course, and attention will be called to some of them further on. But these are the major points covered.

Only through a careful and systematic exegesis can the import of this seemingly routine document be manifested. The first information the text offers is that the solemnization by the court of the celebration at the Minerva was due to Pope Nicholas V (1447-55). I had earlier inferred that this might be the case, but clear documentation was missing to confirm it [6]. De Grassis, invariably reliable in such matters, here has a specificity that adds credence to his words. Moreover, we know from elsewhere that he had access to works, now lost, of Antoine Rébiol, who held de Grassis' position

Gregorian University, Rome, for this information and other kindnesses, as well as for allowing me to use his microfilm of the Ambrosian codex. I have meanwhile travelled to Milan to examine the manuscript itself. Father Dykmans is preparing an edition of de Grassis' *Diarium*.

[6] O'MALLEY, *Renaissance Panegyrics*, p. 175.

during the pontificate of Nicholas and beyond (1450-84) [7]. It is reasonable to assume that this is the source from which de Grassis now draws and that he is thus using an account contemporary with the event.

The significance of Nicholas' action must be stressed. It means that the Curia's celebration of Aquinas' feast in Rome was not a continuation of a medieval tradition, but a deliberate innovation by « the first Renaissance pope ». De Grassis is emphatic that Nicholas was the originator of the solemnity. When we recall how conservative the papal court was in liturgical matters, how resistant to even the slightest change in rubric and protocol, the pope's decision appears all the more noteworthy. It is generally acknowledged that Nicholas was an important figure in the history of the papal liturgies [8]. The present text on the celebration in the Minerva provides significant details to confirm that assessment.

We must not assume, in fact, that Thomas' feast was celebrated annually in all the churches of Europe immediately upon his canonization by Pope John XXII in 1323 [9]. The evidence points in the opposite direction. For instance, out of a sampling of twenty-six editions of the *Missale Romanum* printed in various cities of Europe between 1474 and Pius V's revision in 1570, when the feast was surely stabilized, only three contain the Mass for the feast of Aquinas or make any mention of it on the appropriate day in the body of the text [10]. In many instances his feast is mentioned behind the names of Saints Perpetua and Felicity for March 7 in the calendars prefatory to the text of the missals, but that is the extent of it.

---

[7] See DYKMANS, *Cérémonial de Nicolas V,* p. 787 n. 3, 791 n. 21; ID., *Mabillon,* p. 341; and NABUCO, *Cérémonial Apostolique,* p. 19** n. 35. See also Biblioteca Vaticana, cod. Vat. lat. 5634bis, ff. 2r, 2v-3r, where de Grassis states he used older liturgical books while writing this *Supplementum.*

[8] See, e.g., NABUCO, *Cérémonial Apostolique,* esp. p. 15*-22*.

[9] For John XXII's promulgation of the feast, see A. WALZ, *Historia Canonizationis Sancti Thomae de Aquino,* in *Xenia Thomistica,* ed. S. SZABÓ, III, Rome 1925, p. 150, 154-55. See also W. R. BONNIWELL, *A History of the Dominican Liturgy,* New York 1945, p. 233-36.

[10] See R. LIPPE, ed., *Missale Romanum, Mediolani, 1474,* 2 vols., London 1899-1907 (Henry Bradshaw Society Publications, 17, 33), p. 321; II, p. 181-82. Besides the seventeen missals, including Milan 1474, checked by Lippe and listed, II, p. v, I have myself examined the following:

1) Venice: G. de Rivabenis and P. de Paganinis 1484; 2) Nuremberg: G. Stuchs de Sultzback 1484; 3) Rome: E. Silber 1488; 4) Venice: A. de Zanchis 1501; 5) Venice: L. A. de Giunta 1506; 6) Paris: G. Eustace 1511; 7) Venice: P. Liechtenstein 1536; 8) Paris: I. Keruer 1565.

The three editions that contain the Mass for Thomas are:

1) Venice: hered. L. A. Giunta 1558; 2) Venice: P. Liechtenstein 1558; 3) Paris: I. Keruer 1565. See also M. R. TOYNBEE, *S. Louis of Toulouse and the Process of Canonization in the Fourteenth Century,* Manchester 1929, p. 210 (British Society of Franciscan Studies, 15).

This is true also for a manuscript missal from the chapel of Nicholas V and for another presented to the basilica of Saint Peter by one of its canons in 1475 [11]. From de Grassis' diary for March 7, 1505, it can be inferred, in fact, that the Mass was found only in the Dominican missal at Minerva, not in the ones used in the papal Curia [12].

Why this neglect? It seems to be due to the simple fact that March 7 was already the feast of the ancient Christian martyrs Perpetua and Felicity. These saints were able, out of the sheer inertia of custom, to maintain their place in the missal for that day. Otherwise it is impossible to explain why these same missals almost without exception carry the Masses for King Louis of France and Bernardine of Siena, saints canonized about the same time as Thomas or much later. Seven of the twenty-six missals printed between 1474 and 1570 that I have investigated contain the Mass for Saint Bonaventure, not canonized until 1482.

We know of course that in certain localities Thomas' feast was observed with great solemnity. Padua is an outstanding example, where it was declared a holiday for the entire city as early as 1324 and for the university in 1436 when Thomas became the patron of Arts faculty [13]. Besides the panegyrics from Padua and Rome that survive, we have others — especially by noted Dominicans like Leonardo Mattei (da Udine) and Silvestro Mazzolini (Prierias), but also by the Franciscan bishop of Aquino, Roberto Caracciolo (da Lecce), and at Paris by Josse Clichtove [14]. Outside some special instances like these, however, there is good reason to doubt how widespread during the Renaissance the liturgical cult of Thomas was. On his feast day most priests probably celebrated the Mass for Perpetua and Felicity as they found it in their missals. Even if

---

[11] *Missale Nicolai V*, Biblioteca Vaticana, cod. Archivio S. Pietro, E 4; for a description see SALMON, *Manuscrits liturgiques*. II. *Sacramentaires épistoliers évangeliaires graduels missels*, Città del Vaticano 1969, p. 103 (nr. 229) (Studi e Testi, 253). *Missale basilicae S. Petri*, Biblioteca Vaticana, cod. Archivio S. Pietro, B 72; see SALMON, *ibid.*, p. 100 (nr. 222).

[12] Biblioteca Vaticana, cod. Vat. lat. 12272, f. 70v: « In missa una oratio fuit, videlicet de sancto Thoma, quae est specialis in libris ecclesiae, et incipit Deus qui ecclesiam tuam ». This was the regular prayer for the feast.

[13] See *Del culto di S. Tommaso d'Aquino in Padova*, Padua 1882, and P. RAGNISCO, *Della fortuna di S. Tommaso d'Aquino nella Università di Padova durante il Rinascimento*, Padua 1892. I discuss a few of the panegyrics given there in my *Renaissance Panegyrics*, p. 178-79 and passim.

[14] See O'MALLEY, *Renaissance Panegyrics*, p. 178-80. To the materials listed there should now be added: L. MATTEI, *Sermones aurei de sanctis*, Strassburg c. 1483 (Hain nr. *16126), ff. [114r-119v]; R. CARACCIOLO, *De laudibus sanctorum*, Venice 1490 (Hain nr. 4482), ff. 146v-148r [= 150r]; S. MAZZOLINI, *Quadragesimale aureum*, Venice 1515, ff. 7v-9v.

they bothered to turn to the calendar at the beginning of the missal, they would learn that these saints still had priority of place, and would see no indication what Mass to celebrate for Thomas or even with what prayers to make a commemoration. In such a context, the significance of Nicholas' action is further highlighted.

De Grassis' account of the ceremony in the Minerva emphasizes, moreover, the degree of solemnity that Nicholas established: the entire Sacred College was to participate; the celebration was to be observed annually (« quotannis »), and had in fact continued substantially unchanged from Nicholas' day until de Grassis' own; when the feast fell on a Sunday or on Ash Wednesday, it was transferred to the following day; only the orations for Saint Thomas were used, with no commemoration of the Lenten ferial or of Saints Perpetua and Felicity; it was observed as a *festum* in the Apostolic Palace, which meant inter alia that is was a full holiday with « abstinentia ab opere servili »[15].

It is true that, although de Grassis states that on occasion Nicholas himself assisted at the Mass, there is no further record of any pope doing so. Aside from that fact, March 7 enjoys an extraordinary degree of festivity. The accounts in the diaries of Burchard and de Grassis indicate that practically all the cardinals present in Rome did in fact generally participate, a number that ranged anywhere from about fifteen to thirty. The celebration at Minerva thus became a « cappella cardinalizia »[16]. It is the only such « cappella » for which we have ample documentation during this period and for which we can now construct a continuous history from 1447 forward.

Of special importance is Nicholas' insistence that the Creed be sung. It seems clear from de Grassis' words that this was meant to place Thomas in the same category with Augustine, Ambrose, Jerome, and Gregory the Great. Thomas, considered simply as a « Confessor », would not have merited a Creed. Today we tend to be insensitive to the implications of such liturgical decisions. The matter is clarified by an examination of the bull *Mirabilis Deus* by which on April 11, 1567, Pope Pius V « declared Thomas a doctor of the Church ». In actual fact this document does not « declare » Thomas anything. It simply prescribes that Thomas is to be given

---

[15] See J. HERGENROETHER, ed., *Leonis X Pontificis Maximi Regesta,* 2 vols., Freiburg i. Br. 1884-91, I, p. 289 (Sept. 27, 1513), for the observance of the feast of Saints Cosmas and Damian. Professor Nelson Minnich called this entry to my attention.

[16] On « cappelle cardinalizie », see G. MORONI, *Le cappelle pontificie, cardinalizie et prelatizie. Opera storico-liturgica,* Venice, 1841, p. 358-86, esp. 373-74 on the Minerva.

the same liturgical standing as the four Latin doctors [17]. Thomas was the first saint to receive such honors, and the document was immediately and correctly interpreted as a declaration. Perhaps to forestall any possible misunderstandings, Pope Sixtus V was much more explicit when he took the same action for Saint Bonaventure some years later, in 1588 [18]. The point is that Nicholas anticipated for the papal Curia the action that Pius V took for the universal Church more than a century later.

But to understand the full import of Nicholas' decision and the fidelity with which it was implemented even after his death, we must place the phenomenon in the larger context of the papal liturgies in the Renaissance [19]. There was a general tendency to regularize them and to restrict, rather than to expand, the number of more solemn celebrations, especially if some practice could not be justified from the liturgical books. Even more significant, the feast of Thomas Aquinas was the only feast of a non-biblical saint (except for All Saints) that enjoyed such an elevated liturgical status at the papal court during the Renaissance.

The court did not take any consistent notice of the feasts of Bernard, Francis, Dominic, or Bonaventure, even though the last named was canonized during this period by Sixtus IV. The feast of Saint Lawrence was dutifully observed, but without liturgical pomp. The feast of Saint Nicholas enjoyed a certain standing, at least during the pontificate of Innocent VIII [20]. From time to time and with varying degrees of solemnity some saints were specially honored by the pope and his entourage. Innocent VIII and Alexander VI, for instance, showed in their liturgical actions a personal devotion to Francis of Assisi [21], and Leo X did the same for the pa-

---

17 Pius V, *Bullarium Romanum,* VII, Turin 1862, p. 565: « ...in aliis autem orbis terrae partibus [i.e., outside the Kingdom of Naples], quemadmodum sanctorum quattuor Ecclesiae doctorum festivitates, piae memoriae Bonifacii Papae VIII, etiam praedecessoris nostri, praecepto, celebrantur, sic eundem festum diem sancti Thomae in perpetuum posthac omnes item utriusque sexus christifideles celebrent et venerentur, apostolica auctoritate statuimus ac sancimus ». The significance attributed to Pius' action was challenged in the seventeenth century by the Franciscan, Pedro de Alva y Astorga, *Funiculi nodi indissolubilis de conceptu mentis et conceptu ventris,* Brussels 1663, p. 550-59. The traditional interpretation was defended by the Dominican, S. Piccinardi, *De approbatione doctrinae sancti Thomae Aquinatis libri septem,* I, Padua 1683, p. 218-24. See also A. Walz, *San Tommaso d'Aquino dichiarato dottore della Chiesa nel 1567,* « Angelicum », 44 (1967), p. 145-73, esp. 157.

18 Sixtus V, *Triumphantis,* in *Bullarium,* VIII (1863), p. 1005-12.

19 See O'Malley, *Praise and Blame,* p. 7-35.

20 See J. Burchardus, *Liber Notarum,* ed. Enrico Celani, 2 vols., in *RIS,* n. ed., XXXII, parti 1ª e 2ª, Città di Castello 1906, I, p. 172 (1486), 212 (1487), 313 (1491).

21 On Oct. 4, 1487, Innocent VIII visited the church of St. Francis in Traste-

trons of his family — Saints Cosmas and Damian[22]. But these were intrusions into the regular patterns of the papal liturgies.

The court did not accord any particular attention to the feasts of Ambrose and Jerome. Johannes Burchard describes in his diary seven occasions when the pope and cardinals rode to the church of Saint Gregory to attend a low Mass there, celebrated by the abbot. Except for the elaborate procession from the Vatican to the church, the celebration was devoid of all other solemnity[23].

De Grassis mentions in another of his liturgical *opuscula* that all the cardinals were supposed to attend the Masses at the Minerva for the feasts of Saints Thomas and the Annunciation, with the pope present for the latter, and also the Mass in the church of S. Agostino for that saint[24]. But for Augustine the documentation suggests that this provision was not faithfully fulfilled. The liturgical diaries show in fact, on the few occasions when they describe the feast, that relatively few cardinals attended. Perhaps because of the awkward date during the summer holidays, August 28, the feast seems to have been an occasional rather than an annual observance. No major figure ever took a continuing interest in it; there is no evidence that it was celebrated as a feast in the Apostolic Palace[25]. Gregory and Augustine were Aquinas' only liturgical rivals in Renaissance Rome, and they were weak ones indeed.

There is a further consideration. As I tried to make clear in my recent book, the liturgical occasions at the papal court on which a sermon was allowed or prescribed were severely limited in Re-

---

vere; Alexander VI did the same in 1497, where he assisted at a low Mass. See BURCHARD, *Liber Notarum*, I, p. 208; II, p. 54.

[22] See HERGENROETHER, *Regesta*, I, p. 289, and DE GRASSIS, *Diarium*, Biblioteca Vaticana, cod. Vat. lat. 12275, ff. 66r-v (1513), 128r (1514), 364v (1519), 386v (1520), 411v-412r (1521).

[23] BURCHARD, *Liber Notarum*, I, p. 224 (1488), 299-300 (1490), 339 (1492), 461-62 (1494), 580 (1495), 597 (1496); II, p. 439-40 (1504).

[24] DE GRASSIS, *Caerimoniarum opusculum*, Biblioteca Vaticana, cod. Vat. lat. 5634, f. 16r, « ...in festo Sancti Thomae Aquinatis Annunciationisque gloriosae Virginis et Sancti Augustini ad quorum celebrationem Senatus de more proficiscitur ».

[25] Two panegyrics survive that were preached by A. MASSARI (Ambrosius de Cora) in the presence respectively of Pius II and Paul II, therefore before the new church was built; see his *Vita Aurelii Augustini*, Rome 1481 (Hain nr. *5683), ff. [233r-237v, 241v-247v]. L. DONATO's, *Oratio pro S. Augustini solemnitate habita*, Rome 1482 (?), (GKW nr. 9039), marked the completion of the new church. There is also a panegyric by P. MARSI, *Panegyricus in memoriam sancti Augustini*, Rome n.d. (Hain nr. 10787), probably delivered sometime after Donato's. BURCHARD describes a Mass at S. Agostino's on Aug. 28, 1497, in which seven cardinals took part, *Liber Notarum*, II, p. 50, and P. DE GRASSIS notes a similar celebration there with the same number of cardinals on Aug. 28, 1504, *Diarium*, Biblioteca Vaticana, cod. Vat. lat. 12272, ff. 21v-22r. These are the only times the two diarists mention this feast, whereas the celebration at the Minerva is often described; see below, n. 27.

naissance Rome, more limited in fact than earlier liturgical books prescribed [26]. The mere fact that a sermon was indicated for some occasion eo ipso gave it a special liturgical prominence. De Grassis' *Supplementum* makes it clear that this feast was to have such a « sermo », and the diaries of de Grassis and Burchard testify that this prescription was invariably fulfilled [27]. The sermon at the Minerva was delivered, moreover, « inter missarum solemnia », i.e., during Mass after the singing of the Gospel. This location within the liturgy itself bestowed on the sermon a special dignity as a « sermo sacer et evangelicus » that sermons and orations before or after the liturgy lacked [28].

As important as the fact of a sermon and its rank as « sacer et evangelicus » is the calibre of the person chosen to deliver it. De Grassis' *Supplementum* indicates that during this period the preacher was not to be a member of a religious order, though by the seventeenth century the panegyrist was invariably a Dominican. From the pontificate of Nicholas V until the last years of the pontificate of Julius II, eight panegyrics from the Minerva have survived and been located:

1. 1449/50, pontificate of Nicholas V, by Rodrigo Sánchez de Arévalo [29];
2. 1457, pontificate of Calixtus III, by Lorenzo Valla [30];

---

[26] See Nabuco, *Cérémonial Apostolique*, p. 107-9, for the *Ceremonial* in use from Nicholas V until Sixtus IV. Even Patrizi's *Ceremonial* provided for more occasions than were actually in use; compare Marcello, *Rituum*, ff. 141v-142r, with O'Malley, *Praise and Blame*, p. 14-15.

[27] The entries in Burchard's *Liber Notarum*, which in almost every instance mention the « sermo », are as follows: I, p. 184-85 (1487), 299 (1490), 339 (1492), 405 (1493), 460-61 (1494), 578-79 (1495), 596 (1496); II, p. 18 (1497), 74-75 (1498), 129-30 (1499), 207 (1500), 270-71 (1501), 439 (1504), 473-74 (1505). The entries in the *Diarium* of De Grassis are the following: Biblioteca Vaticana, cod. Vat. lat. 12272, ff. 70r (1505), 148v (1506); cod. Vat. lat. 12269, f. 337v (1510). There are, besides, the actual panegyrics that survive, some of which coincide with the entries in the diaries. They are listed further on in the text above.

[28] See De Grassis, *Caerimoniarum opusculum*, Biblioteca Vaticana, cod. Vat. lat. 5634, ff. 73r-74v, for his important description of the different categories of sermons. See also O'Malley, *Praise and Blame*, p. 7-35.

[29] R. Sánchez de Arévalo, *Sermo factus coram sacro collegio reverendissimorum dominorum cardinalium in die festo Thomae de Aquino ordinis Praedicatorum*, Biblioteca Vaticana, cod. Vat. lat. 4881, ff. 234r-237r. On Arévalo, see esp. the two books: R. H. Trame, *Rodrigo Sánchez de Arévalo, 1404-1470. Spanish Diplomat and Champion of the Papacy*, Washington 1958, and J. M. Laboa, *Rodrigo Sánchez de Arévalo. Alcaide de Sant'Angelo*, Madrid 1973. See also O'Malley, *Praise and Blame*, passim, as well as the further bibliography cited there on p. 90 n. 51. Trame established the date of the sermon, *Sánchez de Arévalo*, p. 72; see also Laboa, *Sánchez de Arévalo*, p. 424.

[30] L. Valla, *Encomium sancti Thomae Aquinatis*, ed. J. Vahlen, in *Opera omnia*, 2 vols., Turin 1962 (Monumenta Politica et Philosophica Rariora, ed. Luigi Firpo, s. I, nr. 5), II, p. 340-52.

3. 1467/71, pontificate of Paul II, by Giannantonio Campano [31];
4. 1485, pontificate of Innocent VIII, by Francesco Maturanzio [32];
5. 1485/90, pontificate of Innocent VIII, by Aurelio Brandolini [33];
6. 1495, pontificate of Alexander VI, by Tommaso « Fedra » Inghirami [34];
7. 1496, pontificate of Alexander VI, by Martinus de Viana [35];
8. 1505/10?, pontificate of Julius II, by Antonio Pucci [36].

---

[31] G. CAMPANO, *In festo sancti Thomae de Aquino oratio,* in *Opera a Michaele Ferno edita,* Rome 1495 (GKW nr. 5939), ff. [90r-93v]. The oration is dated by G. LESCA, *Giovannantonio Campano detto l'Episcopus Aprutinus. Saggio biografico e critico,* Pontedera 1892, p. 143. On Campano's life and works, see now F.-R. HAUSMANN, *Giovanni Antonio Campano (1429-1477). Erläuterungen und Ergänzungen zu seinen Briefen,* Freiburg i. Br. 1968 (Inaugural-Dissertation, Albert-Ludwigs Universität); ID., *Giovanni Antonio Campano (1429-1477). Ein Beitrag zur Geschichte des italienischen Humanismus im Quattrocento,* « Römische historische Mitteilungen », 12 (1970), p. 125-78; and F. DI BERNARDO, *Un vescovo umanista alla Corte Pontificia. Giannantonio Campano (1429-1477),* Rome 1975 (Miscellanea Historiae Pontificiae, 39).

[32] F. MATURANZIO, *Oratio habita Romae in aede divae Mariae in Minerva in laudem divi Thomae Aquinatis, theologorum principis et ecclesiae sanctae doctoris,* Biblioteca Vaticana, cod. Vat. lat. 5358, ff. 33v-45r. The oration is dated by G. B. VERMIGLIOLI, *Memorie per servire alla vita di Franc. Maturanzio oratore e poeta Perugino,* Perugia 1807, p. 29-30. On Maturanzio, see now also G. ZAPPACOSTA, *Francesco Maturanzio umanista perugino,* Bergamo 1970 (Saggi e ricerche di lingua et letteratura italiana, 1).

[33] A. BRANDOLINI, *Oratio pro sancto Thoma Aquinate,* Rome 1485/90 (GKW nr. 5016). The arguments favoring the attribution of this panegyric to Raffaello Brandolini are not convincing; see O'MALLEY, *Renaissance Panegyrics,* p. 176-77 n. 12. On Brandolini, see the article by A. ROTONDÒ in the *DBI,* with the appended bibliography. To that bibliography should now be added: O'MALLEY, *Praise and Blame,* passim; CH. TRINKAUS, *In Our Image and Likeness. Humanity and Divinity in Italian Humanist Thought,* 2 vols., Chicago 1970, I, p. 297-321; II, p. 601-13; and J. M. MCMANAMON, *Renaissance Preaching: Theory and Practice. A Holy Thursday Sermon of Aurelio Brandolini,* « Viator », 10 (1979), p. 355-73.

[34] T. INGHIRAMI, *Panegyricus in memoriam divi Thomae Aquinatis,* Rome c. 1495 (Hain-Reichling nr. 9186). The date of the sermon is known from the entry in BURCHARD, *Liber Notarum,* I, p. 578-79. On Inghirami, see O'MALLEY, *Praise and Blame,* passim, as well as the further bibliography cited there, p. 114 n. 147.

[35] MARTINUS DE VIANA, *Oratio in festo divi Thomae de Aquino,* Rome 1496 (Cop. nr. 6199). Biographical information on de Viana is scarce. He held doctorates in Arts and in Theology, and c. 1494-96 was chaplain to Cardinal Raffaello Riario. He delivered during this time three orations in the presence of Alexander VI. See O'MALLEY, *Praise and Blame,* passim, as well as NICOLÁS ANTONIO, *Bibliotheca hispana nova,* II, Madrid p. 112.

[36] A. PUCCI, *Oratio de laudibus divi Thomae Aquinatis in templo divae Mariae Minervae Romae ad patres et populum habita nonis martiis,* Biblioteca Vaticana, cod. Vat. lat. 3465. This codex is the presentation copy, membrane, to Cardinal Oliviero Carafa; hence, the oration was surely delivered before 1511, the year of Carafa's death. On Pucci, see N. H. MINNICH, *Concepts of Reform Proposed at the Fifth Lateran Council,* « Archivum Historiae Pontifi-

With the exception of the Spanish theologian Martinus de Viana, every one of these panegyrists was a person of considerable cultural or political importance in his day. Valla, Campano, Maturanzio, Brandolini, and Inghirami were all important humanists, though none of the last four is of course of the same stature as Valla. Sánchez de Arévalo and Antonio Pucci were, besides their literary attainments (which for Arévalo were impressive), key figures in setting and implementing certain policies at the papal court and were active there over long periods of time.

Sánchez de Arévalo, Campano, and Valla seem to have been invited to speak by the Dominican friars themselves, although this is not as clear for the first two as for Valla [37]. Maturanzio, Brandolini, and de Viana certainly received their invitations from the cardinal protector of the order, Oliviero Carafa [38]. Since the orations of Inghirami and Pucci fall within the long period during which Carafa acted as protector, 1481-1511, it is reasonable to presume that he issued the invitation to them too. Pucci's oration, like Brandolini's, is in fact dedicated to the cardinal. We thus arrive at a consideration of this major figure at the papal court, whose role at the Minerva is described by de Grassis in the *Supplementum* [39].

During Carafa's lifetime the role of cardinal protector of the Dominican order achieved an importance that it never had before or since. Carafa became in effect a superior of the order, overshadowing in some instances the master general himself [40]. The most lasting monument to Carafa's influence in the order is the chapel dedicated to the Blessed Virgin and to Thomas Aquinas that he had Filippino Lippi decorate in the Minerva [41].

The chapel was constructed, as Lippi himself stated in a letter to Filippo Strozzi, « at immense cost, with no expense spared » [42]. Finished probably sometime before September 8, 1492, it was almost

---

ciae », 7 (1969), p. 163-251, esp. 192-93, and H. Jedin, *A History of the Council of Trent*, tr. Ernest Graf, 2 vols. to date, London 1957-61, I, passim. He wrote *De corporis et sanguinis D. N. Iesu Christi homiliae XIIII virtute*, Bologna 1551.

[37] See Arévalo, *Sermo*, f. 263v; Valla, *Encomium*, p. 349; Campano, *Oratio*, f. [90r].

[38] See Maturanzio, *Oratio*, ff. 34v-35r; Brandolini, *Oratio*, f. [2r], but see also f. [3v] where he says the Dominicans invited him; De Viana, *Oratio*, f. [1r].

[39] See the article on Carafa by F. Petrucci in the *DBI*, with bibliography

[40] See S. L. Forte, *The Cardinal-Protector of the Dominican Order*, Rome 1959, p. 24-29 (Institutum Historicum FF. Praedicatorum, Dissertationes Historicae, 15).

[41] See C. Bertelli, *Appunti sugli affreschi nella cappella Carafa alla Minerva*, AFP, 35 (1965), p. 115-30.

[42] *Ibid.*, p. 115.

immediately honored by a visit of the new pope, Alexander VI. Alexander enriched it with a plenary indulgence for those visiting it on the feast of the Nativity of Mary or on the feast of Aquinas. After the chapel was completed and at least until Carafa's death, part of the annual ritual on March 7 was for the cardinals to repair to the chapel after Mass to pray there and gain the indulgence. This ceremony took place on the feast of Thomas, not on the feast of Mary. It is described in the *Supplementum* and often described in the diaries of Burchard and de Grassis when they speak of this feast.

Carafa's devotion to Thomas Aquinas was not simply a perfunctory corollary to his role as cardinal protector. If anything, his dedication to the Dominicans sprang out of his devotion to Saint Thomas. The cardinal was firmly convinced that, through his mother, he was related to the saint. This was a connection of which he was proud to be reminded [43]. However, he did not allow his relationship to remain on this static and superficial level. According to Cajetan, Oliviero Carafa liked to read Aquinas [44]. Given Carafa's interest in letters and learning, there is no reason to doubt the truth of Cajetan's statement. Even more impressive is the role Carafa played in urging Cajetan to write and publish his commentary on the *Summa theologiae,* as well as some of his other works related to Thomas [45].

Thus we return to the influence Carafa exercised in the Dominican order while cardinal protector. We know for a fact that it was he who summoned Lodovico de Ferrara (Ludovicus de Valentia Ferrariensis) to Rome in 1491 to assume at the papal court the office of procurator general of the Dominicans [46]. He also ap-

---

[43] The relationship is mentioned by BRANDOLINI in the dedicatory letter to his *Oratio,* f. [1r], as well as in the panegyric itself, f. [5r], and by CAJETAN in the dedicatory letter, 1506, to his *Commentaria in Porphyrii Isagogen ad Praedicamenta Aristotelis, ed. Isnardus M. Marega,* Rome 1934, p. lxxxiii.

[44] CAJETAN, *In Isagogen,* p. lxxxiii, « ...quod divi Thomae Aquinatis (cui maternum genus prosapia tua clarissima profudit), operibus summopere delectaris ».

[45] CAJETAN, dedicatory letter, 1507/8, to Carafa, in *Opera omnia iussu impensaque Leonis XIII P. M.,* IV, Rome 1888, p. 4, « ...praesertim cum tu me ad hanc cudendam expositionem adhortatus maxime fueris, vixque dum bene absolutam publicari non solum saepe petieris, verum etiam flagitaveris ».

[46] See T. DE TOTIS, *Oratio de funere Ludovici de Ferraria,* Rome 1496 (Cop. nr. 5843), f. [3r], « ...totius ordinis Praedicatorum procurator generalis in Curia Romana ab illo instituitur ». See also the letter to Lodovico by M. NIMIREUS in Lodovico's edition of Aquinas' commentary on Aristotle's *Politics,* Rome 1492 (Hain-Cop. nr. 1768, GKW nr. 2448), f. 254v, « ...te ad hanc urbem venire iusserit ». I am grateful to Father T. KAEPPELI for allowing me to see the entry for Lodovico in the proofs for the third volume of his *Scriptores Ordinis Praedicatorum Medii Aevi.*

plied pressure to have Vincenzo Bandello elected master general in 1501 [47], to have Cajetan designated procurator general that same year, and to have him elected master general in 1508 [48]. It can hardly be a coincidence that all three of these men enjoyed impressive reputations in their day as teachers of Thomism and as authors of books expounding Thomistic positions.

When Lodovico da Ferrara came to Rome, he immediately set about giving public instruction in Thomistic theology and philosophy in his own « school ». He soon assumed a post at the University of Rome, the Sapienza, where he taught « natural theology and rational philosophy » [49]. In the course of his career he wrote commentaries on several major works by Aquinas, and, more pointedly, composed for Carafa a handbook on Aristotle's *Ethics*, which we can be sure was Thomistic in interpretation [50]. In 1492 he published Aquinas' commentary on the *Politics*, incorporating into the edition not Moerbeke's but Leonardo Bruni's translation of Aristotle [51]. It was his Roman connections that directed his attention to the *Ethics* and *Politics*, that is, to texts that would have a special appeal to Renaissance tastes.

Bandello wrote in Florence, 1474-75, a Thomistic interpretation of human beatitude. This work, directed against Ficino and dedicated to Lorenzo the Magnificent, has recently been edited and studied by Paul Oskar Kristeller [52]. Bandello published in 1475 and 1481 two important works against the Immaculate Conception, in which he espoused the traditional Dominican and Thomistic position on

---

47 See BURCHARD, *Liber Notarum*, II, p. 284.

48 See D.-A. MORTIER, *Histoire des Maîtres Généraux de l'ordre des Frères Prêcheurs*, V, Paris 1911, p. 144-46.

49 See the letter by NIMIREUS, *Politics*, f. 254r.

50 DE TOTIS, *Oratio*, f. [3v]: « ...totam etiam Aristotelis ethicam pro reverendissimo cardinali protectore dignissimo luculenter in capitula clare ac breviter perstrinxit, qui libellus a dominatione sua enchiridion dicitur, eo quod libentius per manibus illum teneat. Primam secundae sancti Thomae ornatissime per modum cuiusdam textus reduxit; primum et secundum Contra gentes mirabiliter declaravit; super librum De ente et essentia quaestiones scripsit; supra primum librum Sententiarum scribere incepit; supra libros De anima ac Priorum commentaria scribebat ». I have not been able to locate any of the works by Lodovico except the edition of the *Politics* and his five orations at the papal liturgies, *Orationes quinque in cappella pontificia*, Rome after 1492 (Hain-Cop. nr. 6983).

51 On the great importance of this edition in the history of the text, see the introduction to the Leonine edition of it, *Sententia Libri Politicorum, Tabula Libri Ethicorum*, XLVIII, Rome 1971, p. A15-A21.

52 The edition is appended to KRISTELLER, *Le Thomisme*, p. 189-278, and entitled *Opusculum quod beatitudo hominis in actu intellectus et non voluntatis essentialiter consistit*. KRISTELLER studied the work at length in *A Thomistic Critique of Marsilio Ficino's Theory of Will and Intellect*, in *Harry Austryn Wolfson Jubilee Volume*, English Section II, Jerusalem 1965, p. 463-94.

this issue[53]. There is no need here to review the career or to list the works of Cajetan, the best known commentator on Aquinas in the history of Thomism[54]. It is perhaps important to mention, however, that while he was procurator general, 1501-8, he too, like Lodovico, taught at the Sapienza.

Cajetan's relationship to Carafa antedates his entry into the Dominican order. The families of Cajetan and Carafa knew each other, and Carafa had met Cajetan when he was a boy or young man[55]. It would be quite natural for Carafa to keep an eye on Cajetan's career and to promote it whenever possible. But it seems clear that Cajetan's devotion to Aquinas would further and more strongly recommend him to the upright and devout prelate — «vir undecumque exemplaris », as de Grassis, echoing the common sentiment, describes him in the *Supplementum*.

Carafa's patronage of the Aquinas chapel in the Minerva and his interest in the celebration of the feast is symptomatic, therefore, of a broader and deeper commitment to the saint. There can be no doubt, however, that his patronage of the chapel and his concern for the feast helped ratify and stabilize the solemnity of the liturgical celebration, again as de Grassis indicates, « interventu reverendissimi domini, Oliverii Caraffae ».

The feast seems, nonetheless, to have been put on a firm footing from the beginning by Nicholas V's clear and emphatic injunctions. The reason Paris de Grassis gives to explain why Nicholas established the feast are credible: his baptismal name was Thomas, and he was elected pope on March 6, the day before the feast. To these reasons we might add that Nicholas was elected pope in the Minerva itself during an unexpectedly easy and brief conclave. By the end of his life, Nicholas had forty-nine volumes of Aquinas' works in his library, by far the largest number for any single author except for the fifty of Augustine[56]. This fact betrays a more intrinsic motivation, consistent with an abiding intellectual interest.

We must ask, however, if there was not a larger context receptive to these initiatives by Nicholas and Carafa that provided a support for them that went beyond the personal enthusiasms of the

---

[53] BANDELLO, *Liber recollectorius*, Milan 1475 (GKW nr. 3237); *De puritate conceptionis Christi*, Bologna 1481 (GKW nr. 3238). For bibliography on Bandello, see L. GARGAN, *Lo studio teologico e la biblioteca dei Domenicani a Padova nel Tre e Quattrocento*, Padua 1971, p. 255-56 (Contributi alla storia dell'Università di Padova, 6).

[54] For some recent studies on Cajetan, which contain further bibliography, see O'MALLEY, *Praise and Blame*, p. 108 n. 123.

[55] See CAJETAN, *In Isagogen*, p. lxxxii.

[56] See L. PASTOR, *Storia dei papi*, ed. ANGELO MERCATI, I, Rome 1958, p. 562.

two men. Thomas was born near Rome and died near Rome; during his lifetime he visited Rome several times. Though quite properly claimed by the Kingdom of Naples, Thomas could almost qualify as a local Roman saint as well. By a curious convergence of circumstances, furthermore, probably the first chapel in the world dedicated to Thomas was constructed on the Aventine shortly after his canonization [57].

But a still sturdier framework than these facts seems required to explain Thomas' popularity in the international atmosphere of the papal Curia. When we recall the presence in Rome especially of the Franciscans and Augustinians, with each of these orders having its own distinguished doctors of theology like Bonaventure, Scotus, Aegidius Romanus — to say nothing of Augustine — the question becomes more urgent.

We might begin with the feast itself. Paris de Grassis states flatly that there was no record in the liturgical books of its being celebrated by the court until the time of Nicholas V. Nonetheless, we know of a similar celebration taking place once before at the Dominican convent in Avignon about 1340 [58]. The Sacred College participated. The preacher that day was no less a person than Pierre Roger, the famous orator and future Pope Clement VI (1342-52). Roger had already preached two important panegyrics on Aquinas — the first in 1324, less than a year after Thomas' canonization, possibly addressed to the students and masters of the University of Paris [59]. From de Grassis' statement it seems clear that these events were not remembered by the Dominicans at the Minerva or by the members of Nicholas' Curia, even though these sermons survive

---

[57] See V. J. KOUDELKA, *La cappella di S. Tommaso d'Aquino in Monte Savello a Roma*, *AFP*, 32 (1962), p. 126-44.

[58] This celebration was probably a unique occurrence, or at least not an annual event. Otherwise Patrizi, Burchard, and de Grassis would have had some record of it from the liturgical books from Avignon that they possessed and consulted. See BURCHARD, *Liber Notarum*, I, p. 217, and NABUCO, *Cérémonial Apostolique*, p. 14*.

[59] See M.-H. LAURENT, *Pierre Roger et Thomas d'Aquin*, « Revue Thomiste », 36 (1931), p. 157-73, esp. p. 165-66. On Roger's fame and skill as an orator, see P. FOURNIER, *Pierre Roger (Clément VI)*, in *Histoire littéraire de la France*, XXXVII, Paris 1938, p. 209-38, and D. WOOD, *The Sermon Literature of Pope Clement VI*, in *The Materials Sources and Methods of Ecclesiastical History*, ed. D. BAKER, Oxford 1975, p. 163-72 (Studies in Church History, 11), as well as the older study by G. MOLLAT, *L'oeuvre oratoire de Clément VI*, « Archives d'Histoire doctrinale et littéraire du Moyen Age », 3 (1928), p. 239-74. See also M.-H. LAURENT, *Autour de la fête de saint Thomas*, « Revue Thomiste », 40 (1935), p. 257-63. For a caution about Roger's « Thomism », see A. MAIER, *Der literarische Nachlass des Petrus Rogerii (Clemens VI.) in der Borghesiana*, « Recherches de Théologie ancienne et médiévale », 15 (1948), p. 356.

today in a number of manuscripts from the fourteenth and fifteenth centuries [60].

Much more important is the general politico-ecclesiastical significance of Aquinas to the popes of Avignon and the Renaissance. Thomas' sanctity was well attested and the process of his canonization altogether regular. Nonetheless, there is no doubt that Pope John XXII saw in Thomas an antidote to some of the problems that plagued him originating from the mendicants. His bull of canonization noted how it was at the invitation of Pope Gregory X that Thomas set out for the Council of Lyons, and it made certain to indicate how Thomas submitted everything he wrote to the correction of the « Roman Church » [61].

In his discourse at the canonization, John emphasized the genuinity of Thomas' understanding of poverty, that question so agitated by the Spiritual Franciscans on which the pope would make a solemn pronouncement just a few months later [62]. The discourse was also intended for the ears of King Robert of Naples who attended the ceremonies and also himself gave a sermon. Robert had at times supported the Fraticelli and promoted their cause. Some of the Fraticelli were, in fact, violently opposed to Thomas' canonization because they considered him a heretic on the question of poverty [63].

Within two years a commission of six papal theologians at Avignon would pronounce against fifty-one propositions of William of Ockham, another Franciscan. In 1329 John condemned a number of propositions taken from the writings of Eckhart, a Dominican master [64]. The chronological proximity of these two events to Tho-

---

[60] See PH. SCHMITZ, *Les sermons et discours de Clément VI, O.S.B.*, « Revue Bénédictine », 41 (1929), p. 15-34. See also J. B. SCHNEYER, *Repertorium der lateinischen Sermones des Mittelalters*, IV, Münster 1972, p. 757-69 (Beiträge zur Geschichte der Philosophie und Theologie des Mittelalters, 43.4). The third sermon was published in part by J. J. BERTHIER, *Sanctus Thomas Aquinas « Doctor Communis » Ecclesiae. I. Testimonia Ecclesiae*, Rome 1914, p. 56-61; LAURENT, *Roger et Thomas*, p. 166-73, published sections from the other two.

[61] JOHN XXII, *Redemptionem misit*, in *Bullarium*, IV (1859), p. 304, « ...multa scripsi in fide Iesu Christi et sanctae Romanae Ecclesiae, cuius correctioni cuncta subiicio, cuncta suppono ». See also ibid., p. 305, « Tu es Petrus et super... ».

[62] See WALZ, *Historia Canonizationis*, p. 146-47. For JOHN XXII's pronouncement against the Fraticelli (Nov. 12, 1323), *Cum inter nonnullos*, see *Enchiridion Symbolorum*, ed. H. Denzinger and A. Schönmetzer, 36a ed., Rome 1973, p. 288-89 (nr. 930-31). On the canonization, see now also WALZ, *Papst Johannes XXII. und Thomas von Aquin. Zur Geschichte der Heiligsprechung des Aquinaten*, in *St. Thomas Aquinas 1274-1974. Commemorative Studies*, I, Toronto 1974, p. 29-47.

[63] See LAURENT, *Roger et Aquinas*, p. 160 n. 3.

[64] See WALZ, *Historia Canonizationis*, p. 146-47, 163.

mas' canonization may not be altogether fortuitous, as a Dominican scholar has suggested [65]. My point is that, in any case, from the very beginning Thomas was seen as eminently orthodox, as a friend and counsellor of the popes during whose lifetimes he lived, and as a theologian docile to papal teaching. This was not true of all other scholastic masters.

It was during the Avignonese residency that the office of Master of the Sacred Palace began to take recognizable and stable form. The Master was the chief teacher of theology in the papal Studium, and eventually assumed other duties like the censorship of sermons to be delivered at the court. He also gave theological instruction during consistories to the cardinals' attendants who awaited them [66]. By 1409 it was already considered an ancient tradition that this office be assigned to a member of the Dominican order, probably because that order was from its earliest years more committed to the academic study of theology than were the others. A legend sprang up, as a matter of fact, that Saint Dominic was the first to hold the office [67]. Even before Thomas' canonization, the Dominicans had taken him as their guide in theology, so that to assign the office of Master to the Dominicans was in effect to commit it to a strong and continuing Thomistc influence. At Avignon it was to the Dominicans that the popes habitually turned for theological counsel [68].

As Thomas was actually interpreted by the Dominicans of the fourteenth and fifteenth centuries, his doctrine came to the support of the papacy in one of its greatest trials. From the beginning of the Schism in 1378 well into the pontificate of Julius II, prerogatives of the papacy were under attack from the conciliarists and their allies. A recent dissertation has shown that during this time the Dominicans were in the forefront in defense of the papacy and of the essentially monarchial structure of the Church [69]. With the

---

[65] *Ibidem.*

[66] See R. Creytens, *Le « Studium Romanae Curiae » et le Maître du Sacré Palais, AFP,* 12 (1942), p. 5-83.

[67] See Creytens, *Le « Studium »*, p. 8-12, and R. Loenertz, *Saint Dominique écrivain, maître en theologie, professeur à Rome et Maître du Sacré Palais, AFP,* 12 (1942), p. 84-97.

[68] See B. Guillemain, *La cour pontificale d'Avignon (1309-1376). Étude d'une societé,* Paris 1962, p. 382-91 (Bibliothèque des Écoles françaises d'Athènes et de Rome, 201).

[69] J. A. Mirus, *The Dominican Order and the Defense of the Papacy in the Renaissance,* Princeton University Dissertation 1973. I used the copy in the Institutum Historicum Fratrum Praedicatorum, Rome. See also Id., *On the Deposition of the Pope for Heresy,* « Archivum Historiae Pontificiae », 13 (1975), p. 231-48.

Dominicans the arguments in favor of papal prerogatives shifted for the most part from the earlier canonical arguments to more strictly theological ones.

Juan de Torquemada of the Order of Preachers is perhaps the most distinguished name we associate with papal primacy during this period [70]. It is important for our purposes to locate him in time and place. Torquemada was appointed Master of the Sacred Palace by Eugene IV in 1435. Without doubt his thorough defense of papal primacy in his *Oratio synodalis de primatu* in October, 1439, led to his elevation to the College of Cardinals within a few months. No later than 1453 he finished his chief work, *Summa de ecclesia,* dedicated to Nicholas V at whose court he still resided. The positions expounded in that work are indicated by its full title, *Summa contra ecclesiae et sedis apostolicae adversarios.* Thus Nicholas would have seen during the difficult days of the Council of Basel and the Council of Ferrara-Florence convincing apologiae for papal positions argued by a Dominican who would be a participant in the conclave that elected him. More broadly, he almost surely would have been aware of the important role other Dominicans played at Florence in support of the papacy during discussions with the Greeks [71].

The Thomistic influence continued in Rome from the time of Nicholas until Carafa. Jacobus Gil had been a reformer in Aragon before he assumed his long tenure as Master of the Sacred Palace, 1453-72/73. He took his office seriously, and left a number of writings, all unedited, in which he undertakes to defend orthodoxy on questions like the poverty of Christ and the Immaculate Conception [72]. On that latter issue he feared the Franciscans were flirting with a form of Pelagianism.

Perhaps the most impressive Thomist in Rome during these same years was Domenico de' Domenichi. This distinguished theol-

---

[70] The literature on Torquemada is abundant. Besides MIRUS' dissertation, some recent studies, with further bibliography, are: V. B. DE HEREDIA, *Noticias y documentos para la biografía del Cardenal Juan de Torquemada, AFP,* 30 (1960), p. 53-148; P. MASSI, *Magistero infallibile del Papa nella teologia di Giovanni da Torquemada,* Turin 1957 (Scrinium Theologicum, 8); K. BINDER, *Wesen und Eigenschaften der Kirche bei Kardinal Juan de Torquemada, O.P.,* Innsbruck 1955; ID., *Konzilsgedanken bei Kardinal Juan de Torquemada, O.P.,* Vienna 1976 (Wiener Beiträge zur Theologie, 49).

[71] See G. MEERSSEMAN, *Les Dominicains présent au Concile de Ferrare-Florence jusqu'au décret d'Union pour les grecs (6 juillet 1439), AFP,* 9 (1939), p. 62-75. See also BERTHIER, *Sanctus Thomas Aquinas,* p. 281-95, for a review of the councils from Lyons I to Lateran V.

[72] See T. KAEPPELI, *Scriptores Ordinis Praedicatorum Medii Aevi,* 2 vols. to date, Rome 1970-75, II, p. 295-97, and R. CREYTENS, *Les écrits de Jacques Gil O. P., AFP,* 10 (1940), p. 158-68.

ogian and churchman, not himself a Dominican, was strongly influenced by Thomistic positions [73]. Like so many at this time, his strongest interest was in politico-ecclesiastical questions. He defended a strong papal authority — just as Cajetan would do later against the *conciliabulum* of Pisa and, along with Prierias, against Luther. Prierias, recommended by Cajetan for the office of Master of the Sacred Palace, which he held from 1515 until 1523, at the same time taught Thomistic theology at the Sapienza.

The point is that Saint Thomas, as he was mediated to the Renaissance popes through their theologians, looked congenial. He was enlisted in their aid in some bitter conflicts. This fact must surely have considerable bearing on the reverence with which he was held in Renaissance Rome. On the other hand, if the popes hoped that the panegyrists at the Minerva would develop this aspect of Thomas' utility, they would have been somewhat disappointed, at least insofar as we can judge from the orations that survive. Thomas' friendship with the popes, his defense of the Church against the Fraticelli, and his refutation of the « errors of the Greeks » who refused to recognize papal primacy are occasionally mentioned, but never given any special prominence. These were already classic themes in the biography of Thomas. His triumph over Averroes, William of Saint Amour, the Fraticelli, and the « errors of the Greeks » were singled out by his first biographer, William of Tocco, as his special achievement [74]. Even in Lippi's depiction in the Minerva of Thomas' triumph over heresy, the saint is shown refuting traditional figures like Arius, Nestorius, and Averroes. I suggest, therefore, that the politico-ecclesiastical uses of Thomas fit into a general and implicit framework of acceptability rather than form part of a deliberate propaganda campaign by the popes for those uses.

Just as Thomas seemed to come to the aid of the popes in their hours of need, so did the popes respond by praising Thomas' sanctity and doctrine. These « testimonia », beginning with John XXII down to the present century, have been collected [75]. Those

---

[73] See O'Malley, *Praise and Blame*, passim, and esp. H. Jedin, *Studien über Domenico de' Domenichi (1416-1478)*, « Abhandlungen der Mainzer Akad. der Wiss. und der Lit., Geistes- und sozialwiss. Kl. », 5 (1957), Wiesbaden 1958, p. 177-300, esp. 297-98.

[74] See William of Tocco's *Vita*, in *Fontes Vitae S. Thomae Aquinatis, Notis Historicis et Criticis Illustrati*, ed. D. Prümmer, Toulouse n.d. [1911], p. 90-96. See also Camporeale, *Valla tra Medioevo e Rinascimento*, p. 21-28, on Averroes, Arius, and Nestorius.

[75] Berthier, *Sanctus Thomas Aquinas*, p. 3-280, esp. 44-87 (John XXII to Leo X). See also S. M. Ramírez, *De Auctoritate Doctrinali S. Thomae Aquinatis*, Salamanca 1952.

from Avignon and the Renaissance are impressive, and there is hardly a pope during those periods who did not have a word of praise for Thomas. Such a record would be difficult to equal.

Impressive though that record was, it seems to have been inadequate for at least one of Thomas' followers. To compensate for it, that person, still to be surely identified, composed sometime around 1473 a tribute to Thomas' orthodoxy and assigned it to « Pope Innocent ». The quotation cannot be found in any authentic papal writings. Its gist is not altogether inconsistent with some of the papal statements about Thomas, but its formulation is much more emphatic. Thomas' teaching is commended in the highest possible terms, and its enemies are accordingly denigrated: anybody who follows Thomas' teaching will never be found to have strayed from the path of truth, whereas the orthodoxy of anybody who attacks him will always be suspect [76].

Bandello already incorporated this quotation into his first work on the Immaculate Conception, 1475, to bolster his position, and he attributed it to « Pope Innocent ». He used it again in his second work on the subject [77]. Maturanzio delivered his panegyric at the Minerva in 1485. He seems to have been aware of the apocryphal lines. In the humanistic manner that preferred allusion and suggestion to direct quotation, he paraphrases the essential point: if you like Thomas, you can know that you will never err in your faith [78].

Martinus de Viana, a scholastic theologian, actually quotes the apocryphal tribute in his panegyric at the Minerva in 1496, attributing it to Pope Innocent IV [79]. The statement, by now quoted by many other authors, has thus early been launched on its course through history. Challenged in the seventeenth century, especially by the Franciscan Pedro de Alva y Astorga, its authenticity was vigorously and, seemingly successfully, defended by the Dominicans [80].

---

[76] Here is the form in which the quotation commonly appears: « Huius [Thomae] doctrina prae ceteris, excepta canonica, habet proprietatem verborum, modum dicendorum, veritatem sententiarum, ita ut numquam qui eam tenuerit inveniatur a veritatis tramite deviasse, et qui eam impugnaverit semper fuerit de veritate suspectus ».

[77] BANDELLO, *Liber recollectorius*, f. 58v; *De puritate*, f. 94r.

[78] MATURANZIO, *Oratio*, f. 43r, « Ille se sciat in fide aberraturum numquam, cui Thomas valde placuerit ». For the humanists' preference for paraphrase over exact quotation, see O'MALLEY, *Praise and Blame*, p. 53-55, 66-67.

[79] DE VIANA, *Oratio*, f. [5r].

[80] See ALVA Y ASTORGA, *Funiculi*, p. 330-71, and, e.g., PICCINARDI, *De approbatione Thomae*, II, p. 23-52. The Dominican D. MORALES dedicated a whole book to an exegesis of this quotation and to a defense of its authenticity. *Laus divi Thomae pro explicatione et defensione doctrinae traditae a R. M. Gravina in Cherubim Paradisi*, Naples 1662.

Though Pope Innocent VI (1352-62) was most often assigned as its author, Popes Innocent IV, Innocent V, and Clement VI were also considered as candidates. This minor, but long-lived and eminently successful piece of Renaissance forgery perhaps achieved its greatest triumph with Pope Leo XIII in 1879. Leo, in his important encyclical *Aeterni Patris,* which gave papal impetus to the Neo-Thomist movement in the Catholic Church, singled out the words of « Pope Innocent VI » as the most fitting tribute any of his predecessors had paid to Saint Thomas [81]. The forgery still passes as genuine, and its history has yet to be written [82].

Thomas had, however, a greater authority than any pope to commend his theology. This brings us back to the Carafa chapel in the Minerva. In the chapel is depicted the miraculous crucifix of the Dominican convent in Naples. From that crucifix, according to the legend, the Savior said to Thomas, « Bene scripsisti de me ». The story is recounted in William of Tocco's life of Thomas, finished in a revised version in 1320/21, just before the canonization [83].

The legend was popular during the Renaissance. It occurs in a majority of the panegyrics at the Minerva and in other works as well. As a recent scholar has accurately noted, « It is, possibly, the best known and most frequently mentioned wonder of his whole life » [84]. No other scholastic doctor, not even any Father of the Church, could boast a similar story.

The legend, however, has not been without its skeptics and critics. The Carmelite, Blessed Baptista Mantuanus, showed a decided reserve towards it in his *Opus aureum in Thomistas,* 1492 [85]. It was attacked, as we might expect, by Alva y Astorga in the seventeenth century [86]. Valla, in his *Adnotationes,* discounted and derided a similar legend according to which Saint Paul appeared to Tho-

---

81 LEO XIII, *Aeterni Patris,* in *Leonis XIII Pontificis Maximi Acta,* I, Rome 1881, p. 276.

82 There is a brief summary of the evidence by the Benedictine editors of the *Cursus Theologicus* of JOHN OF SAINT THOMAS, I, Paris 1931, p. 235 n. 1. The quotation seems to appear for the first time in the Dominican PETRUS DE BERGAMO, *Tabula super omnia opera Thomae Aquinatis,* Bologna 1473 (Hain nr. *2816), f. [3v].

83 WILLIAM OF TOCCO, *Vita,* p. 108. BERNARD GUI also relates the story in his *Vita* of Thomas, published in a revised version in 1324/26, *Fontes Vitae,* p. 189.

84 E. COLLEDGE, *The Legend of St. Thomas Aquinas,* in *Aquinas Commemorative Studies,* I, p. 13-28, esp. 22.

85 B. MANTUANUS (Battista Spagnoli), *Opus aureum,* in KRISTELLER, *Le Thomisme,* p. 152. See also R. ROSA, *Tomismo et antitomismo in Battista Spagnoli Mantovano (1447-1516),* « Memorie Domenicane », n.s. 7 (1976), p. 227-64.

86 ALVA Y ASTORGA, *Funiculi,* p. 462-76.

mas and praised his commentaries on the Epistles [87]. Valla's failure to mention the legend of the crucifix in his panegyric at the Minerva was significant and, almost certainly, deliberate.

Valla's panegyric of Aquinas — in many ways really a counter-panegyric — appears all the bolder when placed in the general context I have described. In 1457 the memory of Nicholas V's recent decisions about the celebration of the feast must still have been vivid. Torquemada was still alive and was possibly in the audience along with the other cardinals. More important still, the liturgical significance of the feast that placed Thomas on a par with the four Latin doctors and that in its solemnity even seemed to raise him above them adds significance to Valla's explicit refusal to do so in the closing words of his *Encomion*. Gasparo Veronese's description of the reaction of Valla's listeners that day takes on new force, even granted his personal antipathy to Valla [88]. When Cardinal Guillaume d'Estouteville criticized Valla and said that he had spoken nonsense, « everybody agreed with him » — « censura huius principis apud omnes valuit plurimum ».

Valla's panegyric has sometimes been taken as typical of humanist reaction to Scholasticism. This does not tally very well with the evidence, even restricted to the sermons at the Minerva. Campano, Maturanzio, Inghirami, and Aurelio Brandolini were certainly, according to everybody's definition, humanists. Yet they found it possible to praise Thomas' writings and doctrine as well as his sanctity. There is no evidence indicating that they were insincere in their praise. It makes more sense to postulate that Valla's originality and genius allowed him to see profound discrepancies that lesser minds did not perceive. In the concordistic atmosphere of Renaissance Rome, it was thought possible to harmonize these diverse systems [89].

I believe a case can be made, as well, for the opinion that there were qualities in Thomas' style that would give him an appeal to humanists that other scholastic authors lacked. Gothic though Thomas' writings were in their structure, method, and relentless attention to detail, they also possessed certain classical virtues like

---

[87] L. VALLA, *Adnotationes*, in *Opera*, I, p. 865. See also ALVA Y ASTORGA, *Funiculi*, p. 492-97. PICCINARDI, *De approbatione Thomae*, II, p. 89-96, defends the legend.

[88] GASPARO DA VERONA, *De gestis tempore pontificis maximi Pauli secundi*, ed. Giuseppe Zippel, in *RIS*, n.ed., III, parte 16, Città di Castello 1904, p. 33. For the best analysis of Valla's treatment in the *Encomium* of Thomas' relationship to the ancient doctors of the Church, see CAMPOREALE, *Valla tra Medioevo e Rinascimento*, p. 56-62.

[89] See O'MALLEY, *Praise and Blame*, esp. p. 161-64.

order, clarity, and simplicity of expression. In fact, these qualities were often singled out for praise by panegyrists at the Minerva [90], just as they had been at Avignon many years earlier by Pierre Roger [91].

There was, besides, perhaps a deeper level on which Thomas would have appealed. Scholars have argued that certain positions of the « via moderna » of Ockham and others corresponded to positions implicit or explicit in some humanists [92]. Perhaps it is possible also to argue that a similar correlation can be made between the « via antiqua » of Thomas and other figures influenced by Humanism, especially when they move in the atmosphere of a court.

Thomas insisted on the harmony that reigned between nature and grace. In his God intelligence clearly governed will. There was thus no capriciousness in the constitution of the universe or in its governance. For Thomas the world was nothing if not ordered. The mark of wisdom, divine or human, was to be able to produce order; it was thus the gift most needed by the ruler. These ideas had classical and patristic equivalents and were easily assimilated into a humanistic world view. They were congenial to a court where order and harmony were postulated as desirable and realizable goals [93].

The story of the papal court during the Renaissance is not, however, one of unrelieved harmony and mutual comprehension even in the court's dealings with the Dominican order. It would be lopsided to bypass mention of these occasional tensions. Pius II effected in 1462 the deposition of the master general [94]. Bandello's works against the Immaculate Conception appeared at just the time Sixtus IV, the Franciscan, was showing official favor towards the doctrine [95]. Then there is the Savonarola case, the most famous

---

90 See SÁNCHEZ DE ARÉVALO, *Sermo*, ff. 235v-236r; CAMPANO, *Oratio*, f. [92v]; MATURANZIO, *Oratio*, ff. 42r-43r; BRANDOLINI, *Oratio*, f. [10]; INGHIRAMI, *Panegyricus*, ff. [11v-13r].

91 See LAURENT, *Roger et Aquinas*, p. 168-69, 172.

92 See H. A. OBERMAN, *Some Notes on the Theology of Nominalism, with Attention to its Relation to the Renaissance*, « Harvard Theological Review », 53 (1960), p. 47-76; ID., *The Shape of Late Medieval Thought. The Birthpangs of the Modern Era*, in *The Pursuit of Holiness in Late Medieval and Renaissance Religion*, ed. CH. TRINKAUS with H. OBERMAN, Leiden 1974, p. 3-25 (Studies in Late Medieval and Reformation Thought, 10); CH. TRINKAUS, *The Poet as Philosopher. Petrarch and the Formation of Renaissance Consciousness*, New Haven 1979, p. 52-89, 111-17.

93 See O'MALLEY, *Praise and Blame*, esp. p. 127-29, 147-49, 231.

94 See R. CREYTENS, *La déposition de Maître Martial Auribelli O. P. par Pie II (1462)*, *AFP* 45 (1975), p. 147-200.

95 See the article by X. LE BACHELET, *Immaculée Conception*, in *Dictionnaire de théologie catholique*, VII, part 2, esp. cols. 1120-24 on Bandello.

instance of altercation between the Holy See and a Dominican friar [96].

Moreover, not all the Dominicans who held official positions in Rome dedicated their full energies to Thomistic philosophy and theology. Sometimes they had other major interests, as is illustrated by the curious Giovanni Nanni (Annio da Viterbo), Master of the Sacred Palace, 1499-1502 [97]. Accordingly, the favor that Lorenzo Valla, Nicholas of Cusa, Aurelio Brandolini, Giles of Viterbo, and similar figures enjoyed at various times imposes caution about trying to reduce the theological and intellectual traditions of Renaissance Rome to a single formula. Nevertheless, the picture that emerges from Rome for the period between Nicholas V and the beginning of the Lutheran Reformation is one of strong support for the papacy by members of the Dominican order and of an extraordinarily consistent influence exercised by them through the authority of their greatest master, Thomas Aquinas.

I should like to conclude this article by summarizing some of the chief points that it has made:

1. Paris de Grassis' document, the *Supplementum,* proves that papal solemnization of the feast of Thomas Aquinas was a Renaissance creation, not a mere continuation of a medieval tradition.

2. Along with other documentation, that text helps establish how unique in Rome the celebration of Aquinas' feast was. He was accorded a liturgical prominence so great that it hardly bears comparison with any other non-biblical saint, even with Augustine.

3. The special insistence on the Creed in his Mass shows that he was honored as much for his doctrine as for his sanctity, and. in effect, was placed on a level with Augustine, Jerome, Ambrose, and Gregory.

---

[96] See esp. R. De Maio, *Savonarola e la Curia Romana,* Rome 1969 (Uomini e dottrine, 15).

[97] On Annio, see esp. E. N. Tigerstedt, *Ioannes Annius and Graecia Mendax,* in *Classical, Medieval and Renaissance Studies in Honor of Berthold Louis Ullman,* ed. Charles Henderson, Jr., II, Rome 1964, p. 293-310; R. Weiss, *Traccia per una biografia di Annio da Viterbo,* « Italia medioevale e umanistica », 5 (1962), p. 425-41; Id., *An Unknown Epigraphic Tract by Annius of Viterbo,* in *Italian Studies Presented to E. R. Vincent,* Cambridge 1962, p. 101-20; F. Secret, *Egidio da Viterbo et quelques-uns de ses contemporains,* « Augustiniana », 16 (1966), p. 371-85; A. Biondi, *Annio da Viterbo e un aspetto dell'orientalismo di Guillaume Postel,* « Bollettino della società di studi valdesi », XCII, n. 132 (1972), p. 49-67; C. Fasoli, *Profezia e astrologia in un testo di Annio da Viterbo,* in « Studi sul medioevo cristiano offerti a Raffaello Morghen per il 90° anniversario dell'Istituto Storico Italiano (1883-1973) », II, Roma 1974, p. 1027-60.

4. This liturgical prominence of Aquinas in Rome corresponds to a theological prominence that had roots in Avignon but that found its most impressive expression in Renaissance Rome with Juan de Torquemada, Domenico de' Domenichi, and Cajetan, as well as with lesser figures.

5. This theological tradition had an institutional counterpart in the office of the Master of the Sacred Palace and, to a smaller degree, in officials of the Dominican order in Rome.

6. Some Dominican masters taught Thomism at the Sapienza, and at least one of them did the same in his own « school ». The influence was also exercised, therefore, outside the strict confines of the institutions of the papal court and the Dominican order.

7. Cajetan spent most of his adult years in Rome. His presence there was not an isolated or insignificant phenomenon, but fitted into the much larger pattern of a convergence of Thomistic influences in and around the papal court.

8. There were many reasons for the favor shown Aquinas in Renaissance Rome, but especially important among them was the identification Dominican authors and their supporters made between Thomas' teaching and various causes dear to the papacy.

9. The intellectual and theological tradition of Renaissance Rome have yet to be studied in a systematic and comprehensive way. Today we know enough only to be certain how complex these traditions were. This article does not pretend to exhaust even the history of Thomism there during the period. Nonetheless, I think it is possible to assert that the single strongest theological influence in Rome was Thomas Aquinas, as interpreted especially by his Dominican confreres.

10. Thus, the chapel dedicated to Aquinas at the Minerva emerges with a new importance. Because of the annual visit of the Sacred College, as well as Nicholas V's earlier directives concerning the feast, it had a liturgical prominence like no other Renaissance monument outside the precincts of the Vatican. More important, it symbolized a theological tradition that was operative in Renaissance Rome far beyond the personal devotion of Oliviero Carafa and the friars of the Dominican church where the chapel is located.

Appendix

TRANSCRIPTION OF DE GRASSIS' TEXT

De missa et festo sancti Thomae de Aquino

Ante tempora sanctae memoriae domini Nicolai papae quinti nullam de hoc festo sancti Thomae Aquinatensis aut de eius missa celebritatem in usu nec eam diem, quae vii martii est, a sacro palatio festificatam fuisse legimus [1]. Sed ipse pontifex, qui etiam Thomas antea vocatus est, ex eo quod cognomines ambo fuerunt et quod in die hoc festum praecedente in pontificem electus fuit, primus missam hanc in ecclesia beatae Mariae supra Minervam fratrum praedicatorum de Urbe, cuius ordinis sanctum Thomam fuisse constat, celebrari et diem ipsam pro festo sacri palatii ab auditoribus et aliis solemnizari quotannis instituit. Ad quam missam in dicta ecclesia audiendam ipse pontifex accedere plerumque consuevit, quod institutum nostris etiam temporibus, sine tamen pontificis praesentia, observatur. Nam et propterea cardinales fere omnes illuc velut ad praecipuam solemnitatem absque eo quod ab aliquo [2] requirantur, sed ultro conveniant sive divi doctoris eiusdem devotione, sive longi temporis assuetudine ducti, sive interventu reverendissimi domini, Oliverii Caraffae, episcopi Ostiensis, cardinalis Neapolitani, viri undecumque exemplaris et impraesentiarum dicti ordinis protectoris, qui etiam ibi sacellum cultu et decore spectabile in honorem numinis [3] illius exstruxit.

Ordo missae [4].

Itaque ipsa die super altare capellae principalis in ecclesia praedicta de Minerva festiviter ornata, missa solemnis ac particularis et propria de sancto per aliquem de familia protectoris prelatum in paramentis albis cum ministris et cantoribus capellae papalis cantatur, in qua « Gloria in excelsis », « Pax vobis », et unica specialis dicitur oratio, sine commemoratione de feria, et « Credo », id est Symbolus, qui [5], licet ab initio institutionis praedictae per aliquos annos iure ordinario omissus fuerit, cum ipse sanctus Thomas de quattuor doctoribus ecclesiae ordinariis non exstiterit, tamen idem pontifex Symbolum praedictum dicendum omnino statuit. Finito evangelio, immediate ante Symbolum, petita benedictione, sermo fieri solet per aliquem potius secularem cum cappa indutum quam per regularem, sed nec per ipsum qui oravit in fine orationis neque per celebrantem in fine missae aliqua indulgentia publicatur, cum ipsa plenaria per diversorum pontificum bullas altare praedictum visitantibus, ut dicitur, concessa sit. Praefatio de communi confessorum. Reliqua more solito fiunt.

A = Biblioteca Ambrosiana, cod. I 185 inf., ff. 233^{v}-234^{r}.
V = Biblioteca Vaticana, cod. Vat. lat. 5634bis, ff. 318^{v}-320^{r}.

1 legimus fuisse *tr.* V
2 aliquo praeinvitentur et [sic! = perinvitentur?] A, cancelled in V
3 nominis A
4 Ordo missae *om.* A
5 quod V

Finita demum missa, cardinalis ipse Neapolitanus, protector modernus, consuevit per caerimoniarium invitari facere praesentes ibidem cardinales ut inde ad sacellum ubi altare est pro adipiscenda indulgentia procedere velint, sicque primo episcopi, tum presbyteri, inde diaconi cardinales ordinate procedunt [6]. Et intra capellam orant, cum quibus est protector in suae promotionis ordine constitutus, qui, ex quo non est in ecclesia sui tituli, ideo sicut nec in ultimo loco post diaconos omnes sedere ita et nullis advenientibus ad ecclesiam cardinalibus obviare nec in fine eis gratias agere decet.

Praelati huic missa, absente papa, non cum cappis, sed quotidianis mantellis interesse debent. Si autem hoc festum venerit aliqua dominica quadragesimae, aut in ipsa die cinerum, tunc transfertur in sequentem diem, et fit missa. In qua tamen advertatur ut prius habeatur indulgentia particularis, quia indulgentiae per bullas concessae intelliguntur in die ipsius festi currentis et non translatione eiusdem. Anno 1490 hoc festum fuit dominica 2ª quadragesimae, et papa Innocentius octavus transtulit festum in die lunae, ac voluit quod ipsa die lunae translati festi missa solemnis consueta ut supra celebraretur ac quod eadem die lunae esset festum palatii. Et similiter anno 1501 idem in omnibus fuit. Et anno 1492 venit in die cinerum et sequenti die ut supra factum est [7].

---

[6] accedunt A

[7] festum palatii. Et anno 1492 venit in die cinerum, et sequenti die ut supra factum est. Similiter et anno 1501. Idem in omnibus factum fuit de mandato papae. V

II

EGIDIO DA VITERBO AND RENAISSANCE ROME

Judging from what we have heard during this conference on Egidio da Viterbo, we have to be impressed by the man. We have been reminded of his role as bishop of Viterbo and as reformer within the Augustinian order. We now see with greater clarity his contribution to the revival of classical learning and to the study of Sacred Scripture. We have a better understanding of his views on contemplation and of the significance of the "Historia XX saeculorum."

Yet nobody knows better than those of us who have participated in the conference that we have left many aspects of Egidio's life and works practically untouched. We want to know more about Egidio the student of the cabala. We want to hear about the impact he may have had on the programs for the ceiling of the Sistine Chapel by Michelangelo and the frescos by Raphael in the Stanze of the Apostolic Palace in the Vatican. We have failed to discuss in any depth Egidio the poet, Egidio the scholastic, Egidio the Platonist, Egidio the visionary and eschatologist, Egidio the papal legate, and Egidio the confidant of Pope Julius II and Pope Leo X. Egidio combined the *vita activa* with the *vita contemplativa* in a way and to a degree that must have impressed his contemporaries as vividly as it does us, and we are intrigued to learn details about it. What I am saying, in other words, is that he seems perfectly to have fulfilled the Renaissance ideal of humanity at its best and most accomplished—Egidio, *l'uomo universale*, as Father Martin has so accurately named him.[1]

Egidio fulfilled that ideal, however, in ways that were peculiarly his own—in ways that represented now one, now another facet of Renaissance civilization, in ways that at times conformed with the values and interests of his contemporaries and that at other

---

[1] Francis X. Martin, "The Writings of Giles of Viterbo," *Augustiniana*, 29 (1979), 144.

times seem to have set him apart from them. The question emerges: how accurately does Egidio represent his age, and how do we fit him into the life and culture especially of Rome in the early Cinquecento? Today we possess a much more sophisticated and detailed understanding of Renaissance Humanism and of Julius II and Leo X than we did even twenty years ago. Where does Egidio stand in this rich and complex scene?

I will address questions like these this morning, but of course in a partial and highly selective manner, for only a *uomo* as *universale* as Egidio himself could do them adequate justice. I will particularly try to analyze the nature of the Renaissance Humanism that he exemplified and the nature of the reforms that he proposed. In treating Egidio under these two broad categories—Humanism and reform—I will compare and contrast him with his contemporaries in an attempt to put his life and accomplishments into historical perspective. I will also try to show a relationship between his Humanism and his reform ideals.

I have no intention of entering into the controversies among scholars as to how the terms "humanist" and "Humanism" are most properly verified in the Quattrocento and Cinquecento.[2] If we take these terms in their broadest sense of indicating the revival and promotion of all those pursuits that we particularly identify with the Renaissance, Egidio surely qualifies. With certain limitations, he also seems to qualify if we narrow the terms to specify the revival of the languages, literature, and literary styles of ancient Greece, Rome, and Palestine—or, the cabala, and what was believed to be a body of sacred literature from the ancient Mediterranean world. Within the framework of the *studia humanitatis* or *bonae litterae*, what profile of Egidio da Viterbo surfaces?

Bonae litterae—what did that expression signify in the Renaissance? It meant the rebirth of literary studies, especially in their two traditional components of grammar and rhetoric. Today few scholars would deny that Renaissance Humanism was "a pursuit of eloquence," as Hanna Gray described it many years ago.[3] But

---

[2] On this issue, see, e.g., WILLIAMS J. BOUWSMA, "The Interpretation of Renaissance Humanism," 2nd ed., Service Center for Teachers of History, Publication Number 18 (Washington, 1966); DENYS HAY, "Storici e Rinascimento negli ultimi venticinque anni," in *Il Rinascimento*: *Interpretazioni e problemi* (Rome-Bari, 1979), pp. 3-41; EUGENIO GARIN, "Interpretazioni del Rinascimento," *Medioevo e Rinascimento* (Bari, 1976).

[3] "Renaissance Humanism: The Pursuit of Eloquence," *Journal of the History of Ideas*, 24 (1963), 497-514.

once the pursuit of eloquence is closely examined, considerable discrepancy appears between those who engaged in it as a pursuit of grammar and those for whom it meant a pursuit of rhetoric. We must examine these categories in more detail.

Rhetoric, as presented in classical treatises on the subject, meant oratory. Scholars today, however, make a useful distinction between "primary" and "secondary" rhetoric.[4] Primary rhetoric is the rhetoric described in Cicero's *De inventione* and in the *Rhetorica ad Herennium*, i.e., the art of speech-making, the art of oratory. This rhetoric is oral; in itself it has no text, though subsequently an enunciation can be treated as a text. It is directed to civic concerns in the law courts, in the senates and parliaments, and in ceremonial settings like weddings, funerals, and inaugurations. The training of public speakers like lawyers and politicians was the single goal of rhetoric undestood in this sense. The primacy of this primary rhetoric is a fundamental fact in the classical tradition through the ages.

"Secondary" rhetoric derives from primary and is an adaptation of it, as the term itself implies. It consists in the apparatus of rhetorical techniques clustering around discourse when those techniques are not being used for their primary oral purpose. In secondary rhetoric the speech-act is displaced by the text. The most frequent manifestations of secondary rhetoric are commonplaces, figures of thought and speech, and tropes in elaborate writing. During the Renaissance one of the first areas for which we have treatises on how to apply rhetorical techniques to a text rather than to a speech-act is epistolography—with Aurelio Brandolini's extensive treatise on it written sometime before 1485 and Erasmus' *De conscribendis epistolis* a half-century later, to say nothing of more modest efforts by others.[5] Historical narrative, diatribes, even philosophical and quasi-philosophical dialogues are further manifestations of secondary rhetoric.

A consistent characteristic of classical rhetoric has been to move from primary into secondary forms. This tendency is sometimes called *letteraturizzazione*.[6] This means a tendency to shift focus

---

[4] See GEORGE A. KENNEDY, *Classical Rhetoric and Its Christian and Secular Tradition from Ancient to Modern Times* (Chapel Hill, 1980), esp. pp. 4-5.

[5] See A. GERLO, "The *Opus de Conscribendis Epistolis* of Erasmus and the Tradition of the *Ars Epistolica*," in *Classical Influences on European Culture, A. D 500-1500*, ed. R. R. BOLGER (Cambridge, England, 1971), pp. 103-14, and my *Praise and Blame in Renaissance Rome* (Durham, 1979), pp. 45-50.

[6] See KENNEDY, *Classical Rhetoric*, p. 5, and VASILE FLORESCU, *La Retorica nel suo sviluppo storico* (Bologna, 1971), p. 43 and passim.

from persuasion to narration, from civic to personal and private contexts, and from speech-making to literature, even including poetry. It is at this point, in fact—at poetry—that secondary rhetoric begins to blur almost imperceptibly into grammar.

In classical times, rhetoric presupposed grammar, but "grammar" meant much more than the elementary skills of reading and writing correctly. These skills had already been acquired under the *litterator* or *magister ludi* before the student entered the classroom of the grammarian. The "grammarian" taught literature, especially poetry, for it was from poetry, not prose, that rules of grammar were originally derived. One of the purposes of grammar was, therefore, to teach good style, to teach accurate and felicitous expression.[7]

Another purpose was to teach how to interpret a text. The grammarian was, indeed, almost myopically attached to his texts. His exposition of them was, in the first instance, philological, and concentrated on a word-by-word or line-by-line reading. When it was necessary to rise above this so-called "atomistic" exegesis to broader meaning, allegory was invoked. Allegory received a Christian benediction from Origen and other early Christian writers, and it was thenceforth the standard method for arriving at the inner, "meta-philological," and most genuine intent of the text. Texts were seen as expressions of philosophical or theological truths artfully masked "under the poetic veil." The grammarian's techniques for interpreting a text moved on two distinct levels, therefore: on a philological level of attention to minute details of usage, orthography, and similar matters, and on another level where allegorical or "poetical" interpretation allowed the scribe to discover philosophical or theological truths of the broadest scope.

Because of the stylistic purposes that constituted an important part of the grammarian's task, he borrowed elements from rhetorical treatises, and thereby appropriated techniques for persuasive discourse that were, strictly speaking, proper to rhetoric. Both in antiquity and in the Renaissance, this meant that often only a fragile barrier separated grammar from "secondary" rhetoric, and that, in turn, separated secondary rhetoric from primary.[8] But if we imagine a poet pouring over a text at one end of the spectrum and at the

---

[7] See H. I. Marrou, *A History of Education in Antiquity*, trans. George Lamb (New York, 1964), esp. pp. 199-242, and id., *Saint Augustin et la fin de la culture antique*, 4th ed. (Paris, 1958), esp. pp. 1-157.

[8] See O. B. Hardison, "The Orator and Poet: The Dilemma of Humanist Literature," *The Journal of Medieval and Renaissance Studies*, 1 (1971), 33-44.

other end a statesman on his feet pleading before the senate for a declaration of war, we perceive more clearly the issues at stake. The poet is the ideal artist turned inward on his own spirit; the orator, as conceived in Roman treatises on rhetoric, is the ideal leader, actively committed to the accomplishment of public and civic goals. The poet is a private person, by preference distanced from the tumult of the marketplace. He is dedicated to the *vita contemplativa* of study rather than to active engagement. In his examination of his texts he descends to the minutest details of punctuation and syntax, whereas the orator must rise to the high level of general ideas on justice, war, peace, and human dignity that were his assigned themes. The orator is totally committed to the *vita activa* as politician, lawyer, and public servant in Church or State.

Where do we locate Egidio da Viterbo on this humanistic spectrum, and what difference does it make? Where do other important Renaissance humanists fit on the spectrum, and are they closer to the grammatical end or to the rhetorical end? My thesis is that most of the major figures, despite what we usually read about them, are located on the area of the spectrum that begins with grammar and then moves into secondary rhetoric rather than the other way around. This was true, it seems to me, for the three greatest Renaissance humanists—Petrarch, Valla, and Erasmus. I have tried to show this elsewhere for Erasmus, but I believe it could easily be demonstrated also for Petrarch and Valla.[9] The touchstones for this demonstration would be some or all of the following: a professional interest in the discovery and editing of texts, the composition of poetry, ambivalence about sacred and secular oratory or even lack of interest in it, a penchant for allegorical interpretations instead of, or along with, philological and historical interpretations; the life-style correlation with this end of the spectrum is to favor the *scriptorium*, the classroom, the villa in the countryside—instead of the fora, the law courts, and the ceremonial halls of the *res publica*. The grammarian is essentially a scribe, and belongs to the scribal tradition of monastery and classroom. The rhetorician is by definition an activist, committed to the public weal by the very definition of his art.

---

[9] On Erasmus, see my "Grammar and Rhetoric in the Theology of Erasmus," in *Paideia*: *Special Renaissance Issue* (1983), id., "Erasmus and Luther: Continuity and Discontinuity as Key to Their Conflict," *The Sixteenth Century Journal*, 5/2 (1974), 47-65; and MARJORIE O'ROURKE BOYLE, *Erasmus on Language and Method in Theology* (Toronto, 1977). On Petrarch, see CHARLES TRINKAUS, *The Poet as Philosopher* (New Haven, 1979), esp. pp. 90-113; on Valla, see SALVATORE I. CAMPOREALE, *Lorenzo Valla*: *Umanesimo e teologia* (Florence, 1972).

These formal elements of the grammarian's or rhetorician's vocation have impact on the content of their writings. For religious persons like Erasmus and Egidio, especially, they have impact on their theology or spirituality. As I believe my study of Erasmus showed, for instance, his spiritual doctrine, for all of the great humanist's attempts to construct a spirituality for people living outside the cloister, has more affinity with the monastic tradition than we have previously been inclined to believe. What about Egidio?

Egidio is difficult to categorize. Prior general of the Augustinian order, papal legate, bishop of Viterbo, he did not retreat from public office. In this regard, his biography differs notably from that of Petrarch, Valla, and Erasmus, and it bears a closer resemblance to public servants like Coluccio Salutati, Leonardo Bruni, and Thomas More. Nonetheless, I believe that Egidio must be assigned a place closer to the grammarian's end of the spectrum than to the rhetorician's.

An examination of his writings verifies, it seems to me, this assessment. He wrote some poetry, and that is a significant fact. But more important, he had a passion for texts—a passion to collect them, to study them, to translate them, to emend them, and to seclude himself with them, as he seemingly did for long periods of time even as bishop of Viterbo. When he interpreted them, he turned to allegory, as is clear from his commentary "ad mentem Platonis" on the *Sentences* of Lombard, and even more dramatically illustrated by his consuming enthusiasm for the cabala. This is the style of interpretation of the mystic, the contemplative, the poet—of the person whose eyes naturally turn inwards, for whom public service is a distraction from what is truly important. Thus we can explain Egidio's reluctance to accept his appointment by Julius II as vicar general of the Augustinians as something more than a convention (though it was probably that as well), and we can also explain his disappearance from the public eye during his many years as bishop of Viterbo, 1523-32.

It is important, therefore, to specify the nature of Egidio's humanism because only thus can we place him in the context of the High Renaissance in Rome. It seems to me that my investigations into the sacred oratory of the papal court allow us to see that a quite different theology or spirituality developed there during the Renaissance that was much closer to the rhetorical end of the spectrum.[10] The immediate dependence of many of the sermons

---

10 See my *Praise and Blame.*

at the court on the principles of classical rhetoric—"primary" rhetoric—helped them develop a message that adapted Christian theology as a readier support for the *vita activa* than had been known before. This spirituality was appropriate for members of the court, who were dedicated to the public service of the Church, but only the art of ("primary") rhetoric provided the rubrics that allow such a spirituality to be articulated. Content was to a large degree dependent upon form.

Here was, then, a "civic spirituality"—I am obviously adopting and adapting Hans Baron's terminology—with an emphasis on *deeds* over speculation, on public service over retirement for contemplation, on insertion into historical circumstances over flight to idealized heavens.[11] The methodological correlate to all this was to discard allegorical and mystical interpretations of Scripture and to employ an historical or literal interpretation. That is precisely what these preachers did. We see in this phenomenon another manifestation of what seems to be a recurring pattern in cultural history. It seems to be almost a replay of the dialectic in the fourth and fifth centuries of Christian antiquity when the orators of Antioch, with their literal interpretation of Scripture, pitted themselves against the speculators of Alexandria, with their predilection for allegory.

Oratory was central to the papal court as to no other Renaissance institution because of its prominent place in the liturgies of the court, and that fact fostered the creation of a "rhetorical theology," in the strict sense of the term, on a scale unknown elsewhere in Europe. This was a theology quite different from what I would term the "grammatical theology" of Erasmus and Valla. As Salvatore Camporeale has observed in this regard: "Si hanno dunque nei secoli XV e XVI due momenti e aspetti molto differenziati dell'incidenza, sulla teologia contemporanea, della cultura umanistica."[12]

Even "due momenti" may be too few, once we begin to analyze "humanistic theology" in detail. It seems possible to distinguish within "grammatical theology" a more properly "philological theology" represented especially by Valla and, with qualifications, Erasmus, and a "poetic theology" represented by others. It is that latter, in any case, that I especially want to contrast with "rhetorical" (or "civic") theology.

---

[11] For BARON'S "civic Humanism," see his *The Crisis of the Early Italian Renaissance*, rev. ed. (Princeton, 1966).

[12] "'Coram papa inter missarum solemnia:' Liturgia della parola e cultura umanistica," *Memorie Domenicane*, N.S. 11 (1980), 631-32.

This "rhetorical theology" is simply the most obvious manifestation of a broader phenomenon at the papal court that we might call "rhetorical culture." We have, it is true, little information at present about the impact of this phenomenon beyond Rome and beyond the early Cinquecento. The central fact for us, however, is that Egidio, present though he was in Rome during the years this theological method developed, seems to have stood outside it. In that regard at least, he does not embody for us one of the most creative and unique characteristics of the religious culture of Renaissance Rome.

Is that assessment justified? What about his sermons at the papal court, the three sermons as bishop of Viterbo recently discovered by Professor Monfasani (Vat. lat. 6320), and the important orations delivered on various solemn occasions for Julius II? Do not these examples of "primary rhetoric" indicate a more "rhetorical theology"? My response to these questions must be based only on his three sermons as bishop and the orations intended for Julius II, for the rest of his oratory does not seem to have survived.

The sermons as bishop are neither homiletic nor scholastic in their form, and in fact are closer to the oratorical form of classical rhetoric than to either of those other standard forms of his day. Nonetheless, the form is "sui generis," as Monfasani has rightly indicated; the sermons have only vague exordia and perorations—to name only two peculiarities. The content, while purportedly dealing with concrete events from sacred history, is nonetheless "sapiential" (Platonic and cabalistic), etymological, allegorical, esoteric, and even apocalyptic. These qualities correlate with the traditional interests and techniques of the grammarian.

The two orations intended for Julius that I edited and published, though exemplifying in various particulars a mastery of the principles and techniques of "primary" rhetoric, can hardly be called orations at all in the form we now have them.[13] They are religious or quasi-philosophical discourses, replete with allegorical interpretations and turned towards the inner world of contemplation and speculation for disproportionately long sections. It is true that they both have effective perorations, but the discourse on "Man's Dignity" lacks even an exordium; in both pieces the other standard "parts" of an oration are difficult or impossible to discover.

---

[13] "Fulfillment of the Christian Golden Age under Pope Julius II: Text of a Discourse of Giles of Viterbo, 1507," *Traditio*, 25 (1969), 265-338; "Man's Dignity, God's Love and the Destiny of Rome: A Text of Giles of Viterbo," *Viator*, 3 (1972), 389-416.

The two orations edited by Dr. O'Reilly cannot be dismissed so easily.[14] Both the inaugural oration before the Fifth Lateran Council and the oration celebrating the reconciliation of Pope Julius II with Emperor Maximilian are anchored directly in the concrete events they celebrate. There is, thus, an emphasis on deeds and facts that is less evident in large portions of the two pieces that I published. But even in these orations there appears at times recourse to allegory regarding the historical facts that is telling and that indicates to me that Egidio, capable though he was of speaking appropriately for such situations, was more at home on the grammatical, the "poetic" end of the humanistic spectrum.

An analysis of the "Historia XX saeculorum" yields the same results. Historical narrative was, in the classical tradition, perhaps the genre of "secondary rhetoric" that most closely approximated primary. Historical narrative by definition concerned public affairs, dealt with deeds and not with abstract doctrines or inner emotions, and often contained important orations, i.e., examples of primary rhetoric. These narratives were meant to promote patriotism and civic virtues, not private relationships between individuals or the observance of the vows of the cloister. Rhetorical though they might be in their literary techniques, they are grounded in verifiable facts that ground the direction of the narrative and the conclusions drawn from them. Think of Thucydides, Bruni, Machiavelli.

Egidio's "Historia," written at the height of his powers between about 1513 and 1518, is about as far removed from such "rhetorical historiography" as we can imagine. It is dominated by a structure derived from the cabala, and its method of interpretation is allegorical and arbitrary in the extreme.[15] It is so far off the spectrum on the poetic end that it can hardly be considered a rhetorical work at all. No one deeply influenced by the principles, methods, and concerns characteristic of primary rhetoric would have produced a work like the "Historia." The same can be said even more emphatically of Egidio's commentary on Lombard, filled as it is with poetic, allegorical, and mythological interpretations of a sober theological text.[16]

---

14 "Maximus Caesar et Pontifex Maximus," *Augustiniana*, 22 (1972), 80-117; "'Without Councils we cannot be saved...:' Giles of Viterbo addresses the Fifth Lateran Council," ibid., (1977), 166-204.

15 See my *Giles of Viterbo on Church and Reform* (Leiden, 1968), esp. pp. 100-38.

16 See Eugenio Massa, *I fondamenti metafisici della 'dignitas hominis' e testi inediti di Egidio da Viterbo* (Turin, 1954).

Egidio's correspondence falls into two clearly distinct categories—the official correspondence as prior general, so capably discussed here by Dr. O'Reilly, and the humanistic correspondence found principally in the codices of the Biblioteca Angelica in Rome and in the Biblioteca Nazionale of Naples. The official correspondence points, by force of the very circumstances of Egidio's office, to the *vita activa,* but does little more in fact than confirm his heavy sense of responsibility for duties that we know he had to perform. The humanistic letters are, broadly speaking, typical of most such correspondence from Renaissance classicists—concerned with affectivity, with personalized and privatized relationships that for that reason bring the letters as close to poetry as their stylistic techniques depend, on the other hand, on rhetoric.

In the latter years of his life, Egidio committed himself ever more passionately to the study of the cabala and to his Christian interpretation of it. This fact irrefutably verifies, in my opinion, his location on the "poetic" segment of the humanistic spectrum. The speculative, fantastic, and protean doctrine of the cabala correlates with its poetic hermeneutics. Egidio quickly moves beyond the "nuda historia" of the text to arrive at the inner meaning—at the "arcana theologia" and at the "divina sapientia." His predilection for the Gospel of John reveals his mentality: "Joannes evangelistarum unus [est] qui Messiae non actiones humanas tantum, ut alii, sed arcanam theologiam et divinam sapientiam conscribendam suscepit."[17]

Egidio's colleagues as preachers at the papal court moved in precisely the opposite direction. Whereas Egidio directed his efforts towards translating the deeds and actions of Christ into abstract and spiritualized doctrines, the typical preachers were, in contrast, attempting to translate doctrines into more concrete representations or narrations. Some of their sermons of the feast of the Ascension, for instance, do not discuss abstract questions like the nature of Christ's risen body, but present for our viewing a panoramic picture of Christ's triumphal procession through the heavenly court, a procession more than vaguely reminiscent of the "triumphs" of the emperors and military heroes through the streets of ancient Rome.[18]

We can distinguish in the Renaissance, therefore, a "poetic theology," a "philological theology," and a "rhetorical theology."

---

[17] *Scechina e Libellus de litteris hebraicis,* ed. François Secret, 2 vols. (Rome, 1959), I, 191.

[18] See my *Praise and Blame,* p. 66.

Pico della Mirandola in fact utilizes the first expression to denote his theological enterprize, and Giles follows in that tradition.[19] His location in that category is confirmed by his dedication to texts, by the nature of the texts to which he devoted immense amounts of time, by the style of exegesis he employed, and by the results that style of exegesis produced. This location is further ratified by what seems to have been, despite his offices as prior general, papal legate, and bishop, his preferred life-style. He liked retirement, study, even seclusion. In the last analysis, he never could forget—never wanted to forget—that he was a member of the Order of *Hermits* of Saint Augustine.

The distinctions between "poetic theology," "philological theology," and "rhetorical theology" are useful in helping us perceive in more orderly fashion the variety that we sometimes mask under the more general terms like humanism and "humanistic theology." We must not allow these distinctions to blind us, however, to the common heritage of classical ideals and ethos that permeates the thinking of Renaissance Humanists of all persuasions and that, to a large extent, played a determinative part in the unexamined assumptions and ideals of almost all men and women of the era because of the common and widely pervasive heritage from classical antiquity. Ingrained into the mentality of the age were certain assumptions about the harmony of the universe, about the legitimacy of the status-quo, about the stability of established institutions, and about the superior value of order over prophecy in the Church. Within the humanistic tradition at least, direct challenge of these assumptions was practically unthinkable, just as indirect and selective challenge of them was almost inevitable. As challenges, they were also for the most part unwitting. This is the point at which we can move from a consideration of Egidio the Renaissance Humanist to Egidio the reformer, for these assumptions correlate with his reform thought and program.

Egidio da Viterbo was unequivocally devoted to the reform of the Augustinian order and to the reform of the Church as a whole. He is thus symptomatic of his age and of that preoccupation with reform that seized Europe for two centuries beginning in 1415 with the battle-cry of the Council of Constance: reform in head and members, reform in faith and morals! Moreover, he enunciated in his oration opening the Lateran Council the famous axiom that no less an authority than Delio Cantimori considered normative and peren-

---

19 See my *Giles of Viterbo*, pp. 55-58.

nial for all reform within Roman Catholicism: men must be changed by religion, not religion by men—"Homines per sacra immutari fas est, non sacra per homines."[20]

This axiom perfectly expressed Egidio's conviction about the basic premise for all authentic reform within the Church, and it betrays the classicism and "substantialism" of his whole intellectual framework. The axiom contains and condenses into one statement the many assumptions of the classical tradition just enumerated and thereby makes Egidio the spokesman for his age. At least in this axiom he spoke for Luther as well as for Leo X and the Council of Trent. A problem arose only when one tried to determine what was *sacra*, what was *humana*, and how the two interacted. But as an enunciation of an abstract principle, Egidio's dictum would have won unexceptional applause.

As such an enunciation, Egidio's axiom may be as valuable today as it was in the sixteenth century. But we understand the peculiarly sixteenth-century meaning that he and his contemporaries attached to it only if we compare it, say, with the principle of *aggiornamento* that dominated Vatican Council II. In that Council Egidio's principle was almost turned around, for the basic premise of *aggiornamento* is that, within certain limits of course, religion is to be changed by men to meet the needs of men.[21]

To put the problem in another way: exegetes in both the sixteenth and the twentieth century confess that the Bible is both word of God (*sacra*) and word of man (*humana*). But, whereas today exegetes are far more aware of the human conditioning of every aspect of the Biblical text and often find difficulty in dealing with its divine character, the situation was precisely the opposite in the sixteenth century. Nowhere is this fact more dramatically demonstrated than with Egidio, the cabalistic exegete.

In the sixteenth century, therefore, the *humana* tended less obviously to intrude themselves into considerations about the text of Scripture than they do today. They did, however, intrude into considerations about the Church and its reform. This fact is obvious with somebody like Luther who loved to contrast "word of *God*" with "church of *men*." Egidio allowed no such dichotomy, and in his "Historia" he puts the Church and its course through the ages

---

[20] *Eretici italiani del Cinquecento* (Florence, 1939), p. 6. See also HUBERT JEDIN, *A History of the Council of Trent*, I (New York, 1957), 169, and ADRIANO PROSPERI, *Tra evangelismo e controriforma* (Rome, 1969), p. 181.

[21] On this issue, see my "Reform, Historical Consciousness, and Vatican II's *Aggiornamento*," *Theological Studies*, 32 (1971), 573-601.

under an impregnable divine plan. Nonetheless, even he allows "homines" a role in the "sacra" that is the Church—a role that may be either beneficial, as with Leo X, or detrimental, as with Alexander VI.

There is, thus, another statement by Egidio that is almost as famous as the axiom for authentic reform that he proposed to the Lateran Council. That statement pertains to the situation of the Church and has been taken by historians as one of the most damning indictments by a contemporary ever hurled against Renaissance Rome. When Egidio tried to summarize the Rome that he knew under Pope Alexander VI, his "j'accuse" was devastatingly comprehensive: greed, violence, and lust reigned supreme.[22]

Like all his Catholic contemporaries, Egidio made an implicit or explicit distinction between the divine substance of the Church (*sacra*) and the defective contingencies in which that substance was immersed. Those defective contingencies were, in a word, the "homines" of his reform axiom. He and his contemporaries were not as troubled as we are with the difficulty that we meet Church most palpably and, therefore, most realistically in the human beings who are its members and in the human words in which its doctrines and rituals are expressed. For our reflections at this conference, however, we are not so much concerned with how Egidio may differ from us as we are with how attune he was to the worldview of his correligionists in the sixteenth century.

Even if we agree that Egidio represents a "poetic theology" and that most of the other preachers at the court represent a "rhetorical theology," on this issue of reform they speak with one voice. What was needed was a reform of morals, a reaffirmation of ancient laws and ancient disciplines, and a more effective realization by the pope that he and his court must act more effectively as an *exemplum* of moral probity and pastoral care for the whole Church.[23] Reform Rome, reform the world. Every sincere reformer in the Eternal City who spoke on the issue of reform seems to have subscribed in some way to that ancient persuasion. Even Ignatius Loyola, so hesitant to speak about reform lest it be interpreted as a criticism of the Church, on at least one occasion allowed himself to say that what was needed was for the pope to reform himself and his household.[24] With Egidio, it is true, apocalyptic overtones sometimes

---

22 "Historia XX saeculorum," Biblioteca Angelica, cod. lat. 502, fol. 260v: "... nihil jus, nihil fas. Aurum, vis et Venus imperabat."

23 See my *Praise and Blame*, pp. 195-237, and *Giles of Viterbo*, pp. 139-78.

24 See Cándido de Dalmases, "Les idées de Saint Ignace sur la réforme Catholique," *Christus*, 5 (1958), 239-56, esp. 249-50. On many points this article is outdated: see my "The Fourth Vow in Its Ignatian Context: A Historical Study," Studies in the Spirituality of Jesuits, 15/1 (St. Louis, 1983).

sounded in his program for reform, but the substance of his message was identical with his reforming colleagues in Rome from the middle of the Quattrocento to the middle of the Cinquecento.

This consensus that moral betterment, especially of leaders in the Church, was the nerve-center of reform was not confined to Romans who were preoccupied with the reform of the papal household and administration. It characterized humanist reformers no matter where they were found, for it coincided with the moral concerns that animated the humanist tradition. Erasmus emerges as a tireless spokesman for the viewpoint that individual reform of morals, of affectivity, and of behavior encapsulates the message of the Gospel. If only theologians—and others—would lead a "theological life," all problems would be solved.[25] In the classicizing viewpoint of humanist reformers, the only change that reform demands is moral change—religion is not to be changed by men, but men are to be changed by religion.

"We are not innovators," Egidio wrote, "but merely fulfill the divine command to bring back to life the ancient discipline."[26] His contemporaries in one way or another echo his words. Do their words, on the other hand, correspond to their actions? We all recognize the wisdom that the French express in their paradoxical observation that the more things change, the more they remain the same. Is there not operative with reformers a different paradox: the more they speak about keeping things the same, the more they are, probably unwittingly, promoting a change?

No reformer of the sixteenth century was more traditional than Ignatius Loyola. That saint had a deep respect for the traditions and holy practices of the Church and would have emphatically denied, like Egidio, that he was in any way an innovator. Yet the life-style he designed for the members of his order was considered to be, and in fact was, a radical turn in the way religious life was conceived and practiced within the Church. Moreover, in his *Spiritual Exercises* he created a pastoral instrument that was, for all the traditional elements upon which it drew, utterly new and would alter the pattern of piety in the Church in notable ways. Simply because Loyola's reforms were not distruptive—or, at least, have not been perceived by most people as disruptive—does not mean that they were not innovations.

---

[25] See my "Erasmus and Luther," esp. pp. 55-56, 64.

[26] Letter to Antonio Pulcri, undated, Biblioteca Comunale, Siena, cod. G. X. 26, p. 261: "Non enim nova facimus, sed leges patrum in ista patria extinctas, Deo ita jubente, suscitamus."

Erasmus is another case in point. He attacked many of the religious practices that prevailed in his day not because he opposed the tradition of the Church but because he saw those practices as deviations from an older and more authentic tradition. These attacks, however, for which he was best known to his contemporaries and best known to us, were peripheral to the really crucial concern of his life. With appropriate purification, he was willing to let these practices continue if they nourished the devotion of the faithful in healthy ways. On one issue he would not retreat—on the reform of theological method.[27]

On this issue, too, he opposed the "modern" to favor the ancient. He despised the scholastics ("the modern theologians") with their innovations and with their ignorance of the Bible and the Fathers, and contrasted them with theologians who based their enterprise more directly on ancient Christian sources. It has taken four hundred years for the assumptions and methodology upon which Erasmus wanted theology to be based finally to prevail and for him finally to be vindicated. In my opinion, the Second Vatican Council was—in the goals it set, in the methodology it advocated, in the mind-set it represented, and in the affectivity it promoted—essentially an "Erasmian Council." Only with the hindsight of four centuries can we fully appreciate the far-reaching consequences of the revolution Erasmus advocated so long ago under the guise of a simple "return to the sources"—*ad fontes*!

There is a direct parallel with Egidio. His conviction that the cabala represented in its method and in its Christianized doctrine the authentic revelation of God led him, at least implicitly, to advocate a revolution in theological method. In his own words, the cabala was the "divine dialectic," the "sapientiae methodus."[28] I repeat what I asserted in my book: "Our imagination staggers at the prospect of what the adoption of the cabala would have meant for the subsequent history of western theology."[29] According to Egidio's own words, no one detested more roundly than he all novelty in doctrine and theology.[30] Yet he devoted most of his adult years to studying and advancing a revolutionary method in theology that perforce would have had a revolutionary impact on the formulation of Christian doctrine.

---

27 See the literature cited in note 9 above.

28 See my *Giles of Viterbo*, pp. 67-99, esp. p. 94.

29 Ibid., p. 187.

30 See ibid., pp. 33-36, 161, and passim.

I am able to report to you what you already know: Egidio's advocacy of the cabala did not succeed with his contemporaries. François Secret has made us keenly aware of an influence that the cabala exercised on Christian theologians that was not inconsiderable and about which we were, until his researches, practically ignorant.[31] Nonetheless, the cabala never entered the mainstream of Christian theology as a major force.

We know from Egidio himself that Pope Clement VII had some interest in his cabalistic studies and that the pope invited him to write his *Scechina*, in the last years of his life.[32] But long before Clement VII, the theological taste of the papal court had definitively turned in another direction. The single most important theological force in Renaissance Rome was already Thomas Aquinas.[33]

We are accustomed to assume that the first revival of Thomism within the Catholic Church took place under Pius V after the Council of Trent, especially through the bull "Mirabilis Deus" of April 11, 1567, by which Aquinas was "declared a doctor of the Church." Aquinas was the first "modern" theologian to be so designated.

We now realize, however, that for the papal court a notable revival of Thomistic theology began under Nicholas V about 1447 that was accompanied by a unique solemnization of the celebration of his feast in the church of Santa Maria sopra Minerva. That celebration symbolized and promoted a devotion to the theological works of Aquinas that was extraordinary and that until recently has gone practically unnoticed. Paradoxical as it may seem, the leading theological authority in Renaissance Rome was, beyond any doubt, the medieval theologian, Thomas Aquinas. The actions of Pius V must be interpreted, consequently, as simply an extension to the universal Church of a pre-eminence that Aquinas had enjoyed in Rome for at least a century.

The factors leading to this development are complex and inextricably tied to the initiatives of certain powerful personalities, especially cardinal Oliviero Carafa, the cardinal protector of the Dominican order. The Dominican Fathers and their superiors were, however, not idle, most especially Egidio's contemporary, Tommaso de Vio, usually known as Cajetan. And that brings us back to Egidio.

---

31 See esp. his *Les kabbalistes chrétiens de la Renaissance* (Paris, 1964), as well as the many articles he has subsequently published on this question.

32 See *Scechina*, I, 66.

33 See my "The Feast of Thomas Aquinas in Renaissance Rome: A Neglected Document and Its Import," *Rivista di Storia della Chiesa in Italia*, 35 (1981), 1-27.

Besides the celebration at the Minerva on March 7 honoring Thomas, there was only one other noteworthy celebration of a non-biblical saint in Renaissance Rome. That was the celebration on August 28 in honor of Saint Augustine at that saint's church near the Piazza Navona. That celebration was, however, a dismal second-best to what occurred each year at the Minerva.[34] Similarly, Augustine did not emerge as a theologian of any particular prominence in Rome during the era, though his name was of course often invoked.

We cannot blame Egidio for the relative neglect of a saint and theologian whom we might have expected for a number of reasons to have been far more seriously studied than he seems to have been. Just as the emergence of Aquinas in Renaissance Rome was the result of a number of converging factors (not least of which was the controlling position the Dominicans enjoyed in the office of Master of the Sacred Palace), so the failure of Augustine to rise to special prominence cannot be assigned to any one cause.

On the other hand, Egidio provides us with little evidence that he took any active measures to promote the celebration of the feast of the supposed founder of his order. Furthermore, although he commended to the members of the order the rule and writings of "Augustini parentis," he does not himself seem to have studied the works of the saint in a degree that resembled his single-minded pursuit of the cabala. This is not to deny that Egidio had read some of Augustine's works and had assimilated some of his theology. But it is to contrast him with his contemporary, Cajetan, who held the same supreme office in the Dominicans as Egidio held in the Augustinians. While Egidio wrote his "Historia" and studied the cabala, Cajetan was hard at work writing and publishing his commentaries on the works of the Angelic Doctor.

Luther, we must remember, believed for a considerable period of time that his doctrine of justification by faith alone was an exact reproduction of the authentic doctrine of Augustine in his battle with the Pelagians. Later in life, he began to have doubts about how perfectly the two doctrines coincided. In 1518, still early in the controversy, Pope Leo X dispatched Cajetan to Augsburg, and it was on that occasion that the fateful exchange between him and Luther took place. Cajetan, the Thomist, tried to engage in theological discourse with Luther, the Augustinian—"Augustinian" in Luther's own estimation still in both senses of the word.

---

[34] See ibid., p. 8, and *Praise and Blame*, passim.

We cannot resist speculating how different the outcome of this meeting might have been if the papal interlocutor had not been somebody trained in Thomistic theology but somebody with an expert knowledge of Augustine's writings on the Pelagian question. In actual fact, as far as I know, there was nobody in Rome who fit that description, at least not anyone of prominence. This lacuna in "the revival of antiquity" in Renaissance Rome had, it would seem, fateful consequences for the future history of western Christianity. Had there been in Rome the same interest in Augustine as in Thomas, had there been as many persons actively engaged in producing commentaries on his writings and in teaching courses in his theology at the Sapienza as there were for Aquinas, Luther may have received a more sympathetic hearing or have been more easily persuaded of the errors of his ways. As it was, a head-on clash was accelerated by the internal dynamism of two radically diverse theological systems and theological vocabularies. In our attempt to place Egidio in the context of his times, we see that in this instance what he was *not* interested in was as important as the concerns that held him in their grasp.

* * *

I have been told that recently at a large American university a seminar was held on the topic, "Rome under Julius II and Leo X." As the semester drew to a close, one of the participants complained that the seminar had not studied Renaissance Rome, but Egidio da Viterbo! I am fair-minded enough to allow that the director of the seminar might have placed too much emphasis on Egidio. I would, on the other hand, seize this opportunity to defend the director as erring in the right direction and to affirm once again what I have said in the past: "We shall never fully undestand the Rome of the High Renaissance apart from the writings of Egidio da Viterbo."[35] The burden of my presentation to you, however, has been to approach these same materials from the opposite direction. My thesis has been, quite simply, that we shall never fully understand Egidio da Viterbo apart from the rich and varied context of Renaissance Rome—apart from the even larger context, indeed, of the exciting age in which he lived.

---

35 "Man's Dignity," p. 391.

III

Content and Rhetorical Forms in Sixteenth-Century Treatises on Preaching

I recently published a book on the sacred oratory of the papal court from about 1450 until the death of Pope Leo X in 1521.[1] The book shows, I believe, that the revival of the *genus demonstrativum* of classical oratory explains the transformation in structure, purpose, and content in the sermons at the court during this period. Besides indicating that the negative judgments historians have commonly made about "Renaissance preaching" need revision,[2] the book provides grounds for suspecting that an examination of how authors of works on preaching deal with the three classical *genera*—judicial, deliberative, demonstrative—is a good entrance into the total network of assumptions that govern their understanding of preaching and its relationship to rhetoric, as well as its relationship to general culture. That is the approach I should presently like to follow for a highly

1. *Praise and Blame in Renaissance Rome: Rhetoric, Doctrine, and Reform in the Sacred Orators of the Papal Court, c. 1450–1521,* Duke Monographs in Medieval and Renaissance Studies, no. 3 (Durham, N.C., 1979).

2. With ill-concealed disdain, for instance, Johann Baptist Schneyer dismisses the whole phenomenon of Renaissance preaching in Italy and Spain with four pages in his *Geschichte der katholischen Predigt* (Freiburg, 1969). This tradition, related though it is to Luther's antipathy for things Italian, derives more directly from Erasmus's caricature of a sermon at the papal court that he describes in his *Ciceronianus*. See my *Praise and Blame*, pp. 29–31. Though it must be used with caution, there is still some useful discussion of the relationship between form and content in P. W. von Keppler, "Beiträge zur Entwicklungsgeschichte der Predigtanlage," *Theologische Quartalschrift* 74 (1892), 52–120, 179–212, esp. 82–103. See also Joseph M. Connors, "Homiletic Theory in the Late Sixteenth Century," *The American Ecclesiastical Review* 138 (1958), 316–32, esp. for a study of rhetorical form in Agostino Valerio and Luis de Granada.

selective sampling of sixteenth-century treatises on preaching. First, however, some background will be helpful.

In Italy by the late fourteenth century, there were sacred orations that broke with medieval traditions of preaching and that show the unmistakable impact of the Renaissance revival of classical rhetoric. The first fully classicizing orations of which I am aware are the panegyrics honoring Saint Jerome composed by Pier Paolo Vergerio in Padua and elsewhere between about 1392 and 1408. Vergerio was a member of the circle led by Giovanni di Conversino da Ravenna that included other notable humanists like Guarino da Verona and Vittorino da Feltre. Vergerio's orations abandon all the features of the medieval *laudes sanctorum*—theme, division, authorities, structure, dialectical style of argumentation—and adopt the principles and *topoi* of the classical *genus demonstrativum*.[3]

By 1410 there is evidence that the adaptation of that *genus* to Christian saints was a standard exercise at Padua, and there is also evidence that at about the same time the *genus* was put to the same use elsewhere in Italy, especially wherever the orations were delivered in Latin.[4] Simultaneously, there was an adaptation of the *genus* to Christian funeral oratory. Poggio Bracciolini's eulogy of Cardinal Zabarella at the Council of Constance, September 27, 1417, is an early and important example of the new approach, which would be widely imitated in the major cities of Italy during the course of the century.[5]

An even more interesting, slightly later, development was the adaptation of this *genus*, of this "art of praise and blame," to doctrinal sermons or sermons dealing with events from the life of Christ. Gasperino Barzizza was among the first to inaugurate this change, which was known in a mature form at the papal court by the middle of the century in several sermons there by Pietro del Monte, the noted canonist and humanist, disciple of Guarino. During the rest of the century, this new form contended at the court with its medieval, thematic rival, and by the death of Leo X it had won a considerable, though by no means total, victory over it.[6] The new form was em-

3. See my *Praise and Blame*, pp. 85 – 86. See also David Robey, "P. P. Vergerio the Elder: Republican and Civic Values in the Work of an Early Humanist," *Past and Present* no. 58 (February, 1973), pp. 3 – 37, esp. 27 – 31.

4. See *Praise and Blame*, pp. 86 – 87.

5. See ibid., pp. 80n, 89 – 90, as well as John M. McManamon, "The Ideal Renaissance Pope: Funeral Oratory from the Papal Court," *Archivum Historiae Pontificiae* 14 (1976), 9 – 70.

6. See *Praise and Blame*, pp. 81 – 119.

ployed outside the court and outside Italy, as Rudolf Agricola's sacred oration at Heidelberg on Christmas Day 1485 clearly proves, but its use seems generally to have been restricted to refined audiences and formal settings.[7]

Though limited in the audiences it reached, this adaptation of classical rhetorical form wrought a change in preaching that was striking. The least important feature of the change was the substitution of classical vocabulary, syntax, and figures of thought and diction for their medieval equivalents. Much more important was the change in the materials with which the sermons dealt — the *res*. These became focused more clearly on God's deeds and actions — his *beneficia* — and less on the abstract doctrines that were the standard materials for the thematic, that is, the scholastic, sermon of the Middle Ages. "History," if you will, replaced "philosophy." Moreover, the very purpose of the sermon was transformed from an exercise in proof and dialectical argumentation to an exercise in praise. Admiration, gratitude, and desire for imitation were the sentiments the sermons were now meant to inspire and for which they now had the appropriate rhetorical techniques. Whereas the thematic sermon emphasized *docere* at the expense of *movere* and *delectare*, the demonstrative oration more effectively coordinated teaching with persuasional aims. Perhaps most important of all, the new style of sermon, through its employment of praise, conveyed a religious vision that was uncommonly positive in its appreciation of God, man, and the world. It was a "rhetoric of congratulation" applied to God and his works, especially man. The emergence of the peculiarly Renaissance theme of the "dignity of man" is due in considerable measure to the employment of the principles of the *genus demonstrativum*.

As far as I have been able to ascertain, this extraordinary development was not heralded by any treatises advocating it or describing how to accomplish it. In 1478, however, Lorenzo Guglielmo Traversagni wrote his *Margarita eloquentiae* in Cambridge. Traversagni's book securely locates all sacred oratory, including even thematic and popular sermons, in the *genus demonstrativum*. This long and still inadequately studied work betrays an awareness of the new type of oratory I described, but the book's influence has yet to be determined and its "modernity" must not be exaggerated.[8]

7. See ibid., pp. 120 – 22.

8. See ibid., pp. 43n, 46 – 47, 49n. Traversagni's *Epitome* of his longer work also locates sermons in the *genus demonstrativum;* see Ronald H. Martin, "The 'Epitome Margaritae Eloquentiae' of Laurentius Gulielmus de Soana," *Proceedings of the Leeds*

Aurelio "Lippo" Brandolini's treatise on letter-writing, completed at the papal court sometime before 1485, is an important and neglected work. Generally speaking, it was the most elaborate of its kind in the Quattrocento, anticipating by several decades Erasmus's similar treatise. Its significance for sacred oratory lies in a few digressions that indicate that sacred oratory pertains to the *genus* of ceremonial oratory, to the oratory of praise and blame. Brandolini criticizes preachers at the court who do not know the difference between a lecture, suitable for the classroom, and an oration, proper to a church. He thus rejects the thematic sermon.[9] Brandolini's few pages document a revolution taking place in certain circles in the Quattrocento due to the revival of classical rhetoric. Nonetheless, during that century it was the medieval *artes praedicandi* that continued to be written and published in Italy and elsewhere.

North of the Alps a modest break comes with Reuchlin's *Liber congestorum de arte praedicandi* of 1504.[10] The *Liber* is brief, sketchy, and noteworthy more for indicating a transition from the medieval tradition than for providing anything coherent to replace it. Without developing the idea, the *Liber* allows the preacher use of all three of the classical *genera.*

Reuchlin pales in importance alongside Melanchthon, his grandnephew, who from his first book on rhetoric in 1519 all through his subsequent career repeatedly addressed the problem of preaching.[11] He had almost immediate impact on other Lutheran theorists like Veit Dietrich and Johannes Äpinus (Hoeck), with whose works on preaching two short treatises of his own were published in Basel in 1540.[12]

Philosophical and Literary Society (Literary and Historical Section) vol. 14, pt. 4 (1971), 99 – 187, esp. 177 – 78. See also James J. Murphy, "Caxton's Two Choices: 'Modern' and 'Medieval' Rhetoric in Traversagni's *Nova Rhetorica* and the Anonymous *Court of Sapience," Medievalia et Humanistica* n.s. 3 (1972), 241 – 55.

9. *De ratione scribendi libri tres* (Cologne, 1573), first published in Basel in 1549. See esp. pp. 94 – 101.

10. (Pforzheim, 1504), esp. fol. [5v] on the *genera.*

11. The most complete study of Melanchthon's theory on preaching is Uwe Schnell's *Die homiletische Theorie Philipp Melanchthons,* Arbeiten zur Geschichte und Theologie des Luthertums, no. 20 (Berlin, 1968). Also useful is Wilhelm Maurer's *Der junge Melanchthon zwischen Humanismus und Reformation,* 2 vols. (Göttingen, 1967 – 1969), esp. 1.171 – 214.

12. *De arte concionandi formulae ut breves, ita doctae et piae, Ioanne Reuchlino Phorcensi, anonymo quodam Rhapsodo [Dietrich], Philippo Melanchthone, D. Ioanne Hepino autoribus. Eiusdem Melanchthonis discendae theologiae rationem ad calcem adiecimus* (Basel, 1540).

Melanchthon at one point was so apprehensive about the *genus demonstrativum* for sacred oratory that he rejected it. Like most sixteenth-century theorists, he also minimized or eliminated the use of the *genus iudiciale* in the pulpit.[13] His most distinctive achievement was the introduction of a new, fourth *genus*, the so-called *genus didascalicum*.[14] This new *genus* had teaching as its purpose. Melanchthon asserted that he in fact transferred the *genus* to sacred rhetoric from dialectics, which he described as the *ars recte docendi*.[15]

Melanchthon wrote his *De officiis concionatoris* in 1529. Though not altogether expressive of his mature thought on preaching, it was, after the revised treatise on rhetoric, his most influential statement on it. In the *De officiis* Melanchthon defines his theory of preaching by employing three *genera:* the *didascalicum*, which teaches true doctrine; the *epitrepticum*, which exhorts to faith; the *paraeneticum*, which exhorts to good morals.[16] The *epitrepticum* and *paraeneticum* are considered exhortations, adaptations of the classical *genus deliberativum*. For such an understanding of the *genus deliberativum*, Melanchthon was influenced by the authority of Erasmus's *Opus de conscribendis epistolis*.[17] In Melanchthon's view, the *didascalicum* and *epitrepticum* are far more important than the *paraeneticum* because they deal with faith, while the *paraeneticum* deals with action.

There are several aspects of Melanchthon's achievement that deserve mention. First, his treatises are more directly and obviously influenced by classical rhetoric than were the medieval *artes*. Second, he nonetheless finds it necessary to add the *genus didascalicum* to the traditional three, to redistribute the *genus deliberativum* into two species of *epitrepticum* and *paraeneticum*, and practically to reject both the judicial and demonstrative except insofar as the latter was an "ornamented" version of the *didascalicum*. Third, Melanchthon specifies the *res* that the sacred orator teaches as the Lutheran doctrines of law, sin, and grace; Scripture is characteristically understood as a

---

Besides Melanchthon's "Ratio" on how to learn theology, his other work published in this volume was the *De officiis concionatoris*.

13. See his *De officiis concionatoris* in *Supplementa Melanchthoniana*, eds. Paul Drews and Ferdinand Cohrs, vol. 5, pt. 2 (Leipzig, 1929), pp. 5 – 7. See also, however, his *Elementa rhetorices*, in *Corpus Reformatorum*, ed. Carolus Gottlieb Bretschneider (1846, rpt. New York, 1963), 13.421 – 23, 429, 448 – 49.

14. See *Elementa rhetorices*, cols. 421 – 28; *De officiis concionatoris*, pp. 5 – 10.

15. See *Elementa rhetorices*, col. 424.

16. *De officiis concionatoris*, pp. 5 – 7.

17. See *Elementa rhetorices*, col. 422.

book of threats and promises; thus Melanchthon's treatises and those of his followers are never doctrinally neutral — *res* and *verba* are inextricably intertwined. Finally, his theory of sacred oratory is considerably more complex than I have here suggested and is intimately related to his teaching on the use of "commonplaces" or *topoi* in theology, on the relationship he postulates between rhetoric and dialectics, and on other major issues like biblical hermeneutics.[18]

It was the *genus didascalicum* that caught the attention of Melanchthon's contemporaries and of succeeding generations. In that *genus* he continues an attention to doctrine propositionally and dialectically articulated that was, surely unintentionally, reminiscent of the thematic sermons of the scholastics. At the same time, he explicitly rejected the emphasis on the deeds of Christ and on the praise of Christ that he quite correctly says characterized Italian "declamations."[19]

Along with Melanchthon, Erasmus is the second figure of towering significance for the theory of sacred oratory in the first half of the sixteenth century. The *Ecclesiastes* of 1535, his last major work, was eagerly awaited for years before it was finished.[20] Though it failed to satisfy Erasmus's contemporaries and his critics through the ages, it was the single most important treatise on the theory of sacred oratory since Augustine's *De Doctrina Christiana,* a work by which the *Ecclesiastes* was profoundly influenced.[21]

In all his writings Erasmus saw Christ as, essentially, a great teacher, and he viewed Scripture as the book containing the "philosophy" that Christ taught. Erasmus thus tends to transform all the books of the Bible into a species of "wisdom literature." We should

18. See, e.g., his *Quomodo concionator novitius concionem suam informare debeat, De modo et arte concionandi,* and *De ratione concionandi,* in the *Supplementa,* pp. 17 – 79. See also Schnell, *Homiletische Theorie,* pp. 46 – 53, 115 – 21; Maurer, *Der junge Melanchthon,* 1.171 – 214; 2.139 – 51, 230 – 63; and Quirinus Breen, "The terms 'Loci Communes' and 'Loci' in Melanchthon," in his *Christianity and Humanism: Studies in the History of Ideas,* ed. Nelson Peter Ross (Grand Rapids, Mich., 1968), pp. 93 – 105.

19. See *De officiis concionatoris,* p. 6.

20. *Ecclesiastes, sive Concionator evangelicus,* in *Opera omnia,* ed. J. Clericus, 10 vols. (Leiden, 1703 – 1706), 5.769 – 1100.

21. See James Michael Weiss, "*Ecclesiastes* and Erasmus: The Mirror and the Image," *Archive for Reformation History* 65 (1974), 83 – 108; Charles Béné, *Érasme et saint Augustin, ou Influence de Saint Augustin sur l'Humanisme d'Érasme,* Travaux d'Humanisme et Renaissance, no. 103 (Geneva, 1969), esp. pp. 372 – 425; André Godin, "Érasme et le modèle origénien de la prédication," in *Colloquia Erasmiana Turonensia,* ed. Jean-Claude Margolin, 2 vols. (Toronto, 1972), 2.807 – 20.

not be surprised, then, that preaching is defined in the *Ecclesiastes* principally as an act of teaching. Though Erasmus located preaching in the charism of "prophecy," he defines the prophet's task not as predicting the future or thundering against sin and misbelief, but as explaining and teaching the mysteries of Scripture, "the philosophy of Christ."[22]

For Erasmus, truly Christian teaching is never dialectical or argumentative, never frigidly abstract, for it must always be persuasive of a godly life. Erasmus constructs five *genera* appropriate to the sacred orator, but at least four of them can be reduced to the *genus suasorium,* that is, an equivalent of the *genus deliberativum* of classical oratory. The fifth, the *genus laudatorium,* represents the demonstrative; Erasmus practically restricts it to panegyrics of the saints and heavily imbues it with elements from the *genus suasorium.*[23]

Erasmus's treatise seems to have been responsible for a widespread tendency among Catholics in the sixteenth century to establish the *genus deliberativum* as the *genus* most appropriate for the pulpit. In 1595 Ludovico Carbone, for instance, stated in his *Divinus orator* that the deliberative was the *genus* proper to the preacher, for the preacher always has some persuasion in mind.[24] Even for Lutherans, under the influence of Melanchthon, the *genus deliberativum* ranked a close second behind the *genus didascalicum* as the *genus* proper to the pulpit.[25]

Erasmus does not explain why he lifts a literary form intended for a deliberative assembly and transfers it to a church setting. His location of preaching in the deliberative genre, as well as his definition of it as teaching, tended to give preaching a more moralistic and professedly didactic quality than was evidenced in the demonstrative sermons at the papal court. Due partly to Erasmus's influence, demonstrative oratory in the sixteenth century becomes, at least in many important treatises, ever more restricted to panegyrics of the saints and to funeral eulogies; it loses its earlier prerogative, apparently taken for granted in Italy in the Quattrocento, as the *locus* for all sacred oratory.

22. See *Ecclesiastes,* cols. 798, 824 – 26.

23. See ibid., cols. 877 – 92.

24. *Divinus orator, vel De rhetorica divina libri septem* (Venice, 1595), esp. p. 125. This Ludovico Carbone (d. 1597) is not to be confused with the fifteenth-century humanist of the same name.

25. See Schnell, *Homiletische Theorie,* pp. 172 – 76; and John S. Chamberlin, *Increase and Multiply: Arts-of-Discourse Procedure in the Preaching of Donne* (Chapel Hill, N.C., 1976), pp. 67 – 91.

The paths through which the influence of Melanchthon and Erasmus was diffused have yet to be explored by modern scholars. At present I will offer a single example of that diffusion, the *De sacris concionibus recte formandis* published in Rome in early 1543 by the Spanish cleric Alfonso Zorrilla.[26] In Zorrilla's dedicatory letter to Juan Alvárez de Toledo, one of the Roman Inquisitors appointed by Pope Paul III in the previous year, he rejects Erasmus's *Ecclesiastes* as too "diffuse, prolix, and confused" to be practical. Somewhat in desperation, then, Zorrilla tells the Inquisitor, he composed the present work "almost as a compendium" of what some others had written on the subject.

Zorrilla's book was influential in Catholic circles. We should not be surprised at this. It seems to have been the first treatise on preaching printed in Italy that broke with the medieval *artes*. It was published, moreover, almost under the auspices of the Inquisition and was singled out for special commendation by Saint Robert Bellarmine about fifty years later. What neither the Inquisitor nor Bellarmine nor anybody else suspected until I recently established it is that Zorrilla's book is constructed out of wholesale borrowings from Lutheran sources — Melanchthon, Dietrich, and Äpinus. Zorrilla made extensive use of the Basel volume of 1540 as well as of Melanchthon's *Elementa rhetorices.* The Lutheran origins of the substance of the book stand as dramatic testimony to the fervid search in the first half of the century for substitutes for the medieval styles of preaching.

Important public documents in the century tend to ignore questions of structure, genre, and rhetoric, and deal largely with content; considerable attention is also given to issues like jurisdiction and the prerequisites of knowledge and virtue in the preacher. Among such documents are the decrees of the Fifth Lateran Council, 1516,[27] of the First Council of Cologne, 1536,[28] of the Second Council of Trier, 1549,[29] of the Council of Trent, 1546 and 1563,[30] of the First Provincial Synod of Milan, under Saint Charles Borromeo, 1563, and the

26. See my "Lutheranism in Rome, 1542 – 43: The Treatise by Alfonso Zorrilla," *Thought* 54 (1979), 262 – 73.

27. See *Conciliorum Oecumenicorum Decreta,* ed. Giuseppe Alberigo et al., 2nd ed. (Basel, 1962), pp. 610 – 14.

28. See *Sacrorum conciliorum nova et amplissima collectio,* ed. Giovanni Domenico Mansi (Paris, 1901), 32.1248 – 55.

29. See ibid., cols. 1441 – 43.

30. See *Conciliorum Oecumenicorum Decreta,* pp. 645 – 46, 739. See also Johann Ev.

saint's influential *Instructiones praedicationis verbi Dei* issued some years later.[31]

Cardinal Gasparo Contarini, the most exciting figure associated with the Roman Curia from about 1536 until his death in 1542, also ignores form in favor of content in his brief "Modus concionandi" of 1540.[32] Like some other theorists in the long history of Christian preaching, Contarini seems to suggest that the study of rhetoric is unnecessary, even dangerous, for the preacher; he requires in him only humility, charity, and a right understanding of the law, sin, faith, and forgiveness. Although Contarini explicitly rejects the "Lutheran pestilence," his teaching on the key doctrines in the "modus concionandi" is only subtly different from Lutheran teaching.

By the time Zorrilla compiled his book in 1542, however, questions of form *(verba)* had become as crucial as questions of content *(res)*. Zorrilla follows Melanchthon (by way of Äpinus) and lists three *genera* for the preacher: *didacticum, demonstrativum,* and *deliberativum.*[33] He accordingly gives special attention to the *genus didacticum* or *didascalicum* and seems to be the first to introduce it, under the unwitting but magnificently orthodox sponsorship of Alvárez de Toledo and Bellarmine, into the Catholic tradition.

Zorrilla makes allowance almost as an afterthought for a fourth *genus,* which he does not name but which is the equivalent of the homily, in the sense of an informal and familiar discourse that follows the text of a biblical pericope—verse-by-verse sometimes, or even phrase-by-phrase.[34] By virtue of this structure (i.e., nonstructure) and by virtue of the patristic models available for imitation, the homily favored allegorical senses of Scripture. There is no doubt that the patristic revival in the Renaissance contributed to renewed interest in this "ancient form."

The homily, known and practiced in the Middle Ages, enjoyed,

Reiner, "Entstehungsgeschichte des Trienter Predigtreformdekrets," *Zeitschrift für katholische Theologie* 39 (1915), 256–317, 465–523; and A. Larios, "La reforma de la predicación en Trento (Historia y contenido de un decreto)," *Communio* 6 (1973), 223–83, which also contains a brief review of preaching theory and practice before and after Trent.

31. See *Constitutiones et decreta condita in provinciali synodo Mediolanensi* (Venice, 1566), pp. 7–14; and the *Instructiones* in *Acta Ecclesiae Mediolanensis,* ed. Achille Ratti (Milan, 1890), 2.1205–48. See also Joseph M. Connors, "Saint Charles Borromeo in Homiletic Tradition," *The American Ecclesiastical Review* 138 (1958), 9–23.

32. Printed in *Regesten und Briefe des Kardinals Gasparo Contarini,* ed. Franz Dittrich (Braunsberg, 1881), pp. 305–9.

33. Zorrilla, *De sacris concionibus,* fols. 25^r–26^v, 59^v–76^r.

34. Ibid., fol. 74.

therefore, new attention in the sixteenth century. Erasmus, for instance, admired its use by his friend, Jacques Vitrier.[35] Despite Erasmus's advocacy of the classical *genera* in the *Ecclesiastes,* he elsewhere seems to favor the homily over them. This great classicist seemed uncertain about just how appropriate for the pulpit were the classical forms of oratory.

The homily, often commended as a "Christian" form in contrast with the "pagan" forms of classical rhetoric, was to a large extent adopted by the Fathers from the classroom style of the "grammarians," the teachers of the pagan classics. Its origins therefore are hardly more Christian than those of its oratorical counterparts. However, once the Bible is perceived as a "wisdom" or a "philosophy" of Christ, the loose and lecture-like structure of the homily is a suitable way to expound it.[36]

Many years after Erasmus, Robert Bellarmine, overtly hostile towards sermons constructed according to principles of classical oratory, particularly commended the homily, as well as sermons from theological *topoi.* According to Bellarmine, use of these forms by the Fathers established their authority. As Bellarmine's preacher expounded Scripture, he would interpret it in the light of the patristic commentaries. But, in the spirit of the Counter Reformation, he would use Saint Thomas and the *Catechism of the Council of Trent* for his exposition of doctrine. Interestingly enough, though Bellarmine approved of Aquinas's doctrine, he was cool towards the thematic (scholastic) sermon.[37]

35. See André Godin, *L'homélaire de Jean Vitrier: Texte, étude thématique et sémantique,* Travaux d'Humanisme et Renaissance, no. 116 (Geneva, 1971), esp. pp. 14–18; *Opus Epistolarum Des. Erasmi Roterodami,* 11 vols. (Oxford, 1906–1947), 4.509. See also Godin, "De Vitrier à Origène: Recherches sur la patristique érasmienne," in *Colloquium Erasmianum* (Mons, 1968), 47–57.

36. See the introduction by Pierre Nautin to Origen's *Homélies sur Jérémie,* eds. Pierre Husson and Pierre Nautin, Sources chrétiennes, no. 232 (Paris, 1976), esp. pp. 112–57; and see also my "Grammar and Rhetoric in the Theology of Erasmus," to appear in *Paideia,* Special Renaissance Issue (forthcoming). For the development of the homily as part of an informal worship service, see James J. Murphy, *Rhetoric in the Middle Ages: A History of Rhetorical Theory from Saint Augustine to the Renaissance* (Berkeley and Los Angeles, 1974), pp. 55–56; 298–300; for the traditional opinion that the homily was a direct outgrowth of the synagogue service and apostolic preaching, see August Brandt, "Abriss der Geschichte und Theorie der Homilie," in Fritz Tillmann's *Die sonntäglichen Evangelien im Dienste der Predigt* (1917; rev. ed. by Paul Goedeke, Düsseldorf, 1965), 19–58.

37. "De ratione formandae concionis," in *Auctarium Bellarminianum: Supplément aux oeuvres du cardinal Bellarmin,* ed. Xavier-Marie le Bachelet (Paris, 1913), pp. 655–57.

One of the most insistent advocates in the second half of the century for a return to patristic forms, homiletic and topical, was Diego de Estella, the renowned Franciscan mystic and stylist. His *Modus concionandi,* first published at Salamanca in 1576 and many times reprinted, urges his "sermo evangelicus," a kind of homily, almost to the exclusion of all other forms. Estella is familiar, however, with the thematic sermon and with the principles of classical rhetoric.[38] Even so, he is reluctant to allow panegyrics even of the saints.[39] Sacred oratory should be based on the text of Scripture, not on the lives of men.

Consonant with the Franciscan tradition and characteristic of Estella is his turning the "teaching" of the sermon to a moral purpose.[40] His preacher will draw copiously on the "moral sense" of Scripture that underlies the literal sense.[41] Estella seems to assume that the audience facing the preacher is invariably living in sin and

---

For a description of the scholastic and nonhumanistic style of Bellarmine's theology, see Robert W. Richgels, "Scholasticism Meets Humanism in the Counter Reformation, The Clash of Cultures in Robert Bellarmine's Use of Calvin in *Controversies,*" *The Sixteenth Century Journal* vol. 6, no. 1 (1975), 53 – 66.

38. *Modo de predicar y Modus concionandi: Estudio doctrinal y edición critica,* ed. Pio Sagüés Azcona, 2 vols. (Madrid, 1951). On Estella, see E. Allison Peers, *Studies of the Spanish Mystics,* 3 vols. (London, 1951 – 1960), 2.171 – 94; and Donat de Monleras, "Estella (Diego de San Cristóbal)," in *Dictionnaire de spiritualité,* 4.1366 – 70. Besides the account by Pio Sagüés Azcona in his edition of the *Modo de predicar* (1.226 – 73), the history of treatises on preaching in Spain in the sixteenth century is reviewed by Félix G. Olmedo in the "prólogo" of his edition of *Don Francisco Terrones del Caño: Instrucción de predicadores,* Clásicos castellanos, no. 126 (Madrid, 1946), pp. lii – clvi; and by Antonio M. Martí, "La Retórica Sacra en el Siglo de Oro," *Hispanic Review* 38 (1970), 264 – 98. Two more general studies are Martí's *La preceptiva retórica española en el Siglo de Oro,* Biblioteca románica hispánica, 1: Tradados y monografías, no. 12 (Madrid, 1972); and José Rico Verdu, *La retórica española de los siglos XVI y XVII* (Madrid, 1973). I am indebted to Professor Donald Abbott of the University of California, Davis, for many of these references. Now see also Hilary Dansey Smith, *Preaching in the Spanish Golden Age: A Study of Some Preachers of the Reign of Philip III* (Oxford, 1978); and Antonio Cañizares Llovera, "La predicación española en el siglo XVI," in *Repertoria de Historia de las Ciencias Eclesiásticas en España, Siglos I – XVI,* 6 (Salamanca, 1977), pp. 189 – 266.

39. See *Modo de predicar,* 2.370 – 75.

40. Saint Francis himself, in his Rule for the friars, set the Franciscan tradition that sermons were to deal with "vices and virtues, punishment and reward." See *Seraphicae Legislationis Textus Originales* (Quaracchi: Collegium S. Bonaventurae, 1897), p. 44. This passage is quoted by Estella, *Modo de predicar,* 2.210. See also the chapter on preaching (esp. no. 118) of "The Capuchin Constitutions of 1536," in *The Catholic Reformation: Savonarola to Ignatius Loyola,* ed. John C. Olin (New York, 1969), pp. 172 – 76.

41. See *Modo de predicar,* e.g., 2.214, 223, 225.

must be moved to virtue and to good works.[42] The preacher will insist on the reality of death, judgment, and hell.[43]

This attitude contrasts with the "rhetoric of congratulation" and the emphasis on the "dignity of man" operative in the Italian demonstrative sermons described earlier. Estella's emphasis on good works is demanded by his moralism, but is also advanced by him as an antidote to the Lutheran heresy. The Venice, 1584, edition of his treatise was dedicated to Charles Borromeo, archbishop of Milan and great saint of the Counter Reformation. Borromeo is known to have been influenced by it and quoted from it, without acknowledgment, in his own important instructions on pastoral care.[44]

Estella's Dominican contemporary and fellow mystic, Luis de Granada, shared some of his pessimism about the low spiritual state of the preacher's congregation and also shared the viewpoint that the preacher's task was principally moral. Following the tradition initiated by Erasmus, he locates preaching in the deliberative genre; it is through use of this genre that men are persuaded to justice and piety and are dissuaded from vice. Granada then reserves the demonstrative solely for panegyrics of the saints, and, seemingly with some reluctance, admits the possibility of the *genus didascalicum* as well as the homily. Consciously dependent though he was upon the classical tradition, he was apprehensive about it and yearned for the day when somebody would create a "fully Christian rhetoric."[45]

That ideal was also espoused and even attempted by the great Lutheran theorist from Marburg, Andreas Hyperius, whose *De formandis concionibus sacris* of 1553 was translated into English by John Ludham a few years later.[46] For Hyperius, Scripture alone is the source from which to draw the forms for preaching. He rejects the attempt to make preaching conform to the three classical *genera,* "as though she [Divinitie] had not furniture and implements sufficient, especially for th'ecclesiasticall function, in hir owne proper house and home."[47] He discovers his five scriptural forms in Paul's Second

42. See ibid., 203 – 5, 210 – 12, 314 – 18. 43. See ibid., 316. 44. See ibid., 1.259.

45. *Ecclesiasticae rhetoricae, sive De ratione concionandi libri sex* (Lisbon, 1576), esp. pp. [viii – ix], 12 – 14, 34 – 35, 69 – 77, 150 – 51, 165, 171, 178 – 87. On Luis de Granada, see Peers, *Spanish Mystics,* 2nd rev. ed. (1951), 1.25 – 61; and Alvaro Huerga, "Louis de Grenade," in *Dictionnaire de spiritualité,* 9.1043 – 54, with excellent bibliography.

46. *The Practis of Preaching, otherwise called, The Pathway to ye Pulpet* (London, 1577). On this treatise, see Chamberlin, *Increase and Multiply,* pp. 67 – 91.

47. *Practis of Preaching,* fol. 18^r.

Epistle to Timothy (3.16), but the first and most important of them in fact corresponds to Melanchthon's "doctrinal or didascalicsk" *genus.*[48] Hyperius, profoundly influenced as he was by the classical tradition, eventually admits that there is correspondence between some of his forms and even the traditional *genera.*[49]

Alfonso García Matamoros, on the other hand, unequivocally reconciles classical rhetoric with the pulpit. His *De methodo concionandi* was first published in 1570.[50] Since the Inquisition in Spain forbade owning and reading Erasmus's *Ecclesiastes,* Matamoros felt an obligation to try to meet the needs of his fellow countrymen that this prohibition created.[51] In fact, while proposing "the life of our Lord and teacher" as material for preaching, he also proposes the typically Erasmian "philosophy of Christ."[52] However, though he respected Erasmus and had studied the *Ecclesiastes,* he judged that in some precepts Erasmus (as well as others) departed from the teaching on eloquence of Cicero and Quintilian. That he could not approve.[53]

Matamoros reproached anybody who would tamper with the three classical *genera* and he rejected as unnecessary all the other *genera,* like the *didascalicum,* that recent authors had invented. According to García Matamoros, a proper understanding of classical rhetoric would show that the three traditional *genera* were sufficient for the sacred orator and that all others could be reduced to them.[54]

More important than García Matamoros's affirmation of the classical *genera* is the theological justification he offers for it. We do not lose our human nature, he asserts, by being Christians, so we should not think it necessary to introduce into the pulpit some new rhetoric fallen directly from heaven. If we accept Aristotle's dialectics and philosophy for use in theology, why not on the same grounds accept classical rhetoric for Christian use? Moreover, Christ by his exaltation on the cross has drawn all things, including rhetoric, to himself and rendered them holy.[55] In this rationalization of García Matamoros, we see a clear instance of an attempt to correlate a vast theologi-

48. See ibid., fols. $18^r - 19^r$.
49. See ibid., fols. $19^v - 20^r$.
50. In *Opera omnia* (Madrid, 1769), pp. 523 – 700.
51. See his *De tribus dicendi generibus,* pp. 436 – 37.
52. See *De methodo concionandi,* pp. 591, 593 – 94, 693. See also, however, p. 622.
53. See ibid., pp. 524, 529. See also pp. 645 – 47 on Erasmus.
54. See ibid., pp. 529 – 33. But see also p. 609 on the *genus didascalicum.*
55. See ibid., pp. 529 – 33, 545 – 46, 551 – 52.

cal position with the relatively pedestrian question of how to use, adapt, or reject classical forms.

Agostino Valerio (Valier), bishop of Verona and later cardinal, is the last author I will mention. His immensely popular *De rhetorica ecclesiastica* was first published in 1574, shortly after Matamoros's treatise. It is more serenely, but no less uncompromisingly, classical than Matamoros's; except for a brief and unobtrusive paragraph on the homily,[56] he never entertains even the suggestion that there might be alternatives to classical oratory.

Just as classical as the preaching theory that Valerio adopts is the *humanitas* that seems to me to animate the treatise. Besides embodying the classical virtues of clarity, order, and simplicity, the treatise emphasizes the human or humane values in Christianity. Valerio, for instance, rejects Stoic apathy and urges the preacher to awaken or instill good affections in his listeners. The preacher should especially arouse the emotion of love—love for God, of course, but also love of parents for their children, of children for their parents, of citizens for their native land, of friends for their friends. He should even try to make the good among his audience love themselves.[57]

Limitations of space now force me to move to the proposal of an agenda for future scholarship. The first task is the completion of the Caplan-King lists of sixteenth-century treatises, especially by taking note of works existing only in manuscript.[58] Second, the sermons preached by the authors of the treatises must be studied to see how practice corresponded to theory.[59] (Ironically, the two most important theorists—Melanchthon and Erasmus—left us no sermons!)[60]

56. See *Libri tres de rhetorica ecclesiastica* (Paris, 1575), fol. 103^r.

57. See ibid., fols. 38^v–42^v.

58. Harry Caplan and Henry H. King, "Latin Tractates on Preaching: A Book-List," *The Harvard Theological Review* 42 (1949), 185–206, esp. 187–95; "Italian Treatises on Preaching," *Speech Monographs* 16 (1949), 243–52, esp. 244; "Spanish Treatises on Preaching: A Book-List," *Speech Monographs* 17 (1950), 161–62; "Scandinavian Treatises on Preaching: A Book-List," *Speech Monographs* 21 (1954), 1–9; "Dutch Treatises on Preaching: A List of Books and Articles," ibid., pp. 235–47; "French Tractates on Preaching: A Book-List," *Quarterly Journal of Speech* 36 (1950), 296–325.

59. Frederick McGinness has completed such a study for preaching at the papal court in the late sixteenth and early seventeenth centuries, "Rhetoric and Counter-Reformation Rome: A Study in the Preaching at the Papal Court, 1563–1621" (Ph.D. diss. University of California, Berkeley, 1982). I am grateful to Mr. McGinness for reading an earlier version of this article and making some useful suggestions.

60. See my "Grammar and Rhetoric."

This would be an enormous undertaking, and judicious samplings will perhaps suffice to disclose dominant patterns. Then comparisons must be made between northern and southern humanism, between Erasmians and anti-Erasmians, between pre-Reformation and post-Reformation, between Catholic and Protestant. Never before had there been such variety in theories of sacred oratory as in the sixteenth century. The very names of the authors of works on preaching — Melanchthon, Erasmus, Contarini, Borromeo, Bellarmine, to name a few — indicate we are dealing with a crucial issue. It is a curious commentary on our scholarship that this phenomenon has never been studied in any systematic or comprehensive way.

It is my persuasion that studies like those I am advocating will uncover not only important information about the history of rhetoric and its adaptation to the Christian pulpit, but will also throw light on larger religious and cultural issues. García Matamoros explicitly relates his stance vis-à-vis classical rhetoric to a theological position. Other authors may be less explicit, but their rhetorical decisions are surely conditioned by their religious anthropology and their doctrinal convictions. In the controversy over rhetorical forms, deeper problems lurked beneath the surface.

Similarly, the authors' understanding of the nature of Scripture — as a book of the "philosophy of Christ," as a book of historical deeds, as a book of threats and promises, as a book of moral precepts — determines their choice of the *genus* that is most appropriate for propounding that book from the pulpit. Their choice of the *genus*, in turn, influences the hermeneutics with which they approach the sacred text, so that rhetoric has implications, here too, for literary interpretation. We can ask, further, what the purpose of a sermon is — to lead to understanding, to faith, to conversion of morals, or to inspiration by the vision of a beautiful deed. This question is implicitly answered by the *genus* in which the author places the sermon. An understanding of the use of the *genera* in preaching is an entrance into the deepest values that sixteenth-century cultures cherished and that its religions reflected and helped create.

IV

FORM, CONTENT, AND INFLUENCE OF WORKS ABOUT PREACHING BEFORE TRENT: THE FRANCISCAN CONTRIBUTION

In the history of Christian preaching there have been some clear turning-points. One of the most important, as is well known, took place in the High Middle Ages when the homilies and sermons of the patristic and monastic tradition were challenged by the methods of the scholastics [1]. Along with other forms, the so-called « thematic » sermon emerged, with a clearly visible structure of theme, pro-theme, prayer for divine aid, and other distinguishing characteristics [2]. Concommitant with the emergence of this new style of preaching based on *definitio* and *demonstratio* was the creation of manuals called *Artes praedicandi* that provided theory about thematic sermons and practical directives as to how to construct and deliver

---

[1] On the distinction between the patristic homily and the patristic sermon, see C. Mohrmann, *Praedicare-Tractare-Sermo. Essai sur la terminologie de la prédication paléochrétienne*, in her *Études sur le latin des chrétiens*, II, Rome 1977, 63-72; Ph. Rouillard, *Homélie*, in *Catholicisme* V (1963) 829-31; and A. Bonfatti, *Oratoria sacra*, Brescia 1964. On patristic preaching in general, see now the survey by Th. K. Carroll, *Preaching the Word*, Wilmington 1984. See also especially P. Nautin, *Origène prédicateur*, in Origen, *Homélies sur Jérémie*, ed. P. Husson and P. Nautin, Paris 1976 (Sources chrétiennes, 232), 136-51, and J. I. H. McDonald, *Kerygma and Didache. The Articulation and Structure of the Earliest Christian Message*, Cambridge 1980.

[2] There are many studies of this phenomenon. See especially Th.-M. Charland, *Artes praedicandi. Contribution a l'histoire de la rhétorique au moyen âge*, Paris 1936; R. H. and M. A. Rouse, *Preachers, Florilegia and Sermons. Studies on the Manipulus florum of Thomas of Ireland*, Toronto 1979; J. Longère, *La prédication médievale*, Paris 1983, Id., *Oeuvres oratoires de maîtres parisiens au XII*[e] *siècle. Étude historique et doctrinale*, Paris 1975 (2 vols.). See also the recent surveys: R. Rusconi, *Predicatori e predicazione (secoli IX-XVIII)*, in *Storia d'Italia. Annali*, IV (Torino 1981), 951-1035, and C. Delcorno, *Rassegna di studi sulla predicazione medievale e umanistica (1970-80)*, in *Lettere italiane* 33 (1981) 235-76.

them [3]. Aside from the *De doctrina christiana* of Augustine, this was for all practical purposes the first time the Christian Church turned its attention in an organized and theoretical way to its principal task, the presentation of its message to the world.

The differences between the « ancient forms » of preaching and the thematic sermon advocated by the scholastics are notable: the former commented more directly and obviously on a single passage of Scripture, whose course was often its only structure; the language of the older forms tended to be literary, even poetic, and made appeal to the affect, rather than to logical demonstration; the older forms were more rhetorical and less structured, whereas the thematic sermons were more dialectical and highly structured.

Thematic sermons never altogether displaced older forms of preaching and, as is well known, they coexisted with the more popular sermons developed by medieval preachers. Persons scholastically trained thus helped develop a rich variety of preaching forms. These forms are clearly distinguishable, nonetheless, from the patristic or monastic homily. By the middle of the Quattrocento, another major turning-point was already under way that would be practically completed almost by the close of the Council of Trent [4]. This phenomenon was

---

[3] See CHARLAND, *Artes*; H. CAPLAN, *Mediaeval Artes Praedicandi. A Hand-List*, Ithaca 1934, and ID., *Mediaeval Artes Praedicandi. A Supplementary Hand-List*, Ithaca 1936, as well as other studies listed in his *Of Eloquence*, ed. A. KING and H. NORTH, Ithaca 1970, 271-72. See also L.-J. BATAILLON, *Les instruments de travail des prédicateurs au XIII*e *siècle*, in *Culture et travail intellectuel dans l'Occident médiéval*, ed J. LONGÈRE, Paris 1981, 197-209.

[4] See especially M. FUMAROLI, *L'âge de l'éloquence. Rhétorique et « res literaria » de la Renaissance au seuil de l'époque classique*, Geneve 1980; P. BAYLEY, *French Pulpit Oratory, 1598-1650*, Cambridge 1980; ID., *Selected Sermons of the French Baroque (1600-1650)*, New York 1983; F. MCGINNESS, *Rhetoric and Counter-Reformation Rome. Sacred Oratory and the Construction of the Catholic World View*, Ann Arbor 1982, and ID., *The Rhetoric of Praise and the New Rome of the Counter Reformation*, in *Rome in the Renaissance*, ed. P. A. RAMSEY, Binghamton 1982, 355-70. See also my studies: *Content*

in part due to widespread dissatisfaction with late-medieval styles of preaching, in part due to many other complex factors during this period of Renaissance, Reformation, and Counter Reformation. The transformation took place in a clearly demonstrable way on the level of theory. On the level of practice, further study is needed, but the change can nonetheless be easily documented in the sermons of a number of prominent preachers. The trends set at this time would continue in a general way into the twentieth century.

Given the inestimably great importance of the Franciscans in the history of preaching from the days of Saint Francis forward, we should anticipate that they would play a similar role in this period of transition. However, this problem has never, so far as I know, been investigated. We possess, of course, competent studies of Franciscan preachers in the fifteenth and sixteenth centuries, but none of these describes in any overarching and systematic way the changes that were taking place and the part the Franciscans played in them [5].

I was asked to address at this Conference the Franciscan contributions to « works about preaching before the Council of Trent, » and, hence, I cannot avoid the larger problem just described. I do not have the competence to treat that problem

---

and Rhetorical Forms in Sixteenth-Century Treatises on Preaching, in *Renaissance Eloquence*, ed. J. J. MURPHY, Berkeley 1983, 238-52; *Erasmus and the History of Sacred Rhetoric. The Ecclesiastes of 1535*, in *Erasmus of Rotterdam Society Yearbook* 5 (1985); *Luther the Preacher*, in *The Martin Luther Quincentennial*, ed. G. DÜNNHAUPT, Detroit 1985, 3-16; *Saint Charles Borromeo and the « Praecipuum Episcoporum Munus ». His Place in the History of Preaching*, forthcoming in studies on Saint Charles from the conference at the Folger Shakespeare Library. October 26-28, 1984, ed. J. M. HEADLEY.

[5] Fundamental is A. ZAWART, *The History of Franciscan Preaching and of Franciscan Preachers*, New York 1927 (Francisc. Studies, 7), and the studies by BONAVENTURA VON MEHR, *Recentes collationes ad historiam praedicationis*, in *Coll. francisc.* 10 (1940) 534-60; *De historiae praedicationis, praesertim in Or. Fr. M. Capucinorum, scientifica pervestigatio, Ibid.* 11 (1941) 373-422; 12 (1942) 5-41; *Über neuere Beiträge zur Geschichte der vortridentinischen franziskanischen Predigt, Ibid.* 19 (1948) 245-58.

in the comprehensive manner it deserves and will therefore limit myself, in the first place, to describing the significance of three Franciscans who have received, at least until recently, little attention in this regard. Despite the restricted nature of this approach, it will throw some light, I trust, on the larger issues. After describing the contributions of these three friars, I will then indicate ways in which the ninth chapter of the *Regula Bullata* of Saint Francis, the chapter that deals with preaching, had a perhaps even more decisive influence on preaching theory during this period and immediately after the Council of Trent than ever before.

The three friars are, in logical rather than chronological sequence: the Italian, Lorenzo Guglielmo Traversagni (d. 1505); the German, Nikolaus Herborn or, to give him his family name, Ferber (d. 1535); and the Fleming, Jean Vitrier (d. 1519). Traversagni was born in Savona in 1425, where twenty years later he entered the Franciscan order [6]. After his studies at Savona and Padua, he traveled widely throughout Europe, lecturing and preaching at intellectual centers like Vienna, Avignon, Toulouse, Paris, London, and Cambridge. In 1485 he returned to Savona, where he died in 1505. A number of his works have come down to us, principally his *Margarita eloquentiae castigatae*, recently published in a critical edition by Giovanni Farris [7]. We also possess some of his orations, which help interpret the sometimes abstract principles of the *Margarita* [8].

Traversagni was described in 1953 by Msgr. José Ruysschaert as « un humaniste franciscan oublié » [9]. He has since then, however, been the object of several studies [10]. None of

---

6 See G. FARRIS, *Umanesimo e religione in Lorenzo Guglielmo Traversagni (1425-1505)*, Milano 1972.

7 Savona 1978.

8 For some transcriptions, see FARRIS, *Umanesimo*, 67-119.

9 *Lorenzo Guglielmo Traversagni de Savone (1425-1503 [sic]). Un humaniste franciscain oublié*, in *Arch. francisc. hist.* 46 (1953) 195-210.

10 Besides the studies by FARRIS and RUYSSCHAERT listed above, see also

these studies, however, assess his place in the critical changes in preaching theory and practice that were already under way in his lifetime.

What were these changes? I have studied them in detail in my book on preaching at the papal court [11]. They can generically be described as a repudiation of medieval forms of public discourse in favor of forms based more directly on the principles of classical rhetoric—more specifically, on the principles of demonstrative or epideictic rhetoric, which is the rhetoric of panegyric, the rhetoric of « praise and blame ». The earliest such sermons of which we at present have knowledge are the funeral oratory and the series of panegyrics honoring Saint Jerome composed by Pier Paolo Vergerio the Elder at Padua in the late Trecento, early Quattrocento [12]. The same principles were applied by others at some later date to sermons on the mysteries of the Christian faith. In circles of high culture these forms were practiced with some consistency in Italy by the last quarter of the Quattrocento, and corresponded to a similar change in secular oratory during this period.

---

the edition by FARRIS of TRAVERSAGNI, *De varia fortuna Antiochi*, Savona 1972; J. RUYSSCHAERT, *Les manuscrits autographes de deux oeuvres de Lorenzo Guglielmo Traversagni imprimées chez Caxton*, in *Bulletin of the John Rylands Library* 36 (1953) 191-96; J. J. MURPHY, *Caxton's Two Choices. « Modern » and « Medieval » Rhetoric in Traversagni's Nova Rhetorica and the Anonymous Court of Sapience*, in *Medievalia et Humanistica*, n.s., 3 (1972) 241-55; R. H. MARTIN, *The « Epitome Margaritae Eloquentiae » of Laurentius Guglielmus de Saona*, in *Proceedings of the Leeds Philosophical and Literary Society (Literary and Historical Section)* 14 (1970-72) 99-187. See also G. FARRIS, *Scuola et Umanesimo a Savona nel sec. XV*, in *Atti e Memorie della Società Savonese di Storia Patria* 10 (1976) 7-53.

11 *Praise and Blame in Renaissance Rome. Rhetoric, Doctrine, and Reform in the Sacred Orators of the Papal Court, ca. 1450-1521*, Durham 1979. See also J. M. MCMANAMON, *The Ideal Renaissance Pope. Funeral Oratory from the Papal Court*, in *Archivum historiae pontificiae* 14 (1976) 9-70; ID., *Renaissance Preaching: Theory and Practice. A Holy Thursday Sermon of Aurelio Brandolini*, in *Viator* 10 (1979) 355-73; and R. WITT, *Medieval « Ars Dictaminis » and the Beginnings of Humanism. A New Construction of the Problem*, in *Renaissance Quarterly* 35 (1982) 1-35.

12 See J. M. MCMANAMON, *Innovation in Early Humanistic Rhetoric. The Oratory of Pier Paolo Vergerio the Elder*, in *Rinascimento* 22 (1982) 3-32.

Although not without precedent in the patristic period, these sacred orations broke new ground in the history of rhetoric. They rejected in practice both the homiletic and more distinctively medieval patterns that until then prevailed, and offered a practical alternative to them. These orations lack all the features that made the thematic sermon odious to many, and, in contrast to the often rambling homily, they hang together as literary units. They have a structure and logical unity that the homily generally lacked, their appeal to the emotions was more artfully designed than in the thematic sermon, and they possessed a literary dignity and restraint not generally manifested in popular preaching. They tend to be positive in outlook, celebrating and praising God's gifts, goodness, and great interventions on behalf of humankind, and are thus in content and mood distinguishable from « penitential » preaching. Their greatest importance, however, consists in the simple fact that classical rhetoric was now applied to preaching in a way and to a degree hitherto practically unknown in the West and that this innovation set off a new movement of discovery and creativity in the forms of preaching.

As part of this movement the patristic homily-sermon began somewhat later to experience a notable revival, partly in reaction, again, to the thematic sermon of the scholastics. The best known practitioner of this form was Martin Luther, although he was not as unique in this regard as is often assumed, and his preaching was influenced by more personal and classical factors as well [13]. By 1535, in other words, the scholastic art of preaching was being challenged by some of the same traditions that that art had several centuries earlier largely displaced. The scene was confused, often polemical.

In 1535 Erasmus published his *Ecclesiastes*, his last major work and his longest [14]. That treatise on preaching (*De ratione concionandi*) enjoyed an immediate success, running through

---

[13] See my *Luther the Preacher.*

[14] See my *Erasmus and the History of Sacred Rhetoric.*

ten printings within a decade of the *editio princeps*. The *Ecclesiastes* was welcomed not only because of the incomparable prestige of its author, but also because contemporaries grasped at it as the first codification and rationalization of developments in preaching that had been under way for over a century. The *Ecclesiastes* is generally recognized as the first treatise on preaching that directly and comprehensively applied classical and patristic rhetoric to the preaching situation. Its importance can hardly be over-estimated. Even later theorists who differed with Erasmus would be profoundly indebted to his great work, little appreciated though it was in subsequent centuries. The history of preaching theory would never be quite the same after late August of 1535.

But was the *Ecclesiastes*, after all, the first work in this period to address the subject of preaching theory in a way different from the scholastic *Artes praedicandi*? Not quite. Aside from Johannes Reuchlin's *Liber congestorum* of 1504, there were two Lutheran works published just before 1535— Philipp Melanchthon's *De officiis concionatoris* and Veit Dietrich's *Ratio brevis et docta piaque sacrarum concionum tractandarum*. The pieces by Reuchlin and Melanchthon were not much more than pamphlets, sketchy in their prescriptions. Dietrich's *Ratio brevis* was somewhat longer, but as much inspired by Lutheran theology as by principles of classical rhetoric. Until at least 1540, they all had quite modest circulation [15].

But there was another work of much greater substance— the *Margarita eloquentiae castigatae* of Traversagni. This work, published in two editions in England, 1479/80, was the result of the lectures on preaching delivered by Traversagni at the

---

[15] See *Supplementa Melanchthoniana*, ed. P. Drews and F. Cohrs, vol. 5, pt. 2, Leipzig 1929, as well as my *Erasmus and the History of Sacred Rhetoric*, and *Lutheranism in Rome, 1542-43. The Treatise by Alfonso Zorrilla*, in *Thought* 54 (1979) 262-73, now reprinted in my *Rome and the Renaissance. Studies in Culture and Religion*, London 1981.

Universities of Cambridge and Paris at about the same time. It is the only reasonably complete treatise on preaching until the *Ecclesiastes* that takes account of the momentous changes then under way in Italy and elsewhere. It is a long work, running 215 pages in the edition by Farris.

Unlike the *Ecclesiastes*, the *Margarita* had little success and diffusion despite its two editions, and even the publication in 1480 of an *Epitome* of it. The printings must have been small, for only a handful of copies survive. Although these three printings within about a year indicate a lively interest in the work in England, it attracted no notice from subsequent generations. We can only speculate about the reasons for this neglect, but a closer examination of its content may be of some help here.

The alternative title to the *Margarita* was « In novam rhetoricam », and that alternative indicates much of the purpose and content of the book. The *Margarita* is for the most part a commentary on the pseudo-Ciceronian *Rhetorica ad Herennium*, known also as the « Nova rhetorica ». Traversagni did not, therefore, like Erasmus, compose a new treatise on preaching, but for the benefit of preaching he applied, adapted, and commented upon the *Ad Herennium*— and to a much lesser extent on the *De oratore* and the *De inventione*. I suspect that this fact largely explains the lack of success of the *Margarita* in Italy, and probably elsewhere. The Italians who were practicing these new forms of preaching were thoroughly familiar with the *Ad Herennium*, which had been the basis of Vergerio's innovations at Padua almost a century earlier, and Traversagni's specific applications of it to preaching in the *Margarita* would tell them nothing about rhetorical theory and its adaptation to preaching that they did not already know.

Does the work, then, lack significance? I do not think so. It is the first work of the Renaissance explicitly to apply classical rhetoric to Christian preaching. It is thus the first treatise since the *De doctrina christiana* of Saint Augustine to theorize about preaching in a way notably different from the tradition of the *Artes*. Secondly, its very lack of success perhaps indicates that the phenomenon for which it tried to prescribe was already so widely practiced at this point, before reflection upon practice began to develop, that contemporaries at least in Italy had little to gain from it. Thirdly, the book contains impassioned theological justifications for the appropriation of rhetoric by the Christian preacher. These are traditional arguments, but they indicate once again that the enthusiasm for rhetoric during this period was not theologically unreflective or uncritical.

Fourthly, the *Margarita* testifies to the variety of Franciscan involvement in the preaching enterprise. Traversagni was a younger contemporary of San Bernardino and a precise contemporary of Roberto da Lecce — they were born in the same year — but he moves at a different level and indicates a different appropriation of Renaissance culture than either of these more famous confrères [16]. The *Margarita* points forward to the great treatises of the sixteenth century that would argue when, why, how, and to what extent classical rhetoric could be applied to the Christian pulpit.

Finally, Traversagni without hesitation locates preaching in the *genus demonstrativum* of classical oratory, bypassing both the *genus judiciale* and the *genus deliberativum* [17]. He here re-

---

[16] See, e.g., *Bernardino predicatore nella società del suo tempo* (Convegni del Centro di Studi sulla spiritualità medievale, 12), Todi 1976; F. A. Mormando, *The Vernacular Sermons of San Bernardino da Siena, O.F.M. (1380-1444). A Literary Analysis*, Ann Arbor 1983; S. Bastanzio, *Fra Roberto Caracciolo. Predicatore del secolo XV*, Isola del Liri 1947; E. V. Telle, *En marge de l'éloquence sacrée aux XVe-XVIe siècles. Érasme et Fra Roberto Caracciolo*, in *Bibliothèque d'Humanisme et Renaissance* 43 (1981) 449-70, and Id., « *To every thing there is a season...* ». *Ways and Fashions in the Art of Preaching on the Eve of the Religious Upheavals in the Sixteenth Century*, in *Erasmus of Rotterdam Society Yearbook* 2 (1982) 13-24.

[17] See *Margarita*, 33: « [...] de demonstrativo vero accumulatius, quoniam illud est quod maxime et proprie spectat ad animorum salubrem conversionem, neque de reliquo quicquam attingendum putassem, nisi connexionem haberet maximam cum demonstrativo genere, et maxime conduceret ad suaden-

flects the Italian consensus of the period. We shall return to this point later. For the moment we must simply note that he introduces the problem of the *genera* and sees it as an issue, which to my knowledge had never before entered into the discussion of preaching theory in a prominent degree.

The next friar to whom I would direct your attention is Nikolaus Herborn. Born about 1480, he spent most of his life in or near Marburg and Cologne [18]. He was a devout and learned man, and he held several important offices in the order, including Provincial of the Cologne Province of the Observants and Vicar General of the ultramontane provinces. He engaged in vigorous polemics against the Lutherans especially in the circle around Philip of Hesse, for which he is best known, but he also wrote one of the first treatises on missionary methods for dealing with the indigenous peoples of the New

---

dum, vel dissuadendum in his que ad bonum publicum, tam ecclesiasticum quam civile pertinere dignoscuntur ».

[18] There is a fair amount of literature on Herborn. Still basic is L. Schmitt, *Der kölner Theologe Nikolaus Stagefur und der Franziskaner Nikolaus Herborn*, Freiburg 1896 (Ergänzunghefte zu den « Stimmen aus Maria Laach », 67). See also his edition of Herborn, *Confutatio Lutheranismi Danici*, Quaracchi (Firenze) 1920, as well as P. Schlager's edition of his *Locorum communium adversus huius temporis haereses Enchiridion (1529)*, Münster 1927 (Corpus Catholicorum, 12). See, as well, Zawart, *Franciscan Preaching*, 413; *Neue Deutsche Biographie* V, 80-81; *Enciclopedia Cattolica* VI, 1412-13; K. Köhler, *Nikolaus Ferbers Methodus praedicandi verbi divini von 1529*, in *Zeitschrift für praktische Theologie* 14 (1892) 305-38; P. Hasenöhrl, *Franziskanische Homiletiker*, in *Kirche und Kanzel* 6 (1923) 123-29, especially 127-29; E. Kurten, *Franz Lambert von Avignon und Nikolaus Herborn in ihrer Stellung zum Ordensgedanken und zum Franziskanertum im besonderen*, Münster 1950; E. Oltra, *Escritura y Tradición en la teología pretridentina*, in *Salmanticensis* 10 (1963) 65-133, especially 88-89; J. Beckman, *Die erste katholische Missionslehre der Neuzeit in einem Basler Druck von 1555*, in *Zeitschrift für schweizerische Kirchengeschichte* 57 (1963) 55-63; J. Nybo Rasmussen, *Herborn og Stagefyr*, in *Kirkehistoriske Samlinger*, ser. 7, 6 (1966) 44-60; J. Beumer, *Erasmus von Rotterdam und seine Freunde aus dem Franziskanerorden*, in *Franzisk. Studien* 51 (1969) 117-29. I have not been able to consult: O. van der Vat, *Collectanea franciscana neerlandica* II, 's-Hertogenbosch (ca. 1931), 395-425, and A. Goetz, *Nikolaus von Herborn. Anleitung zur Heidenbekehrung*, in *Heilige, Märtyrer und Helden*, Aschaffenburg 1957, 135-41.

World. His writing in these genres have come down to us and been studied.

Much less noticed, however, has been his work entitled *Methodus praedicandi verbi divini*, published in a single edition in 1529 in the same volume with a second printing of his anti-Lutheran *Enchiridion* [19]. The *Methodus* runs some sixty pages, and is in the form of a letter to his Franciscan brethren in the cloister at Brühl. In its style and content the *Methodus* is not at all what we would have expected from this religiously besieged and agitated situation.

Unlike Traversagni's *Margarita* and Erasmus' later *Ecclesiastes*, the *Methodus* is not a systematic rhetoric for preachers. Nor is it a set of practical directives or juridical norms, although the latter play some role in the work. What, then, is it? Quite different from the *Artes* in vocabulary, aim, and content, it is a rather unique piece that can best be described as a work on preaching that is in substance a humanistic call « ad fontes », a phrase that recurs in the work [20]. Conditioned as the *Methodus* is by Herborn's passionate opposition to the Protestants, it is a fervent exhortation to base preaching on the text of Scripture and to employ the Fathers of the Church as models for good preaching and as sources for the correct interpretation of the sacred text [21]. Herborn explicitly refers to the *De doctrina Christiana* of Augustine [22]. The *Methodus*

---

19 *Locorum communium adversus huius temporis haereses Enchiridion [...]. Tractatulus eiusdem de notis verae ecclesiae ab adultera dignoscendae. Eiusdem Methodus praedicandi verbi divini concionatoribus cum utilis, tum accomoda [sic]* (Cologne: Pet. Quentel 1529), unnumbered folios. Köhler gives a complete account of its content and criticizes the work from a Lutheran point of view, *Ferbers Methodus*. See also SCHMITT, *Der kölner Theologe*, 139-57.

20 See *Methodus*, e.g., sig. T v^v^, « [...] adeundae sunt divinae scripturae »; sig. T vii^r^: « Sic Moses, sic David, ita Isaias, ita demum & Christus, quoties ad legem, quoties ad prophetas, quoties ad psalmos, porro ad fontes ipsos perpetuam ebullientes sapientiam mittunt »; sig. V ii^r^: « [...] ut ad fontes ipsos confugias »; sig. V vii^v^-V viii^r^.

21 See *Ibid.*, sig. V iv^v^.

22 *Ibid.*, sig. V iii^r^.

also deals with the spiritual life of the preacher and with the subjects about which he should preach.

Altough we know practically nothing about Herborn's education and library, internal evidence in his texts points unmistakably to an Erasmian influence. There is a similarity in vocabulary in certain key phrases like the « celestial philosophy » of the Bible [23] and in the use of the term « Novum Instrumentum » to designate the New Testament [24]. Herborn also occasionally uses Erasmus' translation of the Bible instead of the Vulgate [25]. There is, moreover, a similarity in ideas, including the frank criticism of the venality of some preachers of the mendicant orders [26] and of the disedifying pride of the scholastic masters and their useless, acrimonious disputes [27]. Herborn's statement that many friars prefer the refectory over the library is one of his lesser invectives [28]. He manifests a critical attitude towards canon lawyers and especially towards preachers who cite them [29]. He shows disdain for philosophers, and contrasts the truths of Scripture with the « lies » of Aristotle [30]. But when Herborn makes « peace and concord » (pax et concordia) the first subject the preacher must address, he

[23] See *Ibid.*, e.g., sig. T v^v^; sig. T vi^r^; sig. T vi^v^; sig. X vii^v^. The phrase « a scopo Christo », sig. T iii^r^, is also Erasmian.

[24] See *Ibid.*, e.g., sig. V ii^r^; sig. V iii^v^.

[25] See Schlager (ed.), *Enchiridion*, xxiii, 16, 55, 68, 166; Schmitt (ed.), *Confutatio*, 9, 54, 134, 160, 181, 212, 244, and especially 271. Schmitt explains the frequent use of the *Novum Instrumentum* in the *Confutatio* as the work of the editor (*Ibid.*, 12). Probably not without some basis, this explanation does not suffice, especially for Herborn's usage of the Erasmian text in his other works.

[26] See *Methodus*, sig. Y ii^v^-Y iii^v^.

[27] See *Ibid.*, e.g., sig. X vii^r^: « Quod disceptatiunculis proficitur? [...] superciliosas disputationes »; sig. X vii^v^-X viii^v^: « Inter mundanae sapientiae professores videmus quanta sit aemulatio, quae pugnae, quae dissidia [...]. Neque enim, inquit Paulus, in contentione, non in spinosis syllogismus [sic] [...] ».

[28] *Ibid.*, sig. V i^r^: « Si quidem invenies qui culinae sunt frequentiores quam bibliothecae [...] ».

[29] See *Ibid.*, sig. X vi^v-r^.

[30] See *Ibid.*, sig. V ii^r^-V iii^r^.

is as close as possible to the heart of the Erasmian reform [31].

Herborn later attacked Erasmus in his *Enarrationes Evangeliorum* of 1533. Driven by his hatred of the Protestants, he intemperately accused Erasmus of laying the egg Luther hatched, and he even equates him with the heretics. Erasmus, deeply offended, responded in kind in several letters to friends and tried to have the publication of the *Enarrationes* suppressed [32]. Nonetheless, such a close affinity exists between the *Methodus* and Erasmus' general stance and vocabulary on similar issues that it could almost have issued from Erasmus' pen. The confused relationship between these two men, both of whom considered themselves loyal Catholics, is a microcosm of the complex religious situation of the 1530's.

This relationship must not, however, distract us from an objective consideration of the content and import of the *Methodus*. Where does it fit in the pattern of works about preaching? The *Methodus* is the only substantial work to address the subject directly in a humanistic vein between Traversagni's *Margarita* and Erasmus' *Ecclesiastes*. New *Artes* continued to be published until 1528 [33]; there were the three works by Reuchlin, Dietrich, and Melanchthon; in 1519, moreover, Melanchthon published his *Rhetoric*, which contained applications for preaching; the Fifth Lateran Council issued on December 19, 1516, its decree, « Supernae maiestatis prae-

---

31 See *Ibid.*, e.g., sig. X iii^r. On this issue, see J. K. McConica, *Erasmus and the Grammar of Consent*, in *Scrinium Erasmianum*, ed. J. Coppens, II, Leiden 1969, 77-99, and my *Erasmus and Luther: Continuity and Discontinuity as Key to Their Conflict*, in *The Sixteenth Century Journal* 5/2 (1974) 47-65.

32 See *Opus epistolarum Des. Erasmi Roterodami*, ed. P. S. Allen, H. M. Allen, and H. W. Garrod, 12 vols. (Oxford 1906-58), especially the virulent letter against Herborn to John Carondelet, January 23, 1534: X, 349-50. But see also *Ibid.*, 345-46, 348-49, 358, 364, 368; XI, 21, 34, 50, 52-53, 226-27, 289-90. Beumer touches on this issue, *Erasmus und seine Freunde.*

33 The last new work to be published in the tradition of the *Artes* of which I am aware is the brief piece by Pedro Ciruelo, *De arte praedicandi*, contained in his *Expositio libri Missalis peregregia* (Alcalá: M. de Eguia 1528), ff. 270ra-276ra.

sidio », trying to regulate abuses in preaching. But Traversagni and Herborn are the only two Catholic authors explicitly, clearly, and at length to take account, each in a different way, of a movement calling for the reform of preaching, humanistic in inspiration, that was now widespread. Both of their works look to the future rather than to the past.

When Herborn wrote, the learned world was already awaiting the long-promised *Ecclesiastes*. The failure of the *Methodus* to attract attention is probably due in part to that fact, as well as to the generic nature of its content. But the failure is also probably due to a new defensiveness among Catholics. In a climate of bitter polemics, they would find Herborn's frank criticisms dangerous and unacceptable, just as they found, paradoxically enough in view of the later dispute between Herborn and Erasmus, the similar criticisms of the Dutch humanist.

We now turn to our third Franciscan, Jean Vitrier, best known to us from the famous letter about him and John Colet that Erasmus wrote to Jodocus Jonas, June 13, 1521 [34]. This so-called « Erasmian saint » was born about 1456 at Saint-Omer, where he seems to have entered the order at an early age. He spent most of his life in that vicinity, and met Erasmus there in the winter of 1501-2. He wrote no treatise on preaching theory, but he exercised a decisive influence on the author of the most important such work in the sixteenth century—Erasmus. For that reason he cannot be omitted from our consideration.

The relationship between Vitrier and Erasmus has been examined in great detail in a number of studies by André Godin, especially in his long and impressive book, *Érasme:*

---

[34] See *Opus epistolarum*, VI, 507-27. See also the English translation by J. OLIN, *Christian Humanism and the Reformation, Desiderius Erasmus. Selected Writings*, New York 1965, 164-91, and the French translation and presentation by A. GODIN, *Érasme: Vies de Jean Vitrier et de John Colet*, Angers 1982.

Lecteur d'Origène [35]. Godin has also edited Vitrier's homilary, his only work to come down to us, which confirms the descriptions about Vitrier's preaching style that Erasmus provides on two occasions [36].

According to Godin, Vitrier's influence upon Erasmus was twofold: first, Vitrier impressed Erasmus by a preaching style that was simple, ardent, based directly on the text of Scripture, and thus quite different from how Erasmus evaluated the « sermo modernus » of the scholastic tradition; secondly, he turned Erasmus' attention to Origen in a decisive way [37]. This discovery of Origen would have profound and manifold repercussions on Erasmus, but among them would be for him to find in Origen's homiletic style the ancient counterpart to Vitrier's. There is no doubt from about this time forward of Erasmus' growing admiration for the preaching of the Fathers, of which Origen was the original inspiration and Vitrier the modern representation. Even today we often forget that the revival of the ancient Christian tradition became central to Erasmus' concerns, and even to the Humanist movement in general, and that it conditioned his approach to the classics.

Was Erasmus, then, principally responsible — under the influence of Vitrier — for the renewed interest in the patristic styles of preaching that would be just as important for the later sixteenth century as classical oratory? Of course, Erasmus was only one voice among many. Nonetheless, his was the

---

[35] Geneva 1982. See also his *De Vitrier à Origène. Recherches sur la patristique érasmienne*, in *Colloquium Erasmianum*, Mons 1968, 47-57; *Érasme et le modèle origénien de la prédication*, in *Colloquia Erasmiana Turonensia*, ed. J.-C. Margolin, II, Toronto 1972, 807-20; *Jean Vitrier et le « cenacle » de Saint-Omer, Ibid.*, 781-805; *The Enchiridion Militis Christiani. The Modes of an Origenian Appropriation*, in *Erasmus of Rotterdam Society Yearbook* 2 (1982) 47-79. See, as well, A. Derville, *Jean Vitrier et les religieuses de Saint-Marguerite (1500-1530)*, in *Revue du Nord* 42 (1960) 207-39.

[36] *L'Homéliaire de Jean Vitrier. Texte, étude thématique et sémantique. Spiritualité franciscaine en Flandre au XVIe siècle*, ed. A. Godin (Geneva 1971). See also the review by G. Chantraine in *Revue d'histoire ecclésiastique* 68 (1973) 892-98.

[37] See especially, e.g., *Érasme*, 21-32, 660-85.

most authoritative, at least outside Lutheran circles. His magnificent editions of the texts of the Fathers put their homilies into the hands of his contemporaries so that they could be studied and imitated in a way that had never been possible before.

This brings us to the *Ecclesiastes*, that complex treatise on preaching that even Erasmus recognized was repetitious and difficult to follow. What is the relationship in the *Ecclesiastes* between the homily and the more oratorical forms based on classical rhetoric that Erasmus seems to espouse for preaching? [38] Erasmus for instance places preaching principally in the *genus deliberativum* of classical oratory, in contrast with Traversagni and the earlier Italian tradition that placed it in the demonstrative genre. Erasmus does not call the preachment a « homily » but a « contio », the form of the *genus deliberativum* aimed at popular audiences. In fact, during his lifetime and due to a large extent, we must assume, to his influence, the designation « contio » comes into general usage, and begins to diplace other terms for preaching like « sermo », « homilia », and « oratio ».

I have addressed this issue in some detail elsewhere [39]. In brief, I propose that there is both ambivalence and ambiguity in Erasmus on the relationship between a homily and a « contio ». Had he ever preached himself, he might have resolved the relationship more satisfactorily. On the other hand, along with the ambiguities and ambivalences, there are in Erasmus some clarities about preaching that are even stronger: first, his admiration for the preaching of the Fathers, from Origen to Bernard (some of these texts he knew better than any other person of his times); secondly, his convinction that the literary

---

[38] See Godin, *Érasme*; J. Chomarat, *Grammaire et rhétorique chez Érasme*, 2 vols., Paris 1981; my *Erasmus and the History of Sacred Rhetoric*, and *Grammar and Rhetoric in the Theology of Erasmus*, forthcoming in *Paideia. Special Renaissance Number*, ed. G. C. Simmons.

[39] *Erasmus and the History of Sacred Rhetoric.*

techniques and even the oratorical forms of classical rhetoric had application to Christian preaching; thirdly, his belief that this application should be sober, appropriate to the circumstances and audience, and avoid the exaggerations and every other pitfall of « Ciceronianism », which he opposed so vehemently even for secular literature.

Erasmus seems to have desired in preaching, therefore, some combination of the following: sermons that would be basically *explications de texte*, as were the patristic homilies on the Bible, but he would admit more sophisticated forms as well; sermons that sprang from the deep spirituality of the preacher, as he believed was true for both Origen and Vitrier; sermons that at the same time made use in a sober and restrained way of the techniques of eloquence that classical rhetoric provided; finally, sermons that addressed especially the moral needs of a popular audience, which corresponds to the general situation envisioned by the classical « contio ».

Put in these terms, the Erasmian ideal of sacred eloquence is not far removed from the so-called « severe ideal » that would win the support of Carlo Borromeo and many of his contemporaries later in the century, an ideal so well described by Marc Fumaroli in his recent book [40]. The « severe ideal » was, again, derived from both the patristic and the classical tradition, with clear repudiation of Ciceronianism even in its vernacular transformations. It was also a repudiation of scholastic forms of preaching—a repudiation that by the time Borromeo had arrived in Milan was on this level of theory seemingly unanimous among both Catholics and Protestants [41]. The repudiation is all the more remarkable among Catholics because of the almost simultaneous resurgence of scholastic theology. Even the Jesuit *Constitutions*, completed shortly before the death of Saint Ignatius in 1556, dissuaded members

40 *L'âge de l'éloquence* (note 4 above).

41 See my *Erasmus and the History of Sacred Rhetoric* and my *Borromeo and the Praecipuum Munus*.

of the Society from preaching « in the scholastic style » (IV 8 [402]).

The *Ecclesiastes* was the great watershed in treatises about how to preach. The only works of any length that adumbrated it were by two Franciscans — Traversagni and Herborn — and another Franciscan, Vitrier, helped in a remote but crucial way to inspire it. Within Roman Catholicism many years would pass before the *Ecclesiastes* was digested and alternatives to it proposed. Surely the proscription of the *Opera omnia* of Erasmus by the Roman Index of 1559 sparked the production of new works on preaching within the next two decades, the beginning of the « golden age » of Catholic treatises on the subject.

Once again, the Franciscans played a leading role. Luca Baglioni published at Venice in 1562 the first such treatise in Italian on the subject, *L'arte del predicare* [42]. In 1576 Diego de Estella published his *Modus concionandi*, advocating the patristic homily [43]. The *Modus concionandi* must be listed along with the treatises of two non-Franciscans — Agostino Valier's *De retorica ecclesiastica* (1574) [44] and Luis de Granada's *Ecclesiasticae rhetoricae* (1676) [45] — as among the three most influential works on the subject for centuries to come. Then in 1579 Diego Valades, former missioner to Mexico and later preacher at the papal court, published his wonderfully compassionate *Rhetorica christiana* [46]. At this date no other religious order has in this regard such a claim on our attention.

---

[42] *L'arte del predicare contenuta in tre libri, secondo i precetti rhetorici* (Venice: A. Torrisano 1562).

[43] See the critical edition, *Modo de predicar y Modus concionandi. Estudio doctrinal y edición crítica*, ed. Pio Sagües Azcona, 2 vols., Madrid 1951.

[44] Venice: A. Biochinus 1574.

[45] *Ecclesiasticae rhetoricae, sive De ratione concionandi libri sex* (Lisbon: A. Riberius 1576).

[46] *Rhetorica christiana ad concionandi et orandi usum accommodata* (Perugia: Apud Petrumiacobum Petrutium 1579). H. Caplan and H. King list an edition of this work in 1574, but since Valades explicitly refers, 9, to Granada's book, first published in 1576, that earlier date is impossible; see

The list could continue — I have not even mentioned Francesco Panigarola — but I have already passed the chronological limits set to my subject. Before concluding, however, I want to turn attention to the ninth chapter of the Franciscan Rule and indicate an influence it had in the sixteenth century that has gone practically unnoticed. That short chapter specifies that " vices and virtues, punishment and reward " are to be the subjects about which the friars are to preach. It is never included in lists of " works about preaching ", yet the ninth chapter of the Rule must certainly be considered one of the most important statements in the whole tradition of preaching in the Christian West.

From the study of Zelina Zafarana, we know that that section of the Rule was to a large extent determinative for the content of San Bernardino's sermons and for his general outlook on preaching [47]. We must assume it was similarly operative for many other Franciscan preachers. What is surprising, however, is how often the phrase « vitia et virtutes, poenam et gloriam » recurs in influential texts in the sixteenth century [48]. In 1536 it appears, of course, in the ninth chapter of the Capuchin Constitutions, an amplification of the original

---

their *Latin Tractates on Preaching. A Book-List*, in *The Harvard Theological Review* 42 (1949) 195. Moreover, the dedicatory letter to Pope Gregory XIII is dated 1579.

[47] *Bernardino nella storia della predicazione popolare*, in *Bernardino predicatore*, 41-70. See also G. MICCOLI, *Bernardino predicatore. Problemi e ipotesi per un interpretazione complessiva, Ibid.*, 11-37, especially 14-15.

[48] *Seraphicae Legislationis Textus Originales*, Quaracchi 1897, 44: « Moneo quoque et exhortor eosdem fratres ut in praedicatione quam faciunt sint examinata et casta eorum eloquia, ad utilitatem et aedificationem populi, annuntiando eis vitia et virtutes, poenam et gloriam, cum brevitate sermonis, quia verbum abbreviatum fecit Dominus super terram ». I called attention to the importance of this text in my *Praise and Blame*, 68, 81, and again in *Content and Rhetorical Forms*, 248. I have meanwhile discovered other documents in which the Rule appears, and have been helped by the pertinent pages in the excellent dissertation by MCGINNESS, *Rhetoric and Counter-Reformation Rome*, especially 164-94.

Regula Bullata, and it occurs in subsequent versions of those Constitutions — 1552 and 1575 [49].

By far the most impressive place the phrase occurs is in the decree on preaching of the Council of Trent, June 17, 1546. When the decree specifies the proper subjects for preaching, it paraphrases the Franciscan Rule: « [...] annuntiando eis cum brevitate et facilitate sermonis vitia, quae eos declinare, et virtutes, quas sectari oporteat, ut poenam aeternam evadere et coelestem gloriam consequi valeant » [50]. This fact has, with one exception, escaped the attention of scholars who have studied the decree [51]. All doubt on the issue disappears with an examination of the earlier versions of the decree in the *Acta* of the Council, where we find not a paraphrase or slight amplification but a verbatim quotation, without acknowledgement of source [52]. Almost surely responsible for this insertion of a segment of the Rule into the Tridentine legislation, I venture, was the noted Franciscan preacher and bishop of Bitonto, Cor-

---

49 *Constitutiones Ordinis Fratrum Minorum Capuccinorum Saeculorum Decursu Promulgate*, I, Rome 1980, 65 (1536), 124 (1552), 191 (1575). J. Olin provides a translation into English of the ninth chapter (1536) in *The Catholic Reformation. Savonarola to Ignatius Loyola*, New York 1969, 172-76.

50 *Concilium Tridentinum*, ed. Societas Gorresiana, 13 vols., Freiburg in Br. 1901-57: V, 242.

51 McGinness calls attention to it, *Rhetoric and Counter-Reformation Rome*, 164, whereas Arsenio D'Ascoli barely suggests a relationship between the Rule and the document of the Council in his *Predicazione dei Cappuccini nel Cinquecento in Italia*, Loreto 1956, 66. On the decree, see also the following authors, who do not mention this Franciscan dependency: J. E. Rainer, *Entstehungsgeschichte des Trienter Predigtreformdekrets*, in *Zeitschrift für katholische Theologie* 39 (1915) 256-317, 465-523; A. Larios, *La reforma de la predicación en Trento (Historia y contenido de un decreto)*, in *Communio* 6 (1973) 223-83; H. Jedin, *A History of the Council of Trent*, trans. Ernest Graf, II, London 1961, 99-124; G. Alberigo, *I vescovi italiani al Concilio di Trento (1545-1547)*, Florence 1959, 291-335.

52 See *Concilium Tridentinum*, V, 106 (first version, April 13, 1546): « Parochi quoque diebus saltem dominicis et festis solemnibus suos parochianos pascant salutaribus verbis, annuntiando eis vitia et virtutes, poenam et gloriam, cum aliqua evangelii occurrentis enarratione ». The next two versions (May 1 and May 7) paraphrase the Rule, *Ibid.*, 123, 126.

nelio Musso, a member of the commission at Trent dealing with this subject [53].

After the Council the phrase recurs in several important documents, where its usage may at least in some instances have been encouraged by the stipulation of the Council. The decrees of the synod of Musso's diocese, first published in 1579, explicitly quote the words of Saint Francis [54]. Three other Franciscans do the same in their treaties on preaching — Baglioni [55], Diego de Estella [56], and Valades [57].

But it was quoted beyond Franciscan circles. Gabriele Paleotti, bishop of Bologna, actually structures around it his in-

---

[53] None of the scholars who have studied Musso make the connection. See H. JEDIN, *Der Franziskaner Cornelio Musso, Bischof von Bitonto*, in *Römische Quartalschrift* 41 (1933) 207-75; G. CANTINI, *Cornelio Musso, O.F.M. Conv., predicatore, scrittore e teologo ad Concilio di Trento*, in *Misc. francesc.* 41 (1941) 146-74, 424-63; R. J. BARTMAN, *Cornelio Musso, Tridentine Theologian and Orator*, in *Francisc. Studies* 5 (1945) 247-76; G. ODOARDI, *Fra Cornelio Musso, O.F.M. Conv., padre, oratore e teologo al Concilio di Trento*, in *Misc. francesc.* 48 (1948) 223-42, 450-78; 49 (1949) 36-71.

[54] *Synodus Bituntina Rmi. Patris F. Cornelii Mussi Episcopi Bituntini, totam fere ecclesiasticam disciplinam* [...] *complectens* (Venice: Apud Iolitos 1579), 393: «[...] quibus almus ille heros Catholicus et totus Apostolicus Beatus Pater Franciscus, imperitus sermone forsan, sed non certe scientia, praedicationis summum conclusit, Virtutes inquam et vitia; poenam et gloriam. Nam quae extra haec sunt, ad inflantem potius scentiam, quam ad aedificantem charitatem pertinere videntur».

[55] *L'arte del predicare*, f. 31: « Et perche il fine intento della Predicazione christiana non è altra, per dire in due parole, se non uscire da ogni vitio odiato da Dio, & entrare in ogni virtù da lui amata et necessaria alla salute [...] ».

[56] *Modo de predicar*, II, 210: « Nam si illud de quo habet concionator pertractare de vitiis aut de virtutibus sit, et concionatoris munus sit et vitia texare, et virtutibus alio instruere (sicut et beatus P. Franciscus in *vivendi formula* tradidit, loquens de praedicatoribus dixit: annuntiando eis vitia et virtutes, poenam et gloriam) [...] ». See also *Ibid.*, 212: « Verumtamen, cum supra dictum sit quod materia concionatoris est de vitiis et virtutibus agere [...] ». *Ibid.*, 225: « Verum quia in hac morali doctrina stat omne concionatoris fundamentum atque materia [...] ».

[57] *Rhetorica christiana*, 88: « Ut seraphicus noster pater Franciscus in regula sua c. 9 quasi totam enucleans Rhetoricam monet his verbis: Moneo quoque [...] ».

fluential, several times reprinted, *Instruttione* for preachers, first published in 1578 [58]. Although Carlo Borromeo does not explicitly quote the Rule or the Tridentine paraphrase in his *Instructiones praedicationis verbi Dei*, his reverence for the decree and his familiarity with it is unquestioned, and the content he proposes for sermons corresponds to it: sins, occasions of sin, virtues, and, finally, the sacraments and other holy usages of the Church [59]. Much later, but in the same tradition, is the quotation of the Rule in the influential letter of Francis de Sales to André Fremiot, October 5, 1604, usually known as the Saint's « Treatise on Preaching », many times reprinted [60].

These developments confirmed the moralistic emphases in preaching that were already strong in many sectors of Catholicism in the late Middle Ages and even earlier [61]. For Lutherans and some other Protestants, « the Gospel » was the good news of justification by faith, with its correlative themes of Law-Gospel, works-faith, wrath-grace, and this doctrine was proposed as the foremost and proper subject for sermons. Preaching was primarily doctrinal, not moral, and to structure

---

[58] *Instruttione di Monsig. Illustrissimo et Rever.mo Card. Paleotti* (Bologna: A. Benacci 1586), f. 6r: « Et per hauere qualche regola più ferma da seruare nel progresso de loro ragionamenti, potranno communemente adherire al modo prescritto dal glorioso San Francesco a suoi Predicatori, & commendato da molti altri santi, cioè che nel predicare si debba insistere precipuamente in quattro cose nei vitii, nelle virtù, nella pena, & nel premio con brevità di sermone; talmente che queste siano come le quattro ruote, su le quali sia condotto tutto il corpo ordinario delle prediche, essendo che nelle due prime consiste la giustizia christiana di questa vita [...] ».

[59] See his *Instructiones praedicationis verbi Dei*, in *Acta Ecclesiae Mediolanensis*, ed. A. Ratti, 3 vols., Milan 1890-97: II, 1230-43. See also the decrees of the First Provincial Synod, 1565, *Ibid.*, 34-36; decrees of the Fourth Provincial Synod, 1576, *Ibid.*, 336; *Homiliae nunc primum e mss. codicibus Biliothecae Ambrosianae in lucem productae*, ed. G. A. Sassi, 5 vols., Milan 1747-48: II, 48-49, 418. See also my *Borromeo and the Praecipuum Munus.*

[60] *Oeuvres de saint François de Sales*, 26 vols., Annecy 1892-1932: XII, 305.

[61] For the earlier tradition, see, e.g., the comments by Longère, *Oeuvres oratoires*, I, 279-355.

this doctrinal emphasis the Lutherans, under the influence of Melanchthon, constructed a new rhetorical form, the *genus didascalicum*.

Within Catholicism by the middle of the sixteenth century, « the Gospel » tended to be identified in preaching theory with a turning from vice and an embracing of virtue, under threat of punishment and the hope of reward. Even the Dominican, Luis de Granada, proposed in effect this viewpoint in his *Ecclesiasticae rhetoricae*, an author and a book admired and promoted by Carlo Borromeo [62]. The preaching of the early Jesuits, also, was strongly moralistic [63]. Not doctrine, in the strict sense, but morality held central stage in preaching theory. The *genus deliberativum* was an appropriate form for this message, the *genus* of persuasion and dissuasion, the *genus* for popular and unruly audiences, the « contio ». In treatises on preaching, the more formal, expansive, and elegant *genus demonstrativum* of the Italian Renaissance begins to slip into the background except for funeral eulogies and panegyrics of the saints.

Instructions for preachers and « ecclesiastical rhetorics » of course commended other subjects besides morals to the preacher. Moreover, in the actual practice of preaching, matters were never so simple as theory might imply. In the sermons of Carlo Borromeo, for instance, there appears a strong undergirding of the doctrines of Creation, Fall, and Redemption. The *genus deliberativum* is tempered, often displaced, by the more directly scriptural and affective homily, and sometimes even by the congratulatory *genus demonstrativum*. A stern

---

62 See *Ecclesiastae rhetoricae*, e.g., 73, 76-77. On this tradition in the Dominicans see the letter of the newly elected Master General, 1543, in *Monumenta Ordinis Fratrum Praedicatorum Historica*, IX, ed. B. M. Reichert, Rome 1901, 304. See also V. Th. Gómez, *Crisis de la predicación en vísperas de la contrareforma. La predicación dominicana en las Actas de los Capítulos Generales (1450-1550)*, in *Angelicum* 48 (1971) 171-96.

63 See my « Preaching » in the forthcoming Encyclopedia of Jesuit History (Rome).

morality was admixed with a spirituality based on the transforming powers of divine grace.

In any case, by the end of the Council of Trent Catholic preaching had definitely entered into a new era. The techniques and many of the aims of the thematic sermons (and even of more popular preaching in the late Middle Ages) were repudiated in theory and, we must assume, to a large extent in practice. Preaching was now to be based on patristic or classical models, or on some combination of both. The rich spirituality of the Fathers was now available in printed editions, and great theorists on preaching produced from their reading of them new spiritual classics whose teachings found their way at least into some preaching. Nonetheless, the moralistic and behavioristic emphases in much late-medieval preaching received widespread confirmation; they received official sanction in the Tridentine decree. Catholic theory on preaching tended to be much less prescriptive on doctrinal content than did Protestant theory, but it was at least, if not more, prescriptive about morals. In all these changes, the Franciscan influence was pervasively present.

V

LUTHER THE PREACHER

The corpus of Luther's writings that has come down to us contains an immense amount of material that relates directly and obviously to preaching. Many studies have utilized this material for a more accurate understanding of his theology, but examinations of his "art," of his preaching practice, have been few. The treatment of him in general histories of preaching has often been vague and sometimes uncritically encomiastic.

How is this phenomenon to be explained? Part of the explanation surely lies in the fact that the history of rhetoric has only recently begun to be explored by scholars in a technically adequate way and applied to preaching.[1] It is from the viewpoint of this relatively new discipline that I intend to address Luther here. Although I have been interested in him for years, I can make no claim to a comprehensive knowledge of his writings, and I come at him almost as an outsider. However, by looking at Luther with somewhat fresh eyes, from a somewhat different academic perspective, perhaps some light will be thrown on him, and we will be able to assess his place in a different tradition from the doctrinal and institutional ones in which he is commonly studied. I will build upon a few recent studies of Luther that with technical competence have examined his preaching art, especially Ulrich Nembach's *Predigt des Evangeliums,* and try to carry the examination a step further by placing it in a wider context.[2] I must right off apologize for the highly condensed nature of my treatment, which to be done properly would require a full volume.[3]

Surely another reason for the neglect of Luther's preaching art is that, unlike so many of his contemporaries and near-contemporaries, he left us no specific treatise on how to preach. One of the most characteristic features of theology after the first few decades of the sixteenth century was the proliferation, the veritable explosion, of such treatises.[4] This phenomenon was a continuation of the tradition of the scholastic *artes praedicandi* and at the same time a vigorous reaction against it, as preachers searched the classical and Christian traditions for alternatives to the prescriptions of those manuals.

In this search, despite his failure to write a treatise on the subject, Luther was in the forefront. For the moment, however, we must simply be aware that any study of Luther's art of preaching must be done inductively—from the sermons and sermon materials he left us, and from the *obiter dicta* in these and his other writings.[5] Although we know that we do not possess many of his sermons in the form in which they first left Luther's pen or mouth, we have to work with what we have, and trust that the very volume of his *Nachlass* will be to some extent self-correcting.

The classical treatises on rhetoric isolated three general categories that enter into the assessment of any speech: the speaker, the speech-act, and those to whom the speech is directed. Since these treatises professed to be themselves inductive, we can assume that we have here three categories with which to approach any speech situation, including the Christian pulpit. For economy of space in this short essay, I will concentrate on the second category, in which both form and content must be taken into account. For Luther, both are crucial in assessing him. Unfortunately, I will not be able here to enter into the complex subject of Luther's theology of the Word, essential though that theology is for any comprehensive treatment of his preaching.

Let us, therefore, turn our attention to the form of Luther's sermons and postils, to the form of the speech-act, as we now have it. What do we find? As has often been noted, the structure of a few of the early sermons is heavily influenced by the scholastic or "thematic" sermon as delineated in the medieval *artes*. Luther, however, soon moved away from the thematic model. The trained eye will still detect on occasion some features that correlate with scholastic sermons: Luther sometimes retains the *thema* or scriptural quotation at the beginning; proof-texts still play an important part in most of the sermons; the scholastic *quaestio* does not altogether disappear; there is often no clearly discernible conclusion or peroration.

Yet, despite these seemingly scholastic vestiges, the sermons immediately strike the reader with how different they are from those laid down in the *artes*. Most obviously, they are much freer in their structure than thematic sermons were supposed to be. In this regard they evince a certain variety. For the most part, however, they resemble in a generic way the patristic or monastic homilies in that they progress verse-by-verse through a pericope of Scripture. Not the only, but surely the most clearly visible structure undergirding the sermons, therefore, is the course of the biblical text itself.

What influenced Luther to adopt this homiletic form? Here we must to some extent speculate. It is surely tied to his rejection of scholastic theology for a theology more obviously and directly attached to the text of Scripture.[6] This shift in theological method perforce influenced his preaching style. In this shift we find the most profound reason for the change in his art.

He did not have to search far for this new form. His reading of Augustine would easily have inclined him to it. Moreoever, we know from many examples that in his day the rigid structure prescribed or encouraged by the *artes* was as often followed in the breach as in the observance. That structure was too stiff to be used in its rigor outside formal settings like university audiences. If we examine the sermons of some of the famous preachers who were chronologically close to Luther like Nicholas of Cusa and Thomas à Kempis, two preachers who also had misgivings about scholastic theology or innovated within it, we see that their sermons do not conform to the *artes.*[7] They usually retain the *thema,* as many sermons continued to do until quite recently, but they then move into looser forms similar in some respects to Luther's, and they often manifest a clear relationship to the homily.

We tend to forget the continuing influence of the patristic homily all through the Middle Ages and its renewed influence in the sixteenth century.[8] It is my opinion, for instance, that Erasmus, for all that he has to say about the adaption of classical rhetoric to the pulpit in his *Ecclesiastes* of 1535, still in fact preferred the simple verse-by-verse exposition of Scripture.[9]

Luther made some significant modifications within this form, as we shall see. Nonetheless, in so far as he followed this homiletic pattern, he was not unique among his contemporaries. His practice coincided with and promoted the widespread dissatisfaction with scholastic forms of preaching that characterized the late Middle Ages and that continued well into the sixteenth and seventeenth centuries, even in quarters where we would not be inclined to expect it. The *Constitutions* of the Society of Jesus, for instance, while commending the theology of Aquinas, expressly discouraged the use of the "scholastic manner" of preaching.[10] Robert Bellarmine echoed this distaste for scholastic preaching, and expressly commended the homily, the form ratified for him by its use by the Fathers.[11]

In Luther's day, however, the most innovative attempt to displace the thematic sermon of the scholastics took place in Italy in the context of the humanist movement. This was an attempt to apply classical rhetoric to sacred discourse in a way and to a degree that had hitherto in the history of Christianity been practically unknown. Something must be said, therefore, about the relationship of Luther's preaching to the humanistic revival if we are to place him in the context of his times. One of the limitations of Nembach's book is his failure to locate Luther in this larger context, even though he tries to show that Luther was indeed influenced by a Renaissance enthusiasm for Quintilian.

Relating Luther to the humanistic concerns of some of his contemporaries is a difficult task to accomplish, because we now realize more clearly than ever before how complex a movement Humanism was and how terms like "humanistic theology" or "rhetorical theology" must be broken down into component parts. In the interest of clarity, I shall distinguish within the humanistic tradition a "grammatical" and a "rhetorical" component, corresponding to the traditional stages in classical education, and then subdivide both of these categories once.[12]

"Rhetoric," as presented in classical treatises on the subject, meant oratory. Scholars today make a useful distinction, however, and subdivide rhetoric into "primary" and "secondary."[13] Primary rhetoric is the rhetoric described in Aristotle's *Rhetoric,* in Quintilian's *Institutio oratoria,* and in similar treatises. These treatises deal directly with speech-making, the art of oratory. This rhetoric is oral; in itself it has no text, although subsequently an enunciation can be treated as a text. It is directed to public and civic concerns in the law courts, in senates and popular assemblies, and in ceremonial settings like temples and the courts of princes. The single goal of rhetoric understood in this primary sense is the training of the public speaker.

"Secondary rhetoric" derives from primary and is an adaptation of it, as the term itself implies. It consists in the apparatus of rhetorical techniques clustering around discourse when those techniques are not being used for their primary oral purpose. In secondary rhetoric, the speech-act is replaced by the text, as in epistolography, historical narrative, diatribes, and dialogues. A consistent tendency of classical rhetoric has been to move from the speech-act itself to secondary forms like these. This means a tendency to shift from persuasion to narration, from civic to personal and private contexts, and from speech-making to literature, including poetry. It is at this point, at poetry, that secondary rhetoric begins to blur almost imperceptibly into "grammar."

In classical times and in the Renaissance, rhetoric presupposed grammar, but grammar meant much more than the elementary skills of reading and writing correctly. The "grammarian" taught literature, especially poetry, for it was from poetry that the rules of grammar were originally derived. One of the purposes of grammar was, thus, to teach good style, to teach accurate, appropriate, and felicitous expression. In pursuing this purpose, grammar in fact sometimes becomes almost indistinguishable from "secondary rhetoric."

Another purpose, more distinctive, was to teach how to interpret a text that was being studied in class. The grammarian was, indeed, almost myopically attached to his texts. His exposition of them was, in the first instance, philological, and concentrated on a word-by-word or line-by-line reading. When it was necessary to rise above this so-called "atomistic" exegesis to broader meaning, allegory was invoked. Texts were seen as expressions of philosophical or theological doctrines artfully masked "under the poetic veil." Within grammatical exegesis we have, therefore, two different levels or categories of interpretation—the philological, with attention to minute details of usage, syntax, orthography, and similar matters, and the "poetic," which allowed the scribe or teacher to discover truths of broader scope.

We now have our four categories, useful instruments of analysis even though in practice these sometimes blur into one another: rhetoric, subdivided into primary and secondary, and grammar, subdivided into philology and poetry. Because of the stylistic purposes that constituted an important part of the grammarian's task, he borrowed elements from rhetorical treatises. Nonetheless, an altogether fundamental distinction remained between the grammarian and the rhetorician in the strict sense. Grammar was by definition a text-related discipline, and its practitioners were scribes, schoolmasters, and scholars. Primary rhetoric was not text-related. It was action-related, deed-related, and decision-related, and it looked to public issues like war and peace, like the innocence or guilt of the accused. If we imagine at one end of the spectrum a scribe pouring over his text and at the other a statesman pleading before the senate for a declaration of war, we perceive the issues at stake.[14]

When we apply these categories to Christian preaching, we immediately see how complex the problem is. At least since the days of Origen, who was himself a practicing grammarian before he became a Christian preacher, the Christian art of oratory has been an essentially text-related pursuit. It is concerned with the writings of the Bible. As text-related, it almost eschews the life-related immediacy that primary rhetoric envisioned, and evinces an almost natural affinity for the grammarian's techniques in interpreting a text; yet it is public and communitarian discourse, oratory.

Origen's homilies, despite the relationship they might have to similar practices in the Jewish synagogues, are probably best understood as the application of the interpretative techniques of the classical grammarian to the biblical text.[15] Origen's verse-by-verse exegesis in his homilies closely parallels what must have been his techniques as a grammarian, and he left those techniques as his heritage to the Fathers, most of whom would themselves have been trained in the grammarians' classrooms. His homilies are an *explication de texte.*

How does Luther fit into this scheme, and how does he relate to the humanistic revival of his day? I would maintain that he fits, first and foremost, into the tradition of "the Christian grammarian," and that it is in this category that he was most palpably influenced by the patristic and the Renaissance adaptation of the classical tradition. His sermons generally manifest in their form the characteristics of an *explication de texte.* He saw preaching as a text-related art. He sticks to his text, and he lets it guide the movement of his discourse. Luther's appreciation for the simplicity of the Word of God would make him susceptible to the direct and simple form of the grammarian.

Luther makes use of philological methods, sometimes comparing the Latin or German translation with the Greek or Hebrew original, and he does not hesitate to present this scholarly erudition to his simple audiences, just as a patient teacher would. Luther was dependent in this area on the philological researches of Valla and Erasmus, the two greatest humanists of the Renaissance, whose interests, significantly enough, centered on what I have called grammar and secondary rhetoric, not on primary rhetoric, the art of oratory.[16]

Luther also viewed the text of Scripture as essentially a book of doctrine.[17] Early on he abandoned the traditional four-fold sense of Scripture, yet he wanted, especially when commenting on the Gospels, to get under the actions to the teaching the actions signified. This "sacramental," "spiritual," or "mysterious" level of exegesis, to use his terms, corresponds in a generic way to the allegorical level.[18] He despised the fantasies into which the allegorical method had lapsed, but his own method sometimes has an affinity with a purified version of it. Not so much "under the poetic veil" as "under the historical veil," there lay deeper truths—law-gospel, works-faith, wrath-grace.

Perhaps most fundamental of all, the image that he projects of himself is that of teacher.[19] If the bible is a book of teaching, he is its expositor, laying it open for understanding and appropriation by the student. This explains the lecture-like quality of his sermons. It also explains why only a thin, though important, line seems to distinguish them from his written commentaries on Scripture.[20]

Some of this "grammatical," "scribal," "pedagogical" quality Luther surely drew from the reading of Valla and Erasmus, as well as from his reading of Augustine and other Fathers. But it also relates, I believe, to his training as a scholastic. We tend to be unmindful that Scholasticism early incorporated into itself a grammatical, as well as a dialectical, component, and that that component continued to play a part in the scholastic enterprise, though different in its techniques from the "grammar" of the humanists.[21] Most certainly, the scholastics viewed Scripture as a book of doctrine, almost identifiable in its content with the articles of the Creed.

In a famous passage from the *Tischreden,* Luther defined preaching, basing himself on Romans 12:7-8, as teaching and exhortation—*doctrina et exhortatio.*[22] For him teaching was identical with the practice of dialectics. This, it seems to me, is another link with his early scholastic training. He defined *exhortatio* as the practice of rhetoric, an idea he probably derived to some extent from the scholastic tradition, but more directly from the classical, as I hope to show.

What about Luther and the rhetorical component of the classical tradition? If we focus for a moment on "secondary rhetoric," we see immediately that he did not exercise that art in writing dialogues or historical narratives. He did, however, write letters, treatises, and diatribes. Moreover, he is universally acknowledged as possessing a direct and effective style, which pertains to grammar as well as secondary rhetoric. I do not claim, in fact, the competence to enter into a professional assessment of the literary qualities of his style or to try to trace the sources from which he acquired his stylistic skills. Important though such considerations are for any final assessment of him as preacher, we must on this occasion bypass them and move to primary rhetoric, the art of oratory itself.

We all know from Luther's "Appeal to the Nobility" that he was willing to retain even Aristotle's *Rhetoric* if it could be utilized to produce good preachers.[23] Nembach has demonstrated that Luther esteemed Quintilian.[24] In my opinion, Nembach overstates his case that Quintilian directly influenced the style and structure of Luther's sermons.[25] Nonetheless, his arguments that some of Quintilian's precepts concerning the *contio* (III, 8) are in fact verified in Luther's sermons deserve further study. The *contio* (a term sometimes used by Luther himself) was the form of the classical "deliberative speech" addressed to popular assemblies.[26]

More convincing than Nembach, but independently supportive of his thesis, is the article by Birgit Stolt that analyzes in detail Luther's "Predigt, dass man Kinder zur Schulen halten solle" (1530).[27] This "sermon" completely abandons the homiletical form. Stolt concludes that its structure and rhetorical techniques remarkably correspond to what classical theory envisioned for a speech of the *genus deliberativum* when it was addressed to popular audiences—in other words, the *contio.*

Thus, besides relating to the grammatical component in the classical tradition, Luther's sermons may well have a hitherto unexamined relationship to primary rhetoric. This proposition has a prima facie plausibility, despite a common prejudice that Luther disdained classical rhetoric as a human invention that detracted from a pure presentation of the Word of God. He lived in an age in which primary rhetoric emerged in learned circles with a new prominence. He was in contact with colleagues, enemies, and disciples, especially Melanchthon, who would almost force some of the precepts of primary rhetoric upon his awareness, particularly since he seems to have been born with or early acquired some of the natural gifts of a public speaker.[28]

What is significant is not only that he was, in some way or other, almost certainly in touch with the principles of primary rhetoric, but also that he was influenced by them in a specific way, that is, by ideas found in the classical treatises about the *genus deliberativum*. The fact that Melanchthon was at the same time developing his own theories about the applicability to the pulpit of the *genus deliberativum* and inventing his own new *genus* related to dialectics, the *genus didascalicum* or *didacticum*, provides some external confirmation of this thesis; similar adaptations were being undertaken by Veit Dietrich and Johannes Hoeck, as well as by Erasmus.[29] By the middle of the century it seems that in both Protestant and Catholic circles the *genus deliberativum* had assumed a preeminence over the other two classical *genera—judiciale* and *demonstrativum.*[30] Through a curious act of plagarism from Melanchthon, the *genus didascalicum* made its way into the Catholic tradition in 1543.[31] Luther seems to have played a role in these developments, although his importance has yet to be determined. There is no doubt about the importance of Melanchthon—and, of course, of Erasmus.

What we seem to have in Luther's sermons, therefore, is basically a homiletic form, conditioned in part by the classical *contio*. This combination would allow Luther to fashion his sermons as direct exposition of the text of Scripture, yet give him techniques for public address that were lacking in the homily as such. The sermons certainly possess a strongly doctrinal emphasis and a pedagogical intent, which relates to Melanchthon's *genus didascalicum*. To this intent was conjoined an exhortatory component. This component was directed by him to a popular audience—not to the learned, but to ordinary men, women, and youths, who were assumed to be relatively ignorant and in need of clear directives and motivation. This would correspond to the feisty oratory of the popular assembly, as adapted to an exposition of the *doctrina* of sacred Scripture. The incorporation of elements prescribed for the *contio* would also lift the homily out of the privatized issues that the grammatical form tended to promote, and gave it a more public character, suited to a *Gemeinde.*

To understand the emergence of the *genus deliberativum* in these years, we must examine the humanistic sermons that had come into vogue in Italy in the Quattrocento and that I studied in detail as they were practiced at the papal court.[32] Like Luther, the preachers of these sermons were reacting against the scholastic tradition. However, whereas Luther's sermons were most deeply influenced by the grammatical component of the classical tradition and less clearly by primary rhetoric, the opposite was true in Italy. Moreover, the sermons were clearly constructed according to the principles of the *genus demonstrativum,* the *genus* of ceremonial oratory, the art of praise and blame, the art of panegyric.

These sermons have obvious exordia and perorations. They are less closely attached to individual verses and words of the biblical text, and, rather, focus on the totality of the event, deed, or history they portrayed. Whatever teaching underlies the Gospel story tends to be communicated by a retelling of the story and an elaboration on it, rather than immediately extracting from it a doctrinal proposition. They usually relate more directly to the liturgical feast, season, or solemnity than do Luther's. They are thus more notably historical, narrative, and contextual in their approach. They avoid proof-texts, and their purpose is not so much the defining, proving, or driving home of a doctrine as an attempt to enhance appreciation for a belief already operative and for values already shared. The audience, though frequently reproved for its failings, is more frequently congratulated on its Christian status and dignity. The basic purpose, however, was to praise God for His great acts in history, His mighty deeds—especially Creation and the Incarnation. This is ceremonial oratory, in every sense of the word. It is *oratio,* not *contio.* By placing preaching in the *genus demonstrativum* rather than the *genus deliberativum* (or *didascalicum*) a different product is obtained—a product that tends to fit religion into a different frame of reference. It is this consideration that makes a study of the rhetorical *genera* helpful for understanding religious controversies in the sixteenth century.

Until Melanchthon, Erasmus—and, presumably, Luther—began to relate preaching to the *genus deliberativum* (and, for Melanchothon, to the *genus didascalicum*), contemporaries seem to have assumed that the appropriate *genus* for it was the *demonstrativum.* This is an hypothesis that is somewhat difficult to verify, because until Melanchthon, Erasmus, and others began to write their treatises on preaching, published after Luther began to preach, we possess no contemporary works on the subject that deviate from the *artes,* except Reuchlin's brief and confused *Liber congestorum* of 1504. In any case, by mid-century the *genus didascalicum* and especially the *genus deliberativum* had begun to dominate the discussion wherever there was question of an adaptation to preaching of classical rhetoric. Even in Catholic circles the *genus demonstrativum* seems to have become ever more restricted to funeral oratory and to panegyrics of the saints as the century moved on. The implications of this development for the history of preaching are great, I believe, but I have only been able to suggest a few of them here; a more forcefully didactic and exhortatory quality would be the most obvious result.

In the time left to me, however, I want to isolate some other features of Luther's sermons that made them effective forms of public address. These features correlate with some basic principles of primary rhetoric, but in Luther they correlate just as clearly with his personality, his theology, and the existential situation in which he found himself. I will single out three for special mention.

The first is a clear and untiringly repeated doctrine. The message of works-faith, law-gospel, wrath-grace recurs implicitly or explicitly in practically everything he wrote.[33] This was, at least on one level, a simple message, and one that Luther insisted upon in season and out of season. His message, in other words, had a clear center. What came to be distinctive of Lutheran treatises on preaching, in fact, was how prescriptive they were about precise doctrinal content. Catholic treatises tended to be much less so.

In the second place, Luther's preaching isolated some clear enemies. These enemies—the papists and, later, the *Schwärmer*—were well known to Luther's hearers and designated by him in unmistakable terms as evil.[34] "Clear and present danger" characterized the way these enemies were presented. Such a presentation was almost bound by the nature of the case to excite a reaction.

Finally, from both of the above flowed an agenda for the hearers that was specific and immediate, yet fraught with implications for a better order to come. Luther gave his hearers what every orator longs for: something to *do.* His hearers were urged to read their Bibles instead of their lives of the saints. They were encouraged to eat meat on days of abstinence. Those with vows of celibacy were told they could marry. Abstract though the doctrine of justification might be in its slogan-like formulation, it had, as expounded by Luther, an immediate impact on the way those who heard it viewed themselves and acted. It clashed dramatically with received opinions and with what other preachers had been saying. As such, it had to make an impression.

In summary, then, what do we find in Luther, the preacher, when he is placed in the Western tradition of oratory? First of all, he was deeply influenced by the first step in the training of orators—"grammar." He fits into the tradition of the "Christian grammarian" especially in the basic task he undertook, the exposition of a text. The fundamentally homiletic form of his sermons corresponds in a generic way with that tradition.

His relationship to the rhetorical tradition is much more problematic than his relationship to the grammatical tradition, as is true also of Augustine, Erasmus, and most others who have reflected on the art of preaching. In his style he surely utilized some of the most effective stylistic techniques of secondary rhetoric; just how self-consciously he did so, is quite another question. There is evidence today that either formally or informally he appropriated in some of his sermons principles of primary rhetoric as indicated for the *contio,* the form of the *genus deliberativum* addressed to popular audiences. In any case, that *genus,* along with the new *genus didascalicum,* began to emerge in northern Europe during his lifetime with a new importance for preaching, and shifted the purposes and ethos of the sermon from those envisioned by the Italians who had utilized the *genus demonstrativum.*

It is clear, moreover, that Luther understood some of the most fundamental principles of primary rhetoric, whether he acquired this understanding from formal study or from the exercise of his natural gifts. Included in these would be the central role of a predetermined content—of a clear message made relevant to the concerns of his hearers. He also grasped the importance of explicit directives for action, of having a practical agenda that required decision, and that clearly distinguished friends from enemies, good from bad.

Notes

1. See, e.g., James J. Murphy, "One Thousand Neglected Authors: The Scope and Importance of Renaissance Rhetoric," in *Renaissance Eloquence: Studies in the Theory and Practice of Renaissance Rhetoric,* e.g., James J. Murphy (Berkeley, Los Angeles, and London: University of California Press, 1983), pp. 20-36.

2. *Predigt des Evangeliums: Luther als Prediger, Pädagoge und Rhetor* (Neukirchen-Vluyn; Neukirchener Verlag, 1972). See also Yngve Brilioth, *A Brief History of Preaching,* trans. Karl E. Mattson (Philadelphia: Fortress Press, 1965), pp. 103-18; John W. Doberstein, "Introduction to Volume 51," in *Luther's Works,* ed. and trans. John W. Doberstein, vol. 51 (Philadelphia: Muhlenberg Press, 1959), pp. xi-xxi; Emanuel Hirsch, "Luthers Predigtweise,"

Luther: Mitteilungen der Luthergesellschaft, 25 (1954), 1-23; Alfred Niebergall, "Die Geschichte der christlichen Predigt," in *Leiturgia: Handbuch des evangelischen Gottesdienstes,* 4 vols. (Kassel: Johannes Stauda Verlag, 1954-61), vol. II, pp. 181-353, esp. 257-275; *idem,* "Luthers Auffassung von der Predigt nach 'De Servo Arbitrio,'" in the collection of his studies, *Der Dienst der Kirche: Gesammelte Aufsätze 1954-1973,* ed. Rainer Lachmann (Kassel: Johannes Stauda Verlag, 1974), pp. 85-109; Birgit Stolt, *"Docere, delectare,* und *movere* bei Luther," *Deutsche Vierteljahresschrift für Literaturwissenschaft und Geistesgeschichte,* 44 (1970), 433-474. Studies like the following also deserve mention, although they are less technical in their approach: Harold J. Grimm, "The Human Element in Luther's Sermons," *Archive for Reformation History,* 49 (1958), 50-60; *idem, Martin Luther as a Preacher* (Columbus: Lutheran Book Concern, 1929); Elmer Carl Kiessling, *The Early Sermons of Luther and Their Relation to the Pre-Reformation Sermon* (Grand Rapids: Zondervan Publishing House, 1935); Peter Newman Brooks, "Luther the Preacher," *The Expository Times,* 95 (November, 1983), 37-41. Important, but not so directly pertinent to Luther's preaching are Birgit Stolt, *Studien zu Luthers Freiheitstraktat mit besonderer Berücksichtigung der lateinischen und deutschen Fassung zueinander und der Stilmittel der Rhetorik* (Stockholm: Almquist & Wiksell, 1969); Klaus Dockhorn, "Rhetorica movet: Protestantischer Humanismus und karolingische Renaissance" in *Rhetorik: Beiträge zu ihrer Geschichte in Deutschland vom 16.-20. Jahrhundert* (Frankfurt: Athenaion, 1974), pp. 17-42; Heinz Otto Burger, "Luther als Ereignis der Literaturgeschichte," in his *Dasein heisst eine Rolle spielen* (Munich: C. Hanser, 1963), pp. 56-74.

3. For further background and for elaboration of some of the ideas and categories used in this study, see my "Lutheranism in Rome, 1542-43: The Treatise by Alfonso Zorrilla," *Thought,* 54 (1979), 262-273; "Content and Rhetorical Forms in Sixteenth-Century Treatises on Preaching," in *Renaissance Eloquence,* pp. 238-252; "Grammar and Rhetoric in the Theology of Erasmus," *Paideia: Special Renaissance Issue,* ed. George C. Simmons, 3 vols. (forthcoming); "Egidio da Viterbo and Renaissance Rome," in *Egidio da Viterbo e il suo tempo* (Rome: Augustinian Historical Institute, 1983), pp. 67-84; *Praise and Blame in Renaissance Rome: Rhetoric, Doctrine, and Reform in the Sacred Orators of the Papal Court, ca. 1450-1521* (Durham: Duke University Press, 1979).

4. See my "Content and Rhetorical Forms."

5. Many of Luther's statements on preaching have been collected in *Luthers Werke in Auswahl,* ed. Emanuel Hirsch (Berlin: Walter de Gruyter, 1950), vol. VII, pp. 1-38.

6. On this theological shift, see Nembach, *Predigt,* pp. 118-124; Hirsch, "Predigtweise," pp. 3-5; and Leif Grane, *Modus Loquendi Theologicus: Luthers Kampf um die Erneuerung der Theologie (1515-1518)* (Leiden: E.J. Brill, 1975).

7. See my *Praise and Blame,* pp. 94-101, and Thomas à Kempis, *Opera omnia,* ed. M.J. Pohl (Freiburg i/Br.: Herder, 1910), vol. VI, pp. 7-314.

8. See, e.g., André Godin, *L'Homéliaire de Jean Vitrier: Texte, étude thématique et sémantique* (Geneva: Librairie Droz, 1971), esp. pp. 14-18. Jehan Vitrier is the Franciscan friar whom Erasmus first met in 1501 and described at length in his famous letter to Jodocus Jonas, June 13, 1521; *Opus epistolarum Des. Erasmi Roterodami,* ed. P.S. Allen, H.M. Allen, and H.W. Garrod, 12 vols. (Oxford: Clarendon Press, 1906-58), vol. IV, pp. 507-527.

9. See my "Grammar and Rhetoric in Erasmus."

10. Saint Ignatius of Loyola, *The Constitutions of the Society of Jesus,* trans. George E. Ganss (St. Louis: The Institute of Jesuit Sources, 1970), p. 201 (pt. IV, chap. 8 [402]).

11. "De ratione formandae concionis," in *Auctarium Bellarminianum: Supplément aux oeuvres de cardinal Bellarmin,* ed. Xavier-Marie le Bachelet (Paris: G. Beauchesne, 1913), pp. 655-657.

12. See H.I. Marrou, *A History of Education in Antiquity*, trans. George Lamb (New York: The New American Library, 1964), and *idem*, *Saint Augustin et la fin de la culture antique* (Paris: E. de Boccard, 1958).

13. On this distinction, see George A. Kennedy, *Classical Rhetoric and Its Christian and Secular Tradition from Ancient to Modern Times* (Chapel Hill: University of North Carolina Press, 1980), pp. 3-9.

14. On this issue in the Renaissance, see O.B. Hardison, "The Orator and the Poet: The Dilemma of Humanist Literature," *The Journal of Medieval and Renaissance Studies*, 1 (1971), 33-44, and W. Keith Percival, "Grammar and Rhetoric in the Renaissance," in *Renaissance Eloquence*, pp. 303-30.

15. See Pierre Nautin, "Origène prédicateur," in Origène, *Homélies sur Jérémie*, ed. Pierre Husson and Pierre Nautin (Sources chrétiennes, 232, Paris: Cerf, 1976), pp. 100-191; Howard Marshall, "Palestinian and Hellenistic Christianity: Some Critical Comments," *New Testament Studies*, 19 (1972-73), 271-87; and William S. Kurz, "Hellenistic Rhetoric in the Christological Proof of Luke-Acts," *The Catholic Biblical Quarterly*, 42 (1980), 171-195. See also Hartwig Thyen, *Der Stil der Jüdisch-Hellenistischen Homilie* (Göttingen: Vandenhoeck & Ruprecht, 1955).

16. See my "Grammar and Rhetoric in Erasmus," and Salvatore I. Cámporeale, *Lorenzo Valla: Umanesimo e teologia* (Florence: Istituto Nazionale di Studi sul Rinascimento, 1972).

17. See, e.g., *WA* 10.1.1, 199.

18. See, e.g., *WA* 4, 620; 9, 416-417, 439-442; 10.1.1, 132-136, 382, 384, 391, 422, 619; see also Nembach, *Predigt*, pp. 162-168.

19. See, e.g., *WA* 4, 717; 10.1.1, 75-76, 220, 280, 284; 26, 52; 39.1, 428; *TR* 2199[a], 2216, 4426, 4612, 5082[b]; on the "pedagogical," even catechetical, nature of preaching in Luther, see Nembach, *Predigt*, pp. 13, 25-39, 117, 152.

20. On difference between the two forms, see Nembach, *Predigt*, pp. 175-209, and Doberstein, "Introduction," p. xiii.

21. See, e.g., M.-D. Chenu, *La théologie comme science au XIIIe* siècle (Paris: J. Vrin, 3, 1957), pp. 18-22; *idem*, *La théologie au douzième siècle* (Paris: J. Vrin, 1957); *idem*, *Introduction à l'étude de saint Thomas d'Aquin* (Paris: J. Vrin, 1950), p. 67: "Toute la pédagogie médiévale est à base de lecture de textes, et la scholastique universitaire institutionalise et amplifie ce type de travail."

22. *TR* 2199[a]: "Dialectica docet, rhetorica movet. Illa ad intellectum pertinet, haec ad voluntatem. Quas utrasque Paulus complexus est Rom. 12, quando dixit, Qui docet in doctrina, qui exhortatur in exhortando. Et haec duo conficiunt modum praedicandi." See also ibid., 2216, 4426, 5082[b], and Nembach, *Predigt*, 25-39, 120-124.

23. *WA* 6, 458.

24. *Predigt*, pp. 130-135.

25. *Ibid.*, pp. 135-174.

26. See, e.g., *TR* 3494.

27. "*Docere, delectare*." Further indication that principles of primary rhetoric influenced Luther's sermons comes from the fact that he understood technical terms of rhetoric like *status* and *hypothesis*, and correctly applied them to preaching; see *TR* 3032[b] and 3173[b].

28. See Maria Grossmann, "Humanismus in Wittenberg, 1486-1517," *Luther-Jahrbuch*, 39 (1972), 11-30, and *idem*, *Humanism in Wittenberg 1485-1517* (Nieuwkoop: B de Graaf, 1975).

29. See my "Content and Rhetorical Forms," pp. 241-244. Uwe Schnell, *Die homiletische Theorie Philipp Melanchthons* (Berlin and Hamburg: Lutherisches Verlagshaus, 1968); and Wilhelm Maurer, *Der junge Melanchthon zwischen Humanismus und Reformation*, 2 vols. (Göttingen: Vandenhoeck und Ruprecht, 1967-69), esp. vol. I, pp. 171-214.

30. See my "Content and Rhetorical Forms," p. 244, and Schnell, *Homiletische Theorie,* pp. 172-176.

31. See my "Lutheranism in Rome."

32. See my *Praise and Blame.*

33. I believe this statement is incontrovertible; see e.g. Niebergall, "Auffassung," pp. 86, 103; Gerhard Heintze, *Luthers Predigt von Gesetz und Evangelium* (Munich: Chr. Kaiser Verlag, 1958); and the recent article by Peter Iver Kaufman, "Luther's 'Scholastic Phase' Revisited: Grace, Works, and Merit in the Earliest Sermons," *Church History,* 51 (1982), 280-289.

34. See Brilioth, *History,* p. 112.

VI

Saint Charles Borromeo and the *Praecipuum Episcoporum Munus:* His Place in the History of Preaching

SCHOLARS HAVE LONG RECOGNIZED CHARLES BORROMEO'S IMPORTANCE IN the history of preaching.[1] We possess ample documentation about his activity in the pulpit, about his insistence upon preaching as, in the words of the Council of Trent, the *praecipuum munus* of bishops and pastors, about his authorship of an important instruction concerning it, and about his encouragement of the publication and diffusion of several influential treatises on "ecclesiastical rhetoric." The careful studies of texts of Saint Charles related to preaching by Carlo Marcora and other contemporary scholars confirm his intense involvement in the enterprise. Of the fact, therefore, there is no doubt.

What has been lacking until quite recently, however, have been close analyses of the distinctive character of his contribution and a location of it in the more general history of sacred eloquence. Statements to the effect that he revived or reformed preaching and gave a new impetus to it in the post-Tridentine era, while true and often repeated, fail to indicate either the particular emphases that he promoted or the peculiar junction in the history of preaching in which his activities took place. The history of rhetoric in the postclassical period is, in fact, a relatively new discipline, and the history of sacred rhetoric even newer.[2] Along with the partisanship that has long characterized Counter-Reformation studies, this fact helps explain the generally eulogistic and uncritical nature of many of the assessments of Saint Charles and their detachment from a broader perspective.[3]

Three contemporary scholars have begun, however, to rectify this situation—Peter Bayley,[4] Frederick McGinness,[5] and Marc Fumaroli.[6] Fumaroli, in his massive and erudite study entitled *L'âge de l'éloquence* (1980), has especially inserted Saint Charles into the revival of enthusiasm for eloquence that began in the Italian Renaissance but was transformed and reached a certain culmination in the late sixteenth and the seventeenth centuries, particularly in Italy, Spain, and France. My present study of Saint Charles is profoundly indebted to Fumaroli's book, although originally begun independent of it. On the other hand, I approach Saint Charles with somewhat different concerns and, hence, will be able from another viewpoint to confirm many of Fumaroli's judgments, amplify upon a few of them, and in some instances make them even more emphatic. My particular focus will be the history of treatises on how to preach, the relationship between Saint Charles's theory and practice concerning the *praecipuum munus,* and, in general, the convergence of factors that assured for Saint Charles his unique position in this area of pastoral ministry, the public presentation of the Christian message.

First of all, then, a brief review of the history of treatises or instructions on how to preach.[7] Apart from Saint Augustine's *De doctrina christiana,* there were at the beginning of the sixteenth century no treatises in print on this subject besides the scholastic *Artes praedicandi.* Dissatisfaction with these manuals was, however, already widespread, and alternatives to their prescriptions in the actual practice of preaching have been substantially documented. Forms of the patristic or monastic homily had never died out and were in some quarters experiencing a revival. Moreover, especially in Italy, the principles of classical rhetoric were being applied to sacred eloquence in a way and to a degree hitherto unknown, even in Christian antiquity.[8]

In the early decades of the century, some attempts were made to theorize about new forms for the sermon, notably by Johann Reuchlin, Philipp Melanchthon, and a few others. Without any doubt, however, the great turning point in this development was Erasmus's *Ecclesiastes sive De ratione concionandi* of 1535.[9] That immense treatise, Erasmus's last major work and his longest, for the first time reviewed the whole history of Christian preaching and placed before contemporaries the biblical, patristic, and classical alternatives to the "thematic sermon" of the scholastics and the so-called penitential sermons of the mendicants. The importance of the work was immediately recognized, and within a decade it ran through ten editions, some authorized and some pirated.

But almost as immediately, the *Ecclesiastes* began to run into difficulties. Within a few years after its first appearance, it was criticized with some justification as "diffuse, prolix, and confused."[10] Something better organized, something indeed more practical was needed, but it would take a while for Erasmus to be digested and for alternatives to begin to appear. Only in the 1550s did Protestants like Andreas Hyperius (Gerard d'Ypres) (1553),[11] Niels Hemmingsen (1555),[12] and Niels Palladius (1556)[13] produce their treatises that set off the "golden age" of such works in the Protestant sector—more dependent perhaps upon Melanchthon than upon Erasmus.

Catholics were notably slower to produce effective and widely accepted alternatives to the *Ecclesiastes.* However, the placing of that work on the

"Index of Forbidden Books" in 1559 and the especially rigorous enforcement of the prohibition in Spain now made alternatives to Erasmus imperative. The scholastic method of preaching was by this time as emphatically rejected by Catholic theorists as by Protestant, despite the notable revival of scholastic theology during these years. It was thus that the 1570s came to mark the "golden age" of Roman Catholic treatises on the subject, the crucial decade that coincided with the central years of Charles Borromeo's activities as archbishop of Milan. These treatises symbolize the new and universally diffused enthusiasm for the ministry of the Word that would be a hallmark of the Counter-Reformation.

Now let me review a few well known facts about Saint Charles pertinent to this issue. In the first place, he had no formal theological training and therefore would not have been committed ahead of time to a scholastic theory of preaching that he would have been exposed to "in the schools." Indeed, his background was to a large extent humanistic (literature and law), and we can presume he shared the prejudice against scholastic preaching that was widespread in that environment and even beyond it. Moreover, the circle that he helped form as a young prelate in Rome, the *Noctes Vaticanae*, read and imitated classical and patristic authors, and during this period he underwent a religious conversion somehow related to the *Enchiridion* of Epictetus.[14]

During the sessions of the *Noctes*, various issues of Stoic philosophy were discussed. Also discussed and debated were the uses of the three classical *genera* of oratory—judicial, deliberative, and demonstrative, with a preference seemingly given to the deliberative because of its relationship to prudence and to other moral virtues.[15] This preference coincided in a general way with Erasmus's theory and, in part because of his influence, with that of some other theorists. The only oration certainly by Saint Charles to survive from this circle is in Italian and deals with the so-called Fourth Beatitude, "Blessed are they who hunger and thirst for justice."[16] Loosely demonstrative in its form, the oration is a panegyric of the virtue of justice in its several meanings and is moral rather than theological in its content. He does not deal, significantly enough, with the Pauline concept of "justitia."

Saint Charles was profoundly influenced by the Tridentine legislation pertaining to the episcopal office once he took up residence in Milan, and he gave special attention to its determination of preaching as the *praecipuum munus* of its ideal bishop.[17] That phrase was often on his lips and animated his various efforts to reduce the ideal to effective practice in himself and in other pastors of souls with whom he had contact.[18] It has escaped the notice of scholars, with the exception of McGinness, that among the few lines specifically devoted to the content of preaching in the Tridentine decree of 17 June 1546, is found a paraphrase of chapter 9 of the "Second Rule" of Saint Francis of Assisi, viz., that preaching concerns "virtues and vices, punishment and reward."[19] This specification thus confirmed a moralistic emphasis that characterized much preaching of the late Middle Ages and would help extend it into the new era just beginning.[20]

The first, second, and fourth Provincial Synods of Milan under the presidency of Saint Charles touched on preaching in their various decrees, but only after the fourth, 1576, did Borromeo issue in his own name his famous and widely diffused "Instructiones praedicationis verbi Dei."[21] This was the first, longest, and most influential of a series of such statements composed or authorized at about the same time by other reforming bishops like Gabriele Paleotti of Bologna[22] and Cornelio Musso of Bitonto, himself an important preacher and a member of the commission at Trent that drafted the decree on preaching.[23] Both these bishops quote the Franciscan Rule—not a surprise from the Franciscan, Musso—and Paleotti actually structures his document around it.

In his "Instructiones" Saint Charles quotes neither the "Rule" nor Trent's paraphrase of it, but the content he proposes for sermons corresponds to it in a generic way: sins, occasions of sin, virtues, and, finally, the sacraments and other holy usages of the church.[24] His assessment of the situation of the Christian audience as souls needing constant recall to the "way of the Lord," living as they do under incessant assault by the world and the devil, corresponds to his prescriptions about content.[25] This moralistic, vaguely Stoical, framework stands in contrast to the doctrinal content concerning works-faith, Law-Gospel, wrath-grace that Lutheran treatises insisted upon, and also the more generally doctrinal and affective emphasis in preaching even in other sectors of Catholicism, especially earlier in the sixteenth century.[26]

The moralistic viewpoint extends into the long section of the "Instructiones" that deals with the virtues and knowledge which are prerequisites for the preacher of the Word of God.[27] The preacher must be convinced of the truths he propounds and live according to them. Erasmus had given impetus to such traditional considerations in the long first book of the *Ecclesiastes.* Like that of Erasmus and others, Saint Charles's treatment of this issue can be assessed as a slightly baptized version of the ethos that classical Roman treatises on rhetoric insisted upon for the genuinely successful orator—"vir *bonus,* dicendi peritus."

Admirable though that definition is from many viewpoints, it lacks an important component. What is missing in Saint Charles, as well as in many others who addressed the issue in the sixteenth century, is any developed "theology of the Word" or "theology of the minister of the Word." We know of Saint Charles's reverence for the Bible, and we know that he often read it on his knees,[28] but indications of the suprahuman efficacy of the Word, or suggestions that the task of the Christian preacher is therefore substantively different from the task of the merely secular orator, receive scant attention in his "Instructiones."[29]

He does prescribe a life-style for the preacher that sets him off from the laity, and he even advises him to eschew their ordinary company.[30] One might argue that in this fact recognition is given to the special character of the ministry and minister of the Word. But most obviously indicated here is rather a special, even narrow, ecclesiastical culture, segregated from general culture and thus presumably immune to its contaminations. A higher and distinctive level of virtue is required of the preacher, but the relationship of that virtue to the special energies inherent in the Word of God is only rarely suggested. Perhaps such considerations sounded too Lutheran; perhaps they were considered inappropriate in a document that was, after all, only an instruction, not a treatise; or, more likely, they never occurred to somebody with such a meager theological training, just as they seem to have been ignored even by theorists who had a better background in sacred learning.

Nonetheless, for all its limitations, the "Instructiones" alone would establish for Saint Charles a significant place in the history of post-Tridentine ministry. But that document is only the first such monument, supported by similar legislation he initiated for seminarians and for his Oblates of Saint Ambrose.[31] The second monument is the example he provided his contemporaries of a bishop indefatigable in the *praecipuum munus*. In this he resembled and followed the lead of his colleague, Paleotti of Bologna.

Despite a natural aversion for public speaking and despite a weak voice and a slurred speech pattern that often made him difficult to understand, Saint Charles eventually overcame his hesitancies and sometimes preached as often as three or four times a day, composing a new sermon for each occasion at those times.[32] No representative segment of his sermons was published until the eighteenth century, but the fact of his activity was well known to contemporaries and later generations and was incorporated into the canon of the post-Tridentine ideal of the bishop and conscientious pastor.[33]

Unlike his contemporaries, we are in a position to examine those sermons, principally from the last two years of his life, which have come down to us more or less intact and have been published. Hence, we can ask how his practice conformed to his instructions, and where his sermons were as spiritually and theologically barren as his directives to others suggest. As we read the sermons, we in fact experience a pleasant surprise.

There are, to be sure, some passages in the sermons that are drearily and disconcertingly moralistic in their exaggerated alarm over sometimes innocent pleasures. On 3 July 1583, for instance, he excoriates parents at length for allowing their children to spend so much time playing games; in their games they learn cupidity, the root of all evil, they learn to blaspheme, they waste time and neglect their religious duties.[34] In other sermons he decried what may have been more genuine problems, like indecent plays and obscene literature in circulation in Milan, but one is forced to wonder how objective his judgment was in such matters.[35] Everlasting torment in hell was the penalty for breaking the Lenten fast.[36] Moreover, he preached so consistently the respect due the clergy and the evil of any criticism of the church that we immediately perceive how an insistence on ecclesiastical order extirpated any impulse to prophetic criticism.[37] Finally, he gave special prominence to certain issues controverted by Protestants and explicitly reaffirmed by the Council of Trent, such as the necessity of good works, the superiority of virginity to marriage, the utility of indulgences, and the veneration of relics. In the history of Catholic preaching, an important shift in emphasis was beginning to take place.

Nonetheless, despite a pervasive moralism, the published sermons are relatively inspirational in their language and content, and they rest on a broad basis of the doctrines of Creation and Redemption. This positive teaching finds verification in his so-called "collations" to religious women. Along with a bleak picture of the dangers of the world coexists a presentation of the joys of religious life and of the especially intimate and satisfying relationship with the Lord that it provides.[38]

Even the sermons to general audiences, however, manifest an optimistic view of the spiritual capabilities of humankind, created by God and redeemed by Christ. The workings of grace in the redeemed are described sometimes as a process of deification and its results in peace and joy. Surely somewhat influenced by Trent's pronouncement on this issue, Saint Charles emphasized the role of human cooperation, but rather successfully avoided formulations that sound Pelagian or Semi-Pelagian.[39] In an impressive peroration on the feast of Saint Michael, 1583, he speaks of the dignity of human nature, redeemed and "kissed" by Christ, without any previous merits, and thus raised in excellence above even the angels.[40]

A word that he frequently employs to describe the contents of his sermons is *mysterium*. He thereby intimates the surpassing excellence as well as the transcendence of the message he propounds. Theological elucidations of the *mysteria* are few, it is true. Somewhat like the sacred orators of the papal court during the Renaissance, he contents himself with basic statements about doctrines like Creation and Redemption and then amplifies these by speaking about their significance for Christian behavior, attitudes, and affect. Saint Francis de Sales observed that Borromeo's theological knowledge was meager, but that it was sufficient for effective preaching.[41] The sermons I have examined would, in fact, tend to substantiate both aspects of that judgment.

A related feature of these sermons is their often liturgical starting point.[42] The feast of the day provides the context of the *mysterium*, and some parts of its liturgy provide its content. This means that the sermons tend as much to be as church related as Bible centered. It also sometimes means that Saint Charles begins with certain visual elements immediately perceived by his audience. A dramatic instance of this phenomenon occurs in his sermon in

Milan on the occasion of the death of the queen of Spain, for which he had an immense catafalque erected in the cathedral from which his eulogy took its exordium.[43]

The biblical texts of the liturgy, however, generally provide the starting point and the framework of the discourse. This raises the question of the rhetorical genre into which his sermons fall—a question not easily answered. We know from his activities in Rome, from the works of Cicero in his library, and from his contact with authors of "ecclesiastical rhetorics" that he was not isolated from this issue.[44] In a general way, many of the sermons can be described as homilies in that they are loose commentaries on a verse or passage from Scripture. They do, however, often evince features of "oratory" in the stricter sense, with clear exordia and perorations, and they are certainly marked with the effects of "secondary rhetoric" in their style and literary techniques. Fumaroli is correct in seeing the impact in these sermons of an anti-Ciceronianism, of a "severe ideal," deriving partly from Spanish theorists on preaching, and a desire to return to the simpler style of the Fathers, where the force of the sermon would derive more from its serious content (the *res*) than from elaborate and studied rhetorical techniques (the *verba*).[45] Nonetheless, they are quite different from sermons related to the scholastic and mendicant traditions and must be described, rather, as classicizing. Saint Charles explicitly legislated for his seminarians, in fact, that the lectures for them on sacred Scripture not be done "scholastico more," but according to a more humanistic or patristic methodology, "tamquam theologia positiva."[46] In his sermons the more directly scriptural and affective homily is often admixed with elements from the moralistic *genus deliberativum*, and even with the congratulatory *genus demonstrativum* (panegyric). Without being "masterpieces of pulpit eloquence," the sermons of Saint Charles are intelligent, straightforward, and appropriate for his audiences.

We thus finally arrive at a consideration of the theorists about preaching with whom Saint Charles had contact and whose works he promoted. His activity in this regard constitutes the third monument that established his position in the history of preaching. It came at a crucial and unprecedented moment, as I indicated earlier, and helped set Catholic preaching on a course that would have influence for centuries.

The first Catholic to react to Erasmus was the Spanish cleric Alfonso Zorrilla. He published in Rome in 1543 his *De sacris concionibus recte formandis formula* as a counterpiece to the *Ecclesiastes*.[47] The work had only one printing. It was an act of successful and outrageous plagiarism, principally from Lutheran authors like Melanchthon. Certainly influential in introducing some of Melanchthon's ideas into the Catholic tradition, it was sometimes cited later by orthodox authors. But, perhaps because of its radical nature, it did not inaugurate a trend.

The same can be said of four other works written in Italy in the 1560s that in one way or another dealt with pulpit eloquence: Cornelio Musso's *Discorso intorno all'artificio delle prediche* (1557),[48] Marcantonio Natta's *De christianorum eloquentia* (1562),[49] Luca Baglione's *L'arte del predicare* (1562),[50] and Benedetto Palmio's "De excellentia praedicationis evangelica."[51] The last work, it should be noted, was not published until 1969 but was intended for the eyes of Borromeo and is found in manuscript among his papers. None of these writings was theoretically comprehensive; none attracted wide readership.

It is from Spain, in fact, that books on "ecclesiastical rhetoric" in the strict sense really first derive.[52] After the early publication in 1541 of a book on rhetoric in Spanish for preachers by Miguel de Salinas,[53] the next to be published, in 1563, was the *De formandis sacris concionibus* by the Augustinian friar, Lorenzo de Villavicencio.[54] This work is heavily indebted to the treatise with the same title by the Lutheran, Hyperius. The problem has seemingly escaped the notice of some modern authors but was actually detected in Spain a few years after its publication.[55] The book did, however, have several subsequent printings. For whatever reasons, it did not attract the support of Saint Charles, and its influence was limited.

Besides the two short works on the subject of Andrés Sempere and Alonso de Orozco,[56] the next work of the genre, *De methodo concionandi,* was published at Alcalá (1570) by Alfonso Garciá Matamoros. Written expressly to supply contemporaries with a treatise on the subject of which the suppression of the *Ecclesiastes* had deprived them,[57] it is uncompromisingly dependent on the oratorical precepts of Cicero and Quintilian. This quality perhaps accounts for its limited circulation and the lack of interest Saint Charles showed in it. In 1573 Juan de Segovia published at Alcalá his *De praedicatione evangelica,* a work that also attracted little attention.[58]

This was the situation that prevailed during Saint Charles's first years in Milan. Trent had determined preaching as the *praecipuum munus* of bishops, and by extension, of all pastors, yet there was no received body of literature in existence corresponding to the *Artes praedicandi* produced by the medieval scholastics that told them how to go about it in a way which would satisfy the aesthetic and religious tastes of the day. In this context Saint Charles's importunities to his friend and fellow bishop, Agostino Valier (Valerio) of Verona, to produce a work on "ecclesiastical rhetoric" take on their immense significance. The treatise would be, for all practical purposes, a "first," dependent though it might be on the works that preceded it.

Valier's *De rhetorica ecclesiastica* was published in 1574 and reprinted some twenty-three times thereafter. This book must be immediately conjoined with the similar treatises published just two years later by the Spanish practitioners and theorists, Luis de Granada, a Dominican, and Diego de

Estella, a Franciscan.[59] These three books were characterized by their comprehensiveness, their easy intelligibility, their organizational clarity, and their grasp of both the classical and patristic traditions. In a different way, but along with Erasmus's *Ecclesiastes,* they mark a great watershed not only for the sixteenth century but for the entire history of preaching in the Roman Catholic Church. Like Valier's work, the two works from the Iberian peninsula ran through many editions, published on an international basis. The three together in effect determined the models for the great tradition of treatises on the subject that would mark the seventeenth century, but this fact does not detract from their importance in their own right.

Valier always maintained that he undertook his work only at the insistence of the archbishop of Milan and that Saint Charles was almost a coauthor of it.[60] Given the exaggerations of which the sixteenth century was capable, we might be inclined to dismiss these protestations as flattering, even obsequious, hyperbole. The evidence from the correspondence of Borromeo and his collaborators, however, only confirms Valier's assertions and gives them substance.

Beginning in 1572 the correspondence of Saint Charles with Valier is filled with comments on the drafts of the *Rhetoric* and suggestions for it.[61] He reviewed drafts himself and enlisted others like Pietro Galesino and the two Jesuits—Emmanuale Alvaro and Francesco Adorno—to make emendations. An important letter of Adorno to Valier survives that treats specifically of the book in its formative stages and communicates suggestions from Borromeo.[62] Even before the book was printed, Saint Charles had put a draft of it into use in his seminary.

When Diego de Estella and Luis de Granada published their rhetorics in 1576, Saint Charles was eager to receive copies. He incorporated verbatim a short section of Estella's work in his "Instructiones," and the Venice edition of the rhetoric (1584) was dedicated to him.[63] Saint Charles was even fonder of Luis de Granada, whose published sermons he had been reading for some time and eventually published in Milan for the use of his clergy. He was in personal contact with him through correspondence and through friends in the Iberian peninsula. In a letter of 10 July 1576, Saint Charles requested of a friend in Lisbon that he send him a copy of Granada's book as soon as possible.[64] It is surely due directly or indirectly to Saint Charles that the next year in Rome and the following year in Venice it was published in a single volume together with Valier's treatise.

The first attraction these Spanish texts had for Saint Charles was simply that they existed, filling a gap that had long been recognized. But their content and approach also would commend them. Estella's work was thoroughly Franciscan in the moral purpose it assigned to preaching, with chapter 9 of the "Second Rule" its obvious inspiration. Moreover, it proposed the patristic homily as the appropriate form for preaching, which by this time surely appealed immensely to Borromeo and corresponded in a general way to his own preaching style.[65] Granada's work was more oratorical, favoring the moralistic *genus deliberativum*, but was still "severe" and measured.[66] Moreover, from Granada's other works Saint Charles had already come to esteem and appropriate his theological learning. The pervasive Stoic undercurrent in Granada correlated with similar strains in Borromeo.[67]

Saint Charles's patronage in this sphere went even further. I have already mentioned the work on preaching by Palmio. In 1585, the year after Borromeo's death, Giovanni Botero, another of his collaborators, published his *De praedicatore verbi Dei.*[68] This effort to construct a "fully Christian rhetoric" explicitly owes its origins to Saint Charles's urgings and inspiration.[69] Not nearly so influential as the works of Valier, Granada, and Estella—it had only one printing—the *De praedicatore* is, nonetheless, another significant document in a tradition of "ecclesiastical rhetorics" that can justly be called "Borromean."

The final monument establishing Saint Charles's importance for preaching is his effort to bring to his archdiocese effective preachers for protracted periods of time and the example he thus set for other bishops.[70] The most famous of these was the Franciscan preacher and theorist, Francesco Panigarola, who preached the eulogy of Saint Charles at his funeral[71] and whom Tiraboschi describes in unqualified fashion as "il più eloquente predicatore che sia vissuta in quel secolo."[72] Saint Charles's efforts to bring Panigarola to Milan began as early as 1575, but they did not succeed until 1581, when Panigarola preached for a short while in the cathedral with great success.[73] In 1582 Panigarola returned to Milan after Lent, where he remained off and on even for several years after the death of Saint Charles on 4 November 1584. On 25 August of that year, he had sent to him a copy of his recently published *Modo di comporre una predica.*

In 1579 Saint Charles called Alfonso Lobo, another distinguished Franciscan, to his diocese.[74] Lobo is sometimes considered one of Panigarola's few contemporaries to rival his effectiveness in the pulpit. The Jesuit preachers Benedetto Palmio and Francesco Adorno also responded to Saint Charles's invitation to preach in the cathedral, and the saint's correspondence often indicates his other efforts to bring good preachers into his archdiocese.[75]

* * *

This brief review of Saint Charles's activities regarding various aspects of the ministry of the Word has only touched on issues and personages that deserve more ample study. Much more could be said, for example, about his relationship with the Oratorians and Barnabites in this regard. It is no exaggeration to affirm that a full volume on the subject could easily and profitably be written and that it would illuminate an aspect of the Counter-Reformation and general European culture that until now has received woefully inadequate study. I trust, however, that enough has been indicated here to establish with some detail as well as comprehensiveness his special place in the history of preaching. Fumaroli speaks of the Borromean "atelier" for preaching established at Milan.[76] If anything, that judgment is, in my opinion, too modest. It would be more adequate to the reality to speak of a huge "industry."

This industry consisted of at least four parts, any one of which would point to Saint Charles's importance: first, his "Instructiones" and the related documents; secondly, his example as a bishop who sought indefatigably to reduce the *praecipuum munus* of pastors to practice in his own direct ministry; thirdly, his encouragement of the publication of "ecclesiastical rhetorics" during the crucial years of that new literary genre; fourthly, his efforts to bring to Milan the best preachers of the day and thus share with them some of his already immense prestige.

It is true that other bishops of the period set a good example by their frequent preaching and by promoting in other ways good preaching in their dioceses—notably Gabriele Paleotti of Bologna, with whom Saint Charles was in close contact.[77] But none of these enjoyed the contemporary and posthumous fame of Borromeo. None of these was canonized. Moreover, not even around Paleotti did so many factors converge in such an eminent degree as they did around Saint Charles.

In the history of Christian preaching there have been some critical turning points. There was first of all the long patristic and monastic period, with the homilies of Origen and the *De doctrina christiana* as the most important documents. That tradition was not really challenged until the thirteenth century by the sermons of the scholastics and mendicants along with their correlative *Artes praedicandi.* The humanistic revival of classical oratory and patristic homiletics was in part a reaction to the scholastics and had a long gestation period. Erasmus's *Ecclesiastes* of 1535, along with his other works that dealt indirectly or in passing with preaching, signaled that another great change was in the making—a change which at first would touch only refined and well-educated circles, but that touched off a development which within a century would begin to reach down to more popular audiences. These impulses and scattered efforts were not marshaled, in other words, until the late sixteenth century. Many people collaborated in organizing these impulses and efforts into an effective and more or less coherent program. The new religious orders would be especially important. But without any doubt Saint Charles is a figure who centered these impulses and efforts. No matter what aspect of this phenomenon one investigates, the saint's name appears at every critical juncture. He is a major figure and a chief promotor of that extraordinary enthusiasm for the ministry of the Word in the sixteenth century which, as I said earlier, was just as characteristic of Catholicism as it was of Protestantism, although often not recognized as such.

To be sure, Borromeo's activities in this regard suffer from limitations, and any assessment of them that fails to take these limitations into account would be unbalanced. Although in his own preaching the strongly moralistic tendencies that he explicitly espoused were tempered by a message with a doctrinal and devotional base, he doubtless promoted such tendencies, which were already strong and even canonized by Trent in its decree of 17 June 1546. He thus reflected and helped confirm the assumption, not shared by many Protestants, that preaching was largely moralistic and behavioristic in its aims.

His own culture was broad, but his espousal of a special clerical culture, distinct from general culture and even inimical to it, doubtless worked harm on future generations that did not enjoy the benefits of good family and broad personal contacts as he did. He often focused on ecclesiastical traditions in his preaching, without much historical or even theological perspective on them, and his insistence on church order suppressed an important and traditional aspect of preaching.

These and other limitations are serious. They tarnish the luster of his achievements. Nonetheless, there is no doubt that Charles Borromeo enjoys a place in this critical period in the history of preaching that no other single figure—Catholic or Protestant—enjoys. For the reasons I have adduced, his place is unique and pivotal.

In closing, I can do no better than quote Fumaroli's summary of the achievement of Saint Charles and his generation: ". . . [after the close of the Council of Trent], a veritable 'rhetoric workshop' opened in Spain and Italy, more productive than any of the schools of the ancient Sophists or any humanist Academy. . . . One can also rest assured that no humanist orator, not even the Chancellors of the Florentine Republic, had either the authority or the immediate audience of a Charles Borromeo, heir and imitator of Ambrose in the archiepiscopal see of Milan."[78]

Notes

1. See Herman J. Heuser, "Saint Charles Borromeo as a Preacher," *The American Ecclesiastical Review* 7 (1892): 332–40; Joseph M. Connors, "Saint Charles Borromeo in the Homiletic Tradition," ibid. 138 (1958): 9–23; Federico Barbieri, "La riforma dell'eloquenza sacra in Lombardia operata da San Carlo Borromeo," *Archivio Storico Lombardo,* ser. 4, 15 (1911): 231–62; Angelo Novelli, "S. Carlo Borromeo, oratore sacro," *La Scuola Cattolica* 38 (1910): 108–36; 63 (1935): 313–22; Germano Carboni, "S. Carlo e l'eloquenza sacra," ibid. 57 (1929): 270–90; Balthasar Fisher, "Predigtgrundsätze des hl. Carl Borromäus," *Trierer theologische Zeitschrift* 61 (1952): 213–21; Roger Mols, "Saint Charles Borromée, pionnier de la pastorale moderne," *Nouvelle Revue Théologique* 79 (1957): 600–622, 715–47, esp. 728–34; Carlo Marcora, "La 'Sylva pastoralis' di S. Carlo Borromeo," *Memorie Storiche della*

Diocesi di Milano 12 (1965): 13–98, and Marcora, ed., *Arbores de Paschate* (Milan: Biblioteca Ambrosiana, 1984). Saint Charles is often treated, however, in more general works on preaching in a cursory fashion. See, e.g., Yngve Brilioth, *A Brief History of Preaching*, trans. Karl E. Mattson (Philadelphia: Fortress Press, 1965), p. 143; Emilio Santini, *L'eloquenza italiana dal Concilio Tridentino ai nostri giorni* (Milan: R. Sandron, 1923–28), 1:30; Ernesto Vercesi and Emilio Santini, *L'eloquenza dal sec. XVII ai nostri giorni* (Milan: F. Vallardi, 1938), pp. 14–16; Johann Baptist Schneyer, *Geschichte der katholischen Predigt* (Freiburg: Seelsorge, 1969), pp. 249–50; Werner Schütz, *Geschichte der christlichen Predigt* (Berlin: W. de Gruyter, 1972), pp. 111–12.

2. See, e.g., the comments by James J. Murphy, "One Thousand Neglected Authors: The Scope and Importance of Renaissance Eloquence," in *Renaissance Eloquence*, ed. James J. Murphy (Berkeley and Los Angeles: University of California Press, 1983), pp. 20–36, and my own "Content and Rhetorical Forms in Sixteenth-Century Treatises on Preaching," ibid., pp. 238–52. See also my "Erasmus and the History of Sacred Rhetoric: The *Ecclesiastes* of 1535," *Erasmus of Rotterdam Society Yearbook* 5 (1985): 1–29, and "Luther the Preacher" in *The Martin Luther Quincentennial*, ed. G. Dünnhaupt (Detroit, Mich.: Wayne State University Press, 1984), pp. 3–16.

3. On the present state of Counter-Reformation studies, see my "Catholic Reform," in *Reformation Europe: A Guide to Research*, ed. Steven Ozment (Saint Louis: Center for Reformation Research, 1982), pp. 297–319, and especially the volume under my editorship, *Catholicism in Early Modern History: A Guide to Research* (St. Louis, 1987).

4. See his "Les Sermons de Jean-Pierre Camus et l'esthétique borroméenne," in *Critique et création litteraire en France au XVIIe siècle*, ed. Marc Fumaroli (Paris: CNRS, 1977), pp. 93–98; *French Pulpit Oratory, 1598–1650* (Cambridge: Cambridge University Press, 1980); *Selected Sermons of the French Baroque (1600–1650)* (New York: Garland Publishing Company, 1983).

5. See his *Rhetoric and Counter-Reformation Rome: Sacred Oratory and the Construction of the Catholic World View, 1563–1621* (Ann Arbor, Mich.: University Microfilms International, 1982); "Preaching Ideals and Practice in Counter-Reformation Rome," *The Sixteenth Century Journal* 11, no. 2 (1980): 109–27; "The Rhetoric of Praise and the New Rome of the Counter Reformation," in *Rome in the Renaissance: The City and the Myth*, ed. P. A. Ramsey (Binghamton, N.Y.: Center for Medieval and Early Renaissance Studies, 1982), pp. 355–70.

6. See especially his *L'âge de l'éloquence: Rhétorique et "res literaria" de la Renaissance au seuil de l'époque classique* (Geneva: Droz, 1980).

7. See my studies cited above in note 2.

8. See, e.g., my *Praise and Blame in Renaissance Rome: Rhetoric, Doctrine, and Reform in the Sacred Orators of the Papal Court, c. 1450–1521* (Durham, N.C.: Duke University Press, 1979), and the articles by John M. McManamon, "The Ideal Renaissance Pope: Funeral Oratory from the Papal Court," *Archivum Historiae Pontificiae* 14 (1976): 9–70; "Renaissance Preaching: Theory and Practice. A Holy Thursday Sermon of Aurelio Brandolini," *Viator* 10 (1979): 355–73; "Innovation in Early Humanistic Rhetoric: The Oratory of Pier Paolo Vergerio the Elder," *Rinascimento* 22 (1982): 3–32.

9. See especially my "Erasmus and the History of Rhetoric."

10. This criticism came from the Spanish cleric Alfonso Zorrilla in 1543. On his curious book, see my "Lutheranism in Rome, 1542–43: The Treatise by Alfonso

Zorrilla," *Thought* 54 (1979): 262–73, now reprinted in my *Rome and the Renaissance: Studies in Culture and Religion* (London: Variorum Reprints, 1981), 10.

11. *De formandis concionibus sacris* (Marburg: A. Colbius, 1553). On him, see John S. Chamberlin, *Increase and Multiply: Arts-of-Discourse Procedures in the Preaching of Donne* (Chapel Hill: University of North Carolina Press, 1976).

12. *De methodis libri duo . . . posterior Ecclesiastes, sive methodum theologicam interpretandi concionandique continet* (Rostock, 155); I consulted a subsequent edition (Wittenberg: J. Crato, 1559).

13. *Concionator, seu Regulae quaedam utiles ac necessariae concionatoribus observandae* (Copenhagen, 1556).

14. See, especially, *Noctes Vaticanae, seu Sermones habiti in Academia a s. Carlo Borromeo,* ed. Giuseppe Antonio Sassi (Milan: Bibliotheca Ambrosiana, 1748), and Luigi F. Berra, *L'Accademia delle Notti Vaticanae fondata da San Carlo Borromeo* (Rome: M. Bretschneider, 1915).

15. See, Biblioteca Apostolica Vaticana, cod. Ottob. lat. 2429, pt. 1, fols. 3–7, "Della causa deliberativa."

16. Published in Sassi, *Noctes Vaticanae,* pp. 74–116.

17. On the episcopal ideal, see especially Hubert Jedin, *Il tipo ideale di vescovo secondo la riforma cattolica* (Brescia: Morcelliana, 1950); Giuseppe Alberigo, "Carlo Borromeo come modello di vescovo nella Chiesa post-tridentina," *Rivista Storica Italiana* 79 (1967): 1031–52; Massimo Petrocchi, "L' 'ideal del vescovo' nel Panigarola," *Rivista di Storia della Chiesa in Italia* 8 (1954): 93–95. As background, see also M. Piton, "L'idéal épiscopale selon les prédicateurs français de la fin du XVe siècle et du debut du XVIe," *Revue d'Histoire Ecclésiastique* 61 (1966): 77–118, 393–423.

18. See, e.g., the solemn exordium to his "Instructiones praedicationis verbi Dei," in *Acta Ecclesiae Mediolanensis,* ed. Achille Ratti (Milan: Typographia Pontificia Sancti Josephi, 1890–97), 2:1207; decrees of First Provincial Synod, 1565, ibid., col. 32; *Homiliae nunc primum e mss. codicibus Bibliothecae Ambrosianae in lucem productae,* ed. Giuseppe Antonio Sassi (Milan: Bibliothecae Ambrosiana, 1747–48), 1:106, 238.

19. See *Conciliorum Oecumenicorum Decreta,* ed. Giuseppe Alberigo, et al., 2^d^ ed. (Freiburg im Breisgau: Herder, 1962), p. 645: ". . . annuntiando eis cum brevitate et facilitate sermonis vitia, quae eos declinare, et virtutes, quas sectari oporteat, ut poenam aeternam evadere et coelestem gloriam consequi valeant." The quotation conforms verbatim to the "Rule" in the earlier version of the decree, 13 April 1546. Cf. the "Rule" in *Seraphicae Legislationis Textus Originales* (Quaracchi: Collegium S. Bonaventurae, 1897), p. 44: ". . . annuntiando eis vitia et virtutes, poenam et gloriam, cum brevitate sermonis, ..." The relationship to the "Rule" is noted and given its due importance by McGinness, *Rhetoric and Counter-Reformation Rome,* p. 164, but barely suggested by Arsenio d'Ascoli, *La predicazione dei Cappuccini nel Cinquecento in Italia* (Loreto: Libreria "S. Francesco d'Assisi," 1956), p. 66. On the decree, see also the following authors, who do not mention this Franciscan element: Johann Ev. Rainer, "Entstehungsgeschichte des Trienter Predigtreformdekrets," *Zeitschrift für katholische Theologie* 39 (1915): 256–317, 465–523; A. Larios, "La reforma de la predicación en Trento (Historia y contenido de un decreto)," *Communio* 6 (1973): 223–83; Hubert Jedin, *A History of the Council of Trent,* trans. Ernest Graf (London: Thomas Nelson and Sons, 1957–61), 2:99–124. We can infer, although there seems to be no direct evidence for it, that Cornelio Musso was the person most responsible for this element in the decree. Authors who have studied him do not mention this possibility: Hubert Jedin, "Der Franziskaner Cornelio

Musso, Bischof von Bitonto," *Römische Quartalschrift* 41 (1933): 207–75; G. Cantini, "Cornelio Musso, O.F.M., Conv., predicatore, scrittore e teologo al Concilio di Trento," *Miscellanea Francescana* 41 (1941): 146–74, 424–63; Roger J. Bartman, "Cornelio Musso, Tridentine Theologian and Orator," *Franciscan Studies* 5 (1945): 247–76; Giovanni Odoardi, "Fra Cornelio Musso, O.F.M., Conv., padre, oratore et teologo al Concilio di Trento," *Miscellanea Francescana* 48 (1948): 223–42, 450–78; 49 (1949): 36–71.

20. See, e.g., the thoughtful article by Zelinda Zafarana, "Bernardino nella storia della predicazione popolare," in *Bernardino predicatore nella società del suo tempo,* Convegni del Centro di Studi sulla Spiritualità Medievale, no. 16 (Todi: Accademia Tuderina, 1976), pp. 41–70.

21. The Instruction is found in *Acta Ecclesiae Mediolanensis* 2:1205–48. It was reprinted many times after its first publication.

22. *Istruttione di Monsig. Illustrissimo et Reverendissimo Card. Paleotti* (Bologna: A. Benacci, 1586), first published in 1578. On Paleotti, see Paolo Prodi, *Il cardinale Gabriele Paleotti (1522–1597)* (Rome: Edizioni di Storia e Letteratura, 1959–67), especially 2:75–136.

23. The section on preaching comes towards the end of *Synodus Bituntina Rmi. Patris F. Cornelii Mussi Episcopi Bituntini, totam fere ecclesiasticam disciplinam . . . complectens* (Venice: apud Iolitos, 1579). See n. 18 above for bibliography on Musso.

24. See "Instructiones," cols. 1230–43; *Homiliae* 2:48–49, 418; decrees of First Provincial Synod, 1565, *Acta Ecclesiae Mediolanensis* 2:35; decrees of Fourth Provincial Synod, 1576, ibid., 336.

25. See "Instructiones," col. 1215: ". . . videbit [concionator] diligenter, quanta, et quam summa difficultate ei proponitur, qui in tanta, tamquam perpetua et mundi et Satanae oppugnatione fidelium animas ad viam Domini revocare contendit." See also *Homiliae* 2:15, ". . . ut homines beluarum more vitam ducentes, ad Evangelicam vitam tam numerose converteret. . . ."

26. See, e.g., my *Praise and Blame,* pp. 123–64.

27. See "Instructiones," cols. 1207–15.

28. See, e.g., Agostino Valier, *Vita Caroli Borromei* (Verona: H. Discipulus, 1586), p. 48.

29. There is a suggestion of such a theology, "Instructiones," col. 1215: "Deinde se, qui praedicationis munus aggreditur, ministrum esse, per quem verbum Dei ab ipso divini Spiritus fonte ducitur ad fidelium animas divinitus irrigandas." See also ibid., col. 1217. See also *Homiliae* 1:108–9; 2:23–24, 70; decrees of Fifth Provincial Synod, 1579, *Acta Ecclesiae Mediolanensis* 2:523–24.

30. See "Instructiones," especially cols. 1217, 1228–29; *Homiliae* 2:159, ". . . ut Deo tantum [clerici] vacantes cum Deo loquantur, cum sanctis versentur, in Ecclesiis permaneant, sacris lectionibus et studiis tempus consumant; . . . ideo nec a vobis [laicis] sunt importune perturbandi"; *Discorsi inediti di S. Carlo Borromeo,* ed. Carlo Marcora (Milan: Pro Istituto pei Figli della Providenza, 1965), pp. 101–10. See also Enrico Cattaneo, "La santità sacerdotale vissuta da San Carlo," *La Scuola Cattolica* 93 (1965): 405–26, and Giovanni Moioli, "Temi di spiritualità episcopale e sacerdotale in S. Carlo Borromeo," ibid., pp. 459–88.

31. See "Institutionum ad oblatos Sancti Ambrosii pertinentium epitome," in *Acta Ecclesiae Mediolanensis* 3:49–90, and "Institutiones ad universum seminarii regimen pertinentes," ibid., cols. 93–146.

32. His contemporaries frequently speak of these problems and of his hesitancies. See, e.g., Valier, *Vita,* pp. 10, 29; Carlo Bascapè, *De vita et rebus gestis Caroli S. R. E. cardinalis* (Ingolstadt: D. Sartorius, 1592), pp. 329, 333; Giovan Battista

154

Possevino, *Discorsi della vita et attioni di Carlo Borromeo* (Rome: J. Tornerius, 1591), pp. 45–46; Giovanni Botero, *De praedicatore verbi Dei* (Paris: G. Chaudière, 1585), sig. a ii; Francesco Panigarola, *Il predicatore* (Venice: B. Giunti, G. B. Ciotti, 1609), 1:39.

33. The first major collection of his sermons to be published was *Sermoni familiari di s. Carlo Borromeo,* ed. Gaetano Volpi (Padua: G. Comino, 1720), followed by the five volumes by Sassi, *Homiliae* (1747–48). Other major collections of his sermons, orations, and other religious discourses are: *Discorsi inediti,* ed. Marcora; *Ammaestramenti di S. Carlo Borromeo alle persone religiose* (Milan: Arte Sacra, 1902); *Vingt discours de saint Charles Borromée à des religieuses* (Roulers: J. de Meester, 1910); *Saint Charles Borromée: Homélies, Sermons et Entretiens,* ed. J. B. Gaï (Namur: Soleil Levant, 1961); *Sancti Caroli Borromaei Orationes XII,* ed. Angelo Paredi (Rome and Milan: G. Campi, 1963). The contents of these collections overlap; those edited by Sassi and Marcora are fundamental. Ten volumes of autograph sketches or outlines of sermons survive, principally in the Biblioteca Ambrosiana; see Marcora, *Discorsi,* pp. 9–11.

34. See *Homiliae* 1:392–94. See also ibid. 2:7.

35. See, e.g., ibid. 2:101, 151. See also Carlo Borromeo, *Veri sentimenti di san Carlo Borromeo intorno al teatro* (Rome: G. Zempel, 1753), and idem, *Opusculum de choreis et spectaculis in festis diebus non exhibendis* (Rome: Fratres Palearinos, 1753).

36. See *Homiliae* 2:315–16.

37. See, e.g., ibid. 1:53–54, 88–89, 303; 3:151–52; *Discorsi inediti,* pp. 101–10.

38. The basic collection is still in Sassi, *Homiliae* 5:191–350, in Italian. See also ibid. 2:121–34; 3:58–70.

39. See, e.g., *Homiliae* 1:74–79, 108–16, 239; 2:250; 3:450; *Discorsi inediti,* pp. 55–63, 127–34, 185–89.

40. See *Homiliae* 3:17–19.

41. See his letter to André Frémyot, 5 October 1604, in *Oeuvres de saint François de Sales* (Annecy: J. Niérat [etc.], 1892–1932), 12:301: "Quant a la doctrine, il faut qu'elle soit suffisante, et n'est pas requis qu'elle soit excellente. . . . et en nostre aage, le bienheureux Cardinal Borromee n'avoit de science que bien fort mediocrement: toutefois il faisoit merveilles." This letter is sometimes designated Saint Francis's "Traitté de la prédication." See also his letter to Antoine de Revol, 3 June 1603, ibid., p. 189: "Ayés, je vous prie, Grenade tout entier, et que ce soit vostre second breviaire; le Cardinal Borromee n'avoit point d'autre theologie pour prescher que cella la, et neanmoins il preschoit tres bien." On the relationship between Saint Charles and Saint Francis, see Paul Broutin, "Les deux grands évêques de la réforme catholique," *Nouvelle Revue Théologique* 85 (1953): 282–99, 380–98. Jean-Pierre Camus described Saint Charles as "un pauvre prédicateur selon le jugement ordinaire du monde," in *Homélies panégiriques de sainct* [*sic*] *Charles Borromée* (Paris: C. Chappelet, 1623), p. 142.

42. See decrees of Third Provincial Synod, 1573, *Acta Ecclesiae Mediolanensis* 2:235–36, and Fisher, "Predigtgrundsätze," pp. 216–17.

43. "Concio in funere regina[e] Hispaniarum [Anne of Austria]," 6 September 1581, in *Acta Ecclesiae Mediolanensis* 3:825–40. For a description of the event, see Giovanni Pietro Giussano (Glussianus), *De vita et rebus gestis sancti Caroli Borromei* (Milan: Bibliotheca Ambrosiana, 1751), cols. 591–92.

44. See Orazio Premoli, "S. Carlo Borromeo e la cultura classica," La Scuola Cattolica 45 (1917): 427–40.

45. *L'âge de l'éloquence,* especially pp. 116–52.

46. See "Institutiones ad universum seminarii regimen pertinentes," in *Acta Ecclesiae Mediolanensis* 3:100.
47. See n. 10 above.
48. (Venice: Aldus, 1557).
49. (Venice: Aldus, 1562), not really a treatise on preaching.
50. (Venice: A. Trevisano, 1562).
51. Published by Carlo Marcora, "S. Carlo e il gesuita Benedetto Palmio," *Memorie Storiche della Diocesi di Milano* 16 (1969): 7–53. On this edition, see Mario Scaduto, *L'epoca di Giacomo Lainez* (Rome: Edizioni "La Civiltà Cattolica," 1964–74), 2:514–15, n. 3.
52. The most complete and systematic treatment of this phenomenon is by Antoni Cañizares Llovera, "La predicación española en el siglo XVI," in *Repertorio de Historia de las Ciencias Eclesiásticas en España (Siglos I–XVI)*, vol. 6 (Salamanca: Instituto de Historia de la Theologia Española, 1977), pp. 189–266, with bibliography. See also Melquiades Andrés, "Humanismo español y ciencias eclesiásticas (1450–1565)," ibid., pp. 111–42. Also important are José Rico Verdu, *La retórica española de los siglos XVI y XVII* (Madrid: Consejo Superior de Investigaciones Cientificas, 1973); Antonio M. Martí, "La retórica sacra en el Siglo de Oro," *Hispanic Review* 38 (1970): 264–98; Felix G. Olmeda, ed., *Fray Dionisio Vázquez, O.S.A. (1479–1539): Sermones* (Madrid: Espasa-Calpe, 1943), especially the "Prólogo."
53. On Salinas, see Martí, "Retórica sacra," pp. 280–81, and Verdu, *Retórica española*, pp. 195–99.
54. The edition I consulted was (Cologne: A. Birckmannus, 1575).
55. Bayley states that Villavicencio's work is an "adaptation" of Hyperius, *French Oratory*, p. 61. The problem is not noted by Fumaroli, *L'âge de l'éloquence*, pp. 127–28, or by David Gutiérrez, "De fratribus Laurentio de Villavicentio et Bartholomaeo de los Rios curriculum et documenta," *Analecta Augustiniana* 23 (1953–54): 102–21. The possibility that Lorenzo copied his *De studio theologico* from Hyperius is peremptorily and uncritically rejected by Segundo Folgada Flórez, "Fray Lorenzo de Villavicencio y los estudios teologicos," *La Ciudad de Dios* 177 (1964): 335–44. H. Hurter notes that Lorenzo's *De studio* is copied for the most part from Hyperius, *Nomenclator Literarius Theologiae Catholicae,* 3d ed. (Innsbruck: Libraria Academica Wagneriana, 1907), 3:61n.
56. Sempere, *Methodus oratoria, item de sacra ratione concionandi libellus* (Valencia, 1568), and Orozco, "Epistola X para un religioso predicator," in *Segunda parte de las Obras* (Alcalá, 1570). Orozco also wrote a "Methodus praedicationis" that was never published but is found in manuscript at Valladolid; see Llovera, "Predicación española," pp. 201–2. On Sempere, see Adrián Miró, *El humanista Andrés Sempere: Vida y obra* (Alcoy: La Victoria, 1968), especially pp. 95–100.
57. See his *Opera omnia* (Madrid: A Ramírez, 1769), pp. 436–37. See also my "Content and Rhetorical Forms," pp. 250–51. Also to be noted is Benito Arias Montano, *Rhetoricorum libri III* (Antwerp: C. Plantinus, 1569), written in verse, intended to some extent for preachers. See Martí, "Retórica sacra," pp. 283–85, and Verdu, *Retórica española,* pp. 80–86.
58. See Llovera, "Predicación española," pp. 203–4.
59. Granada, *Ecclesiasticae rhetoricae, sive De ratione concionandi* (Lisbon: A. Riberius, 1576); de Estella, *Modo de predicar y Modus concionandi: Estudio doctrinal y edicion critica,* ed. Pio Sagües Azcona (Madrid: Instituto M. de Cervantes, 1951), done for the most part from the first edition Salamanca, 1576. On these figures, see Llovera, "Predicación española," pp. 199–201, 204–7; Fumaroli,

L'âge de l'éloquence, pp. 143–48; E. Allison Peers, *Studies of the Spanish Mystics* (London: S.P.C.K., 1951–60), 1:25–61, 2:171–94; the pertinent articles ("Estella," "Louis de Grenade") in the *Dictionnaire de spiritualité,* with bibliography.

60. See, e.g., his comments in *Praelectiones tres ab Augustino Valerio,* ed. Giovanni Antonio Possevino (Verona, 1574), sig. B4: "Filii, hoc opus cum erit perfectum, si Cardinalis Borromei opus esse existimabitis; . . . si meum putabitis, quid illud delineaverim, ex patris vestri industria et labore aliquot fructus percipietis."

61. See especially the collection of letters edited by Lorenzo Tacchella, *San Carlo Borromeo ed il Card. Agostino Valier (carteggio)* (Verona: Istituo per gli Studi Storici Veronese, 1972). Valier also wrote a "synopsis" of the book and then, at Saint Charles's insistence, composed a homilary.

62. See *Lettera del padre Francesco Adorno . . . a monsignore Agostino Valiero,* ed. Pietro Bettio (Venice: G. Picotti, 1829), dated 4 May 1572. Valier's undated reply is also printed in this edition.

63. See Azcona's comments in his edition, *Modo de predicar* 1:259.

64. See Alvaro Huerga, "Fray Luis de Granada y San Carlos Borromeo: Una amistad al servicio de la Restauración Católica," *Hispania Sacra* 11 (1958): 299–347, especially p. 344 for the letter of 10 July 1576. See also Ramon Robres Luch, "San Carlos Borromeo y sus relaciones con el episcopado iberico posttridentino, especialmente a través de Fray Luis de Granada y san Juan de Ribera," *Anthologia Annua* 8 (1960): 83–141, and, on a more general level, Benedetto Croce, *I predicatori italiani del Seicento e il gusto spagnuolo* (Naples: Pierro e Veraldi, 1899).

65. See my "Content and Rhetorical Forms," pp. 248–49.

66. See ibid., p. 249; Tacchella, *Borromeo e Valier,* p. 104; Fumaroli, *L'âge de l'éloquence,* pp. 137–40, 143–48.

67. On this issue, see, e.g., M.-J. González-Haba, "Séneca en la espiritualidad española de los siglos XVI y XVII," *Revista de Filosofía* 11 (1952): 287–302; Julien Eymard d'Angers, "Les citations de Sénèque dans les sermons de Luis de Grenade," *Revue d'Ascetique et Mystique* 37 (1961): 31–46; Marcel Bataillon, "De Savonarole à Luis de Granada," *Revue de Litterature Comparée* 16 (1936): 23–39. For more general studies, see Michel Spanneut, *Le permanence du Stoïcisme, De Zénon à Malraux* (Gembloux: Duclot, 1973); Leontine Zanta, *La renaissance du Stoïcisme au XVI*[e] *siècle* (Paris: H. Champion, 1914); Antoine Adam, *Sur le problème religieux dans la première moitié du XVII*[e] *siècle* (Oxford: Clarendon Press, 1959); William J. Bouwsma, "The Two Faces of Humanism: Stoicism and Augustinianism in Renaissance Thought," in *Itinerarium Italicum: The Profile of the Italian Renaissance in the Mirror of its European Transformations,* ed. Heiko A. Oberman with Thomas A. Brady, Jr. (Leiden: E. J. Brill, 1975), pp. 3–60; Alphonse Dupront, "D'un 'humanisme chrétien' en Italie à la fin du XVIe siècle," *Revue Historique* 175 (1935): 296–307.

68. (Paris: G. Chaudière, 1585).

69. See the dedicatory letter to Vincentius Laurus, ibid.

70. See his letter to Paleotti on this subject, transcribed by Prodi, *Paleotti* 2:91–93.

71. *Oratione di Fr. Francesco Panigarola in morte e sopra il corpo dell'Ill.mo. Carlo Borromeo* (Venice: De Imberti, 1585), many times reprinted.

72. Girolamo Tiraboschi, *Storia della letteratura italiana,* (Milan: N. Bettoni, 1833), 4:322.

73. See Paolo-Maria Sevesi, "S. Carlo Borromeo ed il P. Francesco Panigarola,

O.F.M.," *Archivum Franciscanum Historicum* 40 (1947): 143–207. See also Bascapè, *Vita,* p. 64.

74. On Lobo (Lupus), see *Annales Minorum seu Trium Ordinum a S. Francisco Institutorum,* ed. Stanislaus Melchiorri de Cerreto, 2d ed. (Quaracchi: Collegium S. Bonaventura, 1934), vol. 23 (1591–1600), pp. 198–203. On his relationship to Saint Charles, see Federico Borromeo, *De sacris nostrorum temporum oratoribus* (Milan: n., 1632), pp. 49–69.

75. See, e.g., Tacchella, *Borromeo e Valier,* pp. 128, 130–33. Valier says of him, *Vita,* p. 29: "In concionatoribus deligendis mirum studium adhibebat."

76. *L'âge de l'éloquence,* p. 142.

77. See Prodi, *Paleotti* 2:75–136.

78. *L'âge de l'éloquence,* pp. 138, 141: ". . . s'ouvrit en Italie et en Espagne un véritable 'atelier' de rhétorique, plus prolifique qu'aucune école de sophistes antiques ou qu'aucune Académic humaniste. . . . On peut aussi être assuré que nul orateur humaniste, pas meme les Chanceliers de la République florentine, n'eut l'autorité, ni l'audience directe d'un Charles Borromée, héritier et imitateur d'Ambroise sur le siège archiépiscopal de Milan."

VII

*Erasmus and the History of Sacred Rhetoric: The Ecclesiastes of 1535**

IN late August of 1535 Johann Froben published the *editio princeps* of the *Ecclesiastes*. That treatise on preaching—*De ratione concionandi*—was Erasmus' last major work and his longest. The idea for it had been suggested to him as early as 1519 by John Becar of Borsselen, and over the course of years that intervened until 1535 the work was repeatedly and sometimes insistently requested of Erasmus by a number of friends and admirers.[1] These included John Fisher, bishop of Rochester, to whom Erasmus would have dedicated the book if Fisher had not been executed by Henry VIII earlier in the very year it was first published.

Erasmus found the task to which he had committed himself uncongenial, but he labored on it off and on through the years until he brought it to conclusion in the year before his death.[2] Although not altogether satisfied with the results, Erasmus considered the *Ecclesiastes* an important work, and so did many of his contemporaries. Of it, for instance, Wolfgang Capito, the Protestant reformer of Strasbourg, said upon its publication that he could not remember having read any book that was more fruitful for him or for his times; indeed, he found it second only to Paul in its ability to inspire and move him.[3] The book enjoyed, more-

* Presented at the Folger Shakespeare Library (Washington, D. C) on April 25, 1984.

[1] Robert Kleinhans supplies a detailed and concise history of the composition of the *Ecclesiastes* in his *Erasmus' Doctrine of Preaching: A Study of the 'Ecclesiastes, sive De Ratione Concionandi'* (Ann Arbor: University Microfilms, 1969), pp. 7–28; see also Charles Béné, *Érasme et saint Augustin* (Geneva: Droz, 1969), pp. 372–77.

[2] There are different assessments as to why Erasmus procrastinated over the project and lacked enthusiasm for it. See, e.g., Kleinhans, *Preaching*, pp. 19–20, and Jacques Chomarat, *Grammaire et rhétorique chez Érasme*, 2 vols. (Paris: "Les Belles Lettres," 1981), 2:1054–56.

[3] See Alfred Hartmann, ed., *Die Amerbachkorrespondenz*, 5 vols. (Basel: Verlag der Universitätsbibliothek, 1942), 4:375 (#1980), quoted in Kleinhans, *Preaching*, p. 25.

over, an enormously wide circulation. Within the decade after the *editio princeps* in an immense printing of 2,600 copies, it ran through nine other editions—some authorized, some pirated. It was, without doubt, one of the best sellers of the decade.[4]

For all that, the *Ecclesiastes* remains one of Erasmus' least studied works. This neglect is due in part to the long tradition that refused to see Erasmus as a religious thinker and that thereby almost erased from memory Erasmus' central intellectual occupation, the reform of theology and piety. Today, finally, after the "renaissance" in Erasmian studies over the past twenty years, scholars are ready to examine the *Ecclesiastes* and to see it with new eyes, as Professor Telle's lecture on it at the Folger Shakespeare Library for this same audience in 1981 testifies.[5] We now possess several other studies of the *Ecclesiastes*, beginning with Robert Kleinhans' lucid and careful dissertation for the Princeton Theological Seminary in 1968.[6] Charles Béné's *Érasme et saint Augustin* of the following year elucidated certain aspects of it,[7] as have the correctives to his study in the chapters dealing with *Ecclesiastes* in the recent books on Erasmus by André Godin[8] and Jacques Chomarat.[9] In 1974 James Weiss

[4] For the printing history of the *Ecclesiastes*, see Kleinhans, *Preaching*, pp. 28–34.

[5] Emile V. Telle, "'To every thing there is a season . . . ': Ways and Fashions in the Art of Preaching on the Eve of the Religious Upheavals in the Sixteenth Century," *Erasmus of Rotterdam Society Yearbook*, 2 (1982), 13–24; see also by the same author, "En marge de l'éloquence sacrée aux XVe- XVIe siècles: Érasme et Fra Roberto Caracciolo," *Bibliothèque d'Humanisme et Renaissance*, 43 (1981), 449–70.

[6] See n. 1 above. See also his "Erasmus' Ecclesiastes and the Church of England," *Historical Magazine of the Protestant Episcopal Church*, 39 (1970), 307–14, and his "*Ecclesiastes sive de Ratione Concionandi*," in *Essays on the Works of Erasmus*, ed. Richard L. DeMolen (New Haven and London: Yale University Press, 1978), 253–66.

[7] See n. 1 above. See also J. D. P. Warners, "Erasmus, Augustinus en de Retorika," *Nederlands Archief voor Kerkgeschiedenis*, New Series 51 (1971), 125–48.

[8] *Érasme: Lecteur d'Origène* (Geneva: Librarie Droz, 1982). See also his "De Vitrier à Origène: Recherches sur la patristique érasmienne," in *Colloquium Erasmianum* (Mons: Centre Universitaire de l'État, 1968), pp. 47–57; "Érasme et le modèle origénien de la prédication," in *Colloquia Erasmiana Turonenesia*, ed. J.-C. Margolin, 2 vols. (Toronto: University of Toronto Press, 1972), 2:807–20; "Jean Vitrier et le 'cenacle' de Saint-Omer," *ibid.*, 781–805; *L'Homéliaire de Jean Vitrier, Texte, étude thématique et sémantique: Spiritualité franciscaine en Flandre au XVIe siècle* (Geneva: Librairie Droz, 1971), especially pp. 14–18; "The *Enchiridion Militis Christiani*: The Modes of an Origenian Appropriation," *Erasmus of Rotterdam Society Yearbook*, 2 (1982), 47–79.

[9] See n. 2 above.

published a perceptive article on the *Ecclesiastes*[10] and in a dissertation at Yale University on John Fisher, 1967, Thomas Lawler utilized it extensively.[11] It has occasionally been discussed in passing by other scholars, like John Chamberlin in his book on the preaching of John Donne, entitled *Increase and Multiply*.[12]

Much, however, remains to be done. Besides a critical edition, now underway for the Amsterdam series, and a closer examination of the content, we need to set the work in the larger history of sacred rhetoric and treatises on preaching. That is the task I have set myself for the lecture this evening. The only other scholar who can be considered to have attempted this task in any comprehensive way for the Renaissance is Marc Fumaroli in his recent and marvellously erudite *L'âge de l'éloquence*.[13] But even Fumaroli, in a volume that runs to almost nine-hundred pages, devotes only three specifically to the *Ecclesiastes*, and, invaluable though his book is for the history of rhetoric in the Renaissance, he approaches the *Ecclesiastes* with somewhat different concerns than I do.

The history of rhetoric in the post-classical period is, in fact, a relatively new discipline, and within it the history of sacred rhetoric is even newer.[14] This is a second reason for the neglect the *Ecclesiastes* has suffered. It is my contention that this latter history, especially, throws light on questions of much wider significance than its specialized focus would seem to suggest. The history of sacred rhetoric provides a new entrance into some of the basic issues that agitated the sixteenth century, for instance, and thereby causes us to reconsider how they were operative

[10] "*Ecclesiastes* and Erasmus: The Mirror and the Image," *Archive for Reformation History*, 65 (1974), 83–108.

[11] *The English Works of St. John Fisher: A Study of Homiletic and Devotional Method in the Age of Erasmus* (Ann Arbor: University Microfilms, 1968).

[12] *Increase and Multiply: Arts-of-Discourse Procedure in the Preaching of Donne* (Chapel Hill: The University of North Carolina Press, 1976), pp. 72–74.

[13] *L'âge de l'éloquence: Rhétorique et "res literaria" de la Renaissance au seuil de l'époque classique* (Geneva: Librairie Droz, 1980), pp. 106–9.

[14] See George A. Kennedy, *Classical Rhetoric and Its Christian and Secular Tradition from Ancient to Modern Times* (Chapel Hill: The University of North Carolina Press, 1980), and by the same author, *Greek Rhetoric under Christian Emperors* (Princeton: Princeton University Press, 1983). See also the comments by James J. Murphy, "One Thousand Neglected Authors: The Scope and Importance of Renaissance Eloquence," in *Renaissance Eloquence*, ed. James J. Murphy (Berkeley and Los Angeles: University of California Press, 1983), pp. 20–36. The new journal *Rhetorica* (1983–) now carries articles pertinent to this issue.

in its various religious cultures. Form, moreover, influences content. Those are the presuppositions on which my own studies rest. This evening, more specifically, I want to sketch for you some of the achievements and limitations of the *Ecclesiastes*, as seen against the broad canvas of the history of sacred rhetoric until about the middle of the sixteenth century.

The history of sacred rhetoric can be distinguished into two separate but intimately related parts: treatises on how to preach and the actual exercise of the art of preaching. I will briefly review both of these for you up until the publication of the *Ecclesiastes*. First, the treatises.

For all the concern of the Fathers of the Church with preaching, only one work of the whole patristic era received recognition from subsequent generations in the West as dealing explicitly with that subject, the *De doctrina christiana* of Saint Augustine. John Chrysostom's *On the Priesthood* and Gregory the Great's *Pastoral Care* also qualify to a degree as such treatises, but they do not seem to have been generally employed as such in later authors, and hence we can exclude them on this occasion from our consideration.

Augustine's treatise was basically a work on invention—how to discover what to preach—and, therefore, was perhaps more important for scriptural exegesis than for direct application to the art of preaching. In the fourth book, however, Augustine justifies the use of certain principles of classical rhetoric for the Christian preacher, while he at the same time vindicates a distinctively Christian rhetoric based on the text of Scripture. The full history of this book in the early Middle Ages has yet to be written. We know that it influenced persons like Cassiodorus, Rabanus Maurus, Hugh of St. Victor, and Peter Lombard—not, however, precisely as a work on preaching.[15] This aspect of the history of sacred rhetoric remains closed for us at the moment, therefore, so that that history until the twelfth century is almost a non-history.

The situation changed dramatically in the twelfth and particularly in the thirteenth centuries, beginning with Guibert of Nogent's *Liber quo*

[15] See the "Introduction," with bibliography, by D. W. Robertson, Jr., in his translation, *On Christian Doctrine* (Indianapolis and New York: The Bobbs-Merrill Company, 1958), pp. ix-xxii, as well as the pertinent pages in Peter Brown, *Augustine of Hippo: A Biography* (Berkeley and Los Angeles: University of California Press, 1969), pp. 259–69, and the masterful work by Henri-Irénée Marrou, *Saint Augustin et la fin de la culture antique*, 4th ed., rev. (Paris: Editions E. de Boccard, 1958).

ordine sermo fieri debet at the beginning of the twelfth century[16] and Alan of Lille's *Summa de arte praedicatoria* at the end.[17] Neither of these works deal at any length with precisely how to construct sermons or evince any direct influence of either the *De doctrina christiana* or classical rhetoric. Guibert treats principally of exegesis, the importance of preaching, and the spiritual condition of preacher and audience, whereas Alan provides a list of topics that the preacher might profitably employ. Both authors are notably moralistic in their approaches. Alan is especially important for his title, for it stood at the headwaters of an immense stream of works for the next three centuries by scholastic authors that bore equivalently the same title. Alan also provided a definition of preaching as "an open and public instruction in faith and morals."[18] That definition was adopted, modified, and commented upon during the next three centuries in many of the *artes praedicandi* that issued from the pens of scholastic authors.

We tend to forget how central preaching was to the scholastic enterprise.[19] It was the third of the three tasks the scholastics considered peculiarly their own: *legere, disputare, praedicare*—to lecture, to engage in disputation, to preach. By 1936 T.-M. Charland had discovered about one hundred and fifty *artes* written during the scholastic period,[20] and

[16] *PL* 156:21–32. Most of this work has been translated into English in *Early Medieval Theology*, ed. and trans. George E. McCracken with Allen Cabaniss, The Library of Christian Classics, No. 9 (Philadelphia: The Westminster Press, 1957), pp. 285–99.

[17] *PL* 210:111–98, now translated into English by Gillian R. Evans, *The Art of Preaching* (Kalamazoo: Cistercian Publications, 1981).

[18] *PL* 210:111: "Praedicatio est manifesta et publica instructio morum et fidei."

[19] See, especially, Richard H. and Mary A. Rouse, *Preachers, Florilegia and Sermons: Studies on the Manipulus florum of Thomas of Ireland* (Toronto: Pontifical Institute of Mediaeval Studies, 1979). See also, e.g., Jean Longère, *La prédication médiévale* (Paris: Études augustiniennes, 1983); *idem*, *Oeuvres oratoires de maîtres parisiens au XIIe siècle: Étude historique et doctrinale*, 2 vols. (Paris: Études augustiniennes, 1975); Jean-Pierre Torrell, "Frère Thomas d'Aquin prédicateur," *Freiburger Zeitschrift für Philosophie und Theologie*, 29 (1982), 175–88; Robert E. Lerner, "A Collection of Sermons Given in Paris c. 1267, Including a New Text by Saint Bonaventure on the Life of Saint Francis," *Speculum*, 49 (1974), 466–98; and the two recent surveys: Roberto Rusconi, "Predicatori e predicazione (secoli IX-XVIII)," in *Storia d'Italia: Annali* (Turin: Einaudi, 1981), 4:951–1035, and Carlo Delcorno, "Rassegna di studi sulla predicazione medievale e umanistica (1970–80)," *Lettere italiane*, 33 (1981), 235–76.

[20] Th.-M. Charland, *Artes praedicandi: Contribution à l'histoire de la rhétorique au moyen âge* (Paris: J. Vrin, 1936).

others, especially Harry Caplan, have added to his list.[21] This fact alone substantiates the seriousness with which the scholastics took their commitment to preaching. With the *artes*, in fact, this aspect of the history of sacred rhetoric, i.e., treatises on how to preach, really begins.

The so-called thematic sermon, which is the principal burden of the *artes*, has been severely criticized by scholars for its rigid structure, its distance from the text of Scripture, its highly intellectualized approach to Christian doctrine, and its inappropriateness for ordinary audiences. These criticisms, justified as they are at least in some cases, should not blind us to the many virtues of the *artes*. After all, for the first time they directed attention in an organized and reflective way onto the central task of the Christian religion, the presentation of its message in the public forum. Moreover, they were in their design eminently practical manuals or "how-to" books. If one wanted to preach in the scholastic manner, the *artes* provided clear, pithy, and comprehensive directives on how to do so—directives absent from the corresponding works by Augustine, Guibert, and Alan. Finally, trapped as the authors were in the presuppositions of the scholastic system, some of them showed considerable reverence for the patristic and monastic homily and even a nostalgia for it.[22]

The first breaks with the tradition of the *artes* occurred in the late fifteenth and early sixteenth centuries.[23] In 1479/80 and again in 1480, the Italian Franciscan Lorenzo Guglielmo Traversagni published in England his *Margarita eloquentiae castigatae* (also known as the *In novam rhetoricam*), and he later published an *Epitome* of it.[24] The *Margarita* dealt with

[21] See especially Harry Caplan, *Mediaeval Artes Praedicandi: A Hand-List* (Ithaca: Cornell University Press, 1934), and *Mediaeval Artes Praedicandi: A Supplementary Hand-List* (Ithaca: Cornell University Press, 1936), as well as the other studies listed in his *Of Eloquence*, ed. Anne King and Helen North (Ithaca: Cornell University Press, 1970), pp. 271–72.

[22] See, e.g., Johann Ulrich Surgant, *Manuale curatorum praedicandi* (Basel: M. Furter, 1503), fol. XIII; Thomas Waley, *De modo componendi sermones* (ca. 1340), in Charland, *Artes*, p. 344; Robert of Basevorn, *Forma praedicandi* (1322), *ibid.*, p. 247.

[23] I review this phenomenon in my "Content and Rhetorical Forms in Sixteenth-Century Treatises on Preaching," in *Renaissance Eloquence*, pp. 238–52.

[24] See the critical edition by Giovanni Farris (Savona: Sabatelli, 1978). Farris has also edited Traversagni's *De varia fortuna Antiochi* (Savona: Sabatelli, 1972), and published two studies that deal with him: *Umanesimo e religione in Lorenzo Guglielmo Traversagni (1425–1505)* (Milan: Marzorati, 1972), and "Scuola e Umanesimo a Savona nel sec. XV," *Atti e Memorie della Società Savonese di Storia Patria*, 10 (1976), 7–53. See also José Ruysschaert, "Lorenzo Guglielmo Traversagni de Savone (1425–1503 [sic]), un humaniste

preaching and was more obviously influenced by classical treatises on oratory, especially the *Ad Herennium*, than any work on that subject that had preceded it. Traversagni also wrote and delivered some orations that conformed to the new style of oratory then being developed in Renaissance Italy. His labors had the potential for redirecting the course of the history of sacred rhetoric, but they seem to have been singularly ignored by his contemporaries.

Johann Reuchlin, the noted German Hebraist, published his *Liber congestorum de arte praedicandi*, in 1504.[25] Despite the title (*de arte praedicandi*), this book also broke with the tradition of the *artes* in that it more explicitly introduced certain aspects of classical rhetoric and, by omission, rejected the dialectical basis and the highly systematized structure of those manuals. But the *Liber congestorum* was small, flaccid in its organization, and lacking in practical directives. It had only two printings before 1540, and, like Traversagni's works, did not have much immediate impact on contemporaries. It is important more as a symptom of things to come than as in itself a positive contribution. Meanwhile, the *artes* continued to be written and published; the last new work of this genre that I have been able to identify is by Pedro Ciruelo, published at Alcalá in 1528 by Miguel de Eguía, the same publisher who two years earlier had published a Castilian version of Erasmus' *Enchiridion militis christiani*.[26] It consists of only six folios.

In 1519 Philipp Melanchthon, Reuchlin's grand-nephew and Luther's

franciscain oublié," *Archivum Franciscanum Historicum*, 46 (1953), 195–210; *idem*, "Les manuscrits autographes de deux oeuvres de Lorenzo Guglielmo Traversagni imprimées chez Caxton," *Bulletin of the John Rylands Library*, 36 (1953), 191–96; James J. Murphy, "Caxton's Two Choices: 'Modern' and 'Medieval' Rhetoric in Traversagni's *Nova Rhetorica* and the Anonymous *Court of Sapience*," in *Medievalia et Humanistica*, New Series 3 (Cleveland: Case Western Reserve Press, 1972), 241–55; Ronald H. Martin, "The 'Epitome Margaritae Eloquentiae' of Laurentius Gulielmus de Saona," *Proceedings of the Leeds Philosophical and Literary Society (Literary and Historical Section)*, 14 (1970–72), 99–187; Anscar Zawart, *The History of Franciscan Preaching and of Franciscan Preachers*, Franciscan Studies, No. 7 (New York: Joseph F. Wagner, 1927), p. 373; my "Form, Content, and Influence of Works about Preaching before Trent: The Franciscan Contribution," to be published in the *Acta* of the twelfth Convegno di Studi (October, 1984), Società internazionale di studi francescani, Assisi.

[25] (Pforzheim: Anshelm, 1504). There was a second printing in 1508.

[26] "De arte praedicandi," in *Expositio libri missalis peregregia* (Alcalá: M. de Eguía, 1528), fols. 270–76.

best known disciple, published the first edition of his *Rhetoric*.[27] In its organization, scope, and clarity it surpassed any other work on the subject that the Renaissance had produced up to that time. It was a popular book, and in its two editions ran through about ten printings before 1535. Although the aim of the book was broader, it included considerations immediately and explicitly pertinent to preaching, and Melanchthon obviously intended it to be of help for the pulpit. It was not, however, a treatise on preaching as such.

Ten years after the first edition of the *Rhetoric*, Melanchthon composed his *De officiis concionatoris*, published in two undated editions before the first dated one, 1535.[28] At almost the same time Veit Dietrich, a Lutheran colleague, wrote his *Ratio brevis et docta piaque sacrarum concionum tractandarum*, which likewise had two undated editions before the first dated one in 1535.[29] Both these works implicitly rejected the thematic sermon and bear little resemblance to the *artes*. However, they seem until at least 1535 to have attracted little attention outside rather restricted Lutheran circles. In any case, they are sketchy, partisan, and extremely brief works of pamphlet size that did not have an immediate or broad influence.

Meanwhile, in 1529, the German Franciscan Nicolaus Herborn (or Ferber) published his *Methodus praedicandi verbi divini*. This work of some sixty pages was a humanist manifesto on preaching, a call *ad fontes*—especially a call to the Bible, but also to the Fathers. It was demonstrably influenced by some of Erasmus' writings. Significant though this work is as a sign of transition from scholastic to humanistic appreciation of the art of preaching, it contains scarcely any advice on how to construct a

[27] *De rhetorica libri tres* (Wittenberg: J. Grunenberg, 1519). The second edition, *Elementorum rhetorices libri II* (Wittenberg: G. Rhaw, 1531), is reprinted in *Corpus Reformatorum* (Halle: C. A. Schwetsche, 1846), 13:417–506. Melanchthon's *Institutiones rhetoricae* (Hagenau: Thomas Anshelmus Badensis, 1521) seems to have been class-notes transcribed by a student; see *CR*, 13:413–14. On Melanchthon and preaching, see Karl Hartfelder, *Philipp Melanchthon als Praeceptor Germaniae* (Berlin: Weidmannsche Buchhandlung, 1889); Wilhelm Maurer, *Der junge Melanchthon zwischen Humanismus und Reformation*, 2 vols. (Göttingen: Vanderhoeck and Ruprecht, 1969); Uwe Schnell, *Die homiletische Theorie Philipp Melanchthons* (Berlin and Hamburg: Lutherisches Verlaghaus, 1968); and the pertinent articles by Quirinus Breen in his *Christianity and Humanism: Studies in the History of Ideas*, ed. Nelson Peter Ross (Grand Rapids: Wm. Eerdmans Publishing Company, 1968).

[28] The text of this and three other short treatises on preaching, along with a discussion of their genesis, authorship, and publication history, is found in *Supplementa Melanchthoniana*, ed. Paul Drews and Ferdinand Cohrs, vol. 5, pt. 2 (Leipzig: M. Heinsius, 1929).

[29] See *Supplementa Melanchthoniana*, 5, 2:xxxi–xxxvi.

sermon or do exegesis, and had only one, presumably small, printing.[30] The other works on preaching published for the first time in the sixteenth century until 1535—besides those already mentioned, I have located only four—are scholastic in inspiration.[31]

[30] *Methodus praedicandi verbi divini concionatoribus cum utilis tum accomoda [sic]* (Cologne: P. Quentel, 1529), found only in the second edition (1529) of Herborn's *Locorum communium . . . Enchiridion*. Patricius Schlager has edited the *Enchiridion*, Corpus Catholicorum, No. 12 (Münster i/W.: Aschendorff, 1927), and Ludwig Schmitt has edited his *Confutatio Lutheranismi Danici* (Quaracchi: Collegium S. Bonaventurae, 1902). The most comprehensive study of Herborn is still Schmitt's *Der kölner Theologe Nikolaus Stagefur und der Franziskaner Nikolaus Herborn*, Ergänzungshefte zu "Stimmen aus Maria-Laach," No. 67 (Freiburg i/Br.: Herder, 1896). On the *Methodus*, see Schmitt, pp. 139–57; my "Form, Content" (Assisi); Karl Köhler, "Nikolaus Ferbers Methodus praedicandi verbi divini von 1529," *Zeitschrift für praktische Theologie*, 14 (1892), 305–38; Pirmin Hasenöhrl, "Franziskanische Homiletiker," *Kirche und Kanzel*, 6 (1923), 123–29, esp. 127–29. On Herborn, see also *Neue Deutsche Biographie*, 5 (1961), 80–81 (under "Ferber"); Edmund Kurter, *Franz Lambert von Avignon und Nikolaus Herborn in ihrer Stellung zum Ordensgedanken und zum Franziskanertum im besonderen* (Münster i/W.: Aschendorff, 1950); Enrique Oltra, "Escritura y Tradición en la teología pretridentina," *Salmanticensis*, 10 (1963), 65–133, esp. 88–89; Johannes Beckman, "Die erste katholische Missionslehre der Neuzeit in einem Basler Druck von 1555," *Zeitschrift für schweizerische Kirchengeschichte*, 57 (1963), 55–63; J. Nybo Rasmussen, "Herborn og Stagefyr," *Kirkehistoriske Samlinger*, series 7, 6 (1966), 44–60; Johannes Beumer, "Erasmus und seine Freunde aus dem Franziskanerorden," *Franziskanische Studien*, 51 (1969), 117–29. I have not been able to consult: Odulphus van der Vat, *Collectanea franciscana neerlandica*, 2 vols. ('s-Hertogenbosch, ca. 1931), 2:395–425; A. Goetz, "Nikolaus von Herborn. Anleitung zur Heidenbekehrung," in *Heilige, Märtyrer und Helden* (Aschaffenburg, 1957), pp. 135–41.

[31] These works are, in chronological order:

1. Surgant, *Manuale curatorum* (see note 22 above), consisting of 127 small folios. On Surgant's work, see Dorothea Roth, *Die mittelalterliche Predigttheorie und das Manuale curatorum des J. U. Surgant* (Basel: Helbing and Lichtenhahn, 1956), and Fritz Schmidt-Clausing, "Johann Ulrich Surgant, ein Wegweiser des jungen Zwingli," *Zwingliana*, 11 (1961), 287–320.

2. *Modus praedicandi et extendendi diversas materias per colores rhetoricales*, attributed to Michael de Hungaria (O. Min. Observ.) and contained in a collection of works for preachers entitled *Evagatorium*, ed. Jacobus Gaudensis (Cologne, 1505). The *Modus* is a relatively short work, several times reprinted. See Hasenöhrl, "Homiletiker," pp. 126–27.

3. Hieronymus Dungersheim, *Tractatus de modo discendi et docendi ad populum sacra, seu de modo praedicandi* (Landshut: J. Weyssenburger, 1514), consisting of about twenty folios and sometimes employing a classicizing style, much influenced by the *De doctrina christiana*.

4. Bartholomaeus Arnoldi de Usingen, O.S.A., "De recta et munda praedicatione evangelii," in *Libellus de falsis prophetis* (Erfurt: unknown, 1525). The three folios on preaching are simply a scholastic demonstration that only those "in the Church" (therefore, not the Lutheran "faction") are true preachers. The work is not, therefore, an instruction

We have arrived at 1535, the date of the *editio princeps* of the *Ecclesiastes*. We must now backtrack and quickly review that other component in the history of sacred rhetoric, the actual exercise of the art of preaching. The first phase is complex, but some features are clear. At least from the time of Origen, the homily or some more structured variation of it tended to dominate preaching. No matter what relationship that "formless form" had to preaching in the Jewish synagogue at the time of Jesus, and to the Stoic-Cynic diatribe, Origen shaped it as well according to the exegetical practice of the *grammaticus* of the classical tradition.[32] The homily, in the

on preaching in the conventional sense. I have not been able to find a verification for the Würtzburg, 1526, edition mentioned by Harry Caplan and Henry H. King, "Latin Tractates on Preaching: a Book-List," *Harvard Theological Review*, 42 (1949), 195. On Arnoldi, see Primož Simoniti's edition of his *Responsio contra Apologiam Philippi Melanchthonis* (Würzburg: Augustinus-Verlag, 1978), with bibliography.

[32] See especially Pierre Nautin, "Origène prédicateur," in the edition of Origen's *Homélies sur Jérémie*, ed. Pierre Husson and Pierre Nautin, Sources chrétiennes, No. 232 (Paris: Cerf, 1976), pp. 136–51; Marrou, *Saint Augustin*, and his *A History of Education in Antiquity*, trans. George Lamb (New York: Sheed and Ward, 1956). See also James I. H. McDonald, *Kerygma and Didache: The Articulation and Structure of the Earliest Christian Message* (Cambridge: Cambridge University Press, 1980); James J. Murphy, *Rhetoric in the Middle Ages: A History of Rhetorical Theory from Saint Augustine to the Renaissance* (Berkeley and Los Angeles: University of California Press, 1974), pp. 55–56, 298–300; Christine Mohrmann, "Saint Augustine and the 'Eloquentia'," in her *Études sur le latin des chrétiens*, 4 vols. (Rome: Edizioni di Storia e Letteratura, 1958–77), 1:351–70; her "Saint Augustin prédicateur," *ibid.*, 391–402; her "Praedicare—Tractare—Sermo: Essai sur la terminologie de la prédication paléochrétienne," *ibid.*, 2:63–72; Ph. Rouillard, "Homélie," in *Catholicisme*, 5 (1963), 829–31; Jean Leclercq, "Prédication et rhétorique au temps de saint Augustin," *Revue Benedictine*, 57 (1947), 117–31; Robert Dick Sider, *Ancient Rhetoric and the Art of Tertullian* (Oxford: Oxford University Press, 1971); R. P. C. Hanson, *Allegory and Event: A Study of the Sources and Significance of Origen's Interpretation of Scripture* (Richmond: John Knox Press, 1959). See also, on patristic preaching in general, Robert Dick Sider, *The Gospel and Its Proclamation* (Wilmington: Michael Glazier, 1983), and esp. Thomas K. Carroll, *Preaching the Word* (Wilmington: Michael Glazier, 1984). On early medieval and monastic preaching, see Pierre Riché, *Education and Culture in the Barbarian West, From the Sixth through the Eighth Century*, trans. John J. Contreni (Columbia: University of South Carolina Press, 1976), pp. 79–95, and Jean Leclercq, *The Love of Learning and the Desire for God*, trans. Catherine Misrahi (New York: The New American Library, 1961), especially pp. 168–79. On the continuation of the grammatical tradition in the Renaissance, see R. G. G. Mercer, *The Teaching of Gasparino Barzizza: With Special Reference to His Place in Paduan Humanism* (London: The Modern Humanities Research Association, 1979), especially pp. 47, 71; J. Reginald O'Donnell, "Coluccio Salutati on the Poet-Teacher," *Mediaeval Studies*, 22 (1960), 240–56; and Ronald Witt, "Medieval 'Ars Dictaminis' and the Beginnings of Humanism: A New Construction of the Problem," *Renaissance Quarterly*, 35 (1982), 1–35.

strict sense, was a loose exposition of the text of scripture, and often commented on that text verse-by-verse. A more topical approach emerged later in many preachers, but the biblical text, to which both literal and allegorical exegesis was applied, remained by and large the grounding of the discourse. In the West Augustine became the model for succeeding generations, and Leo the Great the exception. The technique was as much that of a schoolmaster teaching his text in the classroom as that of an orator addressing an assembly of citizens, for the homily was basically an *explication de texte*. Literary rather than dialectical in its method, affective rather than cerebral in its vocabulary, these patristic and later monastic forms reflected their poetic origins in the *grammaticus*.

By the early thirteenth century, these forms began to be challenged by the thematic sermon of the scholastics, with its highly developed structure of theme, pro-theme, prayer for divine aid, repetition of theme, division, and (usually) three clearly delimited and often unrelated parts. The thematic sermon was animated not by the technique of the grammarian in the classroom, but by the technique of the dialectician in debate.

Just how frequently the rigid formula of the *artes* was actually reduced to practice is still a matter of dispute, but most sermons as we have them in published form from the late Middle Ages at least show its influence. In any case, a distinctively new way of preaching was now taught and inculcated by the *artes*, and the written evidence might at first lead the unsuspecting to believe that that way utterly dominated the scene. We have considerable evidence, on the other hand, that the homily, sometimes admixed with thematic elements, continued to be practiced in certain circles and regions,[33] and that other sermons followed the thematic model with considerable liberty. This situation continued into the first few decades of the sixteenth century, especially outside Italy.

At the turn of the previous century, however, a new development had begun in and around Padua. Pier Paolo Vergerio the Elder seems to be the person most responsible for it, as evidenced by his funeral oration in 1393 for Francesco da Carrara il Vecchio and his series of panegyrics in honor of Saint Jerome.[34] Vergerio applied to these orations the principles of epideictic or demonstrative oratory, and followed the prescriptions es-

[33] See, e.g., the observations by Waley, *De modo*, in Charland, *Artes*, p. 344.

[34] See John M. McManamon, "Innovation in Early Humanistic Rhetoric: The Oratory of Pier Paolo Vergerio the Elder," *Rinascimento*, 22 (1982), 3–32.

pecially of the *Ad Herennium* in constructing them. Although not without some precedent in the patristic period, these discourses break new ground in the history of rhetoric and reject in practice both the homiletic and thematic patterns that until then prevailed.

In the course of the century, the principles of demonstrative oratory began to be applied in Italy to the central mysteries of the Christian faith, and the sacred *oratio*—as distinguished from the patristic and monastic *homilia* and the scholastic *sermo*—emerged.[35] These orations lack all the features that made the thematic sermon odious to so many, and, in contrast with the often rambling homily, they hang together as literary units. They are real speeches—"holy speeches," but speeches nonetheless, with exordia, perorations, and all the other characteristics that good rhetoric prescribed. They celebrate and praise God's gifts, goodness, and great interventions on behalf of humankind.

Both Melanchthon and Erasmus were somewhat aware of these developments in Italy. They entertained doubts about whether or to what extent demonstrative, that is, "display," oratory was the appropriate Christian adaptation of classical rhetoric to the pulpit, although both believed that there were forms of classical rhetoric that could and should be employed for the reform of preaching.[36] The only treatises that suggest the changes that were taking place were Traversagni's *Margarita* and Herborn's *Methodus*, and there is at present no evidence that either Melanchthon or Erasmus saw or utilized them.

This was, in brief, the situation that prevailed when the *Ecclesiastes* appeared in 1535. Only in such a context does its revolutionary character manifest itself. The *Ecclesiastes* bears a relationship of course to the *De doctrina christiana* and is in many ways dependent upon it,[37] but its differences from that work are more impressive than its similarities. It bears a relationship to the *artes*, for like them it purports to address all the elements required for successful preaching. But the *Ecclesiastes* is in fact an

[35] See my *Praise and Blame in Renaissance Rome: Rhetoric, Doctrine, and Reform in the Sacred Orators of the Papal Court, ca. 1450–1521* (Durham: Duke University Press, 1979).

[36] See Melanchthon, *De officiis concionatoris*, in *Supplementa Melanchthoniana*, 5, 2:6; Erasmus, *Ciceronianus*, *ASD* 1, 2:637–39, 696–97; *Ecclesiastes*, *LB* 5:769–70; *De vidua christiana*, *LB* 5:755. See also Luther's assessment, "An Appeal to the Ruling Class," in *Martin Luther: Selections from His Writings*, ed. John Dillenberger (New York: Doubleday, 1961), p. 419: " . . . [in Italy] no longer are services held or sermons preached," and p. 434: "At Rome preaching and prayer are simply despised."

[37] See the tables in Béné, *Érasme*, pp. 443–48.

anti-*artes* work. Unlike the treatises on preaching by Reuchlin, Melanchthon, and Dietrich, the *Ecclesiastes* had broad circulation and immediate impact; it was incomparably longer and more complete than any of these. It was, furthermore, altogether differently inspired.

In my opinion, the *Ecclesiastes* was the great watershed in the history of sacred rhetoric. First, the *Ecclesiastes*, more than any other single factor, seems to have destroyed, almost at a blow, the powerful and long-standing tradition of the *artes*. As far as I am aware, no new treatise advocating the thematic sermon in its strict form appeared after 1535. Of course, the thematic sermon had been under attack for some time, and other forces were at work that help explain its unlamented demise, especially the early rejection of it by Protestants. True, some elements of the thematic sermons would persist in preaching for centuries. But as a distinct form the thematic sermon ceased to be advocated, even in circles where we might assume it would still be esteemed. For instance, in the *Constitutions* of the Society of Jesus, completed by Ignatius Loyola in the early 1550's, Thomas Aquinas is commended as the principal theologian for the new order. But that document explicitly discouraged members of the order from preaching "in the scholastic manner."[38] Catholics as well as Protestants agreed, therefore, upon the obliteration of the thematic sermon. This almost overnight disappearance of a literary form that held sway for three centuries of religious culture must be an almost unique phenomenon in the history of western civilization.

Secondly, the *Ecclesiastes* was a strikingly original work. Nothing like it had ever been attempted before. Erasmus was the first person to utilize in such a work the whole history of Christian preaching, and to do so with incomparable mastery. He commanded the classical and patristic traditions to a degree that awes us even today. He was a master of the Bible, particularly the New Testament. Although he is not often recognized for it, he also had considerable, even if antipathetic, knowledge of the scholastics, whom he treats with intelligence and unaccustomed

[38] Saint Ignatius Loyola, *The Constitutions of the Society of Jesus*, trans. George E. Ganss (St. Louis: The Institute of Jesuit Sources, 1970), p. 201 (pt. 4, chap. 8 [402]): "In contionibus etiam et sacris lectionibus, eo modo proponendis qui aedificationi populi conveniat, (qui a scholastico diversus est) se etiam exerceant." See my "Preaching" in the forthcoming Encyclopedia of Jesuit History to be published by the Institum Historicum Societatis Jesu, Rome. Erasmus himself comments on how little the thematic sermon in its late-medieval form as practiced by Roberto Caracciolo da Lecce and others was employed in his day, *Ecclesiastes*, *LB* 5:857.

gentleness in the *Ecclesiastes*; but even there he cannot always resist the temptation to ridicule them.[39] He was extraordinarily well informed about his own age, and he had traveled widely throughout Europe. Even granted that his comments about his contemporaries were sometime colored by his prejudices, he was a keen observer of preaching wherever he went. He came to oppose the exaggerations of "Ciceronianism" that he found in both the sacred and profane eloquence of many of those contemporaries. All this vast erudition and subtle judgment came to bear upon the *Ecclesiastes* to make it one of the best informed and most profoundly learned treatises on the subject ever produced, without any doubt far surpassing anything that had preceded it or that would be published for decades to come.

One of the most notable features of the *Ecclesiastes* was the first book on the moral and intellectual qualities required in the preacher. The subject was sometimes dealt with at length in scholastic treatises, especially in the popular *De eruditione praedicatorum* by Humbert of the Romans written in the middle of the thirteenth century and first printed at Hagenau in 1508. But Erasmus gives the subject his own treatment, which reflects his theology and spirituality. That long first book is not a mere prologue to the other three books that treat the preaching enterprise with more technical detail, but is integral to Erasmus' view of what was required to make preaching genuinely successful. Fumaroli's summary of the first book is apposite: "The essence of Christian eloquence consists in the piety that renders the heart docile to the imitation of Jesus Christ."[40]

Moreover, the very title of the treatise indicates a change in perspective even from the Italian adaptation in the Quattrocento of classical rhetoric to sacred subjects. In Italy such sermons were invariably described as *orationes* and located in the *genus demonstrativum*, the genre of ceremonial oratory, the art of praise and blame. But when Erasmus entitled his work *De ratione concionandi* (*contionandi*, more properly) and consistently referred to sermons as *conciones* (*contiones*), he placed the sermon in the genre of deliberative oratory, a shift that would tend to imbue preaching with a more decidedly didactic and moralizing quality than obtained in the *genus demonstrativum*. The *concio* was a specific type of deliberative oratory in which a leader addressed not sophisticated statesmen gathered

[39] See note 5 above.

[40] *L'âge de l'éloquence*, p. 107: "L'essence de l'éloquence chrétienne est dans la piété qui rend le coeur docile a l'imitation de Jésus-Christ."

in the Senate, but a popular and perhaps unruly audience of ordinary people.

One of the first instances in the Renaissance that I have noted of the application of the word *concio* to a Christian sermon is in Erasmus' *Concio de puero Jesu*, now dated 1503 by James Tracy.[41] Thereafter he consistently employed *concio* to designate a sermon. The word was certainly mediated to him and to his contemporaries from the *Elegantiae* of Lorenzo Valla,[42] but Erasmus would find easy confirmation of his usage in Quintilian, on whom he drew heavily for the *Ecclesiastes*. Until Erasmus the word was used rarely by Christian writers, and even more rarely when referring to preaching.

The most important Christian text utilizing the term was Jerome's opening remarks in his commentary on the book of *Ecclesiastes*. He equates the three words *Coeleth* (Hebrew), *Ecclesiastes* (Greek), and *Concionator* (Latin).[43] These lines from Jerome were quoted and paraphrased

[41] Tracy corrects Allen's dating of the piece in 1511. See his "On the Composition Dates of Seven of Erasmus' Writings," *Bibliothèque d'Humanisme et Renaissance*, 31 (1969), 355–64, especially pp. 361–62. An even earlier (1480) example in the Renaissance is in Traversagni's *Margarita*, p. 162: " . . . sive fuerit ad magnates, sive in contione, sive scholastica coram clero et doctoribus, sive quotidianus sermo ad populum." See also the letter of Alexius Celadonius, 1506, to Giles of Viterbo, BN Naples, cod V.F. 20, fols, 171^{v}–177; Professor Nelson Minnich of The Catholic University of America kindly called my attention to this text.

[42] *Elegantiae*, 4, 47, in *Opera Omnia* (Basel, 1540; rpt. Turin: Bottega d'Erasmo, 1962), 1:139: "Concio est populi multitudo congregata vel ex magistratus jussu, vel ex publici sacerdotis, vel interdum sua auctoritate et sponte propria ad audiendum oratorem concionantem in bonum publicum, cuius etiam oratio vocatur concio. In priore significato est Graece εκκλησία, quam nos pro Latina voce habemus. Multique nescio quo jure aedes sacras appellant, quum coetum hominum, ut dixi, significat, non loca." Erasmus, in his *Epitome* of the *Elegantiae*, first published in a pirated edition in 1529, states: "*Concio*, primo est congregatio multitudinis ad audiendum concionantem oratorem, Graeci *concionem*, id est, conventum populi εκκλησίαν vocant. Secundo est oratio habita ad populum. *Ubi fuisti? In concione*," *LB* 1:1081. The opening words of the *Ecclesiastes* are, *LB* 5:769: "Ecclesia Graecis est, quae Latinis *concio*, hoc est, populus evocatus ad audiendum de Reipublicae negotiis. Nam qui multitudinem ad nugas convocant, αγύρται *circulatores* et *circumforanei* vocantur; qui adversus Rempublicam, seditiosi nominantur. Εκκλησιάζειν est *apud concionem verba facere*; εκκλησαστής *qui publicitus orat apud multitudinem*; quod munus apud Ethnicos etiam semper et arduum in primis, et honorificum est habitum." See also *ibid.*, 940.

[43] *PL* 23:1011; *Corpus Christianorum, Series Latina*, 72:250: " . . . et quod nunc dicitur Coeleth, id est Ecclesiasten. Ecclesiastes autem graeco sermone appellatur, qui coetum, id est ecclesiam congreget, quem nos nuncupare possumus concionatorem, quod loquitur ad

by medieval sources dealing with the book of *Ecclesiastes*, including the *Glossa Ordinaria*. I will later comment on the implications in Erasmus of this three-fold correlation from Jerome, with which he surely was familiar. My point for the moment, however, is that until Erasmus the label *concio* was scarcely ever used to designate a sermon, whereas by the second decade of the sixteenth century it was commonly employed that way, surely due in large measure to Erasmus' influence. Moreover, we have now exposed the sources from which Erasmus devised the seemingly curious title for his treatise, *Ecclesiastes sive De ratione concionandi*.[44]

Finally, the *Ecclesiastes* can be viewed as another great humanist manifesto, a call *ad fontes*! It gave warrant to a search of the pre-scholastic past for models and directives pertinent to preaching—a search of Scripture, the Fathers, and the classical tradition of rhetoric. Even those who

populum, et sermo eius non specialiter ad unum, sed ad universos generaliter dirigatur." The word or some variation of it occurs only four times in the Vulgate, twice clearly in a sacred context. (Deuteronomy 9, 10; 18, 16), and twice in a political context (2 Esdras 5, 7; Acts 12, 21). Lactantius uses it to refer to the *conciones prophetarum*, *Divinae institutiones*, 7, 15. The word also occurs in Arnobius, *Adversus Gentes*, 6, 14, as the equivalent of an assembly. The word is used in a secular meaning by some medieval writers, e.g., Alan of Lille, *De arte praedicatoria*, *PL* 210:112; Thomas Aquinas, 4 Sent., dis. 15, 1. 4, a. 1, and in his commentary on Aristotle's *Politics*, 3, 1; Robert of Basevorn, *Forma praedicandi*, in Charland, *Artes*, p. 238. It is also used in a more religious context by Aquinas in his commentary on the *De anima*, 1, 12, and is used by Giles of Rome in his commentary, long attributed to Aquinas, on the Canticle of Solomon; see the Parma edition of Aquinas' *Opera* (1863), 14:388: "Dictus enim fuit Salomon, id est pacificus . . . ; et Ecclesiastes, id est concionator . . . et secundum quod fuit concionator, edidit librum Ecclesiastes." For the *Glossa*, see *Biblia Sacra cum glossa interlineari*, 6 vols. (Venice: [Ziletti], 1588), 3:307^{v}, 308^{r}, 341^{v}, and H. J. de Jonge, "Erasmus und die Glossa Ordinaria zum Neuen Testament," *Nederlands Archief voor Kerkgeschiedenis*, New Series 56 (1975), 51–77. The *Ars concionandi*, attributed to Saint Bonaventure, was not printed or in wide circulation until the edition by Benedetto Bonelli, 1772–74. An index, 1381, to the Assisi codex describes it in fact as "Ars concionandi," as does the London codex from the same century. These are examples of the rare usage as applied to preaching until the sixteenth century. There is no reason to assume that Erasmus or his contemporaries would have been influenced by this work. See Bonaventure, *Opera Omnia*, 10 vols. (Quaracchi: Collegium S. Bonaventurae, 1882–1902), 9:7, 8 n.1. Note also Melanchthon's *Enarratio brevis concionum libri Salomonis, cuius titulus est Ecclesiastes*, 2nd ed., rev. (Wittenberg: Haeredes P. Seitzii, 1557). In the *Ciceronianus* (*ASD* 1, 2:641), Erasmus seems to repudiate a usage of *concio* that he later adopts in the *Ecclesiastes*, *LB* 5:769, 940.

[44] Erasmus was not, however, the first in the Renaissance to use the term *ecclesiastes* to designate the Christian preacher. Herborn, for instance, refers it to himself, *Methodus*, sig. S vii^{v}.

disagreed with the *Ecclesiastes* and found fault with it now knew where to search for an alternative and how to free themselves from the grasp of the *artes*. The thematic sermon could now be effectively displaced because Erasmus pointed to the elements and traditions out of which new forms could be created. The large number of treatises on how to preach that rolled off the presses of Europe after 1535 were thus indebted directly or indirectly to Erasmus' great work. Saint Charles Borromeo,[45] Saint Francis Borgia,[46] Saint Francis de Sales,[47] Saint Robert Bellarmine[48]—to look only at the Catholic side—were some of the eminent personages who authored treatises or instructions on preaching in the aftermath of the *Ecclesiastes*, and especially in the aftermath of its being placed on the first Index of Prohibited Books by the fanatical Pope Paul IV in 1559, as simply part of the *Opera omnia* of Erasmus. That proscription partly explains the proliferation of Catholic treatises in the 1570's.[49]

Long before the Index of Paul IV, however, the *Ecclesiastes* was under criticism. The first book on preaching published by a Catholic after 1535 was the *De sacris concionibus recte formandis* by the Spanish cleric Alfonso Zorrilla. Published in Rome in 1542, it was an act of outrageous and wholesale plagiarism—a covert, scissors-and-paste compilation out of Reuchlin and three Lutheran authors—Melanchthon, Veit Dietrich, and Johannes Hepinus (Hoeck).[50] In his dedicatory letter, audaciously ad-

[45] "Instructiones praedicationis verbi Dei," in *Acta Ecclesiae Mediolanensis*, ed. Achille Ratti, 3 vols. (Milan: Typographia Pontificia Sancti Josephi, 1890–97), 2:1205–48. See my "Saint Charles Borromeo and the *Praecipuum Episcoporum Munus*: His Place in the History of Preaching," forthcoming in the volume of studies from the conference at the Folger Shakespeare Library, October 25–27, 1984, ed. John M. Headley.

[46] "De ratione concionandi," in *Opera Omnia* (Brussels: F. Foppeno, 1675), pp. 469–77.

[47] Known as the "Traitté de la prédication," it is in fact his letter to André Frémiot, October 5, 1604, in *Oeuvres de saint François de Sales*, 26 vols. (Annecy: J. Niérat [etc.], 1892–1932), 12:299–325.

[48] "De ratione formandae concionis," in *Auctarium Bellarminianum: Supplément aux oeuvres du Cardinal Bellarmin*, ed. Xavier-Marie le Bachelet (Paris: G. Beauchesne, 1913), pp. 655–57.

[49] This motive is specifically adduced, for instance, by Alfonso García Matamoros in 1570 in his "De tribus dicendi generibus," in *Opera Omnia* (Madrid: A. Ramírez, 1769), p. 437.

[50] On this curious book, see my "Lutheranism in Rome, 1542–43: The Treatise by Alfonso Zorrilla," *Thought*, 54 (1979), 262–73, now reprinted in my *Rome and the Renaissance: Studies in Culture and Religion* (London: Variorum Reprints, 1981), X. Other works on preaching were being written by Catholics at this time, but were not published. For instance, Cardinal Gasparo Contarini wrote his "Modus praedicandi" in 1540, but it was

dressed to the Cardinal of Toledo, one of the members of the newly founded Roman Inquisition, Zorrilla criticizes the *Ecclesiastes* as "diffuse, prolix, and confused."[51] In a word, it was impractical, almost unfathomable. Although Erasmus himself expressed dissatisfaction with the sprawling and unpolished quality of his treatise, he surely would have been shocked by such an out-of-hand dismissal of a work over which he had labored so long.[52]

There was, however, justification for the criticism, and this fact also helps explain why so many alternatives to it were proposed later in the sixteenth century. Its very length—333 folio columns in the Leiden edition—would daunt all but the most intrepid. As a modern book, it would run, without apparatus, to some thousand pages—with only four, untitled chapters, and without any subdivisions or table of contents. It lacked, therefore, the short chapters, clear progression, and pointed directives that characterized the *artes* and that readers had come to expect. But the difficulties lay deeper, and some of them were endemic, it seems to me, to any attempt to adapt classical rhetoric to the Christian pulpit. They were perhaps all the more insidious for often not being recognized as problems at all.

Discussion about the reconciliation of rhetoric with Christian preaching traditionally centered on whether it was proper or necessary for the Christian to draw upon pagan sources, especially one as suspect as rhetoric. Although Augustine's assessment was riddled with ambivalences, he finally answered in the affirmative. Erasmus was committed to such an ardent affirmative that he does not bother to raise the question in the *Ecclesiastes*. The question continued to be discussed and debated, however, even in the sixteenth century.[53]

It seems to me that there are, rather, at least four other questions that

not published until 1881 in *Regesten und Briefe des Cardinals Gasparo Contarini (1483–1542)*, ed. Franz Dittrich (Braunsberg: von Huye, 1881), pp. 305–9.

[51] Fol. 1^{v}–2: "Erasmus enim Roterodamus de modo concionandi libros aliquot fecit. Adeo tamen opus illud est diffusum, prolixum et confusaneum ut non cuique inde facile sit ea praecepta deligere quae pro sacris concionibus formandis opus sint."

[52] *Ecclesiastes*, *LB* 5:767–68. See Chomarat, *Grammaire* 2:1054–56; and Kleinhans, *Preaching*, pp. 7–28.

[53] See, e.g., Surgant, *Manuale curatorum*, fols. XLIV–XLV^{v}; Andreas Hyperius, *The Practis of Preaching, otherwise called, The Pathway to ye Pulpet* (London: Thomas East, 1577), fols. 18–29; Matamoros, "De methodo concionandi" (first published in 1570), in *Opera Omnia*, pp. 529–33, 545–46, 551—52.

must be raised in this regard, and they have more practical import than that one. The first is, however, closely related to it. It regards the Christian belief in the divine, or supra-human, nature of the word of God. This belief requires that any treatise on preaching must have a component lacking in the classical treatises on rhetoric: a theology of the divine word and the minister of that word. The word of God has a power and acts in a way, by supposition, that is different from the word of a merely human orator.

To Erasmus' credit, he was aware of this issue, and he in fact addresses it more successfully than he does the remaining three. The first book of the *Ecclesiastes*, on the prerequisites of virtue and knowledge in the preacher, is in fact a major contribution to the issue. Erasmus insists that the preacher's words will not accomplish their spiritual goal unless he has the Spirit of Christ dwelling in his heart, who will give his words "a hidden efficacy." Only God transforms hearts.[54] The preacher has a special relationship to the *sermo Dei* or *verbum Dei*, Christ himself.[55]

Theologically profound though passages like these may be, they are few, and they coexist with many others in which the implied model for the preacher follows more political and moralistic presuppositions. These others reflect simply an adaptation of the *ethos* that the Roman oratorical tradition had developed— "vir *bonus*, dicendi peritus."[56] Moreover, we miss in the *Ecclesiastes* the fuller development of Erasmus' ideas on the special dynamism and transforming power of the word of God that passages in his other works, like the *Paraclesis*, might have led us to expect.

The second problem is that preaching at least since the days of Origen had been a text-related enterprise. That is to say, its purpose was somehow to comment upon or simply deliver the words of Scripture. Classical rhetoric did not envision oratory as dealing with a text but with an event, a situation, a person, a practical decision. It was, therefore,

[54] *LB* 5:773. See also *ibid.*, 1013, 1078. See Chomarat, *Grammaire*, 2:1096—1107.

[55] *LB* 5:772. See Kleinhans, *Preaching*, pp. 107–58.

[56] See Quintilian, XII, 1, 14, and Erasmus, *Apologia in dialogum Jacobi Latomi*, *LB* 9:90: "Quod si probatur a rhetoribus definitio, *Orator vir bonus dicendi peritus*, cur nobis displiceat haec, *Theologus est vir pius, de divinis loquendi peritus*; et *Theologia est pietas, cum ratione de divinis rebus loquendi coniuncta?* Quas si recipimus, nimirum par theologiae erit pietas. Quod si judicio Fabii, *non inflammat alios nisi qui ardet ipse, non concitat dolorem nisi qui dolet ipse*, ita non afficit theologus, nisi ipse affectus, non afflat nisi afflatus." See also *Ecclesiastes*, *LB* 5:900–1.

much more immediate and, by definition, less bookish than most Christian sermons. The more closely Christian preaching attached itself to the text of Scripture, a goal Erasmus surely promoted, the more difficult it became to adopt the principles of classical oratory.

In my opinion, the usual solution to this dilemma in the history of preaching has been to abandon primary rhetoric, that is, oratory as such, and to utilize the classroom technique of exegesis of the classical *grammaticus*, while incorporating into the sermon the stylistic and exegetical devices of secondary, or literary, rhetoric. But primary rhetoric, oratory properly so-called, was practically abandoned in the process. The classroom is not the market place; the teacher is not the politician-orator; the text is not an immediate crisis.[57]

What resulted in this process was the homily, or some variation of it. This was Origen's solution, and therefore the solution of Ambrose and, consequently, of Augustine. It was the solution of Thomas à Kempis,[58] Jacques Lefèvre d'Étaples,[59] and, to a large extent, Nicholas of Cusa.[60] With some qualification, it was also the solution of Luther.[61] Moreover, it was the solution of Jacques Vitrier, the Franciscan contemporary so much admired by Erasmus who turned his attention to Origen and whose preaching he several times described and eulogized.[62]

[57] Pertinent to this issue is O. B. Hardison, "The Orator and the Poet: The Dilemma of Humanist Literature," *The Journal of Medieval and Renaissance Studies*, 1 (1971), 33–44.

[58] See his *Opera Omnia*, ed. M. J. Pohl, 7 vols. (Freiburg i/Br.: Herder, 1902–22), 6:7–314.

[59] See his *Epistres et Evangiles pour les cinquante et deux semaines de l'An*, ed. M. A. Screech (Geneva: Librairie Droz, 1964); first edition in 1525.

[60] See my *Praise and Blame*, pp. 98–101.

[61] See my "Luther the Preacher," in *The Martin Luther Quincentennial*, ed. G. Dünnhaupt (Detroit: Wayne State University Press, 1984), pp. 3–16.

[62] Erasmus praises Vitrier's preaching in the famous letter to Jodocus Jonas, June 13, 1521, in *Opus epistolarum Des. Erasmi Roterodami*, ed. P. S. Allen, H. M. Allen, and H. W. Garrod, 12 vols. (Oxford: Clarendon Press, 1906–58), 4:507–27, and again, without actually mentioning his name, in the *Ecclesiastes*, *LB*, 5:987. The letter is translated into English in John Olin, ed., *Christian Humanism and the Reformation: Desiderius Erasmus* (New York: Harper and Row, 1965), pp. 164–91, and into French, with commentary and other documents, by André Godin, *Érasme: Vies de Jean Vitrier et de John Colet* (Angers: Éditions Moreana, 1982). Erasmus' relationship to Vitrier has been the subject of several other studies by Godin (see note 8 above), now incorporated into his *Érasme Lecteur*, especially pp. 13–32, 660–74; see also Chomarat, *Grammaire*, 2:1092–95; Telle, "En marge," p. 450; and

Although in the *Ecclesiastes* Erasmus gives little explicit attention to the homily, his obvious admiration for the preaching of the Fathers, Saint Bernard, and Vitrier indicates his intense study of it.[63] More important, some of his own works based more directly on Scripture resemble homilies, even his *Enarratio* of the fourteenth psalm, written after the *Ecclesiastes*; *enarratio* at times seems to be for Erasmus the equivalent of *homilia*. Throughout his life, in fact, Erasmus showed surprisingly little interest in that fundamental discipline of the classical tradition—oratory, primary rhetoric.[64] He had minimal concern for the training of orators, as the scant attention oratory received in his *De ratione studii* indicates. Only two so-called sermons by Erasmus survive—the *Concio de puero Jesu* and the *De magnitudine misericordiarum Domini concio*. Both are, despite their designations as *conciones*, adaptations of classical panegyric or demonstrative oratory. This fact shows that Erasmus, while having a clear idea of the more technical sense of the term, extended it to include all sermons.

Neither of these sermons seems ever to have been delivered by Erasmus, and the former was in fact intended for delivery by another—by a *puer*. In fact, except possibly for a few instances early in life, this great theorist seems never to have preached in public! Erasmus was painfully aware of this limitation, which surely accounts for some of his discomfort with the subject he addresses in the *Ecclesiastes*.[65] It also accounts for the lack of practical detail that later theorists who were also practitioners,

Georges Chantraine, *"Mystère" et "Philosophie du Christ" selon Érasme: Étude de la lettre à P. Volz et de la "Ratio verae theologiae" (1518)* (Namur: Facultés universitaires, 1971), pp. 53–69. Critical to the issue of preaching is Godin's edition, *L'Homéliaire de Jean Vitrier*.

[63] On Bernard, see *Ecclesiastes, LB* 5:857. While commending the homiletic style in this passage, 856–57, Erasmus also assesses it as practiced by certain ancient writers—Origen, Ambrose, Gregory the Great, et al.

[64] On this issue in Erasmus, see my "Grammar and Rhetoric in the Theology of Erasmus," forthcoming in *Paideia: Special Renaissance Number*, ed. George C. Simmons. The resemblance of the title of my article, first delivered as a lecture at the University of Michigan, Ann Arbor, in 1979, to the title of Chomarat's recent book is purely coincidental. I believe that, even in the face of Chomarat's massive study, my conclusions still stand and, in fact, do not contradict the major theses of Chomarat's two volumes. On the distinction between primary and secondary rhetoric, see Kennedy, *Classical Rhetoric*, pp. 3–9.

[65] See his letter to John Lasky, August 27, 1528, in *Allen*, 7:454.

like Francesco Panigarola, would provide.[66] I would maintain, in any case, that there is an unresolved ambiguity in Erasmus, as in so many other writers, on this basic issue of the relationship between rhetoric and the text-relatedness of preaching and that he does not address the issue in a satisfactory way in the *Ecclesiastes* or elsewhere.

The third problem has to do with the liturgical setting for which the sermon was at least sometimes envisioned. It is true that many sermons took place outside Mass and that in Erasmus' day even sermons somehow connected with the eucharistic liturgy did not always take place after the reading or chanting of the Gospel during the service. Nonetheless, that was the traditional and normative location for the sermon, and treatises about preaching needed to take it into account.[67] Few, if any, did so—certainly not the *Ecclesiastes*.

This setting—*inter missarum solemnia*—put certain time-constraints on the preacher, but it did more than that. It made preaching part of a larger liturgical action, in which some intellectual, affective, and even aesthetic relationship between word and sacrament could rightly be expected. The properly eucharistic part of the liturgy begins with the words: "Lift up your hearts." This directive could serve as a leit-motif for the sermon, which almost immediately preceded it, and would thus caution against reducing the sermon to mere instruction and exhortation, which Erasmus, in concert with a long tradition, generally, though not always, does. In this his scope for the sermon correlates, surely unwittingly, with that of Alan of Lille.

The sermon, in other words, is not just an address on a sacred subject to a popular audience, which would be a fair rendering of Erasmus' understanding of it. For Catholics, at least, it is such an address within a determined, and to some extent determining, setting. The Italians were possibly on more appropriate ground in this regard when they placed preaching in the genre of demonstrative, that is, ceremonial, oratory.

That brings me to the fourth problem: the *genus* of classical oratory in

[66] See especially his *Il predicatore* (Venice: B. Giunti, G. B. Ciotti, 1609), published posthumously.

[67] See my *Praise and Blame*, esp. pp. 7–35. Erasmus seems to assume that the *concio* will not, in fact, take place within the liturgy, *Ecclesiastes*, *LB* 5:966: " . . . praesertim quum olim Evangelii enarratio pars fuerit Missae." In subsequent centuries, most Catholic preaching was done outside the liturgy. See my "Preaching" in the Encyclopedia of Jesuit History.

which preaching is to be placed—judicial, deliberative, or demonstrative.[68] Traversagni, conforming his theory to the practice in Italy in the Quattrocento, locates preaching in the *genus demonstrativum*, assuming rather than arguing that this is the proper place for it.[69] Melanchthon is the first to argue the issue. He constructs, almost without classical precedent, a new *genus*, the *genus didascalicum* or *didacticum*.[70] This *genus* depended more on dialectics than rhetoric, and had teaching as its purpose. Melanchthon allows, however, the use of the *genus deliberativum* or *suasorium* for exhortation, which is also integral to good preaching but subordinate to teaching correct doctrine. While he also makes allowances for the *genus demonstrativum*, he repudiates the way he understood it to be used in Italy. Like almost all other writers on the subject, he minimizes the use in the pulpit of the *genus judiciale*, courtroom oratory of defense and indictment.[71]

By assigning the principal object of sacred oratory to teaching correct doctrine, an object surely in accord with Luther's thinking, a fateful step had been taken for a large tradition within Protestantism. Among other things, this would mean that Protestant treatises on preaching would by and large be much more prescriptive about the doctrinal content of preaching than Catholic treatises. When Melanchthon's works on preaching are correlated with his other writings, especially his influential *Loci communes*, the doctrines of law-gospel and sin-grace would emerge as *semper praedicanda*, whereas certain speculations dear to the scholastics about the nature of the godhead and the metaphysics of the Incarnation would be explicitly excluded. Nonetheless, there is an intellectual affinity

[68] On this issue, see my "Content and Rhetorical Forms."

[69] See *Margarita*, pp. 33, 84–85, 139–67.

[70] Some basis for the *genus* can be found in classical authors. See, e.g., Cicero, *Oratoriae partitiones*, 67, where we find a *disputandi genus*; see also the discussion in Quintilian, 3, 4. Helen North notes, for instance, that Maximus of Tyre adds teaching to the customary three *genera*, "The Concept of *Sophrosyne* in Greek Literary Criticism," *Classical Philology*, 43 (1948), 1–17, esp. 3–4, n. 16. I am indebted to Professor North, Swarthmore College, and to Professor George A. Kennedy, the University of North Carolina, for these references. It is conceivable that Erasmus was influenced by Melanchthon when, basing himself on the authority of Paul, he refers to preachers as διδακτικοι, *Ecclesiastes*, *LB* 5:775, 806–7. But see Chomarat, *Grammaire*, 2:1118–28.

[71] See Melanchthon, *Elementorum rhetorices*, cols. 419–29, and *De officiis concionatoris*, pp. 5–10.

between Melanchthon's *genus didascalicum* and the dialectical nature of the preaching proposed by the *artes*.

With relatively brief justification as to why he does so, Erasmus locates preaching in the *genus suasorium* or *deliberativum*,[72] and he calls the sermon *concio*. As that appellation became normative, especially in Catholic circles, another fateful step had been taken. It meant that persuasion, rather than the presentation of doctrine, would be given greater weight. True, Erasmus uses the term *concio* broadly. Erasmus was also much concerned that correct doctrine be preached, and the fourth book of the *Ecclesiastes* provides a sample listing of doctrinal topics, many of which would have been rejected by Melanchthon as unsuitable for the pulpit, even for theology. But Erasmus was more concerned with inculcating and persuading to good morals and ethically correct behavior than he was to any other end.[73] His placing of the sermon in the *genus suasorium* tends to this kind of emphasis.

By entitling his work *Ecclesiastes*, he also directly alluded to the highly moralistic book of the Old Testament by that name. The book of *Ecclesiastes* pertains to the so-called sapiential or wisdom literature of the Bible. For Erasmus, as I have argued elsewhere, Christianity was a wisdom and the Bible was the book that taught its "philosophy."[74] Although Erasmus locates preaching in the charism of "prophecy," he defines that charism as an exposition of the mystical sense of scripture and a persuasive imparting of its wisdom.[75] His "homilies" or quasi-homilies, like the *enarrationes*, are, therefore, far removed from the blunt proclamations of Jeremiah and Hosea. Erasmus was, moreover, fully aware of the prohibition of apocalyptic preaching by the Fifth Lateran Council, 1516.[76] Not confrontation, but the teaching of prescriptive and ethics-related wisdom was the task of the Erasmian "prophet."

[72] See *Ecclesiastes*, *LB* 5:857–59. See also *ibid.*, 877–87.

[73] See, e.g., Chomarat, *Grammaire*, 2:1128; and Kleinhans, *Preaching*, pp. 107–111.

[74] See my "Grammar and Rhetoric."

[75] See, e.g., *Ecclesiastes*, *LB* 5:798, 818, 825; *Ratio verae theologiae*, *LB* 5:76, 84; *De vidua christiana*, *LB* 5:752; *Commentarius in psalmum secundum*, *LB* 5:206–7.

[76] "Supernae maiestatis praesidio" (December 19, 1516); see *Hyperaspistes*, *LB* 10:1276. For "prophet" as one who knows past, present, and future, see *Enarratio psalmi XIV*, *LB* 5:298–99. Ciruelo's "De arte praedicandi" contains some examples of "prophetic" or apocalyptic preaching. See Jean Delumeau, *La Peur en Occident (XIVe–XVIIIe siècles): Une cité assiégée* (Paris: Fayard, 1978).

These factors helped promote within Catholicism an emphasis on moralistic preaching that was already strong. The treatise by Alan of Lille had long ago codified it. Moreover, one of the most influential lines in the history of preaching—found, significantly enough, not in a treatise on that subject but in the *Second Rule* of Saint Francis of Assisi—prescribed as early as the thirteenth century that the friars should preach about "vices and virtues, punishment and reward."[77] This emphasis would later coordinate with the insistence of the Council of Trent that human cooperation with God's grace issue in meritorious works, good deeds. In fact, among the few lines that Trent explicitly devoted to the content of preaching in its decree of June 17, 1546, are found a paraphrase of the words from the Franciscan Rule just quoted.[78] Those words of the Rule would be quoted again and again in important works about preaching in the late sixteenth and early seventeenth centuries.[79]

Through the studies by Georges Chantraine and others, we have been made aware of the doctrinal grounding and affective, almost mystical, depths of Erasmus' religious thought, and cautioned against reducing it to mere moralism.[80] Nonetheless, the *genus* in which Erasmus places preaching and the very title he gives his work tend to inhibit this spiritual richness from fully manifesting itself, and they mute the warm affectivity and interiority that we find in so many of his other writings.

[77] Chapter IX, "De praedicatoribus," in *Seraphicae Legislationis Textus Originales* (Quaracchi: Collegium S. Bonaventurae, 1897), p. 44: "Moneo quoque et exhortor eosdem fratres ut in praedicatione quam faciunt sint examinata et casta eorum eloquia, ad utilitatem et aedificationem populi, annuntiando eis vitia et virtutes, poenam et gloriam, cum brevitate sermonis, quia verbum abbreviatum fecit Dominus super terram." See *Ecclesiastes*, *LB* 5: 1080.

[78] *Concilium Tridentinum*, ed. Societas Gorresiana, 13 vols. (Freiburg i/Br.: Herder, 1901–57), 5:242: " . . . annuntiando eis cum brevitate et facilitate sermonis vitia, quae eos declinare, et virtutes, quas sectari oporteat, ut poenam aeternam evadere et coelestem gloriam consequi valeant." There is no doubt that the paraphrase is from the Rule, for the first version of the decree, April 13, 1546, quotes it verbatim, without acknowledgment of source, *ibid.*, 106. This fact has generally gone unnoticed. McGinness calls attention to it, *Rhetoric and Counter-Reformation Rome*, p. 164, whereas Arsenio d'Ascoli, *Predicatione dei Cappuccini nel Cinquecento in Italia* (Loreto: Libreria "S. Francesco d'Assisi," 1956), p. 66, barely suggests a relationship between the Rule and the conciliar document.

[79] See my "Form, Content" (Assisi).

[80] See, e.g., "*Mystère*," especially pp. 389–93.

Erasmus betrays himself and the limitations of the form, for instance, when he states at the very beginning of the *Ecclesiastes* that the purpose of the sacred *concio*, patterned as it is after its secular counterpart, is "to explain to the promiscuous multitude the edicts, promises, and will of the supreme prince and to persuade that multitude to accept them."[81] The *genus deliberativum* was the most politically oriented of the three *genera*, and there are indications that Erasmus never fully liberated himself from that political model, concerned as it was with law, order, correct behavior, and obedience. He explicitly defines the *concio* as having to do with "duplex politia," secular and sacred.[82] Moreover, the *concio*, as Erasmus understood it, was addressed to a vulgar multitude, and hence it assumed ignorance and often ill will and vice on the part of the audience.[83] It hardly seems to be the form appropriate to the delivery of Erasmus' sometimes sublime "philosophy of Christ."

Perhaps this problem helps explain why Erasmus felt a continuing attraction for the homily.[84] That form, in its very formlessness and in its employment by so many monastic writers through the ages, allowed for full expression of affectivity, while binding that affectivity closely to certain central Christian doctrines of divine love and human response. As theologians today would express it, Erasmus wanted to rejoin theology with spirituality, healing the divorce that he believed the scholastics had perpetrated.[85] The homily seems more suitable for effecting this recon-

[81] *LB* 5:770: " . . . et sacri [Ecclesiastae], qui summi principis edicta, promissa ac voluntatem exponunt suadentque promiscuae multitudini." See also, *ibid.*, 906.

[82] *Ibid.*, cols. 769–71.

[83] *Ibid.*, cols. 771, 906, 968–69, 976–77, 1046; *Ciceronianus*, *ASD* 1, 2:637: "Habenda est concio apud promiscuam multitudinem, in qua sunt et virgines et uxores et viduae; dicendum est de laude jejunii, de poenitentia, de fructu orandi, de utilitate eleemosynarum, de sanctitate matrimonii, de contemptu rerum fluxarum, de studio divinarum litterarum, ... " On this issue, see also, e.g., Panigarola, *Il predicatore*, 2:284, 643–46.

[84] For his reservations on Origen's homilies, see *Ecclesiastes*, *LB* 5:857, where he also commends the preaching of Augustine and Bernard. See also, *ibid.*, 1000. Fumaroli goes so far as to state that in the *Ecclesiastes* Erasmus makes the Fathers of the Church models for a new type of evangelizing theologians, *L'âge de l'éloquence*, p. 135.

[85] See especially the works by Georges Chantraine, e.g., "*Mystère*"; "Mysterium et Sacramentum dans le 'Dulce Bellum,' " in *Colloquium Erasmianum*, pp. 33–45; "L'apologia ad Latomum: Deux conceptions de la théologie," in *Scrinium Erasmianum*, ed. J. Coppens, 2 vols. (Leiden: E. J. Brill, 1969), 2:51–75; "Théologie et vie spirituelle: Un aspect de la méthode théologique selon Érasme," *Nouvelle Revue Théologique*, 91 (1969), 809–33; "La

ciliation than does the more voluntaristic, even political, *concio*.

Perhaps it was Erasmus' anti-Italian prejudices that caused him to take such a negative view, as he described the Italian situation in both the *Ciceronianus* and the *Ecclesiastes*, of what was happening in Italy.[86] I would propose, in any case, that, had he better understood the Italian situation, he would have found it more congenial to the full breadth of his religious thought. Like the homily, the "sacred orations" of the Italians tended to coordinate teaching and persuading with the elevation of the affections to love, gratitude, and praise. Even while teaching and exhorting, these orations tended to be less dogmatic than what Melanchthon envisioned and less moralistic than what Erasmus proposed. Just how widely this form was practiced after 1535 has yet to be investigated fully, but treatises on preaching did not advocate it after that date, except in some instances for funeral eulogies and panegyrics of the saints. We must presume that Erasmus and his Lutheran contemporaries—Melanchthon, Dietrich, and

musterion paulinien selon les Annotationes d'Érasme," *Recherches de science religieuse*, 58 (1970), 351–82.

[86] See n. 36 above. In the *Ecclesiastes*, Erasmus' criticism of the preaching situation in Italy extends beyond how he perceived the Italians were adapting classical rhetoric to sacred purposes. See, e.g., *LB* 5:798, 857, 954–55, 966, 982, 985–86. The following are the most important recent studies of Erasmus' relationship to Italy: Paul Oskar Kristeller, "Erasmus from an Italian Perspective," *Renaissance Quarterly*, 23 (1970), 1–14; Eugenio Garin, "Erasmo e l'Umanesimo italiano," *Bibliothèque d'Humanisme et Renaissance*, 33 (1971), 7–17; Silvana Seidel Menchi, "Alcuni atteggiamenti della cultura italiana di fronte a Erasmo (1520–1536)," in *Eresia e riforma nell'Italia del Cinquecento*, Biblioteca del Corpus Reformatorum Italicorum, Miscellanea I (Florence: G. C. Sansoni Editore, 1974), pp. 69–133; *idem*, "Sulla fortuna di Erasmo in Italia: Ortensio Lando e altri eterodossi della prima metà del Cinquecento," *Schweizerische Zeitschrift für Geschichte*, 24 (1974), 537–634; *idem*, "La circulazione clandestina di Erasmo in Italia: I casi di Antonio Brucioli e di Marsilio Andreasi," *Annali della Scuola Normale Superiore di Pisa*, 9 (1979), 573–601; Marcella and Paul Grendler, "The Survival of Erasmus in Italy," *Erasmus in English*, 8 (1976), 2–22; and the several articles by Myron P. Gilmore, "Erasmus and Alberto Pio, Prince of Carpi," in *Action and Conviction in Early Modern Europe: Essays in Memory of E. H. Harbison*, ed. Theodore K. Rabb and Jerrold E. Seigel (Princeton: Princeton University Press, 1969), pp. 299–318; "Anti-Erasmianism in Italy: The Dialogue of Ortensio Lando on Erasmus' Funeral," *The Journal of Medieval and Renaissance Studies*, 4 (1974), 1–14; "Italian Reactions to Erasmian Humanism," in *Itinerarium Italicum: The Profile of the Italian Renaissance in the Mirror of its European Transformations*, ed. Heiko A. Oberman with Thomas A. Brady, Jr., Studies in Medieval and Reformation Thought, No. 14 (Leiden: E. J. Brill, 1975), pp. 61–115.

Hepinus—were at least partially responsible for what seems to be the subsequent neglect of this *genus*.[87]

This long discussion of the *genera* was not aimed, however, at electing one of them as more reconcilable with Christian preaching than another, but simply at pointing out that the problem of the *genera* needed to be argued, for the choice of *genus* subtly influenced the content, purpose, and mood of the sermon. Erasmus' seeming failure to perceive all that was at issue here, as in the other three problems relating to the reconciliation of Christian preaching with classical rhetoric, is surely one of the limitations of the *Ecclesiastes*.

But it would not be fitting to conclude this lecture by dwelling on the limitations of the *Ecclesiastes*, on what it failed to accomplish. We must in this final moment put that work in larger perspective. Along with the ambiguities and ambivalences, there are in Erasmus some clarities about preaching that are even stronger: first, his repudiation of the thematic sermon of the scholastics; secondly, his admiration for the preaching of the Fathers, from Origen to Bernard; thirdly, his conviction that the literary techniques and even the oratorical forms of classical rhetoric had application to Christian preaching; fourthly, his belief that this application should be sober, appropriate to the circumstances and audience, and avoid the pitfalls of "Ciceronianism."

Erasmus seems to have desired in preaching, therefore, some combination of the following: sermons that would be basically *explications de texte*, as were the patristic homilies on the Bible, but he would admit more sophisticated forms as well; sermons that sprang from the affect and deep spirituality of the preacher, as he believed was true for both Origen and Vitrier; sermons that at the same time made use in a sober and restrained way of the techniques of eloquence that classical rhetoric provided; finally, sermons that addressed especially the moral needs of a popular audience, which corresponds to the general situation envisioned by the classical *concio*. Put in these terms, the Erasmian ideal of sacred eloquence is not far removed from the so-called "severe ideal" that would

[87] At least in Rome this *genus* continued to enjoy, in practice, considerable favor. See the excellent study by Frederick J. McGinness, *Rhetoric and Counter-Reformation Rome: Sacred Oratory and the Construction of the Catholic World View, 1563–1621* (Ann Arbor: University Microfilms, 1982). See also his "The Rhetoric of Praise and the New Rome of The Counter Reformation," in *Rome in the Renaissance: The City and the Myth*, ed. P. A. Ramsey (Binghamton: Center for Medieval & Early Renaissance Studies, 1982), pp. 355–70.

win the support of Carlo Borromeo and many of his contemporaries later in the century, an ideal well described by Fumaroli in his *L'âge de l'éloquence*.

I return, therefore, to what I said earlier. The *Ecclesiastes* is not simply a major work by Erasmus. It is a major monument in the long history and continuing influence of the classical tradition in western culture. Above all, it is a major monument—perhaps *the* major monument—in the history of sacred rhetoric. Its only rival is the *De doctrina christiana* of Augustine. To that extent, the *Ecclesiastes* is no less than what we would have expected from the pen of Desiderius Erasmus of Rotterdam.

VIII

Grammar and rhetoric in the *pietas* of Erasmus

When Erasmus in both 1523 and 1530 categorized into various *ordines* his writings up to those dates, he designated the "fifth order" as works "pertaining to piety"—*pertinentium ad pietatem.*[1] The number of such works was large, and it was made even larger by subsequent editors who had to account for Erasmus' publications from 1530 until his death in 1536. The fifth volume of the Leiden edition, which corresponds to Erasmus' "fifth order," lists thirty-nine distinct works, contained in 1360 folio columns. This fact alone testifies to the importance that considerations concerning *pietas* held for Erasmus, and confirms beyond question that a reform of piety was one of the major aims of his life.

The term itself was dense with meaning for Erasmus, and "spirituality" renders it only imperfectly into English. The publications "pertaining to piety" include of course the *Enchiridion* and the *Modus orandi Deum*, but also the *Ratio verae theologiae* and the *Paraclesis*. The original list of 1530 included the *Exomologesis*, which, though ostensibly addressed to the penitent, was surely also meant for the confessor. Subsequent editors quite properly added to the "fifth order," therefore, his two later works clearly related to ministry—the *Explanatio symboli, sive Catechismus* (1533) and the *Ecclesiastes, sive De ratione concionandi* (1535). In other words, for Erasmus *pietas* was a reality that by definition could not be dissociated from theology and from the theory and practice of ministry, although it must be admitted that he seems to have grown more sensitive to that latter component only with the passing of years. The reform of *pietas* that he envisioned looked to an integration of "spirituality," theology and, at least after a certain point, ministry. This reintegration would repair the divorce among these three elements that, according to Erasmus, the Scholastics had effected.

Elsewhere I have dealt at length with Erasmian *pietas* and tried to show its many implications and complexities.[2] In this article I wish to

Journal of Medieval and Renaissance Studies 18:1, Spring 1988. CCC 0047–2573/88/$1.50

1. Allen I, 40; VIII, 375–76.
2. See my "Introduction" to CWE 6 (1988).

explore in greater detail one aspect of it that might otherwise escape notice, for it is subtle, and that helps locate Erasmus more precisely among his contemporaries, especially some of his fellow Humanists. I will do this by an examination of two characteristically Erasmian expressions, generally recognized as encapsulating his most cherished interests—*bonae litterae* and *philosophia Christi*.

My curiosity as to what might be distinctive about Erasmian *pietas* was first aroused by my study of the sacred orators at the papal court.[3] In the course of that investigation, I was struck, on the one hand, by a similarity of themes between the orators and Erasmus. In many ways the orators seemed to anticipate him. On the other hand, I thought I detected elusive, yet possibly important, differences. Analyzed, these differences might reveal as much about Erasmus' religious thought as do the usual comparisons of it with the late Middle Ages, the Reformation, and the Counter Reformation. The examination, if successful, would constitute another chapter in that seemingly inexhaustible subject, Erasmus' relationship to Italian Humanism and to Renaissance religious thought in general.[4] Because of his polemic with the Scholastics and his professed admiration for the Fathers, the examination might throw some light even on the general history of Western theology.

Bonae litterae—what did it mean in the Renaissance? It meant the

3. *Praise and Blame in Renaissance Rome: Rhetoric, Doctrine, and Reform in the Sacred Orators of the Papal Court, c. 1450–1521*, Duke Monographs in Medieval and Renaissance Studies, No. 3 (Durham, N.C., 1979).

4. The following are among the most important studies of Erasmus' relationship to Italy: Paul Oskar Kristeller, "Erasmus from an Italian Perspective," *Renaissance Quarterly*, 23 (1970), 1–14; Eugenio Garin, "Erasmo e l'Umanesimo italiano," *Bibliothèque d'Humanisme et Renaissance*, 33 (1971), 7–17; Silvana Seidel Menchi, "Alcuni atteggiamenti della cultura italiana di fronte a Erasmo (1520–1536)," in *Eresia e riforma nell'Italia del Cinquecento*, Biblioteca del Corpus Reformatorum Italicorum, Miscellanea I (Florence, 1974), 69–133; idem, "Sulla fortuna di Erasmo in Italia: Ortensio Lando e altri eterodossi della prima metà del Cinquecento," *Schweizerische Zeitschrift für Geschichte*, 24 (1974), 537–634; idem, "La circolazione clandestina di Erasmo in Italia: I casi di Antonio Brucioli e di Marsilio Andreosi," *Annali della Scuola Superiore di Pisa*, 9 (1979), 573–601; Marcella and Paul Grendler, "The Survival of Erasmus in Italy," *Erasmus in English*, 8 (1976), 2–22; and the several articles by Myron P. Gilmore, "Erasmus and Alberto Pio, Prince of Carpi," in *Action and Conviction in Early Modern Europe: Essays in Memory of E. H. Harbison*, ed. Theodore K. Rabb and Jerrold E. Seigel (Princeton, 1969), 299–318; "Anti-Erasmianism in Italy: The Dialogue of Ortensio Lando on Erasmus' Funeral," *Journal of Medieval and Renaissance Studies*, 4 (1974), 1–14; "Italian Reactions to Erasmian Humanism," in *Itinerarium Italicum: The Profile of the Italian Renaissance in the Mirror of its European Transformations*, ed. Heiko Oberman with Thomas A. Brady Jr., Studies in Medieval and Reformation Thought No. 14 (Leiden, 1975), 61–115.

rebirth of classical literary studies, especially in their two traditional components–grammar and rhetoric. While recognizing ever more clearly the great varieties of Renaissance Humanism, many scholars today would still subscribe to the thesis that it was inseparable from a "pursuit of eloquence."[5] But once the pursuit of eloquence is closely examined, considerable discrepancy appears between those who engaged in it as a pursuit of grammar and those for whom it meant a pursuit of rhetoric. In my opinion, Erasmus is much closer to the former category than were the preachers at the papal court, who without question belong in the latter.

In my book I tried to show that for the preachers in Rome rhetoric, understood as it was understood in the classical and Renaissance treatises on that subject, meant oratory. That at least was its "primary" sense, to use the distinction of George Kennedy.[6] In classical times rhetoric presupposed "grammar" and was thus the third and crowning stage in education in good letters. But "grammar" meant much more than the elementary skills of reading and writing correctly. These skills had already been acquired under the *litterator* or *magister ludi* before the student entered the grammarian's classroom. The "grammarian" taught literature, especially poetry, for it was from poetry, not prose, that rules of grammar were originally derived. One of its purposes was to teach good style, to teach accurate and felicitous expression. Because of its stylistic purpose, it borrowed elements from rhetorical treatises, and thereby appropriated techniques for persuasive discourse that were strictly proper to rhetoric. Both in the Renaissance and even in antiquity this practice blurred the clear distinction between the two disciplines and the two stages in education that strict theory envisioned.[7] Rhetoric tended to move from its "primary" (oral)

5. See the now classic presentation by Hanna Holborn Gray, "Renaissance Humanism: The Pursuit of Eloquence," *Journal of the History of Ideas*, 24 (1963), 497–514.

6. See his *Classical Rhetoric and Its Christian and Secular Tradition from Ancient to Modern Times* (Chapel Hill, N.C., 1980), esp. 3–9.

7. See, e.g., Aubrey Gwynn, *Roman Education from Cicero to Quintilian* (1926; rpt. New York, 1964); H.-I. Marrou, *A History of Education in Antiquity*, trans. George Lamb (New York, 1956); Donald Lemen Clark, *Rhetoric in Greco-Roman Education* (New York, 1957); George Kennedy, *The Art of Persuasion in Greece* (London, 1963), and his *The Art of Rhetoric in the Roman World* (Princeton, 1972); Chomarat, *Grammaire*; W. Keith Percival, "Grammar and Rhetoric in the Renaissance," in *Renaissance Eloquence*, ed. James J. Murphy (Berkeley and Los Angeles, 1983), 303–30; Alex L. Gordon, "The Ascendency of Rhetoric and the Struggle for Poetic in Sixteenth-Century France," ibid. 376–84; and Kees Meerhoff, *Rhétorique et poétique au XVIe siècle en France* (Leiden, 1986).

form to being applied to texts. It tended, according to George Kennedy, "to shift its focus from persuasion to narration, from civic to personal contexts, and from discourse to literature, including poetry."[8]

We tend to forget that Erasmus entered the intellectual world of his day as a "poet."[9] Though in his early years he was occasionally referred to as both "orator" and "theologian," his own enthusiasm, recognized by others, was for studying and writing poetry.[10] Subsequent generations have shown little interest in the neo-Latin poetry of the Renaissance, probably with good reason, and Erasmus himself expressed some disdain for the poetry of his younger days. Yet he wanted it included in the edition of his *Opera omnia* that was being planned in the last years of his life.[11] He continued throughout his life, though with abated enthusiasm, to write and publish poetry. In keeping with the common tradition, he ceaselessly urged the study of poetry as the essential basis for a pursuit of *bonae litterae*, even as his dedication to specifically Christian letters and to the writings of the Fathers of the Church became ever more consuming.

Some years ago, O. B. Hardison wrote a provocative article on "the dilemma of humanist literature."[12] Hardison sees the dilemma as a confusion between poet and orator. For Hardison the orator is "the ideal leader who uses language to persuade." The poet, in contrast, is "the ideal artist who uses language to manifest what Petrarch . . . calls 'an inner force divinely infused in the poet's spirit.' "[13] Hardison shows that the Renaissance failed to observe the distinction between the two, but he warns that we must not if we hope to understand Renaissance texts.

Even a slight elaboration of Hardison's distinction manifests how crucial it is. The orator was conceived in Roman treatises on rhetoric as a public man, actively committed to the accomplishment of public

8. Kennedy, *Classical Rhetoric*, 5.

9. See Reedijk, esp. 61, 63, 67, 85–88.

10. See ibid. 42–101, and Allen, e.g., I, 100, 116–19, 130–31, 162–64, 269. See also Jozef IJsewijn, "Erasmus ex Poeta theologus," in *Scrinium*, I, 375–89.

11. See Reedijk, esp. 85–93.

12. "The Orator and the Poet: The Dilemma of Humanist Literature," *Journal of Medieval and Renaissance Studies*, 1 (1971), 33–44. See also Charles Sears Baldwin, *Ancient Rhetoric and Poetic, Interpreted from Representative Works* (New York, 1924); Wesley Trimpi, "The Ancient Hypothesis of Fiction: An Essay on the Origins of Literary Theory," *Traditio*, 27 (1971), 1–78; Craig R. Thompson, "Better Teachers than Scotus or Aquinas," in *Medieval and Renaissance Studies*, ed. John L. Lievsay (Durham, N.C., 1968), 114–45.

13. "Orator and Poet," 33.

and civic goals. His life was lived in the fora, the law courts, or wherever else the public weal was at stake. The poet was a private person, by preference distanced from the tumult of the marketplace. Even his epic poetry was a step removed from day-by-day political realities. He was dedicated to the *vita contemplativa* of study rather than to active engagement. The successful orator, in touch with the feelings of others, used all his skills to speak "appropriately" for the audience in front of him. The poet was sensitively in touch with his own feelings—in Milton's phrase, quoted by Hardison, in touch with the "paradise within thee happier far."[14] In the *Dialogus de oratoribus*, Tacitus gave classic expression to this conflict between the tumultuous and public life of the orator and the quiet, secluded life of the poet.[15]

What further specifications of the Renaissance "poet" are important insofar as he was the teacher or practitioner of "grammar"? From Marrou and others we know a great deal about how poetry or literature was taught in antiquity.[16] The grammarian was almost myopically attached to his texts. His exposition of them was philological and concentrated on a word-by-word or line-by-line reading of them. When it was necessary to rise above this "atomistic" exegesis to broader meaning, allegory was invoked.

Allegory received a Christian benediction from Origen and other early Christian writers, and it was thenceforth the standard method for arriving at the inner, "meta-philological," most genuine intent of the author.[17] In accordance with Hellenistic practice of this method and its adaptation by Philo and others, literary texts were seen as expressions of philosophical truths artistically masked "under the poetic veil." As Marrou showed, the "grammarian's object was ultimately moral."[18]

14. Ibid. 44. On the distinctive relationships of "eloquence" (oratory) and poetry to feelings, see John Stuart Mill, "What Is Poetry?" in *Literary Essays*, ed. Edward Alexander (Indianapolis, 1967), 57. I am grateful to Professor Philip Rule of The College of the Holy Cross for calling my attention to Mill's essay.

15. See, e.g., esp. 12–13.

16. See Marrou, *Education in Antiquity*, esp. 160–75, 374–83, and his *Saint Augustin et la fin de la culture antique*, 4th ed. (Paris, 1958). See also J. Reginald O'Donnell, "Coluccio Salutati on the Poet-Teacher," *Mediaeval Studies*, 22 (1960), 240–56.

17. See the introduction by Pierre Nautin, "Origène prédicateur," in his edition of Origen's *Homélies sur Jérémie*, ed. Pierre Husson and Pierre Nautin, Sources chrétiennes, No. 232 (Paris, 1976), 136–51. See also R. P. C. Hanson, *Allegory and Event: A Study of the Sources and Significance of Origen's Interpretation of Scripture* (Richmond, Va., 1959).

18. *Education in Antiquity*, 234.

These philosophical, allegorical, and moralistic methods of interpreting literature had an immense impact on the writings of the Fathers of the Church, who were themselves products of the ancient schools of grammar and rhetoric. I will mention only two areas where that impact is most significant for present purposes. First of all, the methods of the grammarian encouraged the development of the homiletic form of preaching.[19] That is to say, it encouraged the method of preaching the Bible that was patterned after the teaching style of the grammarian in his classroom—a familiar, verse-by-verse exposition of the text that had practically no other "scientific" techniques for interpretation besides philology and an acute sense of what the "author"—in this case, God—had said elsewhere in the book. The verse-by-verse technique deprived the homily of oratorical structure and turned it into the "formless form" *par excellence.*

Though the patristic age knew, and sometimes practiced, the oratorical principles spelled out in the classical treatises on rhetoric, it generally spurned them, especially in the West, in favor of the simpler homily. Jerome, Erasmus' great hero, held them suspect; they might produce applause for the orator's skills instead of tears for one's own sins.[20] Augustine's harsh words in the *Confessions* about his career as *rhetor* are well known.[21] He and other Fathers reacted against the pompous and vacuous oratory of their day, the oratory of the Second Sophistic. That oratory lacked content—*res*—and, hence, was to be spurned.

This does not mean that the Fathers could, or wanted to, rid themselves of all they had learned about rhetoric. The pattern of their thinking was often determined by it.[22] Rhetorical figures of thought and diction were discussed and employed. Some sermons from the era bear little resemblance to the homily; in their more narrative and historical character they show a close affinity with classical oratory and with the classicizing Renaissance sermons at the papal court.[23] The

19. See the discussion by Nautin, *Homélies*, 123–36. For the development through the synagogue, see Thomas K. Carroll, *Preaching the Word* (Wilmington, Del., 1984), esp. 9–20.

20. See, e.g., Jerome, *Epistola* 52, 8, *PL* 22, 534. Recall that Erasmus edited Jerome's letters, published by Froben in 1516.

21. See, e.g., 6.6; 8.2; 9.2, 4.

22. See, e.g., Robert Dick Sider, *Ancient Rhetoric and the Art of Tertullian* (Oxford, 1971).

23. See Carroll, *Preaching the Word*, and Jean Leclercq, "Prédication et rhétorique au temps de saint Augustin," *Revue Bénédictine*, 57 (1947), 117–31.

purposes of oratory—to please, to move, to teach—were applied to sacred eloquence, and Augustine expertly discourses on these purposes and on the use of the high, middle, and low styles in the fourth book of the *De doctrina christiana*. But the originality, genius, and even revolutionary quality of that fourth book lie in how far it was removed from the classical treatises on oratory. Augustine assumed in his readers a familiarity with those treatises that would not often be verified in the succeeding generations that looked to the *De doctrina christiana* as the fundamental handbook on Christian oratory.[24]

The second area where the grammarian's techniques had special import was on exegesis. The first three books of the *De doctrina christiana* were an important monument in the history of exegesis. Though they bear some relationship to that part of rhetoric known as invention, they actually are more redolent of the interpretative aims and techniques of the grammarian than of the persuasional aims and techniques of the *rhetor*.

For Fathers like Origen and Augustine, the Old and New Testaments were transformed under the impact of the grammarian's allegory into books of doctrine or "philosophy." Perhaps better said, the sapiential and doctrinal character of some of the books—like Proverbs and the Pauline Epistles—was somewhat extended to them all. Interest in the historical character of many parts of the Bible was thereby considerably reduced. Augustine's very vacillation about how closely "Platonism" approximated Christianity indicates that for him Christianity was a wisdom and the Bible was the book that taught its philosophy.

In Erasmus the tradition of the "Christian grammarian" was strongly operative.[25] He wrote poetry and inculcated the need to study it. He was a man of texts—he edited them, translated them, criticized them.

24. See Marrou, *Saint Augustin*, 505–40; Murphy, *Medieval Rhetoric*, 43–88; Christine Mohrmann, "Saint Augustine and the 'Eloquentia,'" in *Etudes sur le latin des chrétiens*, 4 vols. (Rome, 1958–77), I, 351–70, and her "Saint Augustin prédicateur," ibid. 391–402. See also Pierre Riché, *Education and Culture in the Barbarian West, from the Sixth through the Eighth Century*, trans. John J. Contreni (Columbia, S.C., 1976), 79–95.

25. See, e.g., Chomarat, *Grammaire*, and his "Les *Annotations* de Valla, celles d'Erasme et la grammaire," in *Histoire de l'exégèse au XVIe siècle: Textes du Colloque International tenu à Genève en 1976 réunis par Olivier Fatio et Pierre Fraenkel*, Etudes de Philologie et d'Histoire, No. 34 (Geneva, 1978), 202–28, esp. 227–28. For a wider perspective related to this issue, see Anthony Grafton, "Renaissance Readers and Ancient Texts: Comments on Some Commentators," *Renaissance Quarterly*, 38 (1985), 615–49.

He was stylist—but a stylist in the sector of texts for students and treatises for the literate. His writings are all in some way related to the educational program that he saw as essential for the revival of good letters, good theology, and the "philosophy" of Christ.

Erasmus consistently described the contents of the Bible as a "philosophy." The term is a perfectly accurate description of what he understood the Bible to be. When the "celestial philosophy" Erasmus so tirelessly expounded is analyzed, it proves to be a sapiential understanding of the Christian message. That is to say, the "philosophy" is a body of truths, revealed in the literal sense of Scripture, cunningly concealed in the mystical sense. In that mystical sense, the "arcana" await the delight of the wise and pious person's discovery. Although Erasmus affirmed that Christ was the restorer of human nature, he saw Christ's restoration principally as communication of a wisdom.[26] In the exchange with Luther, he assumed that grace was a gift or power bestowed on the will to enable it to do the good,[27] but throughout his life he consistently viewed Christ's "philosophy" as an enlightenment that was the principal grace or benefit he conferred on the world.

At the end of "The Godly Feast," Erasmus' most sublime colloquy, Eusebius gives four books to his friends—Plutarch's *Moralia*, the Book of Proverbs, the Pauline Epistles, and the Gospel of Matthew. The first two are, without qualification, collections of wise sayings, and the third is principally a book of teachings. Erasmus' reason for singling out Matthew over the other three Gospels seems to rest on the same principle of selection. Whereas the Gospels of Mark and Luke concentrate on actions and the Gospel of John is a fusion of the great signs Jesus did with lengthy discourses to explicate their meaning, Matthew's Gospel most closely among the four approximates a collection of sayings.[28] Even the works of Cicero that Erasmus has Eusebius commend to his friends are not orations but works of a philosophical char-

26. The most impressive statement of this viewpoint, which pervades Erasmus' writings, is the *Paraclesis*, LB, V, 137–44. See also, e.g., *Ratio verae theologiae*, ibid. 84, 89, 91–92, 96–98, 106.

27. See, e.g., Ernst-Wilhelm Kohls, "La position théologique d'Erasme et de la tradition dans le 'De libero arbitrio'," in *Colloquium Erasmianum*, 69–88.

28. See, e.g., John L. McKenzie, "The Gospel according to Matthew," in *The Jerome Biblical Commentary*, ed. Raymond E. Brown et al., 2 vols. in 1 (Englewood Cliffs, N. J., 1968), II, 62: "Mt emphasizes the sayings of Jesus both in discourses and in narratives. . . . In Mt Jesus is contrasted with the scribes, the teacher[s] of Judaism; he is a teacher far superior to them. . . . Mt is as much a presentation of Jesus' teaching as it is a recital of his life. . . . [It is] a handbook of Christian conduct to be used by teachers."

acter like the *De senectute*, the *De amicitia*, the *De officiis*, and the *Tusculan Disputations*. Such preferences are typical of Erasmus and can be verified in his other writings.[29]

Erasmus' choice of texts, therefore, is consistent. It fits with his general approach to literature, sacred and profane. We need only recall that the work that established his reputation with his contemporaries was the *Adages*. Erasmus was proud of that work and continued to revise it during his lifetime.[30] Although he offered it to the public as an instrument by which students might improve their style, he used it as a vehicle for educating his public on moral and religious issues. Perhaps more important, the very structure of the work—the medium, if you will—was much of its message and a good clue to the method of Erasmus' grammatical culture. It was a collection of wise sayings. This "oracular" approach to literature resembles the grammatical techniques of interpretation used by the Fathers, who tended to see the Bible as a vast storehouse of sayings, each of which had some truth to convey.[31]

Anyone who has read the *Adages* will have noted their admonitory and ethically prescriptive character. Much of the philosophy or wisdom Erasmus propounds relates immediately to conduct and has a moralistic emphasis, as critics have often observed. When Erasmus states in his *Ecclesiastes* that the preacher's task is to explain and commend God's "edicts, promises, and will," he more than suggests that he sees Scripture as a book that, while having a supernal power to touch the heart, also to a large extent contains precisely such elements.[32]

What about Erasmus and classical rhetoric? He of course appreciates its stylistic component—"ut copiose splendideque dicas."[33] Like Cicero and other ancient authors, as well as many of his Renaissance predecessors, he demonstrated great ability in widening the scope of

29. For instance, in the *Institutio principis christiani*, he recommends in the first place the Book of Wisdom, Ecclesiasticus, and Proverbs, and, after these, some similar readings from sacred and profane authors, ASD, IV.1, 180–81. See also *Ecclesiastes*, LB, V, 856. See Charles Béné, "Erasme et Cicéron," in *Colloquia Turonensia*, II, 571–79.

30. See Margaret Mann Phillips, *The 'Adages' of Erasmus: A Study with Translations* (Cambridge, 1964).

31. See Hanson, *Allegory and Event*, 367.

32. See the *Ecclesiastes*, LB, V. 770, "edicta, promissa ac voluntatem." See also, e.g., *Institutio principis christiani*, ASD, IV.1, 147 ("Christi imperatoris tui leges"), 179 ("ad Christi regulam"), 210 ("Christi decretis:); *Ratio verae theologiae*, LB, V, 89 ("Christi decretis"), 92 ("decretis Christi"), 97 ("sua decreta"), 98 ("suas leges"), 117 ("praecepta"). According to Erasmus, the secular orator's task consists in persuading the people to accept the monarch's laws and decrees; see *Ecclesiastes*, LB, V, 770–71.

33. *Ratio verae theologiae*, LB, V, 77.

rhetoric from oratory to other forms of discourse and in giving it a more literary cast. The *De copia* of 1511 excellently illustrates his mastery of this element in the rhetorical tradition. Moreover, he was one of the first in the Renaissance to construct a treatise on epistolography derived from rhetorical works. His *Opus de conscribendis epistolis* was among the most influential of such Renaissance treatises.

But insofar as rhetoric means oratory, he was uninterested in it, unsure of how to deal with it. He advocated declamations as a teaching technique, to be sure. Moreover, he composed some himself; two of his most famous works–the *Praise of Folly* and the *Complaint of Peace*–were in fact designated declamations.[34] But the declamation was by tradition and definition a classroom exercise, a fact Erasmus knew full well.[35] The declamations he wrote were essays meant to be read and studied rather than delivered before a live audience.

Erasmus was not interested in training orators, as the scant attention oratory receives in his *De ratione studii* suggests. In the *Ciceronianus* he adopts the position that the judicial and deliberative oratory of classical theory, even if it could now be practiced in Latin, was utterly impractical.[36] He tried his pen once at secular demonstrative oratory, the *Panegyric* of Philip of Hapsburg that he presented to the prince in 1504; he never again wrote a similar piece.[37]

Erasmus severely criticized the "sacred" oratory or preaching of his day.[38] The alternatives he proposed, however, have never been comprehensively studied. Even a general familiarity with his works shows that these alternatives are more complex than even his own complex treatise on preaching, the *Ecclesiastes* of 1535, would indicate. He labored over that treatise, off and on, for many years, and the result was a work whose revolutionary character we are only beginning to

34. Also sometimes classified as declamations are: *Encomium matrimonii*, ASD, I.5, 333–416; *Encomium medicinae*, ibid. I.4, 145–86; *De pueris statim ac liberaliter instituendis*, ibid. I.2, 1–78; *In genere consolatorio declamatio de morte*, LB, IV, 617–24; *Declamatio . . . quae superiori declamationi e Luciano versae respondeat*, ASD, I.1, 516–51; *De contemptu mundi*, ASD, V.1, 39–86.

35. See *Paraphrasis seu potius epitome in elegantiarum libros Laurentii Vallae*, ASD, I.4, 313: "Declamator, qui aut in scholis, aut secum fictam causam agit, ut possit veram rectius agere. Declamare est exercere se in orando ficte. Inde declamationes Quintiliani." See also *Ciceronianus*, ASD, I.2, 633.

36. ASD, I.2, 654. For some Italian opinions in the Quattrocento, see my *Praise and Blame*, 46.

37. For the text, with introduction by O. Herding, see ASD, IV.1, 1–93.

38. See, e.g., *Praise of Folly*, LB, IV, 475–79; *Ecclesiastes*, ibid. V, 771, 953–55; *Ratio verae theologiae*, ibid. 136; *Ciceronianus*, ASD, I.2, 637–39.

appreciate.[39] Nonetheless, he admitted that he found the project uncongenial, difficult to bring to conclusion.[40] Immeasurably important though it was, it failed to satisfy his contemporaries, just as it has failed to satisfy his critics through the ages.[41]

Although in the *Ciceronianus* Erasmus seemingly rejected classical oratory for the Christian preacher, in the *Ecclesiastes* some years later he tries to adapt the classical *genera* of oratory, especially the deliberative *genus*, to Christian purposes.[42] There are, thus, notable discrepancies between this advocacy of the classical *genera* for the pulpit and what he elsewhere recommends by word or example. Even in the *Ecclesiastes* he briefly mentions the homiletic form, though without explicit commendation of it.[43] He even seems to make allowance for use of the "thematic" (dialectical or Scholastic) form of preaching.[44]

Although he was a priest, Erasmus for all practical purposes never seems to have preached in public.[45] Nonetheless, several works that he professedly composed as sermons survive. Two of them—the *Concio de puero Jesu* and the *De magnitudine misericordiarum Domini concio*—are adaptations of classical panegyric or demonstrative oratory.[46] It can be argued that two others betray his more considered judgment

39. See my "Erasmus and the History of Sacred Rhetoric: The *Ecclesiastes* of 1535," *Erasmus of Rotterdam Society Yearbook*, 5 (1985), 1–29.

40. See the prefatory letter to Christoph von Stadion, LB, V, 767–70. The text follows, cols. 769–1100. On the *Ecclesiastes*, see, besides my article cited in n. 39: Charles Béné, *Erasme et saint Augustin, ou Influence de saint Augustin sur l'Humanisme d'Erasme*, Travaux d'Humanisme et Renaissance, No. 103 (Geneva, 1969), 372–425; James Michael Weiss, "*Ecclesiastes* and Erasmus: The Mirror and the Image," *Archive for Reformation History*, 65 (1974), 83–108; and Robert G. Kleinhans, *Erasmus' Doctrine of Preaching: A Study of 'Ecclesiastes, sive De ratione concionandi'* (Ann Arbor: University Microfilms, 1968).

41. See Béné, *Erasme et Augustin*, 425; André Godin, "Erasme et le modèle origénien de la prédication," in *Colloquia Turonensia*, II, 819; and my "Content and Rhetorical Forms in Sixteenth-Century Treatises on Preaching," in *Renaissance Eloquence*, 245.

42. See LB, V, 858–59, 887–92. For the *Ciceronianus*, see ASD, I.2, 654. Gerhard B. Winkler tries to show the influence of the *genera* on some of Erasmus' early theological writings, *Erasmus von Rotterdam und die Einleitungsschriften zum Neuen Testament*, Reformationsgeschichtliche Studien und Texte, No. 108 (Münster, 1974).

43. See LB, V, 953.

44. See ibid. cols. 862–64, 953–55.

45. See Allen I, 37, 146.

46. LB, V, cols. 599–610 and 557–88. I here assume that James Tracy is correct in his redating of the *Concio de puero Jesu* from 1511 to 1503, "On the Composition Dates of Seven of Erasmus' Writings," *Bibliothèque d'Humanisme et Renaissance*, 31 (1969), 355–64, esp. 361–62. Erasmus' *Oratio funebris in funere Bertae de Heyen*, LB, VIII, 551–60, is a consolatory letter, based on principles of demonstrative rhetoric, rather than a sermon or oration.

as to what a real sermon should look like. The first of these is the *conciuncula* contained in the 1525 edition of his liturgy for Our Lady of Loreto.[47] Since this sermon was composed by him in his maturity as an example of liturgical preaching, it surely indicates his thinking on the matter. The *conciuncula* bears practically no resemblance to a classicizing oration, which would have been characterized by an exordium, narration, peroration, and the other parts that rhetoric prescribed. It in fact stands clearly in the tradition of the patristic homily, in that it is for the most part a moralizing and doctrinal commentary on the first two chapters of the Gospel of Luke and on the story of the marriage feast at Cana in chapter two of John's Gospel.

The *In psalmum quartum concio* in even more faithful fashion adheres to the verse-by-verse exposition of the text that is the hallmark of the homily, as distinguished from the oration.[48] In his dedicatory letter to John Longland in 1525, Erasmus explicitly makes the point that he intends this work, in some contrast to his previous publications on the Psalms, as a *concio*. We know, therefore, that the title is deliberate and, for our purposes, important. Erasmus goes on to state that he mightily exerted himself to make this a good sermon, but, as with the *Ecclesiastes*, he is not quite satisfied.[49] In any case, the critical edition of this piece manifests beyond any doubt its patristic inspiration in both form and content. The homiletic form is verified in other works, like the *Concionalis interpretatio in psalmum LXXXV* of 1528, and even in his *Enarratio psalmi XIV* written after the *Ecclesiastes*, shortly before his death.[50]

His esteem for the homilies of the Fathers was, therefore, genuine and lasting. In his little biography of Origen, a preface to his edition of the *Opera*, he admiringly describes Origen's early career as a teacher of grammar, and he gives an accurate and relatively detailed analysis of his homiletic style.[51] This the style he also admired in his friend, the "Erasmian saint," Jacques Vitrier.[52] I submit, therefore, that at a

47. ASD, V.1, 99–107.
48. Ibid. V.2, 191–276.
49. Ibid. 191.
50. Ibid. V.3, 329–427; V.2, 285–317.
51. LB, VIII, 426, 430, 438–49. Béné emphasizes the influence of Augustine's *De doctrina christiana* on Erasmus, *Erasme et saint Augustin*, 372–425, as does J. D. P. Warners, "Erasmus, Augustinus en de Retorika, "*Nederlands Archief voor Kerkgeschiedenis*, NS 51 (1971), 125–48. These studies need to be consulted in conjunction with those by André Godin referred to in the following note.
52. See the studies by André Godin: "De Vitrier à Origène: Recherches sur la

minimum the image he left us of his views on preaching shows that his hand was less steady when he addressed the problem of oratory than when he addressed other problems central to the Humanistic tradition.

The design of his own "homilies," despite his innovative use of the classical term *concio* to designate them, follows the verse-for-verse "formless form" of the Fathers.[53] Like patristic homilies his were, in fact, patterned after the pedantic *explication de texte* of the grammarian rather than the speech of the orator. Erasmus' "homilies" were replete, moreover, with short quotations from Scripture that often follow upon one another in such quick succession that they at first glance read like the litany of proof-texts that characterized Scholastic sermons. But these quotations are perhaps more accurately described as listings of wise sayings, holy adages. Though Erasmus locates preaching in the charism of "prophecy," he defines that charism as a persuasive imparting of wisdom.[54] His own "homilies" are, therefore, far removed from the blunt proclamations of Jeremiah and Hosea. Not confrontation, but teaching, is the task of the Erasmian "prophet."

So much for the structure and form of sacred oratory. What about its content? Erasmus is clear and unwavering. The preacher expounds "the philosophy of Christ." Erasmus on several occasions describes that philosophy as containing major doctrines of Christianity like the Redemption and the Mystical Body.[55] There are, moreover, emphases that are distinctive, like his famous statement in his letter to John Carondelet, 1523, that "the sum and substance of our religion consists in peace and unanimity.[56]

---

patristique érasmienne," in *Colloquium Erasmianum*, 47–57; "Erasme et le modèle origénien de la prédication," in *Colloquia Turonensia*, II, 807–20; "Jean Vitrier et le 'cénacle' de Saint-Omer," ibid. 781–805; *L'Homélaire de Jean Vitrier, Texte, étude thématique et sémantique: Spiritualité franciscaine en Flandre au XVIe siècle*, Travaux d'Humanisme et Renaissance, No. 116 (Geneva, 1971), esp. 14–18; "The *Enchiridion Militis Christiani*: The Modes of an Origenian Appropriation," *Erasmus of Rotterdam Society Yearbook*, 2 (1982), 47–79; and esp. *Erasme: Lecteur d'Origène* (Geneva, 1982). See also his edition of Erasmus' famous letter (#1211) to Justus Jonas, *Vies de Jean Vitrier et de Jean Colet* (Angers: Editions Moreana, [1982]).

53. On Erasmus' use of *concio*, see my "Erasmus and Rhetoric," 14–16.

54. See, e.g., *Ecclesiastes*, LB, V, 798: ". . . nam prophetas appello, qui explanant arcanae scripturae mysteria, et hoc prophetiae genus inter praecipua dona Spiritus commemo[illegible] Apostolus." See also ibid. cols. 824–26, where Erasmus appeals to the example of Jesus, the "prophet," teaching the Samaritan woman at the well (John 4). For a similar use of this passage by Nicholas of Cusa, see my *Praise and Blame*, 99. On "prophecy" in Erasmus, see also his *Ratio verae theologiae*, LB, V, 76.

55. See, e.g., *Ratio verae theologiae*, LB, V, 76; the letter to John Slechta, 1519, Allen, IV, 118.

56. Allen, V, 177: "Summa nostrae religionis pax est et unanimitas."

There is also the strongly Christocentric nature of this philosophy. Christ is, as Erasmus repeats, the "scope" and "aim" of the Christian life.[57] This Christological focus has two characteristics germane to the present discussion. First, although Christ is described in a number of different terms like "leader," "prince," or "head," nonetheless the "image" of him that predominates is that of teacher. Christ's redemptive mission is consequently, sapiential, even educational.[58]

The mystical character of Erasmus' Christology is the second aspect of it that is important for us. This aspect of his *pietas* has received much attention.[59] We now finally see what a great disservice scholars have done to Erasmus by looking upon him simply as a moralist. The ethical and behavorial concerns in his *pietas* are based on inner religious affections, and even on a degree of mystical identification with Christ living in the soul.

It is important to note the transhistorical aspect of this Erasmian Christ; it is important to note the immanentist aspect; it is important to note, as well, Erasmus' relatively scarce interest in the deeds and actions of the Jesus of Nazareth depicted especially in the Gospels of Mark and Luke. Erasmus could have appropriated this particular appreciation of Christ from so many sources that it is perhaps useless to speculate whence it derives. In any event, the sapiential and mystical character of his Christology was appropriate for cultivating the "paradise within" that is the poet's particular domain.

If we now turn to the religious vision projected by the Renaissance orators at the papal court, we have a foil to clarify some of the points under discussion. The first thing to be noticed is that these men, by virtue of their preaching office, could not afford to be ambivalent on oratorical form. As I have shown in my book, the peculiar religious vision they created was due in large measure to their adoption of the *genus demonstrativum* (encomium or panegyric) of classical oratory.

57. See Marjorie O'Rourke Boyle, *Erasmus on Language and Method in Theology* (Toronto, 1977), 72–81.

58. See, e.g., *Ecclesiastes*, LB, V, 769–76.

59. See the studies by Georges Chantraine: "Le mysterion paulinien selon les Annotationes d'Erasme," *Recherches de science religieuse*, 58 (1970), 351–82; "L'Apologia ad Latomum: Deux conceptions de la théologie," in *Scrinium*, II, 51–75; "Mysterium et Sacramentum dans le 'Dulce Bellum,'" in *Colloquium Erasmianum*, pp. 33–45; "Erasme, lecteur des psaumes," in *Colloquia Turonensia*, II, 691–712; *"Mystère" et "Philosophie du Christ" selon Erasme: Etude de la lettre à P. Volz et de la "Ratio verae theologiae" (1518)*, Bibliothèque de la Faculté de Philosophie et Lettres de Namur, No. 49 (Namur, 1971).

This form drew from them a positive and activist appreciation of man and the world. It focused their attention on great deeds, and thus enabled them to see Scripture more clearly as a book of history. The words *gesta*, *facta*, and *magnalia* appeared as often in their vocabulary as did *caelestis philosophia* and *philosophia Christi* in Erasmus. Their sermons were panegyrics of the actions of God, of Christ and of saints of the Old and New Testaments. They felt little need, therefore, to allegorize the text; allegorical interpretations of Scripture are in fact rather rare in their sermons.

All three of the classical *genera* of oratory were constructed with a view to civic and public needs. Thus, by the preachers' adoption of a classical *genus*, their eyes were turned outwards. Their many funeral eulogies were pronounced over popes, cardinals, and jurists—men whose lives had been spent in public office. These orations could therefore easily fulfill the prescription of rhetorical treatises that the virtues to be celebrated in such eulogies were especially those of a public and civic nature. As the eulogies praised such virtues, they validated a concern for this world, even for the building of churches and palaces and for the promotion of the arts. The "civic Humanism" of the Renaissance has a correlate in this sacred oratory and is thereby shown to have a more strongly rhetorical component than is sometimes perceived in it.[60] In such a context the "image" of Christ is less that of a teacher than of a hero who by his *actions* conferred immense benefits on all humanity.

As I earlier indicated, there are a number of recurring themes in the preachers that parallel or anticipate themes we accept as peculiarly Erasmian. Like Erasmus, for instance, the preachers commend the reading of the Bible and the Fathers of the Church as a first step towards true piety; their failure similarly to commend Scholastic authors is significant. They deplore the venality that controls ecclesiastical offices; they call for the reform of the Church and the Curia. They describe and approve what we can properly call "godly feasts," in which good company and good conversation inflame both host and guests with love of God and neighbor. Perhaps most striking, their emphasis

60. The studies by Hans Baron are, of course, central to the discussion, esp. his *The Crisis of the Early Italian Renaissance* rev. ed. (Princeton, 1966). For a vigorous attack on Baron that correctly emphasizes the new rhetorical "paradigm," see Jerrold E. Seigel, " 'Civic Humanism' vs. Ciceronian Rhetoric," *Past and Present*, No. 34 (July 1966), 3–48.

on peace and concord as the societal goal imposed by Christian piety is as insistent and impressive in their writings as it is in Erasmus's.

But, for all that, a different spirit is operative. For instance, the preachers consistently celebrate "the dignity of man," a theme closely related to the practice of epideictic rhetoric. This theme is of course present in Erasmus,[61] but his grammatical practice of rhetoric does not lead him to exploit it to the same degree. More broadly–teaching the philosophy of Christ is not the same thing as celebrating God's great deeds.

Erasmus' location of his "godly feast" in the country, in a secluded place remote from the city, is another symptom of a different spirit. For Cicero, "charming gardens" are alien to the orator's way of life.[62] But in the opening pages of Erasmus' colloquy, Eusebius betrays his prejudice by discoursing on the merits of country over city. Erasmus prefers, in a word, a "monastic" setting over an urban one.[63] He prefers *otium* to *negotium*. Unlike the characters in More's *Utopia*, the guests at the "godly feast" never address the possibility of dedicating their lives to public service and seem content with a life of private, though charitable, piety.[64]

"Monachatus non est pietas," Erasmus emphatically declared in the *Enchiridion*.[65] It is one of his most frequently quoted lines. His criticism of the monasticism of his day was almost as devastating as his criticism of the mendicant friars. To describe his piety as in any way monastic seems to fly in the face of Erasmus' words and actions and to ignore his admirable effort to encourage a deep spiritual life for people in all states of life. It also seems to fly in the face of his increasing efforts to promote more effective instruments for pastoral care, for the public ministry of the Church–one of the most important and

61. See, e.g., *De magnitudine misericordiarum Domini concio*, LB, V, 570–72; *Enchiridion*, ibid., 55.

62. See *De Oratore*, III, 63.

63. See also the "Hieronymi Stridonensis vita," in *Opuscula*. pp. 145–47, 158–59.

64. For a brief comparison of More with the preachers at the court and an attempt to isolate some medieval features in his piety, see my "Thomas More's Spirituality Compared," *Thought*, 52 (1977), 319–23. See also Roger Lovatt, "The *Imitation of Christ* in Late Medieval England," *Transactions of the Royal Historical Society*, 5th ser., 18 (1968), 97–121. On the relationship of *otium* to Renaissance Humanism and its implications for understanding that enterprise, see now the perceptive article by John F. Tinkler, "Renaissance Humanism and the *genera eloquentiae*," *Rhetorica*, 5 (1987), 279–309.

65. LB, V, 65.

distinctive, as well as least appreciated, aspects of his *pietas*.[66] Yet a monastic residue, vague and in the distant background, seems somehow operative even as he moves piety out of the monastery.[67] A city, he after all says, is nothing other than a huge monastery.[68]

Erasmus' commendation of "true monasticism" in his *Life of Saint Jerome* perhaps reveals more of the "true Erasmus" than critics commonly concede.[69] Jerome's companions are his books and the Lord, and his mission is "to write" and to "teach"; even while "in the world," he holds himself aloof from the forum and public office. It was in fact the monks who continued and transmitted the scribal tradition of the grammarians of late antiquity and imbued their spirituality with it.[70] Just as Luther, for all his railing against Scholastic theology and his creation of a new theological style to displace it, was never able to purge from that style all vestiges of his Scholastic education, so the "monk of Steyn" never altogether forsook the monastic influences of his youth.[71]

Erasmus' Humanism is, therefore, grammatical or literary rather than oratorical. Erasmus is interested in "poetry," not speeches; he favors homilies over orations; he will reform society through texts and schools, not public service freely chosen; he is a scribe and teacher, not a politician, lawyer, or civic servant; his location is in the *scriptorium* and classroom, not in the forum, law courts, or council chambers of kings—not even in the pulpit; he is dedicated to the *vita contemplativa* of study rather than to the *vita activa* of engagement; the books he reads and the books he writes are treasure chests of wisdom and celestial philosophy, not stories of great deeds.

66. See my "Introduction" to CWE 66.

67. I am not the first to detect the monastic element in Erasmus' spirituality. See Jean-Pierre Massaut's "Humanisme et spiritualité chez Erasme," in the *Dictionnaire de spiritualité*, VII (1969), 1006–28, esp. 1021–23.

68. Letter to Paul Volz, 1518, Allen, III, 376: ". . . quid aliud est civitas quam magnum monasterium?"

69. "Hieronymi Stridonensis vita," in *Opuscula*, 145–47, 151–52, 154–55, 163, 170. See also the letter to Paul Volz, 1518, Allen, III, 375–76. On Erasmus and Jerome, see Joseph Coppens, "Le portrait de saint Jérôme d'après Erasme," in *Colloquia Turonensia*, II, 821–28; John Olin, "Erasmus and Saint Jerome," *Thought*, 54 (1979), 313–21; and Eugene F. Rice, *Saint Jerome in the Renaissance* (Baltimore, 1985), esp. 116–36.

70. See, e.g., Jean Leclercq, *The Love of Learning and the Desire for God* (New York, 1962), 23–32.

71. See my "Erasmus and Luther: Continuity and Discontinuity as Key to Their Conflict," *Sixteenth Century Journal*, 5, No. 2 (1974), 47–65.

His piety is of the same style. Under the influence of the grammatical tradition, Christ becomes the teacher rather than the prophet; he is found more easily in the secluded garden than in the marketplace; he is more a purveyor of a philosophy than a proclaimer of judgment; he saves through illumination of the soul rather than through action in the city, whether that city be Jerusalem or Babylon. Erasmus himself, speaking in a different context, said it well; "Qualis est philosophia, talem decet esse professorem."[72]

The correspondence, between Erasmus' Christ and the style of Erasmus' own life and culture is consistent. His *pietas* is, therefore, distinctive, different in certain respects from even some of his contemporaries who also were devoted to *bonae litterae*, to the pursuit of eloquence, and to the message of the Bible. Much of this difference can be related to the difference between a grammatical (or literary) and an oratorical appropriation of Humanistic culture.

This article was originally delivered as a paper with a practically identical title in 1979 at the North Central Renaissance Conference, Ann Arbor. I mention this fact only to indicate that the title anticipated the publication of Jacques Chomarat's *Grammaire et rhétorique chez Erasme*, 2 vols. (Paris: "Les Belles Lettres," 1981). The paper was immediately solicited for publication in a volume scheduled soon to appear. Eight years later, with no publication in sight, I felt justified in reclaiming it. After revision I then submitted it for publication to this journal. Despite the similarity in titles, Chomarat and I deal with different, though related, issues.

References

Allen *Opus epistolarum Des. Erasmi Roterodami*, ed. P. S. Allen, H. M. Allen, and H. W. Garrod, 12 vols. (Oxford, 1906–58).

ASD: Desiderius Erasmus, *Opera omnia* (Amsterdam: North-Holland Publishing Company, 1969–).

Colloquia Turonensia: *Colloquia Erasmiana Turonensia*, ed. J.-C. Margolin, 2 vols. (Toronto, 1972).

Colloquium Erasmianum *Colloquium Erasmianum* (Mons, 1968).

CWE *Collected Works of Erasmus* (Toronto, 1974–).

LB Desiderius Erasmus, *Opera omnia*, ed. J. Leclerc, 10 vols. (Leiden, 1703–06).

Opuscula *Erasmi opuscula: A Supplement to the Opera omnia*, ed. Wallace K. Ferguson (The Hague, 1933).

Reedijk C. Reedijk, *The Poems of Desiderius Erasmus* (Leiden, 1956).

Scrinium *Scrinium Erasmianum*, ed. J. Coppens, 2 vols. (Leiden, 1969).

72. *Ecclesiastes*, LB, V, 794.

IX

Early Jesuit Spirituality: Spain and Italy

THE STORY OF IGNATIUS LOYOLA is well known and only a brief resumé of it need be provided here. Born into a noble family at the castle of Loyola in northern Spain in 1491, he had the sparse and chivalric education of his class. His military career ended in 1521 with a severe wound in his right leg received during the siege of Pamplona. During his convalescence he underwent a profound religious conversion while reading two medieval works—Ludolph of Saxony's *Life of Christ* and Jacopo da Voragine's lives of the saints entitled the *Golden Legend.*

He then spent a year in prayer and mortification at Manresa (1522–1523), where he experienced temptations and desolation of spirit, but also deep and refreshing mystical insights. He probably composed the substance of his *Spiritual Exercises* at this time, a sort of objectified recording of his own religious journey for the help of others. The desire to engage in some form of spiritual ministry soon convinced him that he needed a formal education in theology. After studying in several cities in Spain from 1524 to 1528, he finally arrived at the University of Paris, where he remained for seven years (1528–1535).

During all these years of study he guided a number of devout students through the course of his *Spiritual Exercises;* in Paris, finally, he gathered around himself a group of companions who would form the nucleus of the new order he soon founded. In 1537 Loyola and his companions went to Italy, and in 1540 Pope Paul III recognized them as a religious order, the Society of Jesus, with Ignatius as the first superior general. The *Exercises* were approved by the same pope in 1548, thus establishing the text as it had by then evolved as the definitive edition. Meanwhile, Ignatius began to compose the *Constitutions* of his order, the most thorough and systematically designed such instrument known up to that time. Toward the end of his life he was persuaded to tell his "story" to one of his companions, Luís Gonçalves da Câmara, but he got no farther than the events of 1538. Brief and jejune in details, the account nonetheless provides considerable information about "the pilgrim," as Ignatius referred to himself, and especially about his motivations and mystical experiences. These documents, along with segments of his spiritual diary and the over seven thousand letters that comprise his correspondence, are the principal basis upon which we reconstruct his religious message. He died in Rome on 31 July 1556.

Like the founders of other religious orders within the Roman Catholic Church, Loyola left an indelible imprint on the spiritual traditions of the Society of Jesus, and thence upon modern Catholicism. Loyola's imprint was intensified, however, beyond that of many other founders. While he was in Paris as a student, he had, in effect, already set the development of the Jesuit order in motion by persuading each of his companions to go through the *Spiritual Exercises* for a month or more under his guidance. This same experience was prescribed for all those who subsequently entered the order. Ignatius obviously hoped to induce in others a conversion and religious experience similar to his own during the early years of his religious quest. As H. Outram Evennett observed: "[The *Exercises*] were in a sense the systematised, de-mysticised quintessence of the process of Ignatius' own conversion and purposeful change of life, and they were intended to work a similar change in others."[1]

The book of the *Exercises,* intended as a manual for the person guiding others through the program it outlines, is divided into four "weeks" or major parts. The first week presents considerations about the purpose of life, the heinousness of sin, and the necessity and sweetness of repentance. The second week begins with a meditation on "the kingdom of Christ," which is followed by a series of meditations on Christ's incarnation and life up to his last days. The third week is dedicated to his suffering and death, and the final week to the apparitions of the risen Savior and related events. Besides these and other meditations, the book contains a number of directives for the director and the retreatant, some guidelines on fasting, almsgiving, and similar matters, and a number of other considerations. The book is not, in the first place, an exposition of a spiritual doctrine, but a detailed program, in outline form, for a month or more of reflection on one's life and on central mysteries of the Christian religion. It has been called with some accuracy "a recipe for conversion."[2] Among the more important appendixes to the book are several sets of "rules." One of them is for "the discernment of spirits" (313–36), in which the saint gives directives concerning the movement of spiritual consolation and desolation. This set of subtle directives has been the object of a number of studies and is generally considered to be one of the most perceptive parts of the book. It is here that we catch some slight glimpse of the author's own spiritual journey and the temptations and confirmations in spiritual growth that he underwent. Morever, the role of "consolation" in Jesuit spirituality and as a goal in the Jesuits' ministry can hardly be overestimated.

Another of these appendixes is a set of rules for "thinking with the Church" (352–70). Almost certainly inspired by Loyola's antipathy to certain ideas of Erasmus and of the Protestant reformers, it sets the *Exercises* firmly within an ecclesiological context. Here we see that for Loyola genuine spirituality had to be founded on a recognition of one's membership in a larger religious community and of the need to test one's inspirations against the objectified traditions of that community. Though often interpreted in a narrowly Roman Catholic sense, these "rules" are susceptible of a less rigoristic reading.

In its concepts, images, and directives, the book of the *Exercises* stands squarely within the Christian spiritual tradition, so much so that the search for its sources has consistently been frustrated by the very commonplace nature of its ideas. Most commentators are agreed, however, upon some direct relationship to the *devotio moderna,* and Ignatius in fact had a special fondness for the principal document of that late-medieval tradition, *The Imitation of Christ.* Aside from the text of the Gospels, the *Imitation* is the only book specifically recommended to the person following the course of the *Exercises* (100).

Despite the commonplace sources upon which the *Exercises* draws, two features of the book give it special force and have made it one of the most important documents in the history of Christian spirituality. The first such feature is its clear design, aimed at carrying out its stated purpose: "to conquer oneself and to order one's life without being influenced in one's decision by any inordinate affection" (21). That clarity of purpose provided the book with a psychological dynamism that, under an experienced director, proved to be extraordinarily powerful. Though the purpose as stated by Ignatius sounds stoic and rationalistic, it is promoted less by logic than by an activation of the affections, especially through the key meditations and considerations. Of special importance here are the meditation on the "Two Standards" (136–48)—that of Christ and that of Satan—and the reflections on "three classes of persons" (149–57) and on the "three kinds of humility" (165–68). In these exercises the aspirations of the retreatant to generosity and to a sense of *noblesse oblige* are particularly appealed to. Loyola's genius lay, therefore, in his sense of psychological organization. With a laconic, understated style and with a mass of seemingly disparate elements, he constructed a course in which generations have found themselves prepared to respond in a new way to an inner call for intimacy with the divine.

But what is especially remarkable about the course Loyola provides is its nonprescriptive character. This is the second feature of the book that deserves special attention. No line in it better expresses what Loyola expected to happen during the *Exercises* than his advice to the director to "permit the Creator to deal directly with the creature, and the creature directly with his Creator and Lord" (15). The saint had a profound confidence in the direct inspiration of God, which he felt he had himself experienced from the first moment of his conversion. The chief purpose of the *Exercises* was to facilitate the reception of such inspiration and make it effective for the future direction of the retreatant's life. Though Loyola's own experience was formally paradigmatic for the structure of the *Exercises,* he insisted that there was no greater error than to believe that God led all along the same path, and he tried to make ample room for such liberty of spirit in his rubrics and directives in the book.

In summary, I would stress that the book, and with it Jesuit spirituality, while being rationalistic in its language and arguments, is more profoundly concerned with right affectivity; while being logical in the organization of its parts, it is more profoundly psychological in its movement and design; and while being methodical in the aids it provides to prayer and spiritual discernment, it is more profoundly nonprescriptive in the outcome it foresees for the direct divine intervention that is its basic premise.

The book is, nonetheless, clear in the goal toward which it points: an "election," an ordering of life "for the greater service and praise" of God. Thus emerges another essential component in Ignatian spirituality. The single word that best expresses this fundamental element is "service." In the key meditation on "the kingdom of Christ" (91–99), the exercitant is urged to "distinguish himself in whatever concerns the service of the eternal king and Lord of all." The knightly imagery and context in which this meditation is enshrined do not essentially diminish the transcultural nature of its appeal. It is this consideration that led Joseph de Guibert to describe the Ignatian way as essentially a "spirituality of service," a phrase upon which it would be difficult to improve.[3]

From the first moment of his conversion, Loyola was attracted by the great deeds of saints like Dominic and Francis. "If they could so distinguish themselves in the service of the Lord, why cannot I?" was the question he repeatedly asked himself. Especially after the year of retreat at Manresa, Loyola specified the "great deeds" in some form of ministry of the Word for the help of others. At first this ministry of the Word was nothing more than informal conversation with devout persons about "the things of God." He soon began to preach to small groups that gathered around him, and then he began to guide individuals through his *Exercises.* The spiritual doctrine of the Jesuits was thereby from its origins intimately related to ministry, and to a certain extent even subordinated to it. With Ignatius we find one of the first strong expressions of this relationship in the history of Christian spirituality, and he provides us in his correspondence and legislation for the order with numerous practical interpretations of it. It is difficult for us, and perhaps it was difficult even for him, fully to realize what a dramatic break he effected with the monastic traditions of the early church and the Middle Ages. A significant influence on his new way of conceiving of religious life may have been that he had no experience of cloister or established monastic practice until he and his companions decided to found their own order.

The most dramatic symbol of what was involved was his adamant refusal to allow the Jesuits to chant the Divine Office in choir. In his day this practice was considered so central to life in a religious order that many considered that the Jesuits could not be a religious order without it. Eager though Ignatius was to conform himself and his followers to the Catholic tradition in the smallest detail, eager though he was for papal approval of the new order, he would not surrender this point. He doubtless saw it as symptomatic of his whole vision of how his spirituality was "ordered." It was ordered to "service," to ministry, and anything that interfered with that ordering, like the obligation to be present in choir several times a day, had to be excluded.

In several important instructions about the training of the younger members of the order, Ignatius insisted that their time for prayer and their ascetical practices be carefully moderated, so that these not interfere with their direct training for ministry. What he envisioned was a correlation of ministry and spirituality so that one was inconceivable for members of the order without the other. His most telling expression of this vision was in his exhortation (*Constitutions* 288) that Jesuits should "find God in all things"—not just in prayer, not only in the disciplined quiet of their houses, not simply in the solitude of their rooms.

Of all his disciples, Jerome Nadal (1507–1580) is the one who gave most powerful articulation of this idea with his celebrated phrase "contemplative in action."[4] Nadal's idea, genuinely reflecting Loyola's, implies the contemporaneity or at least reciprocity of contemplation and ministry. One of Nadal's effective illustrations of his point is his description of the habitation of the members of the order. Their "most perfect dwelling-place is in travel and pilgrimage from place to place, by which they seek to gain for Christ those lost sheep that are perishing."[5] There could hardly be a more dramatic contrast with the typically monastic vow of stability, by which the monk promised to spend his whole life within the confines of the monastery he had entered. This commentary by Nadal gives force to Ignatius's requirement in the *Constitutions* (588) that the members of his order be ready to travel from place to place for the sake of their ministry. The *Imitation of Christ,* one of Loyola's favorite books, warned that the person who traveled much could not expect to attain holiness. Ignatius turned this axiom around by insisting that it was only by engaging in the pilgrimage implied in ministry that the Jesuit could hope to attain the sanctification proper to his vocation.

Once again, it is the ideal of service that underlay this provision. Put in other terms, it was an ideal of availability for the needs of others. This ideal was institutionalized in the Society of Jesus by the famous "fourth vow" of obedience to the pope that professed members pronounced. As universal pastor, the pope had, in Loyola's understanding, the large vision of where the greatest pastoral needs prevailed. The Jesuits wanted to put themselves at his disposition to meet these needs. This was clearly the purpose of the vow as the original members of the order conceived it, and it fits perfectly with the ministerial intentionality with which Ignatian spirituality is imbued. In commenting on this vow, Nadal insists that the Jesuits are to be sent to minister where there are no ministers, where no one else wants to minister, and they are to do this without regard for their personal convenience or preference.[6] Thus a new asceticism begins to emerge that is not dependent for its practice on self-imposed austerities to curb one's own disordered tendencies, but on the rigors and hardship imposed by total dedication to an ideal of ministry in the world of ordinary people, with their often undisciplined needs and demands.

This brings us to the "world-affirming" quality of Ignatian piety. The expression is dangerous, for it can be interpreted as suggesting a compromise with the transcendent or a surrender to its opposite. That interpretation would utterly contradict everything that Loyola had experienced of the divine action within himself and that he hoped for in others. Nonetheless, the term does highlight an engagement with human reality, with all its contingencies, and a positive appreciation for human values that was characteristic of him and his piety.

It is, indeed, possible to trace a gradual evolution in Loyola's thinking on this issue from the days at Manresa, where a rigorous asceticism, a desire for eremitical seclusion, and a distaste for anything that might ingratiate him with his fellows—even cleanliness and a neat appearance—prevailed. This is quite different from the later Ignatius, who heartily recommended to his disciples that, while giving a preeminence to the "supernatural" means of serving God like prayer, they employ all the "natural" means that time and circumstances offered for the advancement of their ministry.

This reconciliation of the natural and the supernatural perhaps found its theological grounding in Loyola's study of Aquinas at Paris, for the great scholastic subscribed to the principle that "grace builds on nature" and fully articulated it in his system. Its true origins, however, relate to his earlier mystical experiences. Be that as it may, Loyola's most sublime expression of this sense of reconciliation was in his "Contemplation for Obtaining Divine Love" at the end of the "fourth week" of the *Exercises* (230–37). Here the exercitant sees "all things as creatures of the goodness of God and reflections of it." He is urged to relish this profound religious truth. Ignatius thus moves the Christian tradition of asceticism away from the ideal of the *contemptus mundi* that characterized much of the spirituality of the Middle Ages and was found in a marked degree even in the *devotio moderna*, from which he originally drew some of his own inspiration.

Although this theological insight can be correlated with the medieval system of Aquinas, it also corresponded in a general way with one aspect of the religious culture of the Italian Renaissance in which the early Jesuits moved. Especially at the papal court in the sixteenth century, a group of preachers influenced by the humanistic movement formulated a similar style of piety of "service" for persons whose lives were lived outside the cloister in the public life of church and state. This piety, too, was remarkably world-affirming. I have elaborated on this important development elsewhere,[7] but have discovered no clear evidence of influence one way or another between it and the first Jesuits. I call attention to the parallel here, however, because it provides further substantiation for the break with medieval spirituality that the Ignatian system, for all its medieval roots, suggests, and it also intimates why that system proved attractive to so many persons in the early years of the Society. It was attuned to the times.

Another correlation of Ignatian spirituality with the religious culture of the sixteenth century is possible; this time a line of influence can be unmistakably detected. The Lutheran doctrine of "justification by faith alone" caused Catholics to search their tradition on this issue more carefully than before. By the time the Council of Trent dealt with the matter in Session IV in 1547, Catholic theologians were aware of the dangers of Pelagianism and Semi-Pelagianism that the Lutherans accused Catholics of teaching. The Council tried to avoid any formulations that might seem to support the save-yourself tenets traditionally ascribed to the Pelagians, but at the same time it insisted on the necessity of human cooperation in the process of justification. As interpreted in a popular way, this meant an insistence on the role of "free will" in attaining salvation, while still maintaining the prevenient and constitutive role of grace.

Loyola raises this issue in the book of the *Exercises* where he counsels that grace should be spoken of only in such a way that "works and free will" are not slighted (369). The early Jesuits were involved in discussion on this issue within the Council of Trent and in polemics on it outside the Council. Since Lutherans "denied free will," the Jesuits especially emphasized it. There is a direct relationship between this Jesuit emphasis in the controversies with the Protestants in the sixteenth century and their position vis-à-vis the Dominicans over many of the same problems in the so-called *De Auxiliis* controversies a century later.

What this means for Jesuit spirituality is that it tended to have a decidedly activist character and helped promote the activist piety that Evennett found characteristic of the Counter-Reformation in general. Evennett's summary is worth quoting: "The spirituality of the Counter Reformation sprang from a triple alliance, as it were, between the Tridentine clarifications of the orthodox teaching on Grace and Justification, the practical urge of the day towards active works, and certain new developments in ascetical teaching and practice which promoted this outlook."[8] That last element—the "new developments"—was particularly characteristic of the spirituality developed by Loyola.

This activist character manifested itself in the varied and energetic ministries the early Jesuits undertook—in their works of mercy directed toward orphans, prostitutes, prisoners in jails, the sick in hospitals, and especially in their schools and their preaching. For all of Trent's emphasis on sacramental ministry and the Jesuits' promotion of it, especially the frequent reception of the Eucharist and penance that Jesuit preachers urged from the beginning, their real contribution lay, as I mentioned earlier, in some form of "ministry of the Word." This was typical of most Protestant ministry at the time and is generally recognized as such. It is not so clearly recognized how typical it was of the early Jesuits. The motivations for this general interest are complex and relate inextricably with the personal histories of the great leaders like Loyola, Luther, Calvin, and others, but certainly part of the impetus derives from the invention of printing, from the humanists' new concern with the recovery of ancient texts, and from their new interest in rhetoric and in other disciplines related to verbal communication in classroom, pulpit, and other public forums. The word—printed and oral, human and divine—emerged as a new focus for the intellectual and spiritual life of the day.

For the Jesuits the ministry of the Word took a number of forms, especially the most traditional one of preaching. But even in this form their ministry showed an energy and an imagination that were notable, if not altogether original. They not only preached from the pulpit of churches but also sought listeners in hospitals, piazzas, prisons, and even inns. Ignatius insisted that his men undertake this ministry wherever they went, and he followed their efforts with keen interest. Both Juan Ramírez and Francesco

Borgia–Jesuit contemporaries of Ignatius–composed treatises on how to preach.

Jerome Nadal left an important exhortation on this ministry of the Word in its various forms.[9] Peculiar to the Jesuits was the emphasis that Ignatius and Nadal placed on informal conversation, with individuals or groups, about "the things of God." In his exhortation Nadal gives sensible directives about how this practice could be made most effective.

We do not have as clear information as we would like about the content of the formal sermons the Jesuits preached. Loyola wanted "the errors of the heretics" to be refuted when occasion demanded it, but he tempered this advice with the warning that charity and good example would be more forceful means to winning them over than confrontation and controversy. His frequent instructions to the members of the Society were that they preach both by their words and by their example. This coupling of word and deed, almost a truism in the Christian tradition, was notably revived in the sixteenth century by the humanists. But it seems to have had a special significance for Ignatius in that he so consistently joined the two as almost to equate them. "Example" is a message to the affections and noble aspirations of persons rather than directly to their minds, as the humanists never tired of saying, and it looks to behavior as well. This is what concerned Loyola all his life, and this is the orientation that he expected all "ministry of the Word" to have.

The point I am making is that in an age so agitated by dogmatic differences that, on one level, controversy was its distinguishing intellectual characteristic, Loyola showed himself in practice singularly detached from that controversy. His interest, quite simply, lay elsewhere, and he conceived "doctrine" in a different way than did many other leading figures of his time. For him "Christian doctrine" dealt in the first place with virtue, prayer, repentance, and conversion, and then "consolation"–with reform of life. Luther proposed that right thinking and preaching about justification were essentially what the world needed. For Loyola the central issue was right living and loving, based on a general spirituality in which certain affectivities were fostered and sustained. This position coincides perfectly with the basic character and emphasis of the *Spiritual Exercises,* whose stated purpose was "the ordering of one's life" (21).

The most distinctive form of this Jesuit ministry of the Word was in fact the guiding of devout persons through the *Spiritual Exercises.* This task implied constant recourse to the text of Scripture, for most of the meditations in the book deal with some aspect of the life of Christ. In these meditations the retreatant confronted the *deeds* of the Savior and was then asked to respond in kind, for he did "all this for me" (116). The retreatant is urged "not to be deaf to His call, but prompt and diligent to accomplish His holy will" (91). What is induced is a sense of companionship with Christ in ministry, suffering, and, finally, glory—a companionship intimated by the name Loyola insisted on for his order, "Compagnia di Gesù."

Further questions are put to the retreatant: "What have I done for Christ, what am I doing, what ought I to do?" (53). These questions once again point inexorably to the activist, even dynamic, nature of Ignatian spirituality. This dynamism, a contrast with the repose of monastic contemplation, is indicated by Loyola in a number of ways, but particularly by his favorite expression, "the greater glory of God." The phrase occurs countless times in the *Constitutions* of the order. The comparative form—"greater"—suggests a questing, a restlessness, almost an insatiability. This is the Ignatian "más," "magis," "more" that commentators have often noted.

For Ignatius, this "more" was meant to translate itself most directly into an ever greater and more generous oblation to the divine will and divine grace. The prayer he composed for the retreatant at the end of the "Contemplation for Obtaining Divine Love" in the *Spiritual Exercises* encapsulates this deep yearning of the saint: "Take, Lord, and receive all my liberty, my memory, my understanding, and my entire will, all that I have and possess. Thou hast given all to me. To Thee, O Lord, I return it. Dispose of it wholly according to Thy will. Give me Thy love and Thy grace, for this is sufficient for me" (234).

Loyola himself achieved this surrender to the divine in an eminent degree. Throughout his adult life he experienced a deep sense of the divine presence that often produced tears of consolation and joy. His perception of God was specified by the Christian doctrine of the three divine persons of the Trinity, with a strong sense of their individuality—Father, Son, Spirit. The trinitarian aspect of his personal mysticism has been the subject of a number of studies. But what must be emphasized here is that in Ignatius the dynamism of his spirituality found its source in the divine action within his own being. It was not the result of a self-induced compulsion or of a drive for some merely extrinsic behavior modification. He was a saint, and he was revered even during his lifetime for a union with God that seemed to manifest itself clearly to those who had to deal with him.

Unfortunately, the same cannot always be said of the spirituality that the order fostered. The early companions of Ignatius were close enough to him to have understood the spirit of his directives. When Ignatius observed in the *Exercises* that "love ought to manifest itself in deeds" (230), they knew that this was not meant in some pedestrian sense. Nonetheless, the insistence on the practice of the virtues, the importance attached to sacramental confession of sins and the "reform of life," and the insistence in

1. Gian Lorenzo Bernini, *Cathedra Petri*, 1657-1666.

Ignatius's writings to his fellow Jesuits on the practice of obedience could easily lead, in less expansive minds, to a moralism and a behavioralism that were far from the true intent of the saint.

A graphic illustration of an eclectic and superficial grasp of the spirituality of the order is the book published in 1609 by the Spanish Jesuit Alonso Rodríguez (1526–1616) entitled *Ejercicio de perfección y virtutes cristianas.* (This author is not to be confused with the Jesuit lay brother St. Alfonso Rodríguez [1531–1617].) Rodríguez had been for a number of years master of novices, responsible for the first training in spirituality of new recruits to the order. The audience he originally had in mind for his ideas must be noted for an understanding of his book, but he in fact composed it out of a number of exhortations that he gave to Jesuit communities in various cities of Spain.

Divided into three parts, each containing three treatises, the book follows no systematic plan. It draws on the mainstream of Christian asceticism in a presentation of virtues and in practical recommendations about prayer, mortification, silence, and similar matters. Rodríguez illustrates his points with numerous anecdotes and *exempla* drawn from John Cassian, the *Vitae patrum,* and the lives of the saints. Often quaint, sometimes amusing, these illustrations betray the author's preoccupation with reducing spirituality to conventional practicality.

The book's success was immediate and enormous, probably because of the simplicity of its presentation, its avoidance of controversial matters, and its comprehensiveness. Like Alice's medicine, there were so many good things in it that there was something to suit everybody's needs. Joseph de Guibert commends also the "robust realism" of the book and finds in that quality another reason for its success.[10] It is quite true that the book is filled with precise and concrete counsels, though these are sometimes irreconcilable with each other and are never related to any clearly distinguishable theological foundation. By 1626, in any case, there were seven Spanish editions as well as translations into English (partial, 1612), French (1617), Italian (1617), Latin (1621), German (1623), and Dutch (1626). The book continued to be popular well into the present century and has run through over three hundred editions in twenty-three languages.

Is this book an authentic reflection of early Jesuit spirituality? Its favorable reception in the order immediately upon its publication and the continued commendation it received from Jesuit authorities through the centuries would seem to indicate that it is. There can be no doubt that it caught one important aspect of the spiritual message of St. Ignatius and the early Jesuits. While appreciative of the higher forms of prayer, it insists that every interior inspiration be tested against the deeds it produces. If the deeds are virtuous, the inspiration is holy. Even the highest gifts of prayer are suspect, ultimately unacceptable, if they fail in this regard. The avoidance of sin, the observance of the duties of one's state in life, adherence to the traditions of the church and respect for its authority—these were the Jesuit touchstones for authenticity from the very beginning. Rodríguez never lets his reader forget them.

Viewed in this perspective, Rodríguez's book has an authentically Jesuit character. Loyola, moreover, doubtless considered these qualities to be perennially valid foundations for a solid spiritual edifice. Yet there were historical circumstances of his era that gave them a particular incisiveness and led some of his followers in the order like Rodríguez to exaggerate them, especially toward the end of the sixteenth century.

These circumstances were not so much the presumed dangers of Protestantism, as we might first suspect, but rather the spiritualism of the indigenous mystical tradition in Spain whose adherents came to be known as the *Alumbrados.* Originating in the late fifteenth century, this movement was perceived by ecclesiastical authorities as a danger because it attributed an undue importance to visions, revelations, raptures, and similar phenomena. Loyola himself was charged at Salamanca in 1527 with being tainted by the movement, and he was careful for the rest of his life to make clear his distance from it. Moreover, he fought within the order a tendency, especially in Spain and Portugal, to subordinate ministry to contemplation and to multiply the hours spent each day in prayer.

These problems reached a point of crisis under the fourth general of the order, Everard Mercurian (1573–1581). Mercurian took a number of measures to meet the crisis. In his opinion he was not reforming a spirituality gone astray so much as forming one that was still in its infancy. He imposed a greater regimentation in prayer and religious observance within the order, but especially emphasized the practical, non-Illuminist character of the spirituality of the Jesuits. Somewhat forgetting the other styles of prayer allowed or suggested in the *Exercises,* he put great emphasis on examination of conscience and on the form of "meditation" described by Ignatius in the section of the book entitled "Three Methods of Prayer." Sober and methodical consideration of such matters as the Commandments, the duties of one's office, various virtues and vices—even if the purported subject matter of the prayer was the text of Scripture—seems to have been his ideal. He even forbade the reading, without special permission, of medieval mystics like John Tauler, Jan van Ruysbroeck, Henry Suso, and others.

Mercurian's measures against two Spanish Jesuits—Antonio Cordeses (1518–1601) and Balthasar Alvarez (1534–1580), confessor for six years to Teresa of Avila—indicate the narrowness with which he conceived the spirituality of the order and his misunderstanding of some of the central teachings of the saint who founded it. He forbade Cordeses to promote "affective prayer," and he judged Alvarez's style too contemplative.

Alvarez is particularly important. Although he published nothing in his lifetime, his Jesuit disciple, Venerable Luis de la Puente, wrote a remarkable biography of him (1615), admired even today for its comprehensive design, the accuracy of its narrative, and the grace of its style. The biography ranks as one of the great works of spiritual biography produced in Spain in its golden age. Most important of all, La Puente summarized the teachings of Alvarez and thereby transmitted them to his contemporaries and to subsequent generations. The biography in effect vindicated Alvarez and allowed him to influence masters like the English Benedictine Augustine Baker (1588–1685), the Jesuit Louis Lallemant (1587–1635), and, later, St. Alfonso Liguori (1696–1787). This recognition of him as one of the leading figures in Spanish spirituality in the sixteenth century eventually led to the publication in modern editions of his exhortations, meditations, letters, and treatises.

Alvarez advocated a prayer of quiet and silence, into which he himself had moved about 1567 from a more discursive style and after a long period of aridity. His descriptions of this form of prayer are surely influenced by St. Teresa, John of Avila, Francisco de Osuna, and other contemporaries. The prayer consists essentially in placing oneself in the presence of God and of keeping oneself in a state of repose before him. In Alvarez it resulted in an interior sense of the corporal presence of the humanity of Christ. This experiential and mystical sense of Christ's presence within was at the heart of his teaching.

Throughout his life Alvarez held positions of high responsibility in the Society of Jesus. He was, for instance, several times rector and master of novices, and at the very end of his life (1580) he was named superior of the province of Aragon of the Society. Nonetheless, from about 1573 on he was subjected to repeated scrutiny by his superiors in the Society because his teaching on prayer was suspected of fostering illusions and of deviating from the teaching of the *Exercises,* as interpreted by Mercurian and others. His explanations failed to give satisfaction, and in late 1577 he submitted to the decision against his teaching.

Mercurian's motivations were sincere. He wanted to consolidate a spirituality that still lacked a large corpus of literature to sustain it, and he wanted to preserve it from influences that would lead it back into an essentially monastic mode. Within the order, especially in the Iberian peninsula, there flourished a strongly contemplative tendency, a desire in some cases for eremitical withdrawal from the *saeculum* and sometimes a cultivation of the suspect phenomena associated with the *Alumbrados.* All this forms a background for understanding the success of an author like Rodríguez and the approbation he enjoyed.

Mercurian's vision, fortunately, did not altogether prevail even during his generalate, and his successor, Claudio Aquaviva (1581–1606), was a person of larger spirit, who encouraged a less rigid and narrow interpretation of the charism of the order. As early as 1582 he delivered an important exhortation in Rome on the gifts of the Holy Spirit—traditional in its doctrine, but indicative of a spirituality irreducible to moralism and external discipline. At about the same time in Rome and Naples, Roberto Bellarmino (1542–1621), a respected theologian and later a cardinal and canonized saint of the order, delivered a series of exhortations on the same subject and, more important, a series on "liberty of spirit."

There were, then, at least two general strains to "Jesuit spirituality" by the beginning of the seventeenth century. One was cautious and soberly ascetical, favorable almost exclusively to a methodical and even moralistic style of prayer, suspicious of contemplation and other higher forms of prayer as inimical to the active ministry to which the order was committed. It ran the danger of reducing Loyola to a small-minded master of hackneyed precepts. The other strain was more expansive, more syncretistic within the broad tradition of Christian spirituality, and intent on developing the implications of the affective and even mystical elements in the life of the founder of the order. It bordered at times on the Illuminism that Loyola had so emphatically eschewed and wanted to exclude among his followers. Most Jesuit writers on spirituality whose books were actually published during these decades tended to strike a balance between extreme expressions of these two tendencies and were able more or less to perpetuate the synthesis that Loyola represented.

Among the early associates of the saint, none had done this better than Jerome Nadal (1507–1580), already mentioned several times. Born at Palma de Majorca, he pursued courses of study at Alcalá and Paris and was present in the latter city while Loyola was there gathering his first companions. At that time he refused to have anything to do with the group and in 1537 went to Avignon, where he was eventually ordained a priest and promoted to doctor of theology.

Sometime after his return to Majorca, he felt an attraction to the new order, now confirmed by the Holy See, and in 1545 he journeyed to Rome to join it. He immediately won the special confidence of Ignatius and soon was constituted by him as his special envoy to promulgate and explain the *Constitutions* of the order in various parts of the Society. In the judgment of Juan de Polanco, Loyola's secretary, Nadal grasped Ignatius's ideas better than any other,[11] and therefore came to be considered an authentic interpreter of them. In his many writings—dialogues, letters, and especially the exhortations and instructions to Jesuit communities—we have a secure elaboration of the central themes of early Jesuit spirituality. Moreover, most Jesuits of his day, especially in Spain during his three official visits there, actually heard him speak about the Society and its spirit. His impact was, therefore, direct and enormous.

Most characteristic of Nadal is the evident theological and biblical basis on which he contructed his interpretation, and he has been described as "the theologian of Ignatian spirituality."[12] He clearly depended on a theological tradition represented by Aquinas and Bonaventure. Distinctive of him was the doctrine of "contemplative in action." This was, as I have indicated, simply a fuller articulation of Loyola's exhortation to his followers "to find God in all things." God was the goodness active in the world from which all other good descended. God was the author of both nature and grace, who impressed his own good on all reality. Here is the source of the world-affirming spirituality that would continue to mark the spiritual vision of many Jesuits through the centuries and that helps explain how some Jesuit missioners like Matteo Ricci (1552–1610) in China and Roberto de Nobili (1577–1656) in India could so easily affirm the values of the indigenous cultures in which they labored. Any study of early Jesuit spirituality that ignores the enterprises and cultural magnanimity of missioners like these misses a central element of the tradition.

Nadal's rhetoric on issues like these is even bolder than Loyola's. On a number of occasions he affirmed straightforwardly that for the members of the order "the world" was their "house." Although he of course recognized that for many Jesuits the houses of the professed members of the order would be the place from which they would normally exercise their ministry, he returned again and again to the idea that the Society was essentially a group "on mission," ready at any moment to travel to any point where there was need for its ministry. In Nadal's writings we find the most emphatic statements in the early history of the Jesuits of their break with the more monastic tradition.

Nadal's balance is evident in the way he encouraged and exemplified affective and even mystical prayer while at the same time insisting on its correlation with ministry and with the necessity of a balanced asceticism. He cautioned against the excesses of the *Alumbrados* and at the same time rejected a frigid moralism and intellectualism, which he also saw as dangers as well.

One of Nadal's most innovative teachings concerned the "grace of vocation," especially within the context of a religious order of the Catholic Church. According to him, the "grace" of each institute within the church was specific, somewhat like the specific grace conferred by each of the sacraments. The grace proper to each institute was articulated in the life and gifts of the founder and was meant to be transmitted to each member of the order. In his exhortations Nadal made extensive use of Ignatius's *Autobiography*, dictated to da Câmara, as encapsulating the grace of the Jesuit vocation. Thus, the teachings of Loyola were for Jesuits something more than the teachings of a holy man whom all revered. Nadal imbued them with an exemplarity that required their appropriation by all members of the order. These teachings were articulated in the *Spiritual Exercises* and the *Constitutions* of the order, which spelled out the ideal of "contemplative in action" in a way that made it, according to Nadal, accessible to all Jesuits.

For this ideal, Nadal seems to have seen the biblical base clearly as Pauline. In a suggestive statement in 1557, he indicated that "Paul signifies the ministry of our Society."[13] Cryptic though this statement is in itself, Nadal expands on its implications in his other writings. In them "the ministry of the Word"–in a wide variety of forms–has preeminence over all others. The Pauline ideal of evangelization–of "becoming all things to all men," of intimate and mystical identification with the Christ, and of total expenditure of oneself "to gain all" for Christ–is spelled out by Nadal in detail. This same affinity with the doctrine and ministry of the "Apostle to the Gentiles" is discernible, in fact, in Ignatius himself.

Here we see another correlation of Jesuit spirituality with a more general phenomenon of the sixteenth century, a renewed interest in St. Paul. There is evidence of this revived interest in the humanistic tradition that preceded Luther, but without doubt Luther's affirmation of the Pauline doctrine of "justification by faith alone" is its most powerful and best known expression. Luther extracted from Paul a theological or doctrinal maxim; Loyola and his followers saw in Paul a pattern for ministry and an exemplar for loving identification with the Savior. These positions may not be quite so distant from each other as they at first seem. It is important, however, to note the differences between them and also to recall that neither of the parties involved seemed to be aware of any affinity with the other.

Nadal's writings were not published in any coherent form until their critical editions in this century. Indeed, as I mentioned, the spirituality of the Society of Jesus had no corpus of published writings to support it except those of Ignatius himself until toward the end of the sixteenth century, and this fact makes Mercurian's apprehensions about its being dissipated through the assimilation of other traditions more comprehensible. Nonetheless, the teachings of masters like Cordeses and Balthasar Alvarez, despite Mercurian's misgivings, began to have effect, at least in a modified form.

In 1608 Jacobo (Diego) Alvarez de Paz (1560–1620) published his *De vita spirituali ejusque perfectione.* Rodríguez's *Ejercicio* was published the next year, but the two works were quite different in their approach. Alvarez de Paz was a theologian and a contemplative. His book, though dense in its details, rests on a coherent theological base and emphasizes affective prayer. Its most distinctive characteristic is the elaborate discussion of "infused contemplation," a technical category to describe an advanced form of prayer that transcends methodical meditation. For our purposes, the book is important for its clear validation of an ideal like this sort of contemplation within the larger Jesuit tradition.

Perhaps the most important Jesuit author in this regard is another Spanish Jesuit, Luis de la Puente (1554–1624), the disciple of Balthasar Alvarez. He was beatified by Pope Clement XIII in 1759. Besides several important works published posthumously, he saw into print five major treatises during his lifetime: two volumes of *Meditaciones de los mysterios de nuestra sancta fe* (1605); *Guía espiritual* (1609); four volumes of *De la perfección del christiano en todos sus estados* (1612–1616); *Vida del Padre Baltasar Alvarez* (1615); and *Expositio moralis et mystica in Canticum canticorum* (1622). The volume of *Meditaciones* was his best known work, frequently republished, translated, summarized, and adapted.

The sources on which La Puente draws are the Scriptures, the fathers, Aquinas, and the *Exercises* of Loyola, from which he continually takes his inspiration. With his discussion of infused contemplation, he obviously sees higher forms of prayer as part of the Jesuit tradition, and his subsequent beatification eventually gave official, even if indirect, ratification of this interpretation of Jesuit spirituality. Moreover, his preoccupation with grounding his teaching on theological doctrine is a good exemplification of the *docta pietas* that Ignatius tried to instill in the order with his insistence on a long and exacting course of studies for those who joined the Society.

La Puente nowhere showed himself a more faithful disciple of the founder of the order, however, than in his *De la perfección del christiano en todos sus estados.* This seems to be the first work of such breadth in the history of Christian spirituality that applies that spirituality to the different states of Christian life, including the laity. The very conception of the work reflects Loyola's own conviction that genuine piety was not restricted to the cloister and further articulates Loyola's efforts to make such piety available to all through the course of the *Spiritual Exercises.*

During the first half century of the order there were in Italy no masters of spirituality of the same stature as these Spaniards. However, some of the works of the Spaniards were originally written in Latin, and others were soon translated into Latin or Italian; thus the writings were made available to brethren in that part of the world. Roberto Bellarmino, already mentioned, was important, but his major interest lay more strictly in the fields of exegesis and in speculative and controversial theology.

Italy was, in fact, less agitated by controversies and extremes in these matters than was Spain. Symptomatic of this fact was the volume by Bernardino Rossignoli (1547–1613), rector of the Roman College, *De disciplina christianae perfectionis,* published at Ingolstadt in 1600. Rossignoli dedicated the book to the general of the order, Claudio Aquaviva, whose moderate views were in fact well exemplified in it.

Aquaviva's tenure as general was not altogether untroubled, however, by the issues that were so live for his predecessor, Mercurian. Achille Gagliardi (1537–1607), a Jesuit born in Padua, undertook in 1584 the spiritual direction of Elisabetta Berinzaga, a visionary and mystic in Milan. He soon helped write and edit several works inspired by Berinzaga. Gagliardi almost immediately found himself embroiled in controversies that eventually required the intervention of Aquaviva and even of Pope Clement VIII. The details of this complicated affair need not detain us, much less an attempt to do justice to all the parties involved. But it is important to note that Gagliardi was subjected to the now standard accusation of trying to introduce a monastic spirit within the Society. Certainly, the influence of the Rhineland mystics, whose reading was prohibited by Mercurian, is evident in the writings for which he was at least partly responsible, especially the most widely circulated of them, the *Breve compendio intorno alla perfezione cristiana,* first published in French translation in Paris in 1596 and in Italian in Brescia in 1611.

Influenced by Gagliardi was Giuseppe Blondo in his *Essercitii spirituali di P. Ignazio,* published in Milan in 1587. The work was variously received in Jesuit circles, but eventually the attacks on it became so violent that Aquaviva "for the sake of peace" ordered it retracted from circulation in 1589. In France it probably had, nonetheless, an influence on Pierre de Bérulle (1575–1629) and through him on others in the seventeenth century. It is certain, in any case, that Bérulle knew and esteemed the *Breve compendio,* of which his own first published work, *Bref discours de l'abnégation intérieure,* is an adaptation. The development of French spirituality in the late sixteenth and the seventeenth century, including that of the Society of Jesus, is treated in chapter 3 of this volume.

The instruments the Jesuits devised or characteristically promoted to inculcate their spiritual doctrines and to assist people in appropriating them are perhaps as important for understanding Jesuit spirituality as the doctrines themselves. Here we find a significant reciprocity of form and content, the one influencing and being influenced by the other.

The first such instrument developed by the Jesuits was the "retreat." Although the practice of spending a period of time alone in contemplation is older than Christianity itself, there existed no widely recognized codification of it until the *Spiritual Exercises* of Ignatius of Loyola. The book not merely contained some of the saint's most important ideas but also provided a new framework in which to spend a limited period of time in prayer and reflection. Structure, progression, rubrics, "methods," and clear purpose were harmonized in such a way that these "forms" influenced the shape of the spirituality that emerged, as I indicated above.

A Jesuit who was asked to direct someone in retreat knew what was expected of him, and he had a ready-made plan to follow. Thus was inaugurated a new era in Christian spirituality in which a periodic retreat became a regular feature in the pattern of piety followed by many religiously minded persons. To aid the Jesuit in guiding someone through the *Exercises,* moreover, the Jesuits composed a *Directorium,* first published in Rome in 1599. Although this official document relied on some preliminary versions, it was in effect the first book of its kind—an official set of instructions on how to lead people, under the inspiration of God, through a set of considerations leading to "reform of life."

In substance, the *Directory* does little more than paraphrase, expand, specify, and put into better order instructions that Loyola indicated in the book of the *Exercises* itself. A clear humanity characterizes the *Directory,* as when it states that the person who is to direct the *Exercises* should be "of sweet rather than of stern disposition" (V.2). The same care is operative as in the *Exercises* that "God be allowed to dispose of His own creature, according to the good pleasure of His divine Goodness" (V.5). In prayer, however, the safe and sure "Three Methods" receive the most explanation and commendation, although "other methods are [not] excluded, such as the Holy Ghost is wont to teach" (XXXVII.13). More significant, the *Directory* explicitly related the "weeks" of the *Exercises* to the three traditional "ways" of Christian spirituality—purgative, illuminative, and unitive. The *Directory* thereby suggests that the *Exercises* are more than a "recipe for conversion"; they are a recipe for *ongoing* conversion that leads to higher prayer and an ever more interiorized spirituality (XXXIX). It thus reflects the viewpoint of Claudio Aquaviva, the superior general of the Jesuits who authorized its publication.

"Spiritual direction" is a second instrument that the early Jesuits developed to a high degree. This practice is, again, older than Christianity itself. But there is no doubt that it emerged with a new prominence in Catholic Europe in the sixteenth and especially in the seventeenth century—and precisely as a formalized and continuing relationship between the two persons involved. The book of the *Exercises* and, with it, the later *Directory* were the most important factors in promoting this development. Furthermore, the *Constitutions* of the Society insisted on the practice of spiritual direction for members of the order; thus it easily became normative for those to whom the Jesuits ministered.

Aquaviva published an important instruction in 1599 on the formation of spiritual directors in the Society, and in the next year he composed a small treatise on the subject that deftly combines experience with traditional teaching. We should not be surprised, therefore, that Rossignoli also insists on the indispensability of a *magister idoneus.* Alvarez de Paz, Luis de la Puente, and others do the same. Spiritual direction had by now become an essential component of Jesuit doctrine and practice.

Sometimes given in the sacrament of penance, sometimes outside it, the practice of direction by the early Jesuits had a number of aims. It was meant to give comfort in time of temptation and to advise in cases of doubt. As we might expect in this period, it was also seen as a way to safeguard against illusion and against the suspect mysticism of the *Alumbrados* and their kind. But it was especially aimed at helping the individual "discern" what "movements" were taking place within him and whence they came. All this was directed in the Jesuit system to greater intimacy with "the divine Goodness," which in turn was somehow to be expressed in greater "service" of that same Goodness.

The third instrument that the Jesuits adopted, modified, and then widely propagated was confraternities of various kinds, which they sometimes called "sodalities." These associations had been an important part of late medieval life, so there were models available for Jesuits to use. In Italian cities like Florence, such confraternities seem particularly to have flourished in the fifteenth century; their members sometimes dedicated themselves to specific works of mercy like burying the dead or nursing the sick, and they met regularly for prayers and sermons. Many confraternities also sponsored banquets, festivals, and similar activities for their members, which played a part in the development of local culture.

In Rome in 1563 a young Belgian Jesuit, Jan Leunis, founded the first such sodality for students attending the Roman College, the original Jesuit educational institution in the city, later known as the Gregorian University. About two decades later, Pope Gregory XIII recognized this organization and empowered its Roman headquarters to affiliate other sodalities willing to adhere to the rules approved by the Holy See. Sodalities quickly sprang up in Jesuit schools, where they became almost an integral part of the education offered there. An impressive body of spiritual literature was produced for the members of this organization, who were principally young men of good families.

This development was consonant with what the Jesuits were doing outside their schools. As early as 1547 Loyola had formed a group of devout and charitable men in Rome whom he brought together regularly and encouraged to engage in works of mercy. In Parma, the "Company of the Most Holy Name of Jesus" traced its beginnings back to the Jesuit Pierre Favre's stay in the city in 1540. We still possess the program drawn up by Favre for these laymen: daily meditation, daily examination of conscience, daily Mass, weekly reception of the Eucharist, and regular engagement in works of mercy. This is roughly equivalent to what was later prescribed for sodalists in the schools. As sodalities spread outside schools in the seventeenth century, they generally drew their members from homogeneous groups, so that we find sodalities of students, of artisans, of nobles, of businessmen, of sailors, of clergy, and on occasion of doctors, of lawyers, of judges—and even of prisoners in jails!

Continuous though the Jesuits' confraternities and sodalities were with their medieval paradigms, they also manifested some noteworthy differences. In general, the later institutions were more exclusively religious in character, more codified in their practices of devotion and of works of mercy, more likely to be based in some larger institution like a school, more securely placed under the direction of a priest. These were changes that were self-consciously introduced, not changes that spontaneously happened. Were they, however, changes for the better, as they were certainly meant to be? This question leads into the historiographical problem of how to fit early Jesuit spirituality into the larger context of the Counter-Reformation and how to see it as both reflection of that period in the history of Roman Catholicism and an agent within it. And that contextualization leads, in its turn, into the problem of how to evaluate early Jesuit spirituality.

The problem is too complex to deal with here except in the broadest way. Some historians, in brief, judge that the Counter-Reformation tended to force religion into ever more codified and institutionalized forms that were deviations from an earlier, healthier tradition. These historians would see the strength of the older medieval confraternities, for instance, in their close relationship to family and local culture, whereas the new confraternities, including the Jesuits' sodalities, made piety more formalized and removed it from the context in which people actually lived their lives. The confraternities are for these historians, however, only one aspect of this larger pattern of institutionalization and centralization that began to dominate the religious practice of the Catholic Church in the last years of the sixteenth century, after the close of the Council of Trent. In this viewpoint, the Counter-Reformation, for all its vitality and creativity, had finally a deleterious effect on religion and, therefore, on spirituality. Insofar as this criticism is justified and applied to the early Jesuits, it means that their efforts to create a spirituality that would enable persons to "find God in all things" became so structured, so institutionalized, and so transformed that it made those same persons strangers to their own culture and "natural kinships."

The problem raised by such criticisms of the Counter-Reformation is real, although we must recognize that most of the criticism has been directed against changes in popular forms of piety, especially among the rural poor, rather than against the more intellectualized, urban patterns of spiritual doctrine and practice that have been the subject of this article. Moreover, it is quite possible to admit that early Jesuit spirituality was susceptible of some of the bad effects attributed to the religious forms promoted by the Counter-Reformation without at the same time denying the many positive achievements of that spirituality. In fact, the formalizing elements in the spirituality of the Counter-Reformation simply reflected these same tendencies in society at large in the late sixteenth and early seventeenth centuries. It was an age fascinated with "method"–in science, politics, and philosophy. We should not wonder that spiritual writings and practices felt these same pressures and evinced these same tendencies.

Most important of all for assessing early Jesuit spirituality, however, is the fact that its primordial and most authoritative sources–the writings of Loyola and of his best interpreter, Nadal–do not give first rank to these formalistic tendencies. These two authors proposed, in fact, a spirituality that in its aims as well as in the strategies it proposed to achieve those aims tried to assure "liberty of spirit" and to foster in individuals an adaptation of divine inspiration to every condition of life. If Jesuit spirituality later in the century fell into more stylized modes of thought and presentation, this change was rather a product of the later culture in which it was immersed than an inevitable development of Ignatius of Loyola's original legacy.

Notes

1. H. Outram Evennett, *The Spirit of the Counter Reformation,* 45.
2. Ibid., 65.
3. Joseph de Guibert, *The Jesuits: Their Spiritual Doctrine and Practice,* 176–81.
4. *Monumenta Nadal* (Monumenta Historica Societatis Jesu [hereafter MHSJ]), IV, 651; V, 162, ". . . simul in actione contemplativus."
5. Ibid., V, 153–54.
6. Ibid.
7. J. O'Malley, *Praise and Blame in Renaissance Rome* (Durham, NC: Duke University Press, 1979).
8. H. O. Evennett, *The Spirit of the Counter Reformation,* 32.

9. *Monumenta Nadal* (MHSJ), V, 820–65.
10. J. de Guibert, *The Jesuits,* 264.
11. See *Ignatii Epistolae* (MHSJ), V, 109.
12. Miguel Nicolau, "Nadal," in *Dict. Sp.,* 11, col. 13.
13. *Orationis Observationes,* ed. Miguel Nicolau (Rome: Institutum Historicum Societatis Jesu, 1964) 151.

Bibliography

Sources

All the texts of Loyola are published in the MHSJ. The correspondence and some of the other documents relating to his first companions are also published in that series, but other important texts are published elsewhere; some still await publication. On these editions, as well as translations into languages other than the original, see L. Polgár, *Bibliographie.*

Studies

The following series and journals regularly present studies relating to Jesuit spirituality: *Archivum Historicum Societatis Jesu* (AHSJ), *Christus, Geist und Leben, Manresa, Review for Religious, Studies in the Spirituality of Jesuits* (St. Louis), *The Way.*

Bangert, William V. *A History of the Society of Jesus.* St. Louis: Institute of Jesuit Sources, 1972.

Brodrick, James. *Saint Ignatius Loyola: The Pilgrim Years.* New York: Farrar, Straus, & Cudahy, 1956.

——. *The Origin of the Jesuits.* London: Longmans, Green, 1940.

——. *The Progress of the Jesuits.* London: Longmans, Green, 1947.

Conwell, Joseph F. *Contemplation in Action: A Study of Ignatian Prayer.* Spokane, WA: Gonzaga University Press, 1957.

Donnelly, John Patrick. "Alonso Rodriguez' *Ejercicio:* A Neglected Classic." *The Sixteenth Century Journal* 11/2 (1980) 16–24.

Dudon, Paul. *St. Ignatius Loyola.* Translated by William J. Young. Milwaukee: Bruce, 1949.

Egan, Harvey D. *The Spiritual Exercises and the Ignatian Mystical Horizon.* St. Louis: Institute of Jesuit Sources, 1976.

Evennett, H. Outram. *The Spirit of the Counter Reformation.* Edited by John Bossy. Cambridge: University Press, 1968.

Fessard, Gaston. *La dialectique des Exercises Spirituels de Saint Ignace de Loyola.* 2 vols. Paris: Julliard, 1956, 1966.

Gilmont, Jean-François. *Les écrits spirituels des premiers jésuites: Inventaire commenté.* Rome: Institutum Historicum Societatis Jesu, 1961.

Guibert, Joseph de. *The Jesuits: Their Spiritual Doctrine and Practice.* Translated by William J. Young. Chicago: Loyola University Press, 1964.

Guichard, Alain. *Les jésuites: Spiritualité et activité.* Paris: B. Grosset, 1974.

Iparraguirre, Ignacio. *Orientaciones bibliográficas sobre San Ignacio de Loyola.* Rome: Institutum Historicum Societatis Jesu, 1957.

——. *Contemporary Trends in Studies on the Constitutions of the Society of Jesus.* Translated by Daniel F. X. Meenan. St. Louis: Institute of Jesuit Sources, 1974.

——. *Répertoire de spiritualité ignatienne (1556–1615).* Rome: Institutum Historicum Societatis Jesu, 1961.

Nicolau, Miguel. "Espiritualidad de la Compañía de Jesús en la España del siglo XVI." *Manresa* 29 (1957) 217–36.

——. *Jeronimo Nadal, S.I. (1507–1580): Sus obras y doctrinas espirituales.* Madrid: Consejo Superior de Investigaciones Científicas, 1949.

O'Malley, John W. "De Guibert and Jesuit Authenticity." *Woodstock Letters* 95 (1966) 103–10.

——. "The Fourth Vow in Its Ignatian Context: A Historical Study." *Studies in the Spirituality of Jesuits* 15/1 (1983).

——. "The Jesuits, St. Ignatius, and the Counter Reformation: Some Recent Studies and Their Implications for Today." *Studies in the Spirituality of Jesuits* 14/1 (1982).

——. "To Travel to Any Part of the World: Jerome Nadal and the Jesuit Vocation." *Studies in the Spirituality of Jesuits* 15/5 (1983).

Polgár, László. *Bibliographie sur l'histoire de la Compagnie de Jésus.* Vol. 1. Rome: Institutum Historicum Societatis Jesu, 1981.

Rahner, Hugo. *Ignatius the Theologian.* Translated by Michael Barry. New York: Herder & Herder, 1968.

——. *The Spirituality of St. Ignatius Loyola.* Translated by F. J. Smith. Chicago: Loyola University Press, 1953.

Ravier, André. *Ignace de Loyola fonde la Compagnie de Jésus.* Paris: Desclée de Brouwer, 1973.

Ruiz Jurado, Manuel. "La espiritualidad de la Compañía de Jesús en sus Congregaciones Generales." AHSJ 45 (1976) 233–90.

Scaduto, Mario. *L'epoca di Giacomo Laínez.* 2 vols. Rome: Institutum Historicum Societatis Jesu, 1964, 1974.

——. "Il governo di s. Francisco Borgia 1565–1572." AHSJ 41 (1972) 136–75.

Schneider, Burkhart. "Die Kirchlichkeit des heiligen Ignatius von Loyola." In *Sentire Ecclesiam,* 268–300. Edited by Jean Daniélou and Herbert Vorgrimler. Freiburg i/Br.: Herder, 1961.

Toner, Jules. *A Commentary on St. Ignatius' Rules for the Discernment of Spirits.* St. Louis: Institute of Jesuit Sources, 1982.

Wulf, Friedrich, ed. *Ignatius of Loyola: His Personality and Spiritual Heritage, 1556–1956.* St. Louis: Institute of Jesuit Sources, 1977.

X

RENAISSANCE HUMANISM AND THE RELIGIOUS CULTURE OF THE FIRST JESUITS

The historiography of the relationship between Renaissance Humanism and the first generation of Jesuits emits conflicting signals. Most studies of Ignatius Loyola affirm that he embraced for his new religious order that aspect of Renaissance culture known as Humanism, sometimes seeming to imply he was himself a learned exponent of it. We know, however, that his own and his early companions' education and culture were basically eclectic and late-medieval. Many Jesuit historians have called attention, moreover, to a story about how Ignatius's religious devotion was cooled early in life by reading Erasmus's *Handbook of the Christian Soldier* and that he therefore later in life issued a blanket prohibition for the Society of Jesus of the works of the Prince of the Humanists.[1]

In any case, all serious studies of the Society of Jesus recognize its special and important relationship to Renaissance Humanism in the secondary schools that the Jesuits began to operate after 1548, but the precise impact that Humanism had on the ministries, theology, spirituality and self-understanding of the Society is practically never detailed. One is left with the impression that it was superficial and even peripheral.

The problem is vast and enormously complicated. All that I can hope to do in these few pages is sketch its basic contours. My thesis is simple: Renaissance Humanism, despite reservations some of the Jesuits entertained about certain aspects of it, had a profound and determinative impact on the Society by the time Ignatius died in 1556, and we shall never understand the subsequent history of the Society unless we take that impact into account. I believe that the first Jesuits, including Ignatius, were not always fully aware of the consequences of their attitudes and decisions regarding Humanism; but that fact does not mitigate the immensity of its influence henceforth on the Society.

Perhaps the most fundamental reason for the confusion in the historiography of the Society in this regard stems from a confused historiography about Renaissance Humanism itself. By the time Ignatius and his companions arrived in Rome in 1537, Humanism had been the most exciting and dominant cultural phenomenon there for at least a century. None the less, with the outbreak of the Reformation, suspicions became rampant that when Humanism attempted to deal with religious questions, especially theological questions, it overstepped its bounds. Criticism focused particularly on Erasmus, the most widely read and the most articulate spokesman for the Humanist cause who, as the contemporary slogan put it, 'laid the egg that Luther hatched'.[2] When the *opera omnia* of Erasmus were listed in 1559 on the first papal *Index of Prohibited Books* and in that same year on the similar Spanish *Index*, the fury reached its climax. Its long aftermath would taint all subsequent historical writing by Catholics. The stylistic elegance that Humanism advocated would continue to be much appreciated, but direct relationship to theological method would be viewed with caution — at least in certain highly-placed circles. After Luther's dramatic repudiation of Erasmus in 1525, a similar, but less virulent, antipathy generally held sway in historians from the Protestant churches.

Only in the past thirty years have we acquired a comprehensive understanding of what Humanism was all about and been able to dismiss the misconception that in some of its advocates it represented a thinly disguised neo-paganism and that its more properly theological aspects were unorthodox.[3] Studies of Erasmus in particular have vindicated him on almost every theological and religious issue, showing him to have been more orthodox, Catholic, and far-sighted than his adversaries. The customary portrait of him in both Protestant and Catholic historiography as a weak and vacillating theological dilettante has been replaced by an ever deepening appreciation of him as one of the towering religious thinkers in the whole of the Christian tradition.[4]

This recovery of the religious aspects of Humanism, especially in Erasmus, has been, however, part and parcel of a more general enterprise of Renaissance scholars that has enabled us to define with much greater precision than heretofore the general contours of the phenomenon and trace its history more accurately.[5] I need to say a word about that enterprise, for unless one is a specialist in the Renaissance one still might succumb to the confusions that the term Humanism engenders.

Today 'Humanism' is sometimes used to signify an ideology that would exclude God from consideration — so-called 'secular Humanism'. Such Humanism bears little, if any, relationship to its Renaissance counterpart. The contemporary antithesis of 'secular Humanism' is so-called 'Christian Humanism', an expansive designation that would include figures as different as Francis of Assisi, Thomas Aquinas and Mother Theresa. This 'Humanism', which at times seems to indicate nothing more than a benign attitude towards nature and other human beings, also has little relationship to the much more specific and definable phenomenon with which we are concerned.

What, then, was *Renaissance* Humanism? In its beginnings in Italy in the mid-fourteenth century, it was primarily a literary movement that believed that the style and content of the ancient Latin authors like Cicero and Virgil held the key for a cultural revival in which good literature and good morals would go hand in hand. Francesco Petrarcha was the most influential spokesman for this conviction, and he proposed it as an antidote to the barbarous style of his own day, exemplified most tellingly in the jargon-ridden prose of scholastic lawyers, philosophers and theologians. As a contemporary scholar has noted, when Petrarch besought his contemporaries to close their Aristotle and open their Cicero, the Renaissance had properly begun.[6] In Petrarch's view and that of his followers, good literature was essentially didactic, so that an ethical component was inherent in Humanism from its very origins.[7] Moreover, the movement clearly specified good literature as the Latin classics, and implied a certain disdain for Greek metaphysics and natural science.

In the two hundred years between the Petrarchan call to arms and the founding of the Society of Jesus in 1540, the Humanist movement remained remarkably faithful to its original inspiration, but had undergone some significant developments, only the most important of which can I even barely suggest here. First of all, the corpus of approved literature had been expanded to include the literary and historical classics of ancient Greece, as well as the Latin and Greek Fathers of the Church, whose appealing style of presentation of the truths of Christianity differed so remarkably from the crabbed style and impenetrable technical terminology of 'the modern theologians' — Scholastics like Thomas, Scotus and Ockham. The Fathers were theologians who could be read with profit by all literate persons, and their style, presumably, would enkindle one's heart with a desire for a more godly life — the ultimate purpose, according to the Humanists, of all genuine theology.

Secondly, beginning in the early fifteenth century the movement had centred on classical rhetoric as its primary discipline, now understood not simply as good epistolary style but as the art of oratory, and therefore the proper training for lawyers and statesmen.[8] Almost immediately in Italy this art began to be applied to preaching, in the hope of displacing the medieval and scholastic styles so favoured since the thirteenth century.[9] The movement thus began to have implications for Christian ministry. This development reached a watershed in 1535 with the publication of Erasmus's *Ecclesiastes*, after which no new treatises advocating the scholastic style were ever published.[10]

Thirdly, the movement found an institutional embodiment in primary and secondary schools where the Latin and Greek classics were the centre of the curriculum.[11] With oratory as their central discipline, the schools aimed at producing graduates who would take the active life of the *polis* as their goal, whether as churchmen or statesmen. Moreover, the ethical concerns inherent in the movement from the beginning expressed themselves in the conviction that the true aim of education was not learning for its own sake but the formation of character, which is what the study of the best literature would produce.

Upright lawyers, governors, bureaucrats, statesmen, bishops and pastors — and thus an ethically renewed society — would be the result. The curriculum, the relationship between teachers and students, and everything else in the school would be geared towards teaching the most profound art, the *ars bene beateque vivendi* — the art of living a happy and socially productive life for the benefit of oneself and others. It is easy today to smile at the almost utopian optimism of this conviction and to question the adequacy of the methods employed to achieve these high goals, yet one cannot gainsay the force or long-lived appeal of the ideal.[12]

Finally, the Humanist movement early began to develop a more technical side. From the beginning it had been interested in texts — first of all in recovering the complete corpus of ancient Latin and Greek classics, and then in establishing the most reliable text among the many manuscripts thus recovered. This led to the beginnings of the science of textual criticism, which reached a certain culmination in the early sixteenth century with Erasmus's first critical editions of the Greek New Testament and of the Greek and Latin Fathers of the Church.[13]

This monumental achievement was acclaimed by some, but decried and greeted with alarm by others because it challenged the hallowed status of the Vulgate and especially because it practically coincided with the outbreak of the Reformation. In any case, it supported the conviction of Erasmus and others that the whole theological enterprise had to be re-thought, so that it be based on a more historical, less proof-text reading of the sources and be modelled more on the rhetorical style of the Fathers, which would thereby overcome the divorce between theology, spirituality and ministry that scholastic theology had, in their opinion, brought about.

This broad description of the nature and course of Renaissance Humanism until the founding of the Society of Jesus will have to suffice for our purposes. It will at least serve to distinguish Renaissance Humanism from the late twentieth-century phenomena that have appropriated the name, and will provide us with the basic tools we need to understand its relationship to Ignatius and the other Jesuits of the first generation. What I have to say on that relationship I will divide into two parts: I will first speak in more general terms about the relationship of Humanism to the style of spirituality, ministry and theology that the Jesuits espoused, and then I will speak more specifically about the impact on the Society of the decision to operate secondary schools according to the Humanist model.

Let me begin with a word about the misgivings about Humanism some Jesuits held. They were wary of the displacement of the Vulgate and of the doctrinal implications of certain emendations. Even Jerónimo Nadal, who among the inner circle most thoroughly appropriated Humanist ideals, betrayed some caution. Probably while he was at Paris he learned how the Humanists were stigmatized as mere 'grammarians' when they intruded themselves into the realm of theology.[14] When Nadal urged the necessity of scholastic theology because otherwise one 'stuttered and stammered' over the grave issues of doctrine, he almost certainly assigned that failing to the Humanists.[15]

None the less, he and his colleagues recognized the necessity of knowledge of the Biblical languages and, within limits, the legitimacy of textual criticism. At one point Ignatius went so far as to state that the study of languages was to be used to defend the Vulgate on every point — '*deffender en toto*'. Diego Laínez and Alfonso Salmerón, his trusted advisers who had been present at Trent and understood how qualified the Council itself had been in its approbation of that text, rushed to change Ignatius's obvious intent by interpreting him to mean 'everything that with reason and honesty can be defended'.[16] While more open-minded on this issue than many of their contemporaries, therefore, the Jesuits still opted for a notably cautious course.

The new editions of the Bible gave impetus to new vernacular translations, whose wide diffusion the invention of the printing press made possible. Erasmus and his colleagues centred much of the piety they advocated on a devout reading of the sacred text, thus giving added impetus to this traditional practice. Early Jesuit sources, except for the *Spiritual Exercises*, are subdued in this regard. They never condemn the practice, but only occasionally commend it, perhaps rendered cautious by the suspicions and antagonisms about it that antedated the Reformation but that were much exacerbated by it. From the very nature of the *Exercises* with their many meditations on the life of Christ, however, we almost have to infer that the Jesuits were more favourably inclined towards this practice than their silence might otherwise suggest.

No Humanist wrote more about the godly or devout life than Erasmus; none was more widely read. By 1550, however, the furious and fanatical vendetta against everything he wrote crested into a violent rage in certain ecclesiastical circles in Rome and elsewhere. During the first few decades of the Society, the Jesuits for the most part stood aloof from this bitter campaign, hardly taking notice of Erasmus's many works on the spiritual life. Their neutrality, or perhaps silent antagonism, prevented them from discovering how much in that perspicacious genius was congenial to their own *pietas* and to the peculiar emphases in theology that they advocated.

We are almost certainly justified in regarding the story about Ignatius and the *Handbook* as a fabrication.[17] There is in fact no evidence that Ignatius had firsthand knowledge of anything Erasmus wrote. Had he read works like the *Praise of Folly* or some of the *Colloquies*, he surely would have been distressed by their caustic and sardonic criticism of abuses, venality and superstition in the Church, but we have no clear statement from him on the issue.

Ignatius did on several occasions try to limit the use of Erasmus's works as textbooks in the Jesuits schools, explaining simply, 'Since the author is not in favour, it is not appropriate for students to get to like his books'.[18] But he never altogether prohibited them, as Laínez in 1557 reassured Jesuits at Ingolstadt and Padua to quiet their scruples.[19] Even after the *Index* of 1559, some Jesuit schools continued for a while to use Erasmian texts.

A great deal more could be said about the hesitations and ambivalences of the first Jesuits concerning Humanism, but more important was their enthusiasm for much that it proffered. Perhaps the best entry into this complex problem is the eleventh rule in the 'Rules for Thinking with the Church', a kind of appendix to the *Spiritual Exercises* that was most probably composed by Ignatius about 1535 at the end of his seven years as a student at the University of Paris. In that rule Ignatius commends both scholastic and patristic theology — the first for its clarity and precision and the latter because by it we are 'moved to love and serve God our Lord in all things'.

The rule suggests several important things about Ignatius. First, he was aware of the basic distinction between the two styles of theology. Secondly, in his usual detached and even-handed manner, he puts the best interpretation on both of them, refusing to enter into the contemporary controversy. Thirdly, he adumbrates the subsequent cultural history of the order he would found, in which both styles would be considered reconcilable with each other and each of them would have an important role to play.[20]

If we now try to place this important statement in the larger context of Ignatius's life and vision, does he in fact seem to favour one above the other for the theological enterprise of his Society? The most obviously strong case can be made for Scholasticism. Although he and his companions would have been exposed to some aspects of Renaissance Humanism at both Alcalá and Paris, the philosophy and theology they studied was professedly scholastic. Moreover, the *Constitutions* of the Society, for which Ignatius was ultimately responsible, determined that Thomas Aquinas was to be the principal theological authority prescribed for the order.[21] That would seem to answer the question.

Precisely what led to the Jesuits' choice of Aquinas among the scholastic theologians is not altogether clear, but his unquestioned orthodoxy would surely be among them. The clear organization and comprehensiveness of the *Summa Theologiae* would be another. Moreover, for decades before the Jesuits arrived in Rome, Aquinas had enjoyed special favour there, and this phenomenon could not have gone unnoticed by them.[22]

We might conjecture about more intrinsic reasons. Chief among them would be the basic assumption in the Thomistic system of the compatibility between 'nature and grace', which surely coincided with Ignatius's own conviction, born of his personal experience, that in ministry one should not only rely on God's grace but also make use of all human means, as the *Constitutions* prescribed.

Despite this and other convergences in basic viewpoint, on one crucial issue the first Jesuits surely differed from Thomas. In the opening question of the *Summa*, Thomas states unequivocally that theology is principally a 'contemplative' discipline, i.e., academic or, to use the Jesuits' term for it, speculative'.[23] The *Summa* as a totality provides convincing substance to the integrity with which Thomas carried out that basic presupposition. The highly intellectualized character of that speculation meant that it was addressed to the head, not the heart, as Humanist adversaries of Scholasticism never failed to point out.

A strong case can be mounted for the opinion that the most pervasive aim of Ignatius's life after his conversion was his desire to move others 'to love and serve God our Lord in all things', which is precisely how he described patristic theology and which could equally well be applied to the theological reform advocated by Erasmus and others. It was also the most fundamental aim of the *Spiritual Exercises*, and it was an aim directed at the affections, at the human heart. It was the aim of his ministry.

When Jerónimo Nadal, his disciple and most reliable interpreter, referred to Ignatius as 'the theologian', he said: 'Here then you see the necessity for the course of studies in the Society: to be able to preach and to become skilled in those ministries that the Church deems ordered for the help of our neighbour. Here is our father, the theologian'.[24] Theology for Ignatius, as Nadal presents it, was not the abstract and speculative discipline practised by the scholastics of his day, but was an instrument for the help of souls, and, if we take the *Exercises* as the basic paradigm for all Jesuit ministry, that help was centred on the right ordering of the affections. These orientations obviously looked to a conjoining of theology, ministry and spirituality.

It was no accident, therefore, that some of the first Jesuits inveighed bitterly against reducing theology to 'speculation alone', often directing their criticsm specifically against the Faculty of Theology at the University of Paris where so many of them had studied. Nadal excoriated those theologians for not going out into the cities and town to announce the kingdom of Heaven according to the example of Christ and the Apostles, and for being 'only speculative theologians and treating all disciplines in only a speculative fashion'.[25] The words could have been spoken by Erasmus.

What Nadal and Juan de Polanco, Ignatius's secretary and *alter ego*, would substitute for such speculation was what they called 'mystical theology'. By mystical they did not mean the transports and ecstasies usually connoted by the term, but an inner understanding and relish of the truth that is then translated into the way one lives. There is no need to underscore how closely this understanding of theology correlates with the *Spiritual Exercises*. We must observe, however, that it also bears a close affinity to the way the Humanists conceived the scope of the theological enterprise.

Aside from this theological affinity on the most general level, there were in my opinion three quite specific ways in which Humanism had a clearly palpable impact on how Jesuits went about their ministry. All three of these ways are directly related to rhetoric, the art of oratory or persuasion.

The first of them, as one might expect, is their preaching. Polanco, who had carefully studied Erasmus's *Ecclesiastes* while he was a student of theology at the University of Padua, is probably responsible for the provision in the Jesuit *Constitutions* that members of the Society are not to preach in 'the scholastic manner'.[26] What that had to mean in the concrete was that they were to preach according to what Humanists were advocating as substitutes — either a revival of the patristic homily or some adaptation of the principles of classical rhetoric to the Christian pulpit.

All the first Jesuits, including Ignatius, spoke with one voice when they repeated again and again that preaching was directed to 'arousing the affections' and thereby to moving listeners to a more godly life. They would have imbibed this conviction from many sources, but, once again, it coincides with what the Humanists proposed, for it coincides with the basic assumptions of classical rhetoric.[27]

But here we have more than coincidence. Ignatius himself advocated the use of Cicero and other classical orators for the training in preaching of recruits to the Society and implicitly built those orators into the curriculum for them laid out in the *Constitutions*. Nadal, like some others of his day, looked forward to a time when a 'properly Christian' art of oratory might be composed, but even such an art would according to him have to draw on classical rhetoric, most especially on the parts that deal with 'moving the affections'.[28] He also argued that whereas in the 'primitive Church' an artless style was required so that it be clear that the power of the Gospel was not due to human persuasion, now it was appropriate that what was founded on divine foundation be extolled with every human art.[29]

In 1565 Pedro Perpinyá, a distinguished teacher of rhetoric at the Jesuits' Roman College, argued in a memorandum intended for Jesuit leadership in Rome that, if unadorned truth excited love for it, how much more would the feelings be aroused when the language in which the truth was expressed was more commensurate with the sublimity of the subject.[30] This typically Humanist argument would have fallen on willing ears.

Although the first Jesuits do not seem explicitly to have made the connection, the practice of rhetoric, i.e., oratory, coincided with their 'way of proceeding' on another profound and pervasive level. Essential to the orator's success was his ability to be in touch with the feelings and needs of his audience and to adapt himself and his speech accordingly. Beginning with the *Exercises* themselves, the Jesuits were constantly advised by Ignatius to adapt in all their ministries what they said and did to time, circumstances and persons.

If we may judge from Ignatius's *Autobiography*, he derived this principle from his personal experience of ministry in the early years of his conversion. It was deepened, surely, by his experience as superior general of an order that from the beginning had to learn to operate in the very different cultures of sixteenth-century Europe, as well as in exotic places like India, Japan and Brazil. None the less, it found confirmation and rationalization in the precepts of rhetoric that either directly or indirectly he had come to know. The 'rhetorical' dimension of Jesuit ministry in this sense transcended the preaching and lecturing in which they were so assiduously engaged and fanned out to become characteristic of all the activities in which they were engaged.

That brings me to the third way in which classical rhetoric influenced them, perhaps unawares. While it is true that in his *Autobiography* Ignatius depicted himself as engaging primarily in various 'ministries of the word of God' and that such ministries held pride of place in the fundamental documents of the Society, such ministries found their centre and culmination in the Sacrament of Penance.

For everybody to whom the Jesuits ministered, Ignatius heartily recommended frequent, i.e., weekly or monthly, confession as a way of remaining in the way of the Lord and making progress in it. This meant that the Jesuits were consistently called upon to deal with a wide variety of cases of conscience in all their complexity. This meant that they had to become skilled in the then developing art of casuistry, i.e., the art of applying general rules of morality to specific instances, in which the morality of the case was largely determined by particulars of time, places, persons and other circumstances.

To help his fellow Jesuits ply this art, Ignatius ordered Polanco to write a book on it. Polanco set about the task, and in 1554 he published his *Breve directorium* on the subject, the first book on ministry by a Jesuit.[31] That book helped set the Society on a course in which its members' skill in casuistical art would become part of their tradition, making them in the next century an easy target for Pascal's ridicule in his *Provincial Letters.*

The flexibility in dealing with diverse penitents that casuistry advocated was certainly open to abuse, whose dangers would be increased when the Jesuits much later subscribed to probabilism, but its fundamental insight was sound. It echoed, in any case, the kind of advice that Ignatius gave the director of retreats in the *Spiritual Exercises* and his more general and insistently repeated advice to Jesuits in his correspondence to adapt to time, places and circumstances.

We have been schooled to believe that casuistry developed out of medieval Scholasticism, which it most immediately did. But, as the recent book by Albert Jonsen and Stephen Toulman has shown, classical rhetoric provided in its injunctions to the orator to adapt to circumstances the remote and fundamental elements upon which casuistry drew.[32] Jonsen and Toulman put the matter well: 'Rhetoric and casuistry were mutual allies. It is not surprising to find the Jesuits, who were dedicated to teaching classical rhetoric in their colleges, become the leading exponents of casuistry'.[33]

That quotation brings me nicely to the second part of what I have to say about the relationship of Renaissance Humanism to the early Society of Jesus. It brings me to the schools. I hope that I have at least been able to suggest thus far that Humanism had an impact on Ignatius and the Society even apart from what was effected by the schools, Humanism's most characteristic institution — soon to become the most characteristic institution of the Society of Jesus. None the less, the impact of the decision to operate secondary schools according to the Humanist model would be, if possible, even more determinative of the subsequent character of the Society.

With the benefit of hindsight, we can see how Ignatius and his early associates might have been susceptible to the idea of undertaking schools as a ministry. They were educated men, and from their earliest arrival in Rome some of them had been engaged in temporary teaching assignments at the Universities of Rome, Ingolstadt and elsewhere. None the less, they considered permanent positions in such institutions contrary to the humble and largely itinerant nature of their vocation.

When Ignatius agreed to open in Messina in 1548 what was in effect the first Jesuit school, he was motivated principally by the hope that it would provide funding for the education of young Jesuits, while at the same time providing classes for other students. From the first moment, however, the latter reality overpowered the former. Under the leadership of Nadal, the venture at Messina became an immediate and resounding success. It not only offered hope of the formation of the laity in piety, character and good letters — three aspects of the same reality in the Humanists' viewpoint — but also provided a marvellous base for the other ministries of the Society.

Although relatively few of Nadal's letters from this period survive, they had to help convince Ignatius to move with bold, even precipitous, speed along a path where previously he had taken only a few tentative steps. Within a month after the Collegio di San Nicolò opened in Messina, thirty members of the Senate at Palermo petitioned Ignatius for a similar school in their city, and Ignatius acceded.

Word reached distant Cologne of what had happened in Messina and Palermo, and on 4 October 1549 Leonard Kessel wrote to Ignatius registering his surprise but also his enthusiasm: 'If it has come to the point that the brethren have begun to teach publicly', he said, then it would be a splendid idea to do so in Cologne, where there is hope of 'gaining all youth to Christ'.[34] The college at Cologne would have to wait for a future date, but within two years Polanco wrote in Ignatius's name to the provincials of Spain and Portugal urging them to undertake colleges like the ones in Italy that by then had been begun in Messina, Palermo, Ferrara, Florence, Rome, Naples, Bologna and elsewhere.[35] The Society had taken a dramatic turn in its road. By the time Ignatius died in 1556 it was operating at his insistent urging well over thirty schools, eighteen of them in Italy, with negotiations under way in places as distant as Warsaw and Mexico.

Why must this turn be considered so dramatic? The reasons are many. First of all, no religious order had ever taken on formal schooling as an explicit ministry. Surely among the reasons that impelled Ignatius and the first Jesuits to this decision was the Humanists' propaganda that linked their style of education so intimately with piety, good morals and the formation of character.

For the Jesuits, moreover, the schools soon became not one ministry among many, but the ministry that enjoyed a certain preeminence over all the others. On 10 August 1560 Polanco wrote in the general's name an important letter to all superiors of the Society. He said: 'Generally speaking, there are [in the Society] two ways of helping our neighbours: one in the colleges through the education of youth in letters, learning and Christian life, and the second in every place to help every kind of person through sermons, confessions and the other means that accord with our customary way of proceeding'.[36] The Jesuits' decision opened a new era in the way ministry would be conceived in the Catholic Church, as the history of so many orders of women and men founded subsequently has shown.

That much is obvious and has generally been acknowledged. But we must look at the repercussions of the decision on the very character of the Society itself — repercussions that could hardly have been foreseen in the beginning. The decision helped determine, for instance, to which classes of society the Jesuits would tend to minister.

As Paul Grendler has shown, two major types of schools existed in Italy by the mid-sixteenth century: the Latin (or Humanist) School and the Vernacular School.[37] The former appealed to the upper classes of society, whereas the other, a more 'practical' form of education, appealed to those of the lower classes who desired the basic skills of reading, writing and arithmetic. Humanists like Erasmus believed that a Humanist education was appropriate and desirable for all, but the fact was that it simply did not appeal to all.

Ignatius and the first Jesuits were adamant in their conviction that their ministries should be offered gratis to anybody who desired them, regardless of their gender, race, socio-economic class and, to some extent, even their religion. True, in the *Constitutions* Ignatius laid down as one of the norms for 'the distribution of members of the Society in the vineyard of the Lord' that 'spiritual aid given to important and public persons ought to be regarded as more important' because such persons had great influence for better or worse on others.[38] None the less, what strikes one when reading the reports Jesuits wrote back to Ignatius about their ministries is how marvellously indiscriminate they were in the choice of people to whom they ministered, although they had a special concern for those in dire spiritual or physical need.

That same desire not to restrict their ministry to any particular class animated them in the operation of their colleges. They insisted that the schools accept indiscriminately the poor and the rich, that they accept, as Polanco wrote to the Jesuits opening a new college at Ingolstadt in 1556, 'every kind of person . . . in order to animate and console them'.[39] In Lisbon in 1555 'a great friend of the Society' made known his opinion that the Jesuits should not teach Latin grammar to boys from the lower social classes, for if those classes got a taste for study there would be no artisans or craftsmen left. The opinion displeased the Jesuits immensely, as they reported to Ignatius, and they refused to conform to it.[40]

The fact is, however, that this determination had to do battle with the dynamics intrinsic to the Latin School itself, so that with time the Jesuits' ministry of education was directed towards the middle and upper classes to an extent that seems not to have been foreseen in the original decision, and some schools were explicitly founded for that purpose.

Historians have in fact sometimes exaggerated this shift in clientele. It has been reckoned, for instance, that well into the eighteenth century, sixty to sixty-five per cent of the students in Jesuit schools in France were from the 'working classes', and that the 'overall enrolments showed a remarkable closeness to the broadest social representation one could expect'.[41] None the less, a significant shift did take place over time — not so much because of a deliberate decision in that regard but because of a prior decision whose ultimate implications were not fully understood.

The decision to take the operation of schools as a primary ministry profoundly affected even the way the Jesuits would conceive of themselves. There can be little doubt that in the beginning and for the first ten years the ultimate model for ministry that the Jesuits held up for themselves was intinerant preachers of the Gospel as described in chapter 10 of Matthew's Gospel and in the Acts of the Apostles through the story of the evangelizing Paul. Especially the fully professed members of the Society were to hold themselves in readiness to travel anywhere in the world for ministry at a moment's notice.[42] Long-term residence in the houses of the Society for those members who had finished their education seems to have been almost precluded by the itinerant nature of the Jesuit vocation. Whereas Benedict saw the monk as constituted by his vow of stability, the *Constitutions* of the Society stipulated that 'the first characteristic of our Institute' was to travel to various parts of the world.[43]

Once the schools were founded, however, this ideal had to compete with the reality of being resident schoolmasters. Early in the 1550s Ignatius discovered that chaos resulted from moving Jesuits too frequently from the schools to which they were assigned, and complaints from both students and parents poured into Jesuit headquarters when a popular teacher was transferred. Ignatius adapted accordingly. Few stronger indications of the esteem in which he held the schools exist than his willingness to modify in practice this original and basic understanding of how Jesuits were to operate and conceive of themselves.

Ignatius had likewise to modify another of his most cherished proposals for the Society. From the first days of his conversion he had been attracted to Francis of Assisi and to the ideal of religious poverty to which the Franciscans aspired. One recalls the pivotal role that 'actual and spiritual poverty' plays in the *Spiritual Exercises*. Learning from the troubled history of the Franciscan order, Ignatius realized how difficult it was to translate that ideal into a form that would be viable for an institution like the Society.

Learning also from his own experience as a student at the University of Paris, he determined in the *Constitutions* that the students in the Society could live in houses (called 'colleges') that enjoyed an endowment, thus freeing them to concentrate on their studies without worry about where the next meal was coming from. Those members of the Society who had finished their education, however, would live strictly off alms — hand-to-mouth, one might say

— in so-called 'professed houses'. The colleges would presumably be few, since in this original formulation the only ones the Society would operate would be for its own members. The professed houses would be many — and would be the norm.

Hardly had the ink dried on those parts of the *Constitutions* that deal with this matter before the reality outstripped the theory. In the last five years of Ignatius's life, schools were founded at breakneck pace, so that it had to become apparent that most members of the Society would live in endowed institutions. The most astounding aspect of this development is that it happened not despite Ignatius but with his blessing. In the last years of his life, he for the most part would not accept an invitation for Jesuits to establish themselves in a given location if it meant not a school but a professed house. As Polanco wrote to a superior in 1555, a year before Ignatius's death: 'Our father's intention is that, especially in these initial stages, the schools must multiply rather than the houses'.[44] This 'intention' turned out to be the blueprint for the future.

Finally, the decision to operate schools in the Humanist mode profoundly affected the relationship of the Jesuits to learning and culture. Ignatius and his companions, graduates of the University of Paris, were well educated according to the standards of their day. As Ignatius stated several times in his *Autobiography*, he early determined to pursue further studies in order to help his ministry. The idea was widespread in his day, ardently promoted by the Humanists, that a better educated clergy was one of the most urgent needs of the Church. We have every reason to believe that, even if he had not made the momentous decision to take schooling as a ministry for his order, he would have prescribed for its members a rigorous education.

That decision had, none the less, a peculiarly determinative influence. In the first several years of the Society, for instance, some members were convinced that the writing and publishing of books was something alien to their itinerant and pastoral vocation.[45] As evidenced by Polanco's *Directorium*, this persuasion did not last long. What seem to have especially commended themselves to them were works on ministry like the *Directorium* or works to 'refute the heretics'.[46]

Jesuits indeed began to produce books along these lines, but once the schools were opened they discovered, like so many teachers before and since, that the textbooks available were not to their liking. They soon began to publish, therefore, works on Latin grammar and rhetoric and their own editions of the classics appropriate to the classroom. In a word, they began an engagement — modest enough at first — with secular culture that would become one of their trademarks. This engagement, we must observe, was more than a propensity; it was intrinsically interwoven with the very fabric of their understanding of their ministry.

Moreover, one of the basic premises of the Humanist tradition was that religious and moral inspiration could be found even in pagan authors. No Jesuit, so far as I know, went so far as to echo Erasmus's famous prayer, 'O Saint Socrates, pray for us', but some of them came close.[47] One recalls the words of the distinguished Jesuit exegete, Cornelius a Lapide, in the late sixteenth century commenting on a passage from the philosopher Epictetus: 'O wonder! These words ring of the Gospel, not pagan philosophy'.[48]

In the *Constitutions* of the Society of Jesus inspired by Ignatius, the conviction runs deep that grace builds on nature — a conviction born of Ignatius's personal experience and reinforced by the teaching of scholastic theologians like Aquinas whom he commended to his order. One aspect of that conviction was that transcendent religion and human culture mysteriously interpenetrate and are reconcilable.

That conviction was also fundamental to the religious thought of Renaissance Humanism. When Ignatius committed his Society to the ministry of formal education and thus approved the Humanist curriculum of classical authors, he gave the conviction an institutional articulation in the legislation of the Society. It is not implausible to postulate that this conviction helped incline later Jesuits like Matteo Ricci and John de Britto towards their notably benign attitudes towards the ancient cultures of China and India.

The nascent Society of Jesus had its basic charter in the *Spiritual Exercises* of Saint Ignatius, later supplemented by his *Autobiography* and then the *Constitutions*. There can be no doubt that these three documents provided and reveal the foundational elements of the character of the Society. More specific delineations of that character resulted, however, from decisions made along the way and from cultural forces acting upon it in ways not altogether foreseen. Renaissance Humanism was one of those forces. I hope I have shown, within the modest limits of a brief article, that the impact of Humanism on Ignatius and the Society was manifold, profound and of lasting significance.

Notes

1 See John C. Olin, 'Erasmus and St Ignatius Loyola', in his *Six Essays on Erasmus* (New York, Fordham University Press, 1979), pp.75-92.

2 See Silvana Seidel-Menchi, *Erasmo in Italia 1520-1580,* Turin, Bollati Boringhiere, 1987, and Erika Rummel, *Erasmus and His Catholic Critics, II: 1523-1536,* Nieuwkoop, De Graaf Publishers, 1989.

3 See Paul Oskar Kristeller, 'Paganism and Christianity', in his *Renaissance Thought: The Classic, Scholastic, and Humanist Strains* (New York, Harper & Brothers, 1955), pp.70-91, and now Albert Rabil, Jr. (ed.), *Renaissance Humanism: Foundations, Forms and Legacy*, 3 vols., Philadelphia, University of Pennsylvania Press, 1988.

4 See my 'Introduction', in *Spiritualia*, Collected Works of Erasmus, vol.66, Toronto, University of Toronto Press, 1988.

5 See Rabil, *Renaissance Humanism* (note 3 above).

6 R.R. Bolger, *The Classical Heritage and Its Beneficiaries: From the Carolingian Age to the End of the Renaissance* (New York, Harper & Row, 1964), p.255.

7 See Craig R. Thompson, 'Better Teachers than Scotus or Aquinas', in *Medieval and Renaissance Studies*, ed. John L. Lievsay (Durham, The University of North Carolina Press, 1968), pp.114-45.

8 See John M. McManamon, 'Innovation in Early Humanist Rhetoric: The Oratory of Pier Paolo Vergerio (the Elder)', *Rinascimento*, n.s. 22 (1982), pp.3-32, and his *Funeral Oratory and the Cultural Ideals of Italian Humanism*, Chapel Hill, The University of North Carolina Press, 1989.

9 See my *Praise and Blame in Renaissance Rome: Rhetoric, Doctrine, and Reform in the Sacred Orators of the Papal Court, c.1450-1521*, Durham, Duke University Press, 1979.

10 See my 'Erasmus and the History of Sacred Rhetoric: The *Ecclesiastes* of 1535', *Erasmus of Rotterdam Society Yearbook* 5 (1985), pp.1-29.

11 See Paul F. Grendler, *Schooling in Renaissance Italy: Literacy and Learning, 1300-1600*, Baltimore, The Johns Hopkins University Press, 1989.

12 For a discussion of the limitations of the pedagogy, see Anthony Grafton and Lisa Jardine, *From Humanism to the Humanities: Education and the Liberal Arts in Fifteenth- and Sixteenth-Century Europe* (Cambridge, Harvard University Press, 1986), especially pp.1-28.

13 See, e.g., Erika Rummel, *Erasmus' Annotations on the New Testament: From Philologist to Theologian*, Toronto, University of Toronto Press, 1986, and John C. Olin, 'Erasmus and the Church Fathers', in his *Six Essays* (note 1 above), pp.33-47.

14 See *Pláticas espirituales del P. Jerónimo Nadal, S.I., en Coimbra (1561)*, ed. Miguel Nicolau (Granada, Facultad teológica de la Compañia de Jesús, 1945), p.133.

15 *Monumenta Nadal*, in *Monumenta Historica Societatis Jesu* (henceforth MHSJ), 5:829.

16 *Monumenta Ignatiana: Constitutiones* (MHSJ), 1:191, 393-94.

17 See Olin, 'Erasmus and Ignatius' (note 1 above).

18 *Monumenta Ignatiana: Epistolae* (MHSJ), 9:721-22.

19 *Monumenta Laínez* (MHSJ), 2:304.

20 See Marc Fumaroli, 'Définition et description: Scholastique et rhétorique chez les jésuites des XVIe et XVIIe siècles', *Travaux de linguistique et de littérature* 18 (1980), pp.37-48.

21 *Constitutions* [464].

22 See my 'The Feast of Thomas Aquinas in Renaissance Rome: A Neglected Document and Its Import', *Rivista di Storia della Chiesa in Italia* 35 (1981), pp.1-27.

23 *Summa Theologiae*, 1.1.4.

24 *Monumenta Nadal* (MHSJ), 5:282-84. See also my 'The Fourth Vow in Its Ignatian Context: A Historical Study', *Studies in the Spirituality of Jesuits* 15/1 (January, 1983), especially pp.8-14.

25 *Fontes Narrativi*, 2nd ed. (MHSJ), 2:56.

26 *Constitutions* [401]. See Angelo Martini, 'Gli studi teologici di Giovanni de Polanco alle origini della legislazione scolastica della Compagnia di Gesù', *Archivum Historicum Societatis Jesu* 21 (1952), especially pp.254-66.

27 See Hanna Holborn Gray, 'Renaissance Humanism: The Pursuit of Eloquence', *Journal of the History of Ideas* 24 (1963), pp.497-514.

28 *Monumenta Nadal* (MHSJ), 5:828, as well as 4:645, 5:824-30; Nadal, *Scholia in Constitutiones S.I.,* ed. Manuel Ruiz Jurado (Granada, Facultad de Teologia, 1976), pp.386-87.

29 *Monumenta Nadal* (MHSJ), 4:831-33.

30 *Monumenta Paedagogica* (MHSJ), 2:661-63.

31 *Breve directorium ad confessarii et confitentis munus rite obeundum concinnatum*, Rome, Ant. Blado, 1554.

32 *The Abuses of Casuistry: A History of Moral Reasoning*, Berkeley, University of

California Press, 1988. See also John Mahoney, *The Making of Moral Theology: A Study of the Roman Catholic Tradition*, Oxford, Clarendon Press, 1987.

33 Jonsen and Toulman, *Abuses* (note 32 above), p.88.

34 *Litterae Quadrimestres* (MHSJ), 1:172.

35 *Monumenta Ignatiana: Epistolae* (MHSJ), 4:5-9, 11-12.

36 *Monumenta Paedagogica* (MHSJ), 3:305-6.

37 *Schooling in Renaissance Italy* (note 11 above).

38 *Constitutions* [622, e].

39 *Monumenta Paedagogica* (MHSJ), 1:485.

40 Polanco, *Chronicon Societatis Jesu* (MHSJ), 5:562.

41 See Aldo Scaglione, *The Liberal Arts and the Jesuit College System* (Amsterdam and Philadelphia, John Benjamin Publishing Company, 1986), p.118.

42 See my 'To Travel to Any Part of the World: Jerónimo Nadal and the Jesuit Vocation', *Studies in the Spirituality of Jesuits*, 16/2 (March, 1984).

43 *Constitutions* [626]. See also ibid., [82], [92], [304], [308], [588], [603], [605].

44 *Monumenta Ignatiana: Epistolae*, 9:82.

45 *Monumenta Salmerón* (MHSJ), 1:46-47.

46 *Monumenta Nadal* (MHSJ), 5:665-66.

47 Spoken by Nephalius in 'The Godly Feast' (*Convivium religiosum*), in *Opera omnia* (Amsterdam, North Holland Publishing Company, 1972), 1/3:254. See *Ten Colloquies of Erasmus,* ed. Craig R. Thompson (New York, Liberal Arts Press, 1957), p.158.

48 Quoted in François de Dainville, *La Naissance de l'humanisme moderne* (Paris Beauchesne et ses fils, 1940), p.223.

XI

ATTITUDES OF THE EARLY JESUITS TOWARDS MISBELIEVERS

TEXTBOOKS AND POPULAR LITERATURE on the sixteenth century depict Saint Ignatius and his early companions as the spearhead of the Catholic attack on the Reformation especially in Italy and Germany, and they leave the impression that the Society of Jesus was founded in 1540 with precisely this 'defence of the faith' as its primary objective. Scholars have long realized that such depictions fail to take full account of what the first Jesuits were about, but by and large they have not analysed Jesuit attitudes towards Protestants—or towards others of different religious beliefs, like Jews or the pagans with whom they worked in places like India and Brazil. I shall briefly address the issue.

To forestall any possible misunderstanding, however, it must be stated clearly at the outset that the early Jesuits were to a man utterly convinced that the Roman Catholic Church of their day held in its dogmas and essential religious practices the unique key to every human being's eternal salvation. For this conviction they were willing, if God gave them the grace, to suffer a martyr's death at the hands of heretics, schismatics, infidels, Jews or pagans. In this supreme sacrifice they considered that they would simply be doing their Christian duty.

With that preamble firmly in place, we can begin to descend to a few particulars about their basic religious attitudes that will correct some common misapprehensions. The first such misapprehension is that the Society was founded to fight the Reformation. The original statement of its purpose, the so-called 'Formula of the Institute', 1540, reads simply, 'for the progress of souls in Christian life and doctrine and for the propagation of the faith'.[1] In their earliest years the Jesuits were much more concerned with the conversion of the infidels in Jerusalem than with the Lutherans in Wittenberg.

In 1550, however, the phrase 'defence of the faith' was added to the statement of purpose in the 'Formula', an indication of growing awareness of the threat of Protestantism.

This does not mean that Ignatius and his companions were previously unaware, as the documentation surviving from the period incontestably indicates. Given the turmoil over Protestantism in Paris when Ignatius and his first companions were studying there, 1527–35, and in Italy where they subsequently arrived, what is remarkable about that documentation, however, is the relatively small role Protestantism plays. It is scarcely mentioned, for instance, in Ignatius' *Autobiography*, completed in 1555, the year before his death, and it in effect nowhere appears in the *Constitutions* he composed for the Society. If we except for a moment the special problem posed by the 'Rules for Thinking with the Church', it plays no role in the *Spiritual Exercises*.

But beginning about 1550, more attention began to be paid to it by Jesuit leadership in Rome, although it would always remain only one concern among many. The reasons for this shift in emphasis are manifold. Among them surely would be the ever more desperate plight of the champion of the Catholic cause, Emperor Charles V, and his final defeat in 1555, codified in the provisions of the Peace of Augsburg.

More pertinent, however, were certain developments internal to the Society. In 1550, after a brief sojourn in Italy, Peter Canisius returned to Germany, which he would in effect never again leave until his death in 1597. He became the great catalyst for the Society's extensive ministries in the Empire. Almost by definition those ministries dealt either directly or indirectly with Lutheranism. His insistent demands on Jesuit headquarters in Rome for reinforcements in manpower signalled a new alert. Moreover, in 1555 Jerónimo Nadal, trusted confidant of Ignatius and itinerant troubleshooter for the nascent Society, made his first trip to the Empire, where he was utterly appalled by what he found. He would thereafter be an especially strong voice in the Society for assigning high priority to the German situation.

Nadal seems to be the first person in history, in fact, to propose in bold fashion the interpretation of the origins of the Society that linked it intrinsically with the battle against Protestantism. As early as 1554, Ignatius had come close, with the benefit of hindsight, to saying the same thing.[2] His secretary, Juan de Polanco, took up the idea.[3]

Once Ignatius was dead, however, the temptation to compare and contrast him with Luther was too great to resist. The very year after his death, Nadal suggested the theme in an exhortation to the Jesuits at the Roman College.[4] In his second *Dialogue* some five years later he pits Ignatius, the new David, against Luther, the Goliath.[5] He reminded the Jesuits at Cologne in 1567, with some confusion of dates, that in the year Luther was called by the devil Ignatius heard the call from God.[6] The now familiar diptych, so beloved of historians, with Luther on the one side and Ignatius on the other, was first painted by the early Jesuits themselves.

Perhaps more important, Nadal and others began to interpret certain practices in the Society in a way that could lead to the impression that they were undertaken specifically as antidotes to Protestant errors. He refers, for instance, to frequent confession and to the special vow of the professed to obey the pope 'concerning missions'.[7] Antidotes they may well have become, but all the things to which Nadal refers had their real origins in some other cause.

The distorted view of how and why the Society came into being to which we have become accustomed began, therefore, with some of the first Jesuits themselves. Why, then, *was* the Society originally founded? Scholars who are aware that it was not founded specifically to counter the Reformation sometimes state that it was founded to 'reform the (Catholic) Church'. This comes closer to the mark. But we need to be aware that, although the expression 'reform of the Church' was on practically every thinking Catholic's lips, it was rarely employed by the first Jesuits—and practically never to describe what they themselves were about.

As the expression was then commonly employed, it meant a reform of ecclesiastical legislation that would effect more genuinely pastoral practice and attitudes in the bishops, especially the Bishop of Rome, and in the pastors of parishes. This was the understanding enshrined in the 'reform' legislation of the Council of Trent. The Society, a religious order exempt from episcopal jurisdiction and as one that had explicitly foresworn undertaking parochial ministry, never officially spoke of its scope as 'reform of the Church' in this sense.

The word 'reform' (*reformatio*) does appear frequently, however, in Jesuits' letters and other documents. While it sometimes refers to their efforts to bring convents and monasteries back to a stricter discipline, it more often applies to the result they hoped to effect in individuals of every class of society by their various ministries.

It stands as a close equivalent to what we usually mean by 'conversion'—conversion away from a life of sin or conversion from a mediocre Christian life to a much closer following of Christ. If we should wish to make this type of reform mean the same thing as 'reform of the Church', we must be willing to apply the same designation to phenomena like the Fransiscan movement in the thirteenth century. In so doing, we must admit that we are using the designation differently from the way in which it was used in the sixteenth century—a rather questionable procedure.

The Jesuits' understanding of 'reform' echoes its meaning in the *Exercises* (Exx 189). As practically everybody who has written on the Jesuits agrees, we must turn to that book for our fundamental understanding of what they thought they were about. There is no doubt that it is about conversion of life and conversion of heart—conversion from sin in the First Week and conversion to a more efficacious following of Christ in the Second, to be confirmed in the Third and Fourth.

The purpose is betrayed even more generically in the Fifteenth Annotation: 'to permit the Creator to deal directly with the creature, and the creature directly with his Creator and Lord'. Amidst all its structure, suggestions and directives, what finally emerges in the *Exercises* is its basically non-prescriptive character regarding the outcome of those dealings. Although the *Exercises* are obviously biased towards a life of 'real' poverty by adherence to what were known as the 'counsels of evangelical perfection', they are clear that, for various reasons, this may not be literally possible or best for everybody. For precisely that reason they were held in great suspicion by some important Catholic contemporaries of Ignatius.[8]

We are here touching not only on what is central to the *Exercises* but also on what was central to Ignatius' own religious experience, which he distilled for others in his book. No more significant passage appears in his *Autobiography* than where he relates how at Manresa he was directly taught by God [Exx 27]. The 'word of God' to which he and his fellow Jesuits made such frequent reference was often specifically this personal word spoken within. In many ways that is what the Rules for the Discernment of Spirits in the *Exercises* are all about.

For him and them the 'word of God' also referred to the scriptures, as is clear from the way the last three Weeks are organized. In them was the objectified counterpart to the inner word. But what kind of book were the scriptures as they are presented in the *Exercises?* They are not a data base from which to draw dogma and theological doctrine in the ordinary senses of those terms, which is how scholastic theology viewed them. They are, rather, a book about living the Christian life. As such, they were intended for every human being on the face of the earth. Noteworthy about the *Exercises* in this regard is that they propose no dogmatic theses for adherence and that the dogmatic assumptions about the Christian religion they assume would belong to the common heritage. In that sense they were about *Christianitas*, as that term was understood in the Middle Ages and in Ignatius' own day.[9]

What was the teaching of *Christianitas?* Nadal tells us in an impassioned passage from his *Apologia* for the *Exercises* against their detractors: 'What did Christ and what did the Apostles, what have the saints and the Church ever taught except that mortals should love God above all things, with their whole heart, their whole mind, their whole soul, and their whole being?' According to him, this was the essential message of the *Exercises*. It was a message written in every human heart.

The point of this important passage is, in fact, that the *Exercises*, or at least parts of them, can therefore with profit be engaged in not only by Protestant heretics but even by pagans.[10] Nadal states this idea as his 'personal opinion', but his opinions always carried a great deal of weight. In the early days of the Society some few Protestants did in fact make the *Exercises*.[11] Although the Jesuits who guided these persons clearly hoped that they would thereby be cured of their heresy, the point is that even in the sixteenth century some persons saw in the *Exercises* transconfessional validity.

There were of course elements in the *Exercises*, like the confession of sins recommended at the end of the First Week, that would require considerable adaptation if the *Exercises* were given to persons who were not practising Roman Catholics. Many traditional commentators on them, however, would see the largest obstacle in the 'Rules for Thinking with the Church', i.e., with the Catholic Church. Some have in fact tended to see these 'Rules' almost as the hermeneutical key for interpreting the whole book. Interpreted in that sense, the *Exercises* become a manifesto of Roman Catholic orthodoxy. Even today that is the impression conveyed by many textbooks and general studies of the sixteenth century.

Several considerations need to be kept in mind if we are to understand those 'Rules'. First of all, although the wording of a few of them sometimes seems particularly emphatic, even those like the notorious thirteenth rule about believing what seems to me white to be in fact black if it is so defined by the Church, do not differ from what other Catholics would have believed, as has recently been shown precisely for that thirteenth rule.[12] They do not represent some exaggerated or special orthodoxy.

Secondly, they are in their essence statements of attitudes that generally bear on pastoral practice and do not attempt to settle in any specific way controversial issues. In this regard, they are perfectly in accord with Ignatius' customary posture.[13] When he wrote to the Jesuits present at the first period of the Council of Trent, for instance, his only counsels concerning doctrine were that they were to avoid favouring any position that might seem to approach that of 'heretics and sectarians' and avoid taking sides on issues on which Catholics were divided among themselves.[14]

Finally, important though the 'Rules' are in other ways, they were rarely commented upon by the early Jesuits and were not seen by them as integral to the *Exercises* as such. Juan de Polanco, Ignatius' secretary and *alter ego*, equivalently states this when in his *Directory* for the *Exercises*, 1573–75, he joins them with three other sets of 'Rules'—for almsgiving, scruples, and the use of food: 'About these four the following can be said in general. They should not be proposed to everybody, but only to persons who seem to need them and for whom it is worth the effort'.[15]

The *Exercises* are not, therefore, about correct dogma, but about conversion of *heart*. If we had to sum up the Jesuits' agenda in all their ministries in one expression, that would be it. That was what was important to them, for they believed that that was what was most important in life. If that could be effected, all else would fall into place. Contrariwise, the root of all evil in individuals as well as in society lay in not having undergone such a conversion. They accordingly subscribed to the ancient persuasion that the root of heresy lay in some other sin. With conversion of heart, the heretic would abandon his or her heresy.

This persuasion helps explain their sometimes benign, if perhaps condescending, attitude towards Protestants. In 1541 Peter Faber, the first Jesuit to have direct contact with the Lutherans in Germany, recorded a list of those for whom he explicitly prayed on a regular basis: 'The Pope, the Emperor, the King of France, the King of England, Luther, the Sultan, Bucer, and Philipp Melanchthon'.[16] He noted that God had given him a great love for heretics and for the whole world, especially for Germany—'*esta pobre nación*'.[17]

In 1558 Diego Laínez, already elected to succeed Ignatius as superior general of the order, told a lay audience in Rome that, although some persons maintained the contrary opinion, it was praiseworthy to pray for heretics, schismatics, and excommunicates. He especially exhorted them to do so for the first group, misled because of their own sins but also 'scandalized by our rottenness and simony'.[18] If the Lutherans could undergo a conversion of heart, he implies, they would no longer be susceptible to the heresy of their leaders.

In 1545 Faber expressed sentiments of compassion for both Henry VIII and Luther.[19] By about 1560, however, other Jesuits began at least on occasion to fall into explicit vilifications of Luther that practically never occurred during Ignatius' lifetime. Laínez said he was perverse.[20] In 1577 Canisius went so far as to call him a 'hog in heat'—*subantem porcum*.[21] Nadal became perhaps the worst and most consistent offender, for whom Luther was 'disturbed and diabolical', 'an evil and bestial man', 'a wicked, proud, enraged, and devilish monk'.[22] Revealing though such passages are in Nadal, they in fact occur relatively infrequently.

It has never been established that Nadal ever read Luther, and, like practically all the leading Jesuits of his generation except Canisius, he was surely incapable of doing so in German. His occasional sketches of Luther's teaching were suspiciously brief and repeat the usual Catholic distortions. Nadal is particularly important for our topic because he directly instructed most of the Jesuits in Europe about the meaning of their vocation. Other leading Jesuits of the period like Laínez and Alfonso Salmerón, and most certainly Canisius, read some of the Protestant writings, but most of the others, if they had any interest in the matter, seem to have derived their knowledge from Catholic polemicists. As far as we know, Ignatius never read any of the Protestants with the possible exception of Bernardo Ochino, whose writings he expressed a desire to see in 1545 in order that he might help him be reconciled to the Catholic Church.[23]

In any case, Nadal did not invent the bad-monk interpretation of Luther. It had been in circulation for decades among Catholic polemicists before he adopted it. Besides being an example of the vituperative rhetoric common to all parties in that religiously disturbed period, it helped promote among Catholics thenceforth a persistently moralistic reading of the Reformation. Furthermore, if immorality—first of all their own and then that of various Protestant leaders—had been the cause of the Reformation, a more devout and morally upright life would be its cure. When the Jesuits took it into their heads to counter the Reformation, whether they were dealing with Catholics or directly with Protestants, they believed that it was towards that cure that they best direct their efforts. This belief happened to coincide with what the *Exercises* had in any case indicated as their goal for anybody unto whom they ministered.

A passage from one of Laínez' Roman lectures in 1558 illustrates the point well. He said: 'I am not a Lutheran, but I believe that we have given occasion for the trouble by our pomp, sensuality, avarice, simony, and by usurping for ourselves the goods of the Church. And now what? We can now restore what we have ruined and scandalized, but how do we do it? In my opinion we cannot do it with beautiful words alone or with conferences and similar things without accompanying them with deeds, because it was with the deeds of a bad life that we did evil. All right, now we want to do better? Contraries are cured by contraries. We must therefore lead good lives.'[24]

Laínez prefaced these words with a condemnation of even a 'just war' because of the great damage it inflicts on the innocent, especially to women and children. This seems in context to be an obvious allusion to the war just ending that Pope Paul IV had waged against Philip II of Spain, but it would seem to apply to wars against heresy.

The doctrinal issues of the day were, in any case, to a certain extent a somewhat secondary concern to the early Jesuits. Not that they thought them unimportant but that they were best not addressed in the first instance. Ignatius' most consistent advice on the way to deal with doctrinal controversies was to avoid, whenever possible, polemics and direct confrontations, especially in the pulpit, and be content with a positive exposition of Catholic teaching.[25] Faulty though Nadal's understanding of Luther may have been, he had a masterful grasp especially of the best Catholic theology of grace and was skilled in speaking about it. Even he underscores in his first *Dialogue* that avoidance of contention, which leads only to bitterness and hatred, was meant to be characteristic of the

Jesuits' general way of proceeding concerning controverted doctrines.[26] The overheated religious situation of the sixteenth century, however, did not suffer the sage principle always to prevail.

Much more could be said about the attitudes of the early Jesuits towards Protestants, but we must move on to a hasty glance at their attitudes towards two other categories of misbelievers for whom they had concern—Jews and pagans. Regarding the first category, we must recall that most of the leading Jesuits of the founding generation were from the Iberian peninsula where anti-Jewish sentiment raged and had found its most virulent expression in the decrees of expulsion from Spain in 1492 and from Portugal in 1496.

These decrees had repercussions in Italy, where new restrictions began to be imposed on Jews within a few decades. In 1516, for instance, the Republic of Venice forced Jews to live in a designated quarter of the city. Pope Paul IV imposed a similar ghetto upon them in Rome during 1555 and enforced some of the most stringent restrictions on their freedom in all of Italy. Since most of the first Jesuits were concentrated in Iberia and Italy, they could not avoid the issue.

Ignatius not only seems to have approved of the papal bull of 1555 but actually helped propagate it.[27] He had strong feelings against the Jewish religion and all who practised it. As with the Protestants, this bigotry had an epistemological root: the truth of Christianity was clear; only moral perversity could explain failure to embrace it.

If we distinguish between race and religion, however, Ignatius notably transcended most of his peers in his open-mindedness towards the Jews as a race of people. He on several occasions severely shocked people by saying that he would consider it a great grace from God to have been born, like Jesus, from Jewish lineage.[29] He warmly welcomed into the Society Italian converts from Judaism.

This attitude is illustrated most dramatically in his insistence on allowing so-called 'New Christians' in Spain to enter the Society. By the middle of the sixteenth century, the major and most influential religious orders in Spain refused to admit novices who could not boast of *limpieza de sangre*. The pressure on the young and fragile Society of Jesus to follow suit was almost overwhelming, but Ignatius refused to budge.

Nadal, who often had to bear the brunt of Jesuit policy in Spain, faithfully implemented it in this regard and defended it to both clergy and laity. When in 1551 the formidable Archbishop of Toledo, primate of all Spain, forbade Jesuits to do ministry in his diocese, the principal reason for his animosity seems to have been their practice of admitting New Christians into their ranks.[29] Not all Jesuits agreed with Ignatius on this policy, but the best indication of support for it was the election of Laínez as his successor as general. Laínez' great-grandfather had been a Jew, and therefore Laínez himself was considered one.

The early Jesuits' attitudes towards the indigenous populations of India, Brazil, and elsewhere was as complex as their attitude towards Protestants and Jews. They were of course intent upon conversion to Christianity, with all that that implies about their attitudes towards certain aspects of the indigenous culture.

Deserving emphasis, however, is the consistently positive assessment of the peoples themselves. Their talents and their inherent goodness often elicited praise from them, as well as unflattering comparisons to their European counterparts.[30] The Jesuits were highly critical of the 'military' mode of evangelization of other European missionaries.

The advanced culture of the Japanese presented special problems. When Francis Xavier arrived there in 1549, he eulogized their virtues and intelligence.[31] His successors there recognized that to win converts they would have to emphasize how Christianity was consonant with 'reason'.[32] Although the first Jesuits in Brazil were gratified to learn that idolatry was unknown among some of the Brazilians, they were soon dismayed to realize that this meant they had no concept of God whatsoever.[33]

For boys and girls in India and Brazil they tried to provide a catechesis, a basic education in reading and writing, and training in basic skills the equivalent to what they provided in Europe, and in their schools accepted boys into classrooms with the sons of European parents, often over the objections of the latter.[34] When they taught catechism to children in India, they also taught them Portuguese, while at the same time the children taught them their language.[35] They immediately recognized in certain sections of Brazil the extraordinary musical talent of the people, taught and themselves learned songs in the native languages, tried to develop native talent in other imaginative ways and, of course, to capitalize on it for their own evangelizing purposes.[36]

While to twentieth-century minds these efforts may smack of paternalism and a misguided sense of European cultural superiority, they were not engaged in by the Jesuits without some feeling of mutuality. For all their problems, they surely contrast positively with the attitudes and practices of many other Europeans who settled in those places. As was true for them regarding Protestants and Jews, they often evince prejudices that are foreign to us today and repulsive. They also sometimes managed to rise above them in significant ways.

NOTES

[1] *Formulae Instituti*, in *Constitutiones Societatis Jesu* (Rome: *Apud Curiam Praepositi Generalis*, 1937), p xxiii.

[2] *Epistolae*, in *Monumenta Ignatiana* (MHSJ), 12:259.

[3] *Monumenta paedagogica* (MHSJ), 3:335.

[4] *Fontes narrativi*, in *Monumenta Ignatiana* (MHSJ), 2:5.

[5] *Monumenta Nadal* (MHSJ), 5:607.

[6] *Ibid.*, 780.

[7] *Ibid.*, 5:315-21.

[8] See Ignacio Iparraguirre: *Historia de la práctica de los Ejercicios Espirituales de San Ignacio de Loyola*, 2 vols (Bilbao and Rome: *Institutum Historicum Societatis Jesu*, 1946–55), 1:83–117.

[9] See John Van Engen: 'The Christian Middle Ages as an historiographical problem', *American historical review*, 91 (1986), pp 519–52.

[10] *Monumenta Nadal*, 4:849–52.

[11] Iparraguirre: *Historia*, 1:136.

[12] See Marjorie O'Rourke Boyle: 'Angels black and white: Loyola's spiritual discernment in historical perspective', *Theological studies*, 44 (1983), pp 241–57.

[13] See my 'The fourth vow in its Ignatian context: a historical study', *Studies in the spirituality of Jesuits*, 15/1 (January 1983), pp 8–21.

[14] *Epistolae*, 1:386–89, and Polanco, *Chronicon* (MHSJ), 1:177–83.

[15] *Exercitia spiritualia*, in *Monumenta Ignatiana* (MHSJ), 2:292.

[16] *Monumenta Fabri* (MHSJ), p 502.

[17] *Ibid.*, pp 107, 507.

[18] '*De oratione*', in the Roman Archives of the Society of Jesus, cod. 73, fols. 151–52.

[19] *Monumenta Fabri*, p 674.

[20] '*De oratione*', fol. 74.

[21] See James Brodrick: *Peter Canisius* (London: Sheed and Ward, 1935), pp 72–74.

[22] *Monumenta Nadal*, 4:773; 5:317, 321.

[23] *Epistolae*, 1:343–44.

[24] '*De oratione*', fol. 202v.

[25] *Epistolae*, 1:386–87; 10:690–91; 11:359–65, 372, 541.

[26] *Monumenta Nadal*, 5:576.

[27] On this issue and his general attitude, see James W. Reites: 'St Ignatius of Loyola and the Jews', *Studies in the spirituality of Jesuits*, 13/4 (September 1981).

[28] *Fontes narrativi* (MHSJ), 2:476.

[29] *Epistolae mixtae* (MHSJ), 2:625–26.

[30] See Polanco's *Chronicon*, e.g., 1:200; 2:383; 394; 3:463; 5:618, 656.

[31] *Ibid.*, 1:461–64.
[32] *Ibid.*, 4:649.
[33] *Ibid.*, 5:632–33.
[34] *Ibid.*, 5:657.
[35] *Ibid.*, 1:474.
[36] *Ibid.*, 4:640.

XII

WAS IGNATIUS LOYOLA A CHURCH REFORMER? HOW TO LOOK AT EARLY MODERN CATHOLICISM

Almost fifty years ago, Hubert Jedin published his highly influential essay entitled *Katholische Reformation oder Gegenreformation?*[1] In it he reviewed in masterful fashion the tangled historiography concerning the Catholicism of the fifteenth through the seventeenth centuries and especially the efforts of historians to invent designations that would adequately indicate its character. When I recently reread the essay, I was again impressed with the subtlety, sensitivity, and breadth of information of surely one of the greatest historians of the Catholic Church in this century, then still a relatively young man with thirty-four of his most productive years still ahead of him. To reduce the essay to a few generalities distorts it badly, but to provide a *mise en scène* for what I have to say in relatively few pages about Saint Ignatius and its implications for Jedin's thesis I am compelled to do precisely that.

Although Jedin recognized some validity in terms like "Catholic Restoration" and even "Catholic Renaissance," he ultimately rejected them. He rejected "Counter-Reformation" even more emphatically, because it implied that whatever of importance happened in Catholicism during the period postdated the Protestant Reformation, was reactive to it, and consisted to a large extent in efforts to repress it through force and intimidation. His solution to the problem is well known and has today become normative among historians of almost every persuasion. It is enshrined in

[1](Lucerne, 1946).

textbooks around the world, sometimes in ways that do not do full justice to Jedin.

In any case, Jedin answered the question he posed in the title of the essay by substituting an "and" for the "or" (*oder*), so that according to him the proper way to designate the phenomenon was "Catholic Reform *and* Counter-Reformation." He thus recognized the valid elements in the latter term, but emphasized by the former an earlier, originally independent, and continuing reality, for which he gave many examples. Subsequent historians have greatly amplified these examples, with the result that there can be no possible doubt about the existence of "Catholic Reform" as Jedin described it. In fact, historians today confirm this aspect of Jedin's thesis by inclining to see both the Protestant Reformation and its Catholic counterpart as two different expressions of the same reforming impulses that antedate 1517. Sometimes in fact they designate every aspect of the Catholic phenomenon simply as "Catholic Reformation."

Despite its widespread acceptance, however, Jedin's thesis has not been without its critics, sometimes explicit, sometimes implicit. In the former category, for instance, is Gottfried Maron, who argues that Jedin failed to take account of the repressive impulses in "Counter-Reformation" that after about 1542 gave even "Catholic Reform" its character.[2] Among the latter we might place Jean Delumeau, as indicated by the title of his *Le Catholicisme entre Luther et Voltaire,* in which he eschews both "Catholic Reform" and "Counter-Reformation" and extends forward the chronological limits beyond what Jedin seems to suggest as valid.[3] In his more recent books Delumeau again implicitly challenges Jedin's chronology by dealing with the thirteenth to the eighteenth century as a cohesive unit.[4]

Wolfgang Reinhard, following the lead of Ernst Walter Zeeden, has taken a different tack for the period after about 1550 by insisting on the similarities between Catholicism and Protestantism in what he calls the "confessional age."[5] In that age Reinhard sees the churches as expressions of the

[2]"Das Schicksal der katholischen Reform im 16. Jahrhundert," *Zeitschrift für Kirchengeschichte,* 88 (1977), 218–229.

[3](Paris, 1971). The subtitle, *A New View of the Counter-Reformation,* was added to the English-language edition (London and Philadelphia, 1977).

[4]See, e.g., *La peur en Occident, XIVe-XVIIIe siècles* (Paris, 1978), and *Le péché et la peur: La culpabilisation en Occident, XIIIe-XVIIIe siècles* (Paris, 1983).

[5]See, e.g., "Zwang zur Konfessionalisierung? Prolegomena zu einer Theorie des konfessionellen Zeitalters," *Zeitschrift für historische Forschung,* 10 (1983), 257–277; "Reformation, Counter-Reformation, and the Early Modern State," *The Catholic Historical Review,* 75 (July, 1989), 383–404; and the discussion by Robert Bireley, "Germany," in *Catholicism in Early Modern History: A Guide to Research,* ed. John W. O'Malley (St. Louis, 1988), especially pp. 11–13.

"modern world" and of forces within it toward what he calls "*Modernisierung.*" It must be mentioned that Jedin himself intimates the possibility of such an interpretation, for he sees the age of "Catholic Reform and Counter-Reformation" as essentially transitional, already manifesting some of the characteristics of the "modern church."[6] It must also be mentioned that Reinhard sees the Jesuits as manifesting aspects of modernity.[7]

What these examples and the many others that could be adduced indicate is that, whereas nobody questions the aptness of the designation "Reformation" for the phenomena that began with Martin Luther in 1517, despite the great diversity among them, some historians still find themselves uncomfortable with Jedin's designations, even while they recognize that they captured something important and basic.[8]

It is at this point that I should like to introduce Saint Ignatius and with him the early Society of Jesus. Jedin mentions the official founding of the Society in 1540 as among the first events of the Counter-Reformation, and at another point describes the spirit of battle with which Ignatius, the former soldier, imbued the Society especially through the *Spiritual Exercises.*[9] He correctly cautions, however, that Ignatius and the Society must also be seen as part of Catholic Reform, reminding us that our categories of interpretation convey a neatness that does not perfectly correspond to the complexity of historical reality.[10] His treatment thus indicates that Ignatius and the early Jesuits are best understood as some combination of Catholic Reform and Counter-Reformation.

Jedin's analysis is confirmed by the treatment other historians accord the early Society. It is exemplified, for instance, by the entry under "Jesuits" of the *Oxford Dictionary of the Christian Church* (2nd edition), which specifies the purpose of the order as "to foster reform within the Church, especially in the face of the acute problems posed by the Reformation." The diptych is familiar: on the Protestant panel is Lucas Cranach's portrait of Luther and on the Catholic is Jacopino del Conte's portrait of Ignatius.

An immense amount has been written about Luther's evolution that finally brought him in 1520 to publish his "Appeal to the German Nobility," the document that more than any other signaled he was ready to assume

[6] *Katholische Reformation,* pp. 44–49.

[7] "Reformation, Counter-Reformation," pp. 386–389.

[8] See, e.g., Eric Cochrane, "Counter-Reformation or Tridentine Reformation? Italy in the Age of Carlo Borromeo," in *San Carlo Borromeo: Catholic Reform and Ecclesiastical Politics in the Second Half of the Sixteenth Century,* ed. John M. Headley and John B. Tomaro (Washington, D.C., 1988), pp. 31–46.

[9] *Katholische Reformation,* pp. 33, 34, 35–36.

[10] *Ibid.,* p. 37.

leadership in a program of disciplinary, ritual, and structural changes in the Church that, while based ultimately on his doctrinal positions, had ecclesial and ecclesiastical repercussions certainly not foreseen by him or others in 1517. With the "Appeal" he dramatically entered center stage to begin his career as among the two or three most influential church reformers of all times. Few historical personages have been subjected to more searching and systematic scrutiny than Luther or undergone more revisionist interpretations, yet no scholar has ever challenged that Luther was a reformer of the Church or that at a certain point he claimed that role for himself.

Ignatius Loyola has not benefited—or suffered—from the same quantity and quality of historical analysis. This situation is part and parcel of the stagnant condition in which scholarship on his side of the situation languished until quite recently. For the past two decades French and Italian historians have been turning their attention to this field with new zeal and new methods, but have applied curiously little of their zeal and methods to the Jesuits and their founder. True, reliable and helpful works on the subject appear with regularity, but they tend to be long on information, short on analysis; they concentrate on leaders like Ignatius, Francis Xavier, Diego Laínez, and Peter Canisius; they tend to interpret these figures and the Society in familiar categories without giving them the more precise definitions that contemporary scholarship makes possible and demands. Among these familiar categories for Ignatius is "reformer of the Church."

I do not know precisely when or how historians first began to speak of Ignatius and the Jesuits of his generation as concerned with that issue. One thing is certain: the expression appears with surprising infrequency in the immense amount of documentation that has come down to us from those Jesuits and, as far as I know, never do they apply the term to themselves, certainly not in the way it was understood in the sixteenth century. That fact should itself give us pause.

How was the expression understood? The sixteenth century was heir to ideas about the reform of the Church first articulated during the Investiture Controversy of the eleventh and twelfth centuries that centered on the disciplinary and moral reform of the episcopacy by means of a thoroughgoing implementation of the ancient canons, authentic and forged. Once formulated, these ideas took on a powerful life of their own, contributing greatly to the bitter controversy among lay and clerical leaders of the Church that marked the high and late Middle Ages. By a curious historical twist in the fifteenth century, they were turned against the papacy, which had originally created them, so that reform of the Church sometimes meant first and foremost reform of the papacy and papal curia. From that reform would follow the reform of the rest of the episcopacy, from which would follow reform of the pastors of parishes and parochial ministry.

You will note that reform of the Church centered on *offices* in the Church—papacy, episcopate, pastorates—and hoped to accomplish its moral and pastoral goals principally through canonical discipline. This understanding of the term is attested to by the legislation of the councils of Constance and Basel, by the numerous other synods of the fifteenth and sixteenth centuries, and most obviously and forcefully by the massive legislation of Trent *de reformatione*.

This definition of reform already suggests why Saint Ignatius and his fellow Jesuits used the term so infrequently. They did, however, occasionally employ it. In Ignatius' correspondence it recurs with unaccustomed frequency at the time of the election of Pope Marcellus II in 1555. As Cardinal Marcello Cervini, that Pope had showed himself friendly to the Jesuits in many circumstances. Ignatius and his collaborators knew him well, and therefore their hopes for "reform of the Church" were high.

The issue seems to have come up in informal conversations at the Jesuit *casa professa* after the election. Ignatius is reported to have said that the Pope should reform himself, the papal "household" or curia, and the cardinals of Rome; if he does that, everything else will fall into place.[11] The sentiment was hardly original, but it indicates a significant strand of thinking in the Society about reform of the Church not confined to Ignatius.

When Marcellus after a pontificate of less than a month was succeeded by Paul IV, the Jesuits tried to look on the bright side of that volatile fanatic, which was the zeal for the reform of the Church for which he had been known for decades. The new Pope initiated a flurry of activities to reform the Roman curia. In private correspondence the next year Juan de Polanco, Ignatius' talented secretary and *alter ego,* showed himself realistic: "They are beginning to deal with reform [of the curia], and it seems in earnest, even if the procrastinations of the past prove that we should not easily believe these things until we see them accomplished."[12]

Despite the concern that these statements indicate, they are more remarkable as exceptions in Jesuit documentation from the period. The reasons are clear. The Jesuits deliberately forswore for themselves the very offices with which reform was concerned—papacy, espiscopacy, pastorate.

[11] *Monumenta Ignatiana: Fontes Narrativi,* Monumenta Historica Societatis Jesu (henceforth cited as MHSJ) (Madrid and Rome, 1894–   ), I, 719.

[12] *Monumenta Ignatiana: Epistolae,* MHSJ, XI, 245; X, 665.

Such reform did not concern them directly or touch the way they wanted to live their lives or do their ministries. Moreover, the "humility" that they saw as distinguishing their vocation made them loathe to program juridical changes for these venerable offices. More basically, such reform was not what they were about.

What were they about? Although the first Jesuits rarely indeed spoke about reform of the Church, they with some regularity used the term *reformatio.* By it they meant two things. Sometimes it referred to their work in helping convents elect better superiors and otherwise deal with their morale and religious observance. Much more often it referred to the change of heart effected in individuals through the *Spiritual Exercises* and the other ministries in which the Jesuits were engaged. It meant conversion. It was thus closer to the biblical and patristic sense than that of church reformers since the eleventh century.[13] It was at the heart of the *Exercises* and therefore of their mission.

Another term that comes close to encapsulating that mission is *christianismum* or *christianitas,* the object of Jesuit catechesis as specified in the papal bull approving the new order, September 27, 1540. *Christianitas* was a term in wide usage and of immense significance in the Middle Ages, as John Van Engen showed in his brilliant article in the *American Historical Review* four years ago.[14] What it means is the making of a Christian, and that is certainly what the Jesuits hoped to accomplish by teaching catechism. *Christianitas* did not consist in memorizing abstract orthodoxies but in introducing the individual to the essential and traditional practices of the Christian religion and to the social responsibilities and opportunities of the believer especially through the spiritual and corporal works of mercy. It was a patristic and medieval idea. Although not quite the same thing as *reformatio, christianitas* is related to it as its framework. The more I study the first Jesuits the clearer it becomes to me how the teaching of catechism was emblematic of all their ministries and why they attached such importance to it.

To some extent the Humanists of the fifteenth and sixteenth centuries were simply updating the term *christianitas* when they spoke of *pietas* as the object of their educational program. While that program insisted on the acquisition of information and skills, its true object was what the Germans

[13]See Gerhart B. Ladner, *The Idea of Reform: Its Impact on Christian Thought and Action in the Age of the Fathers* (Cambridge, Massachusetts, 1959).

[14]"The Christian Middle Ages as an Historiographical Problem," *American Historical Review,* 91 (June, 1986), 519–552.

call *Bildung*—the formation of character—in this case the formation of Christian character.

True, *pietas* had important classical resonances that *christianitas* did not, but these ideas resembled each other in the importance they attached to the appropriation of right sentiments and the necessity of living according to them. I believe that this correlation was probably the principal reason the first Jesuits so easily made the humanistic program of education their own. The Jesuit schools were not, of course, merely schools of catechism—far from it!—but *christianitas* in the broad sense was what they wanted them to accomplish in their students.

In 1551 Polanco wrote an important letter to Antonio Araoz, the provincial of Spain. He encouraged him to open colleges similar to the ones just beginning in Italy. He also listed fifteen "benefits" to be derived from the enterprise—a list as important for what it does not say as for what it does. Nowhere, for instance, is the problem of the Reformation alluded to. In general the "benefits" do not admit interpretation related to reform as we generally understand the term.

The last one comes closest to it when it states: "Those who are now only students will grow up to be pastors, civic officials, administrators of justice, and to fill other important posts to everyone's profit and advantage."[15] In a broad way this benefit can be taken as an aspect of "Catholic Reform." The Jesuits occasionally referred to it as *reformatio,* but understood the term as an articulation of what the Humanists hoped to accomplish by their educational program, more or less independent of the agitated religious issues of the day. The Jesuits seem to have understood the "benefit" as one of the ways they could work toward the medieval goal of the "common good," as the bull of papal approval enjoined upon them, and as an effective way "to help souls" through what they saw as this means that had exponential effects.

In my opinion the expression that best captures the self-definition of the first Jesuits was, in fact, "the help of souls." It is only a slight exaggeration to say that it or its equivalent occurs on almost every page of the voluminous correspondence they left behind. It occurs with telling frequency in Ignatius' so-called *Autobiography,* importuned from him by his colleagues toward the end of his life as a kind of testament or "mirror" in which they would discover the true meaning of their vocation.

Curious about the *Autobiography* from our viewpoint is that, even as late as 1555, when Ignatius finished dictating the text, the year before his

[15]*Monumenta Ignatiana: Epistolae,* MHSJ, IV, 7–9.

death, he scarcely mentions the Reformation, although he had ample opportunity to do so. As he looks back and interprets his life at this late date, moreover, nowhere does he speak about reform or suggest that he or the Society has anything to do with it. The text is remarkable, in fact, for its detachment from all the urgent issues facing the Church, more than suggesting that they had little or nothing to do with his vocation. The military imagery so often attributed to the founder of the Society is almost entirely absent. It occurs, of course, at several key points in the *Exercises,* but, *pace* Jedin, is less pervasive, for instance, than in Erasmus' *Handbook of the Christian Soldier.*

The *Autobiography,* of course, does not tell all. In the Empire after about 1550 and then in other localities especially in northern Europe, the Society took up the struggle against the Reformation with special earnestness, and it did this with Ignatius' blessing.[16] Even before that date Ignatius and his colleagues showed themselves eager to stop the advance of "Lutheranism" in Italy and elsewhere. Ignatius supported the establishment of the Roman Inquisition in 1542 and founded the German College in Rome a decade later. In 1554 through Peter Canisius he urged King Ferdinand to repressive measures against "the heretics" in his domains.[17]

Ignatius and his fellow Jesuits came to believe, furthermore, that some of their ideals and practices could be powerful stimuli to needed changes in Catholic ministry. Their adamant refusal to accept alms for the hearing of confessions, for instance, surely helped banish in certain localities the persuasion that a confession was not valid unless one "paid" for it. They knew well the power of example in effecting change. In religious practice their advocacy of more frequent Communion grew out of their conviction that such was the way of the "primitive Church."

When all is said and done, therefore, did not the pursuit of personal *reformatio,* of *Christianitas,* of *pietas,* of "the help of souls" by Ignatius and the first Jesuits contribute enormously to the betterment of Catholicism and therefore to its reform, making them church reformers after all? Have we not merely been splitting hairs, engaging in a *lis verborum,* and making distinctions of no real import if the result was the same in any case? I reply that if we wish to make reform synonymous with renewal, religious revival, "great awakening," "new flowering," and a host of similar terms, that may well be true, but I think we generally want to denote something different when we speak of reform.

[16]See my "Attitudes of the Early Jesuits towards Misbelievers," *The Way,* Supplement 68 (Summer, 1990), pp. 62–73.

[17]*Monumenta Ignatiana: Epistolae,* MHSJ, VII, 398–404.

What is in a name, you still urge, for a reform by any other name would smell as sweet? In response I would simply quote Alfred North Whitehead: ". . . definitions—though in form they remain the mere assignment of names—are at once seen to be the most important part of the subject. The act of assigning names is in fact the act of choosing the various complex ideas which are to be the special object of study. The whole subject depends on such a choice."[18]

My contention is that our habitual way of naming what happened in Catholicism in the sixteenth and seventeenth centuries is often inexact and therefore obscures what we otherwise know to be true. It has derived to a large extent from German—and, more broadly, northern European—historiography. Thus the Reformation and Catholic efforts to counter it have rendered other aspects of the story secondary. The Society of Jesus, we must realize, was more strongly based in Italy and the Iberian peninsula, and directed much of its attention to India, Japan, and Brazil. True, we cannot understand what happened in all those territories apart from the controversies aroused by the Reformation, but we need to look at it with other lenses as well.

For instance, the intense study of the Renaissance in the past thirty years has taught us that, unlike what earlier scholars assumed, "Renaissance" and "Humanism" are not interchangeable terms, even though neither can be understood without the other. We need to apply somewhat the same kind of rigorous analysis to what I choose to call Early Modern Catholicism, on the one hand, and "Catholic Reform and Counter-Reformation" on the other. As in the example I adduced, they cannot be understood without each other, but they are not precisely the same thing. The first is broader, and helps us take account of important elements that only with difficulty can be forced under the umbrella of the latter. The latter does not capture the full reality and, indeed, in significant measure sometimes distorts it. It forces us despite ourselves into a somewhat narrowly conceived ecclesiastical history and inclines us to slight considerations of the more general shifts in culture that affected religion.

I believe that Saint Ignatius and the Society of Jesus are most appropriately placed under the former rubric, and only then should they be related, as they must be, to "Catholic Reform and Counter-Reformation." But they are not thus unique phenomena. Two others are outstanding.

For the future of Catholicism, first of all, few enterprises in the fifteenth

[18]*The Axioms of Projective Geometry* (Cambridge, 1906), p. 2, as quoted in Ladner, *op. cit.*, pp. 427–428.

and sixteenth century had greater ultimate impact than the missions in newly discovered lands. The motivation of the explorers, missioners, and their patrons was complex, and in some cases not devoid of escatological dreams of an end-time of "one flock under one shepherd" or of relationship to the cataclysmic politico-religious situation in Europe.[19] Nonetheless, this enterprise would have gone forward pretty much as we know it, independent of such motivation—even when it existed. It seems, in any case, to have played practically no role with the Jesuits in their ventures overseas. We must recall, moreover, that the missionary activities of the period are not even mentioned in all the decrees of Trent, and, almost as a consequence, not mentioned in any significant way in Jedin's essay.[20]

The papacy provides the second example. While "reform of the papacy" was a crucial issue, well treated by Jedin in his volumes on Trent, that reform never eventuated in ways that were generally desired and foreseen, as is more than suggested in Barbara Hallman's recent book.[21] Paolo Prodi argues, however, that the institution underwent significant changes in the functioning and understanding of papal political authority and that these changes were due not to "Catholic Reform" but to other forces operative in the great shift in culture from the Middle Ages into what we call Early Modern Europe.[22]

One might question, moreover, just how closely "reform" was related to the Thomistic revival, to the development of casuistry, to the development of social ethics, and to similar phenomena of the era.[23] While there undoubtedly was such a thing as what is called "Counter-Reformation Art," there was also much religious art done under Catholic patronage that does not fit what that category would seem to designate. To what degree and in what precise ways, for example, were Caravaggio and Bernini "Counter-Reformation (or Catholic Reform) artists"?

[19]See Pauline Moffitt Watts, "Prophecy and Discovery: On the Spiritual Origins of Christopher Columbus's 'Enterprise of the Indies,' " *American Historical Review,* 90 (February, 1985), 73–102, and my "The Discovery of America and Reform Thought at the Papal Court in the Early Cinquecento," in *First Images of America: The Impact of the New World on the Old,* ed. Fredi Chiappelli *et al.* (2 vols.; Berkeley, Los Angeles, London, 1976), I, 185–200.

[20]See the passing observations, *Katholische Reformation,* pp. 72–73.

[21]*Italian Cardinals, Reform, and the Church as Property, 1492–1563* (Berkeley, Los Angeles, London, 1985).

[22]*The Papal Prince: One Body and Two Souls: The Papal Monarchy in Early Modern Europe,* trans. Susan Haskins (Cambridge, 1987).

[23]See, e.g., Jared Wicks, "Doctrine and Theology," in *Catholicism in Early Modern History,* especially pp. 237–241.

Taking my cue, therefore, from Erwin Panofsky and other historians who have tried to analyze what distinguishes those historical phenomena we properly designate as "renaissances" from other cultural peaks that we do not,[24] I would say that for "reform" some intentionality is required, some self-conscious *intention* not merely to reanimate existing institutions but to reorganize them according to some clear pattern or to displace them with new ones. As I have been suggesting, such intentionality was not absent from Saint Ignatius and his disciples, especially in certain particulars and with the passing of the years, but it was neither their starting point nor their center.

Of course, if we wish to apply the term "reformer" to every religious figure of great intensity who had social or cultural impact, it applies to Ignatius (and to Philip Neri, Jeanne Françoise de Chantal, Joseph Calasanctius)—just as it would apply to Saint Benedict and Saint Francis. In a somewhat different way, it would apply to Thomas Aquinas and the whole enterprise of Scholastic theology—rarely has such a revolution been effected in the traditional pattern of thinking and behaving, which resulted in the creation of a new institution, the university. But we do not generally apply "reformer" or "reform" to these figures or movements because they never declared reform as their intention. Changes like these, even changes supposedly for the better, are not the same thing as reform.

Such changes are quite different from Reformation and from "Catholic Reform and Counter-Reformation"—from Luther and Calvin, from Gasparo Contarini, from Marcello Cervini, from Pope Paul IV, from Carlo Borromeo. They are to some extent different from Teresa of Avila, for she was a late expression of the observantist reform movement of the mendicant orders. Although it is different from the Capuchins, their motivations for a reformed observance were strongly influenced by the "spiritualist" movement in the Franciscan order that had roots back almost to the beginning of the order.[25]

What I am trying to say can perhaps be clarified by an example that has nothing to do with the Church. Perhaps no one in history has had greater impact on the rehabilitation of alcoholics than Bill Wilson and "Doctor Bob," the founders of Alcoholics Anonymous. Nonetheless, we do not generally speak of them as reformers in that field because they never set out on such a crusade or conceived of themselves in such a role. Their object

[24] *Renaissance and Renascences in Western Art* (New York, 1960).

[25] See Thaddeus MacVicar, *The Franciscan Spirituals and the Capuchin Reform,* ed. Charles McCarron (St. Bonaventure, 1986).

was "to help souls," in this case drunken souls. Alcoholics Anonymous, of course, became incorporated into the institutional treatment of those suffering from the dread disease, but it did so without losing its independence or its original intention, philosophy, and methods.

I suggest that "reformer" came to be applied to Saint Ignatius largely through osmosis. Since so many leading figures of the age defined their principal concern as reform, he must have done the same. But he did not. Since he lived in an age of aberrant or lax religious practice and of the loose morals of the Renaissance (so the argument goes), he must have been aware of this situation and set out to rectify it. But historians of our generation question this assessment of the religious situation, and, in any case, Ignatius manifests little awareness in the main that he lived in a particularly irreligious or immoral age.

Since he lived in the Tridentine age, he might even be described as a Tridentine reformer. But he—and the vast majority of his colleagues—seem remarkably detached from the doings of the Council. That assertion needs amplification and analysis.

A pervasive but unexamined assumption in much that is written about sixteenth-century Catholicism is that the Council of Trent set the agenda and that all fervent Catholics, including the Jesuits, fell to in implementing it. I have even heard the Jesuits described as essentially agents for the implementation of Trent. While they undoubtedly supported the Council and a few of them were directly involved in it, they had an agenda of their own, generically related to the agenda of the Council but specifically independent of it and different from it.

Within the framework of personal *reformatio, Christianitas,* and so forth, the Jesuits' agenda consisted in their ministries. If we examine those ministries, those efforts "to help souls," the discrepancies with Trent emerge. Trent was concerned with providing the traditional rhythm of Word and Sacrament by the *pastor* to the *faithful* in their *parishes* on Sundays and holydays, reinforced by canonical penalties.

Jesuits ministered to the faithful by Word and Sacrament, but relied on persuasion and operated outside the parochial structure. Moreover, they had an array of other ministries that Trent altogether ignores or at best barely mentions—elaborate programs of adult education in Scripture and moral issues through their so-called "sacred lectures"; preaching programs in the streets, shipyards, hospitals, and barracks; engaging volunteer corps of adults and children in the teaching of *Christianitas*; fostering confraternities under lay management for the spiritual and corporal works of mercy; promoting so-called "ministries of interiority" like retreats and spiritual direction; evangelization of the heretic, schismatic, infidel, and pagan; the schools.[26] They had an altogether special relationship to Renaissance Humanism.[27]

Perhaps the best indication of how the early Society related to the Council comes from Ignatius himself in the instruction he sent in early 1546 to Laínez, Alfonso Salmerón, and Claude Jay as to how they should deport themselves in Trent.[28] Divided into three parts, the document (once again!) is as important for what it does not say as for what it does. The first part counsels that they should be modest in presenting their opinions, listen with respect to the viewpoint of others, always present and consider both sides of any disputed point. The second instructs them to carry on the usual ministries of the Society—preaching, catechism, the *Exercises,* visiting the sick and poor, "even bringing them a little gift, if possible." Contrary to what we might expect, Ignatius designates these ministries as the principal reason he allowed the Jesuits to be sent to Trent, and, hence, this must be considered the most important part of the instruction. The third part concerns their life-style and regimen.

What is missing, of course, is any word concerning the great issues facing the Council. Ignatius obviously assumes that, whatever those issues are, the Jesuits will have something helpful to say when occasion requires. He looks upon them, however, more as mediators than as proponents of specific agenda.

Polanco's account of the Jesuits' contribution to this first period of the Council manifests the same detachment from specific issues under debate. But he adds the significant detail that, since in Ignatius' opinion the Council in 1546 was moving at such a snail's pace, he considered recalling Laínez and assigning him to Florence.[29] In the early summer of 1546 Ignatius had in actual fact written to the three Jesuits asking whether it might not be to God's greater glory for them to withdraw from the Council and engage in the *consueta ministeria* of the Society elsewhere. Salmerón replied that they were of the unanimous opinion they should remain at Trent, and Ignatius acquiesced.[30] Just before the troubled adjournment of the Council in 1547, nonetheless, he assigned Jay to Ferrara, seemingly without second

[26]See my "Priesthood, Ministry, and Religious Life: Some Historical and Historiographical Considerations," *Theological Studies,* 49 (June, 1988), 223–257, especially 237–248.

[27]See my "Renaissance Humanism and the Religious Culture of the First Jesuits," *Heythrop Journal,* 31 (October, 1990), 471–487.

[28]*Monumenta Ignatiana: Epistolae,* MHSJ, I, 386–389.

[29]*Chronicon Societatis Jesu,* MHSJ, I, 177–183.

[30]*Monumenta Salmeron,* MHSJ, I, 16.

thought that the Council at that critical moment in its history ought to have priority.[31]

The attitude Ignatius here manifests was, as best I can tell, by and large typical of the vast majority of Jesuits at the time. What the Council hoped to accomplish was, of course, important to them, but it was not exactly their business. Convinced of their own orthodoxy, they did not need to take special note of the doctrinal decrees. The disciplinary decrees were pertinent to bishops and pastors of parishes, not directly to them. In fact, like members of the mendicant orders, they feared the consequences for themselves of one of the principal aims of the council, viz., an emphasis on the jurisdiction of bishops that might result in restriction of their ministries and curtailment of their many pastoral "privileges."

From the experience many of us have had of Vatican Council II, we easily imagine Jesuits of the sixteenth century pouring over the documents of Trent and rushing around the world with them in their hands. That is not how it was. Few of them probably ever saw the decrees.

There were, of course, notable and well-known exceptions. Laínez and Salmerón were present for all three periods of Trent over its eighteen-year history, a distinction enjoyed by few other participants in the Council. For them the Council accounts for important years of their lives as Jesuits, and they knew its documents well and contributed to their formulation. Jerónimo Nadal, the person after Ignatius most responsible for the cohesion in the early Society, obviously studied and assimilated the great decrees on Original Sin and Justification. In 1565 Peter Canisius by special request of Pope Pius IV carried the *corpus* of Tridentine legislation with him back to the German bishops after the completion in Rome of the Jesuits' Second General Congregation, and, because of the peculiar situation in which he found himself in the Empire, was subsequently much concerned with that *corpus*. But to judge the rest of the Society by these examples is to engage in unabashed history "from above."

Helpful to the process of osmosis by which Ignatius and the Society began to be designated as focused on the reform of the Church would be a superficial recognition by roles in relationship to Trent played by a few leading Jesuits. If one examines the evidence in its entirety, however, one sees how the Society was in fact riding a trajectory independent of the direct concerns of the Council. In the great bulk of correspondence from Jesuits working in the ministries of the Society, it is amazing how seldom the Council is even mentioned.

[31]Polanco, *Chronicon,* MHSJ, I, 225.

In the broadest possible perspective, of course, the Jesuits were in perfect tandem with Trent in so far as it represented opposition to the Reformation. It was in this regard that the early Jesuits themselves made statements that would promote the osmosis. Nadal made his first trip to the Empire in 1555 and was appalled at what he found. Although opposition to the Reformation is only implicit in such foundational Jesuit documents as the *Exercises* and the *Constitutions,* Nadal after 1555 became a strong voice in the Society for assigning a high priority to the German situation. His reflections after that date on Jesuit origins began to see retrospectively a providential relationship to Protestantism.

Once Ignatius died in 1556, Nadal found the temptation to compare and contrast him with Luther too great to resist. The very next year Nadal suggested the comparison in an exhortation to the Jesuits at the Roman College.[32] In his second *Dialogue* some five years later, he portrayed Ignatius as the new David pitted against Luther, the Goliath.[33] In 1567 he reminded the Jesuits at Cologne, with some confusion of dates, that the year Luther was called by the Devil Ignatius heard the call from God.[34]

Sometime later Pedro Ribadeneyra paralleled the two figures in a passage in his biography of Ignatius, the first ever published and probably the most influential. Luther and his followers were destroying the faith; Ignatius and his were raised up by God to confirm and defend it.[35] Other Jesuits took up the theme and its variations, as place and occasion suggested it was appropriate. The facile diptych that has helped create the confusion and further the process of osmosis first derived from the Jesuits themselves. Even as the Jesuits painted it, however, they did not speak of Ignatius as a reformer. Moreover, while the idea was rhetorically effective, it did not for that reason represent the full reality of Jesuit activity everywhere in the world even at that late date.

Was, then, the great saint of the Counter-Reformation a Counter-Reformation saint? Strong in him was his opposition to the Reformation, without doubt, but in his early years his eyes were set on Jerusalem, not Wittenberg. Even in his later years his self-understanding and his understanding of the Society he founded did not primarily define themselves in relationship to that problem, perhaps even less in relationship to "Catholic Reform" as his age understood it. In retrospect some of his disciples eulo-

[32] *Monumenta Ignatiana: Fontes Narrativi,* MHSJ, II, 5.

[33] *Monumenta Nadal,* MHSJ, V, 607.

[34] *Ibid.,* p. 780.

[35] "Vida del Bienaventura Padre San Ignacio de Loyola," in *Historias de la Contrarreforma,* ed. Eusebio Rey (Madrid, 1945), pp. 140–152.

gized him by comparing and contrasting him with Luther, but these were rare flights into metahistory generally in the course of more factual accounts.

This hasty review of Ignatius and the first Jesuits can serve as a sort of test-case for Jedin's categories. Although it has vindicated their utility, it has also shown how they fail to take account of certain features that are important. They were a great step forward in our analysis of the Catholicism of that troubled period and helped give impetus to almost fifty years of scholarship that have intervened since it was published. This scholarship has, in the meantime, allowed us to see things from a somewhat different perspective. It has, moreover, allowed us to see the limitations under which Jedin worked.

What are some of those limitations? I will mention two. First of all, Jedin's focus was the Council of Trent and, therefore, the abuses in what we have come to call the "institutional church" in the sense of its hierarchy and official leadership. Crucial problems, surely, and often scandalous, but not the whole picture. In that framework, "reform" was the burning issue, and it was easy to latch onto the term and to sweep all changes and religious enthusiasm under its label.

Secondly, even though Jedin was properly critical, he was mightily influenced by Burckhardt, Huizinga, and Pastor in his assessment of the general religious situation and in his understanding of the Renaissance and late Middle Ages. His judgment, like theirs, was largely negative. Social historians in the past several decades have shown how lively religious practice was among most of the faithful, carried on in large measure in confraternities and other institutions that fell outside strictly parochial confines. Misguided that practice perhaps may have been in some ways, but not for that reason is it summarily to be dismissed as in every way unhealthy or as crying for reform. Moreover, not all historians would agree that the changes that de facto occurred in the sixteenth and seventeenth centuries as a result of "Catholic Reform" or other causes were in every instance for the better—*in melius.*

Renaissance historians have discovered the religious and moral issues that the Humanists tried to address, and they evaluate them positively. They have dismissed from the scene the category of "pagan Humanists" of whose existence earlier generations were so thoroughly convinced. They do not, of course, fail to see deficiencies in the humanistic enterprise, but they have radically revised many of the assumptions and conclusions of Burckhardt, Huizinga, and Pastor.

From these limitations flow in some measure the limitations of "Catholic Reform and Counter-Reformation" as an adequate category to capture the complexity of the phenomenon under discussion. Just as Jedin objected to "Counter-Reformation" as an adequate category because it took the Reformation as its point of reference, so might we object that "Catholic Reform" in a more subtle way does the same. Wherever Protestantism penetrated, there Reformation was the definition of the game. Not every place where Catholicism extended did "Catholic Reform," "Counter-Reformation," or the combination of the two always define the reality, even where religious enthusiasm was heightened. Catholicism, with its sluggish continuities as well as its new realities, was bigger than "Catholic Reform and Counter-Reformation."

I propose that "Early Modern Catholicism" is a better designation. It suggests both change and continuity and leaves the chronological question open at both ends. It implicitly includes Catholic Reform, Counter-Reformation, and even Catholic Restoration as indispensable categories of analysis, while surrendering the attempt to draw too firm a line of demarcation among them. It does not silently deliver Renaissance Humanism to an early grave. It is open to "confessionalization" when and where that becomes operative. It seems more welcoming to the results of history "from below" than "Catholic Reform" and "Counter-Reformation," which indicate more directly concerns of religious officialdom. Most important, it suggests that important influences on religious institutions and "mentalities" were at work in "early modern society" that had little to do with religion or "reform" as such, and it is thus more sensitive to the theses like those about "modernization" proposed by Reinhard and Prodi. It accounts, in brief, for more of the data.

Our categories of historical analysis do not easily yield their hold on our imaginations, and, even though "Catholic Reform and Counter-Reformation" is a mouthful, its otherwise obvious merits make it deserving of special respect. For reasons I have adduced, I think it might well be replaced by "Early Modern Catholicism," bland and all-too-neutral though such an alternative might sound for that contentious age. I conclude, in any case, not so much with a plea to do so as with the more modest and perhaps more realistic request that we exercise caution in applying Jedin's construct to the sprawling and complex reality he designated by it. That would be a tribute worthy of him.

XIII

PRIESTHOOD, MINISTRY, AND RELIGIOUS LIFE: SOME HISTORICAL AND HISTORIOGRAPHICAL CONSIDERATIONS

THIS ARTICLE has a simple thesis: the categories with which we customarily think about religious life are inadequate to the historical reality and that inadequacy is to a large extent responsible for some of the confusion in the Church today about religious life, especially about the relationship to priesthood and ministry of the "regular clergy," i.e. priests living in a religious order or congregation under a rule. This confusion, I further maintain, is harmful to religious orders and congregations, even those that do not have ordained members, and is also harmful in the long run to the Church as a whole.

The confusion has roots deep in our past, but it remained latent or at least virtually unnamed until quite recently. Forcing it ever more into our awareness have been the implications and implementation of certain documents of Vatican Council II, especially *Presbyterorum ordinis* on the "ministry and life of priests," *Optatam totius* on the "training of priests," *Christus Dominus* on the "pastoral office of bishops," and *Perfectae caritatis* on "the renewal of religious life." An altogether crucial question has emerged: How do religious priests fit in the ministry of the Church?

If we turn to the Council, we do not find an altogether satisfactory answer, although we are left free to infer that the specific difference between religious and diocesan priests lies in the fact that the former take vows of poverty, chastity, and obedience, whereas the latter do not. The ideals that these vows entail, however, are so vigorously enjoined upon diocesan priests themselves in *Presbyterorum ordinis* that in the long run the difference seems to be at most one of emphasis or consists simply in the juridical fact of public vows, or perhaps life in community.[1] The difference seems thus reducible to some rather subtle particularities of spirituality which in fact are almost impossible to define. The conclusion that seems to follow is that there is one priesthood,[2] but priests can be animated by different spiritualities.[3] There are no further differences. Although *Presbyterorum ordinis* concedes that its provisions are to be

[1] Nos. 15–17.

[2] See ibid., no. 7.

[3] See *Christus Dominus* (henceforth *CD*), no. 33.

applied to regular clergy only insofar as they "suit their circumstances," the document seems to assume that they in fact "suit their circumstances" quite well.[4] The topic sentence of the opening paragraph sets the tone for everything that follows: "What is said here applies to all priests."[5]

Some things surely do apply to all. The Council, for instance, locates priestly identity to a large extent in ministry, a location surely pertinent to both diocesan and religious clergy.[6] Yet it is with this very issue of ministry that the problem begins to manifest itself. The basic design in *Presbyterorum ordinis* for priestly ministry, implicit though it is, has three essential components: it is a ministry by and large to the faithful; it is a ministry conceived as taking place in a stable community of faith; it is a ministry done by clergy in "hierarchical union with the order of bishops."[7]

This design corresponds to the ministerial traditions and situation of the diocesan clergy. But does it correspond to the traditions and situation of the religious clergy? Not so clearly. In fact, it practically contradicts them—as I hope to make clear in this article, if it is not clear already. Moreover, we must note that the Council ties ministry to questions of church order when it speaks so repeatedly and insistently of "hierarchical union with the order of bishops." Yet, the major religious orders and congregations have lived in a tradition of exemption from episcopal jurisdiction, to a large extent even for their ministry. If we are to understand the sense of dislocation in some religious at the present time, I therefore contend, we must direct our attention not so much to issues of spirituality, in the conventional sense of the term, but to issues of ministry and church order.

As a background to Vatican II, I will review these two issues in the history of religious life from about the 13th to the late-16th centuries, when traditions that affected the modern Church were set. I deal explicitly with clerical orders and congregations of men, for it is only with them that the question of ordained priesthood arises. Ministry is, however, an issue also for most orders and congregations of women and for nonclerical congregations of men. It is an issue for the laity. For lack of

[4] *Presbyterorum ordinis* (henceforth *PO*), no. 1. Unless otherwise noted, English translations are from *Documents of Vatican II*, ed. Austin P. Flannery (Grand Rapids: Eerdmans, 1975).

[5] Ibid.

[6] On the unresolved conflict in *PO* between the "classic" theology of priesthood and a "poco tradizionale" presentation of ministry, see Christian Duquoc, "La riforma dei chierici," in *Il Vaticano II e la chiesa*, ed. Giuseppe Alberigo and Jean-Pierre Jossua (Brescia: Paideia, 1985) 399–414.

[7] *PO*, no. 7. The idea recurs, e.g., ibid., nos. 2, 4, 5, 6, 8, 12; *CD*, nos. 28, 34; *Optatam totius* (henceforth *OT*), no. 2.

space and competence, I do not address these aspects of the problem, but I assume that where my observations and conclusions might apply to these women and men will be clear. For the same reasons I have had to restrict myself almost exclusively to the Dominicans, Franciscans, and Jesuits, but I believe that what I say applies *mutatis mutandis* to others.

SOME HISTORIOGRAPHICAL TRADITIONS

We cannot examine "what happened" until we examine the categories in which we frame what happened. We must therefore examine certain historiographical traditions. I am convinced that the origin of part of our confusion about priesthood and ministry in religious orders and congregations lies in some inadequate but popular and widely appropriated historical grids. That is to say, whether we realize it or not, we think about these issues in historical frameworks that we do not question.

The historiography of any phenomenon falls into patterns that form at certain moments and then tend to persist for decades, generations, or even longer. This is especially true for standard and general histories, for it takes a long time for monographic studies to challenge the received wisdom that such texts tend to repeat without re-examination. Moreover, the historiography of any given phenomenon tends to take on a life of its own, isolated from the historiography of even related phenomena, so that integration of the results of research from different areas or disciplines is a slow and usually imperfect process.

We are in fact dealing in this article with the history of five imperfectly distinct phenomena: (1) ministry and priesthood, (2) church order, (3) religious life, (4) spirituality, (5) church reform. Although in some of their basic premises the historiographical traditions of these phenomena are quite valid, they suffer from certain defects along the lines I indicated above, which in many instances can be reduced to the fallacy of misplaced emphasis. At this point I want simply to describe the patterns, in as brief and clear a manner as possible, and to suggest how they might need to be modified. My critique goes somewhat as follows.

1. Histories of priesthood and ministry, as we now have them, deal almost exclusively with data from the biblical and patristic periods, to the almost complete neglect of the traditions of the Church during the Middle Ages through the modern period up to Vatican II.[8] That neglect

[8] Typical of this tendency is the otherwise excellent survey by Nathan Mitchell, *Mission and Ministry: History and Theology in the Sacrament of Order* (Wilmington, Del.: Glazier, 1982). See also Edward Schillebeeckx, *Ministry: Leadership in the Community of Jesus Christ* (New York: Crossroad, 1981); Joseph Lécuyer, *Le sacrement de l'ordination* (Paris: Beauchesne, 1983); Albert Vanhoye, *Old Testament Priests and the New Priest according to the New Testament* (Petersham, Mass.: St. Bede's, 1986). In his second book on ministry, Schillebeeckx' treatment of our period is still brief, but especially perceptive and helpful:

of some 1500 years, I propose, gives us a curiously unbalanced and incomplete picture of our traditions of these important institutions.

2. The scant attention that these histories sometimes concede to that long period consists almost exclusively in *ideas* about priesthood or sacred orders that Aquinas or the Council of Trent, for instance, proffered. They thus do not deal with what was actually *happening* in ministry, in church order, in culture at large, and therefore, for this portion of their presentation, woefully brief, they fall into simply a history of ideas. I propose that what Aquinas and Trent *said* about ministry and priesthood did not necessarily correspond to the *experience* of ministry and priesthood even for their own times. What we desperately lack at present is a comprehensive study of the history of ministerial *practice* from the 12th to the 20th centuries, although we are now beginning to possess the monographic studies in *social* history that would make such a synthesis possible.[9]

3. Whereas histories of ministry do sometimes deal with institutions as well as ideas when they discuss the biblical and patristic periods (though not subsequent periods), general histories of spirituality for all periods have fallen almost exclusively into the pattern of the history of ideas. Their concern is what saints and spiritual authors *thought* about prayer, mortification, spiritual reading, the sacraments, and even religious experience itself. Generally missing, therefore, is any indication of how these devout persons might fill up a day or, more important, how they engaged in ministry, what instruments they might have devised for ministry.[10]

4. The title of David Knowles's little classic on the history of religious life, *From Pachomius to Ignatius*, clearly indicates the pattern with which we habitually frame this complex phenomenon.[11] We see religious life as

---

The Church with the Human Face: A New and Expanded Theology of Ministry (New York: Crossroad, 1985). The only book of which I am aware that attempts a chronologically evenhanded treatment is Bernard Cooke, *Ministry to Word and Sacrament: History and Theology* (Philadelphia: Fortress, 1976). Commendable though this book is in so many ways, it approaches these centuries with a somewhat different perspective than myself and without utilizing the same information.

[9] The current tidal wave of social history has made practically no impact here. See, e.g., B.-D. Marliangeas, *Clés pour une théologie du ministère* (Paris: Beauchesne, 1978). For some issues connected with social history and for bibliography, see Peter Burke, "Popular Religion," forthcoming in *Catholicism in Early Modern History: A Guide to Research*, ed. John W. O'Malley (St. Louis: Center for Reformation Research, 1988).

[10] See, e.g., the survey of literature by Massimo Marcocchi, "Spirituality," in *Catholicism*. See also, however, my "Introduction" to the so-called *spiritualia* of Erasmus, to be published in Vol. 66 of the *Collected Works of Erasmus* (Toronto: Univ. of Toronto, 1988).

[11] Oxford: Clarendon Press, 1966. See now also Philip Rousseau, *Pachomius: The Making of a Community in Fourth-Century Egypt* (Berkeley: Univ. of California, 1985).

a continuous development, out of the cenobitic traditions, of the search for personal perfection. The matrix for the development is thus decidedly monastic. True, there was an "active" element in monasticism almost from the beginning. True, as time moved forward some monasteries and other institutions enriched the tradition by being even more "active" in the world. But, I ask, do not the "active orders" constitute more of a break with the tradition than the from-Pachomius-to-Ignatius pattern superficially suggests? If those orders are viewed not as the institutional embodiment of an ascetical tradition traced back to Pachomius, but as a critically important phenomenon in the history of ministry claiming "apostolic" inspiration, different appreciations and new issues emerge. In other words, at least from the 13th century, the history of religious orders pertains as much to the history of ministry as it does to the history of institutional asceticism.

5. The history of the religious orders, especially when incorporated into larger histories, is often seen as pertaining to the history of church reform. This is most obviously verified in the foundations of the Counter Reformation like the Jesuits and the Capuchins, but it is no less true for foundations in other periods. Most histories that deal with church reform tend to treat it in moralistic-disciplinary terms and, to a much lesser extent, in terms of doctrine. The religious orders are seen, therefore, usually in the context of their spiritualities, as "reforming morals and confirming doctrine," which is how the Council of Trent described its own task.[12] This historiographical tradition, which absolutely dominates the way most Catholics think about reform, ignores the important shifts in culture, ministry, church order, religious rhetoric, and propaganda that almost invariably accompany any reform and that in the long run are probably more important than any "moral reform" or "doctrinal confirmation" that might have taken place.

6. This situation is to a large extent the result of the tendency in the West to view church history from the perspective of a universalist ecclesiology. As Giuseppe Alberigo has recently observed, "The efforts made to elaborate a history of the Church 'from the base' or focused on popular religiosity remain largely inadequate and are still far from giving a satisfactory vision of the development, spatial and temporal, of the Christian experience as a communion of local communities."[13] Thus the various ways that ministry was effective or ineffective, especially in the long run, remain unstudied, or at least unincorporated into general

[12] See, e.g., the treatment of the mendicants and of the Jesuits in *Handbook of Church History*, ed. Hubert Jedin and John Dolan, 4 (Montreal: Palm, 1970) 172–83; 5 (New York: Seabury, 1980) 446–55.

[13] "The Local Church in the West (1500–1945)," *Heythrop Journal* 28 (1987) 125–43.

presentations.

7. Although rarely recognized in standard histories, every reform program rests upon ecclesiological constructs like "the true Church," "the apostolic Church," "the evangelical Church," "the well-disciplined Church," the "herald Church," the "sacramental Church."[14] There is an ecclesiology under every reform, and every ecclesiology relates directly to assumptions about ministry and church order. These ecclesiological constructs need to be exposed.

8. General histories that deal with church reform tend to rely too heavily upon official documents, like the decrees of Trent, and upon the *ideals* expressed by reformers, thereby neglecting what was actually happening "in the field."[15] Such histories need to be counterbalanced with *social* histories, which are concerned not with what people wanted to happen but with whether and how anything did happen and with its impact on the institutions of society.

9. Moreover, historians often fail to realize that the official documents of religious orders, including the documents of the founders themselves, express even the ideal only imperfectly. In particular, those documents find it easier to articulate how they are in continuity with the tradition than how they are innovating within it, for by the very nature of the case the latter reality lacks as yet a precise vocabulary. Those same documents are also incapable of rising above the historical realities in which they are immersed.[16] Only with the hindsight of generations or centuries does the *sensus plenior*, the full implication, emerge.

10. Finally, a general tendency in the historiography of all these phenomena must be mentioned: a tendency to read the past as a history of progress. Religious life, church reform, ministry, and similar institutions in this view thus move almost inexorably towards the balanced, comprehensive, and presumably definitive settlements of the contemporary Church, especially as expressed in the documents of Vatican II. One of the consequences of the subtle (and flattering) prejudice towards the present that underlies this tendency is that it admits no regress to a previous situation or condition. Paradoxically, it also does not admit

[14] I have shown this in great detail for one figure in *Giles of Viterbo on Church and Reform* (Leiden: Brill, 1968). See also, e.g., Gerhart B. Ladner, "Two Gregorian Letters: On the Sources and Nature of Gregory VII's Reform Ideology," *Studi Gregoriani* 5 (1956) 221–42.

[15] See, e.g., a standard text like Justo L. González, *The Story of Christianity* 2 (San Francisco: Harper and Row, 1984) 14–121.

[16] See, e.g., my "The Fourth Vow in Its Ignatian Context: A Historical Study," *Studies in the Spirituality of Jesuits* 15, no. 1 (St. Louis: Seminar on Jesuit Spirituality, 1983), and "To Travel to Any Part of the World: Jerónimo Nadal and the Jesuit Vocation," ibid. 16, no. 2 (1984).

much possibility of progress beyond the present. According to this style of thinking, the reforms of Vatican II, for instance, become definitive culminations of historical development, now frozen in their perfection, and they do not of themselves invite us to further reflection and action in relationship to a reality that, by definition, can never achieve perfect expression in this world and that therefore requires constant readjustment.

TOWARDS A CRUCIAL TURNING POINT

What I now intend is to provide some historical evidence to support and illustrate the foregoing generalizations and show in more detail their implications. I will deal with just a few crucial moments in the period from the 13th century to the present. I am painfully aware that to accomplish adequately the task I have set myself would require several volumes dense with documentation, but for the moment I have to settle for nothing more than an interpretative essay, with all the perils inherent in such an enterprise.

I must assume that the reader is already familiar with some well-established findings about ministry, church order, and religious life from the period of the New Testament into the Middle Ages. These findings are extremely important for our purposes, but limitations of space indicate that nothing more than the briefest of summaries can be provided here.

The New Testament does not yield an altogether clear or consistent picture about church order, about the relationship between authority and community. Itinerant preaching is the pattern for ministry that emerges most obviously from these same documents, but different origins of missioning and commissioning for that ministry seem operative. Evidence for patterns of church order well into the second century is scarce, but eventually the now familiar pattern of a bishop surrounded by his presbyters emerged. From this point forward most of what we know about ministry during the patristic period derives from this now stable situation, in which the bishop and his clergy assume ever more fully certain traits of the Roman civil servant; the episcopacy becomes an *officium*, and the presbyter a *sacerdos*. Meanwhile, by the fifth century monastic and quasi-monastic communities have developed, and some few of these engage in ministry in collaboration with the bishop.[17]

[17] On these developments see, e.g., Mitchell, *Mission and Ministry;* Schillebeeckx, *Ministry;* Gerd Theissen, *Sociology of Early Palestinian Christianity* (Philadelphia: Fortress, 1978), and his *The Social Setting of Pauline Christianity* (Philadelphia: Fortress, 1982); Wayne Meeks, *The First Urban Christians: The Social World of the Apostle Paul* (New Haven: Yale Univ., 1983); Raymond E. Brown, *The Churches the Apostles Left Behind*

With the breakdown of public order in the early Middle Ages, some members of monastic communities began to take an ever-larger role in ministry. By now often without any relationship to the episcopacy, they became the great agents of evangelization until the tenth century. By the end of that century, however, "ministry," whether done by monks or "local" clergy, consisted to a large extent in various rituals and blessings and in the celebration of the liturgy. Evangelization, catechetics, and other traditional forms had practically disappeared in any organized form, and even preaching was considerably curtailed.[18]

With the 11th century a series of immensely important changes began to take place in society as trade, cities, law, literacy, kingship, and other institutions took on new vitality. A great turning point had been reached, and "the making of Europe" had begun. The Church was so integrally present to these phenomena that it can hardly be distinguished from them. For our purposes, however, two manifestations of change are particularly important.

The first is a phenomenon that took place at the upper level of European society, the so-called Investiture Controversy or Gregorian Reform, whose most dramatic expression was the battle unto death between Pope Gregory VII and Emperor Henry IV. The ramifications of that Reform for the internal life of the Church were incalculably great and are still being felt today. The most obviously direct of these ramifications was the emergence of a strong and centralized papacy and the concomitant emergence of a stronger episcopacy. The latter was a result both of the Gregorian insistence on the ideal of episcopal independence from lay magnates and of the growth of cities, over which bishops presided. The revival of canon law that the Gregorians promoted gave support to an ideal of the bishop that emphasized his status in the hierarchical society of the times and vindicated his authority over certain properties and processes as over against his lay rival, the local nobility. The bishops' relationship to ministry as such was for a number of reasons not much considered in any direct fashion. In any case, the feudal age when abbots ruled the Church from their rural monasteries had begun to fade, as this important shift in church order took place.

The second phenomenon did not occur on the level of bishops and popes, but on a lower level of society. It included some clergy and monks, but also lay elites and rabble, and was in many ways more spontaneous than its Gregorian counterpart. Although it took a number of forms, it was unified by an enthusiasm for the "apostolic life," *vita apostolica* or

(New York: Paulist, 1984); Adolar Zumkeller, *Das Mönchtum des heiligen Augustinus* (Würzburg: Augustinus, 1950).

[18] See, e.g., *Handbook of Church History* 3, 307–12, with bibliography.

vita evangelica.[19] With differing emphases that ideal included itinerant preaching, disdain for material goods, shunning and often denouncing the honors and social position that both Church and society offered. Increased literacy seems to have contributed somewhat to this ideal, for the "apostolic life" was vindicated on the basis of the way the "apostles" were presented in the New Testament. The "apostolic life" sought to recover the "apostolic Church."

This complex phenomenon was surely to some extent a "protest movement," reacting against the ostentatious wealth and status, especially of some of the upper clergy, that the new economic, social, and ecclesiastical conditions had already begun to produce. In some localities the enthusiasm for the "apostolic life" eventually turned sour. By the late-12th century, heretical movements like the Waldensians and the Albigensians—resulting from a strange mixture of learning and ignorance, of high ideals and smoldering resentments—became a widespread and public problem.[20]

THE DOMINICANS AND FRANCISCANS

As we know so well, one "answer" to these heresies was the Dominican and Franciscan orders, both founded in the early-13th century.[21] They "answered" effectively because they were themselves part of the same enthusiasm for the *vita apostolica*, which included certain assumptions about ministry. We must look carefully, therefore, at the ministry of the friars. One of its most notable features was its origin. The ministry of the Dominicans clearly derived from a special and specific *need*, from a circumstance that fell outside the capabilities of the pastoral structures that were normatively in place. Those structures were impotent to deal with the Albigensians. For this period of church history, we can only with reservation describe those structures as "parochial," because parishes were not at this point the sociological reality they would eventually

[19] See, e.g., M.-H. Vicaire, *L'Imitation des apôtres* (Paris: Cerf, 1963).

[20] See, e.g., Tadeusz Manteufel, *Naissance d'une hérésie: Les adeptes de la pauvreté volontaire au Moyen Âge* (Paris: Mouton, 1970), and *Handbook of Church History* 3, 453–65; 4, 98–109, with bibliography.

[21] See, e.g., William A. Hinnebusch, *The History of the Dominican Order* (2 vols. New York: Alba, 1965–73); M.-H. Vicaire, *Dominique et ses prêcheurs* (2nd ed. Paris: Cerf, 1979); idem, *Histoire de saint Dominique* (2 vols. Paris: Cerf, 1982); Cajetan Esser, *Origins of the Franciscan Order* (Chicago: Franciscan Herald, 1970); Stanislao da Campagnola, *Le origini francescane come problema storiografico* (Perugia: Università degli Studi, 1979); Lazaro Iriarte, *Franciscan History: The Three Orders of St. Francis of Assisi* (Chicago: Franciscan Herald, 1983); Lawrence C. Landini, *The Causes of the Clericalization of the Order of Friars Minor, 1209–1260, in the Light of Early Franciscan Sources* (Chicago: n. publ., 1968).

become.[22] But we can say that the structures were those under the local clergy that looked to the "normal" sacramental practice of the faithful. The Albigensians were, however, a radically alienated group, heretics, who scorned that practice and condemned the life-style of its ministers. Out of this situation was born the aptly-named Order of Preachers.

If we take the life of St. Francis as somewhat paradigmatic for the origins of Franciscan ministry, we have a somewhat different picture. It is true that the Franciscan movement cannot be understood apart from the history of the Waldensians and similarly heretical groups, but the direct inspiration for Francis' preaching seems almost certainly to have been the impelling force he felt within himself to speak of the Lord and of His love for all creatures. While the origin of Dominican ministry was a quite specific situation "out there," a need, the origin of Franciscan ministry was more internal to Francis' spirit. The origins of these two ministries were similar, however, in one extremely important regard. Neither of them derived from office.

The origins of the concept of *officium* are ancient, but the most influential description of it came from St. Isidore of Seville in the seventh century. For Isidore it signified the functions connected with major and minor orders, which he understood to be largely ritual and liturgical functions. Gratian and especially later canonists, bearing the burden now of the social and economic legacy of the feudal periods, inextricably linked benefices to *officium*, because benefices were the way those in major and minor orders received their living.[23]

Thus in the clerical state office and benefice were two aspects of the same reality. Even more important from my point of view, however, is that, while office implied the care of souls in some form or other, it did not always in fact so issue. Where it did, furthermore, it looked to stable, established, and well-defined positions, whose functions did not vary from generation to generation.

The Gregorian Reform and its aftermath accelerated and accentuated developments like these in the ministerial apparatus of the Church. In its quest for order in the Church, it aided and abetted closer definition of *officium*, just as it aided and abetted a hierarchical mode of thinking about the clerical state that already had grounding in the patristic period with the graduated *cursus honorum* of minor through major orders.

[22] See, e.g., Luigi Nanni, "L'Evoluzione storica della parrochia," *Scuola cattolica* 81 (1953) 475–544.

[23] See, e.g., Donald Edward Heintschel, *The Medieval Concept of an Ecclesiastical Office* (Washington: Catholic University of America, 1956); see also Thomas Peter Rausch, *Priesthood and Ministry: From Küng to the Ecumenical Debate* (Ann Arbor: University Microfilms, 1976) esp. 98–144.

The Gregorian Reform marks the strong articulation, therefore, of what we have come to call the "institutional Church," or, to use Ernst Troeltsch's term, "the church-type." We can still take a hint from Troeltsch's brilliant, though faulty, analysis of the aftermath of the Reform and postulate that the Dominicans and Franciscans represent the "sect-type," an almost inevitable reaction to the church-type.[24] The church-type, whose essence is "its objective institutional character,"[25] would be constituted even in its ministry by order, status, office, and stable functions. In the wake of the feudal and monastic cultures of the early Middle Ages, those constitutive elements of ministry would be further specified as ritual and sacramental.

The sect-type, by definition "a voluntary community,"[26] even in its ministry would be almost the antithesis, evidencing by its flexibility and adaptibility the inward inspiration that was its source. Whereas the church-type would find its scriptural warrant in the Pastoral Epistles, the sect-type like the Dominicans and Franciscans would clearly find its warrant in the ministry of Jesus and his first disciples in the Synoptics and in the egalitarian principles in the early chapters of Acts. Francis underscored that egalitarianism when he consistently referred to his group as a *fraternitas*.[27]

For the friars this distinction between the two types cannot be pressed too far, for in many important respects it does not correspond to the facts, nor does it correspond in the main to the friars' self-understanding. "Types" are, after all, artificial constructs designed to make an admittedly too sharp distinction. Neither the Dominicans nor the first followers of Francis defined themselves as against the Church or apart from it, and they found justification for their ministry precisely in the licensing of a bishop, the bishop of Rome. Nonetheless, we must pay attention to the realities that the distinction makes more manifest to us.

It is at this point that the "spirituality" of the early mendicants must enter into consideration. Dominic chose poverty and rejected nominations to the episcopacy so that he might preach in freedom.[28] Asceticism and ministry are thus closely conjoined for the Dominicans. Francis' romance with Lady Poverty may in some ways seems to antedate and be more independent of his own early ministry, if we may thus speak of it, but here too the fusion of spirituality and ministry is early. Both founders

[24] *The Social Teaching of the Christian Churches* 1 (New York: Harper and Row, 1960) 328–82.

[25] Ibid. 338.

[26] Ibid. 339.

[27] See Esser, *Origins* 17–52.

[28] See Vicaire, *Dominique et ses prêcheurs* 222–35.

were engaged in a ministry of discipleship.[29]

The New Testament, but especially Acts 4:32–37, taught the late-12th and early-13th century a great deal about the "apostolic life," for which it showed such great enthusiasm. That apostolic life did not mean only a life of "apostolate" in our sense of the word, but included a life-style modeled on the way the early disciples or "apostles" were supposed to have lived, which to many did not seem to correspond to what they found in the Church of their day. The vows pronounced by the friars, especially the vow of poverty, thus had an important relationship to ministry, even though superficially they might seem to relate only to the ascetical tradition. The apostles, like Jesus, preached, moved around from place to place, shared their goods, and based their relationship to one another on direct personal fellowship. A certain egalitarianism was implied because of the implied recognition of the validity of a variety of charisms in a setting where charism was the foundational value. All these factors, plus others, had impact on the internal structures of the early mendicants, articulated into a system of capitular government—in some contrast to the "monarchy" that was emerging ever more decidedly in the papacy as well as in the episcopacy—and of superiors elected for definite and indefinite terms, quite unlike abbots united to their monasteries and bishops united to their dioceses until death, and even unlike other clerics united to their benefices in almost the same way.[30]

Another telling difference between the diocesan clergy and the friars developed almost immediately: the concern of the latter for systematic programs of education for their recruits. The friars came into being just as the universities attained their mature organization at the beginning of the 13th century. Although diocesan priests and even monks sometimes attended the universities, the friars had a relationship to them that was systemic. This is not to say that every member of these orders who engaged in ministry attended a university, but rather that explicit programs of education were formulated within them that were based on the same principles that undergirded the university programs.

These programs were created by the internal government of the orders and never suffered any episcopal, or even papal, restraints upon their formulation and implementation. They were the first systematic attempts to formulate and implement programs of education for the clergy that were generally incumbent upon them. The *raison d'être* for such programs was without question the kind of ministry in which the friars principally engaged in the various forms it might take—preaching. Preaching under-

[29] See Brian E. Daley, "The Ministry of Disciples," *TS* 48 (1987) 605–29, and Avery Dulles, "Imaging the Church for the 1980's," *Thought* 56 (1981) 121–38.

[30] See, e.g., Hinnebusch, *Dominican Order* 1, 217–50; Esser, *Origins* 53–135.

went its powerful revival in the 13th century because it figured so clearly in the "apostolic life." It also happened to correspond to the *needs* of a population that was increasingly urban, more curious and critical, even more literate.[31]

If we should at this point construct a profile of the friar, therefore, we would note that his ministry originated in charism and need, that the minister transcended local lines and moved about "like the apostles," that his ministry consisted to a large degree in preaching and thus required an education, that it related to personal life-style and to the style of governance within the order, which in effect removed him from the governance operative in the church-type. If this profile is inserted into the history of religious life as we now have it, strong continuities emerge because of the ascetical tradition involved. If this profile is inserted into the history of ministry and of church order, however, we perceive a sharp break not only with the preceding monastic and feudal era but to some extent even with the presumably more normative paradigms of, say, the fourth and fifth centuries.

Finally, we must at this point recall that from the beginning both orders enjoyed certain privileges and exemptions from the Holy See, which grew more numerous with passing years. On the surface this fact does not seem terribly remarkable, for it seems to fit into a tradition that goes back to the monastery of Bobbio in the seventh century, but more immediately to the monastery of Cluny in the tenth, when Cluny was taken under the patronage of St. Peter, i.e. the papacy, so that it might be free in its internal affairs from the interference of local patrons—lay and episcopal. This juridical reality gained in clarity and application in the 11th and 12th centuries. What is important for us, however, is not the similarity between the exempt status of Cluny and the later mendicants, but the immense difference.[32]

Cluny was a monastery, and in medieval theory and practice the right of monks to engage in ministry was hotly contested, even forbidden by

[31] See, e.g., Hinnebusch, *Dominican Order* 1, esp. 3–98; Hilarin Felder, *Geschichte der wissenschaftlichen Studien im Franziskanerorden bis um die Mitte des 13. Jahrhunderts* (Freiburg i/Br.: Herder, 1904).

[32] See, e.g., E. Fogliesso, "Exemption des religieux," in *Dictionnaire de droit canonique* 5 (Paris: Letouzey, 1953) 646–65; J. Dubois, "Esenzione monastica," in *Dizionario degli istituti di perfezione* 3 (Rome: Paoline, 1973) 1295–1306; and J. Fernández, "Facultà e privilegi negli istituti di perfezione," ibid. 1378–85. See also Burkhard Mathis, *Die Privilegien des Franziskanerordens bis zum Konzil von Vienne (1311)* (Paderborn: F. Schöningh, 1928), esp. 91–115. Even after the publication of the first Code the Jesuits, e.g., issued an *Elenchus praecipuarum facultatum nostris ad auxilium animarum concessarum* (2nd ed. Rome: Curia Praepositi Generalis, 1936).

canon 16 of Lateran Council I, 1123.[33] The "exemption" granted to Cluny was, therefore, in favor of the interior development of the monastery, to try to ensure the election of abbots who would promote its special regimen, especially the long and powerful intercessory liturgies of the monks, which in Cluny were considered their foremost duty.

The similar juridical status granted the Dominicans and Franciscans looks, of course, to their internal governance, but the most striking difference from Cluny, Citeaux, and like establishments was that it also looked to ministry. The *ministry* of the friars was exempt from the supervision of the episcopacy, for the friars engaged in ministry in a particular way and, like "the apostles," they transcended local boundaries. This development is a tribute to the stronger papacy that the Gregorian Reform set on its course, as well as to those bishops who supported such exemption for the friars because, whatever its juridical complications, it helped get needed ministry done.

From the viewpoint of church order, of course, this development is astounding. It created in effect a church order (or several church orders) within the great church order, and it did this for the reality to which church order primarily looks—ministry. It is no wonder, therefore, that all through the rest of the Middle Ages well into the 17th century the conflicts between the episcopacy and the religious orders were so many and so characteristically bitter. It *is* a wonder, however, that these various church orders worked together in fact as well as they did and provided such an abundance of ministerial diversity in the Church.

We consistently fail to take account of this *de facto* variety in church order, which goes beyond the familiar patterns of local order and universal order. In the Celtic Church, responsible for so much of the evangelization of barbarian Europe, the abbots governed.[34] In the great monastic centuries, and even beyond, abbots were often the equals of bishops in sacramental powers and in many cases at least their equal in practice, if not in theory, in church order. We forget that, while some 400 bishops celebrated Lateran Council IV, 1215, the greatest and most effective of the medieval councils, their number was dwarfed by the 800 or so abbots who attended—besides some lay magnates and their vicars.[35] The local clergy often had little relationship to the bishop in matters like appoint-

[33] G. Alberigo et al., eds., *Conciliorum oecumenicorum decreta* (2nd ed.) 193; henceforth *COD*.

[34] See, e.g., James Bullock, *The Life of the Celtic Church* (Edinburgh: St. Andrew, 1963); Kathleen Hughes, *The Church in Early Irish Society* (London: Methuen, 1966); and John Ryan, *Irish Monasticism: Origins and Early Development* (Ithaca: Cornell Univ., 1972).

[35] See Raymonde Foreville, *Latran I, II, III et Latran IV* (Paris: L'Orante, 1965) 251–52; see also Georgine Tangl, *Die Teilnehmer an den allgemeinen Konzilien des Mittelalters* (Weimar: H. Böhlaus, 1922) 219–32.

ments, and only in the late Middle Ages did urban parishes as such begin to achieve in fact more central status in church life.[36]

The role of monarchs and lay magnates in church order is, of course, of a different character. We must nonetheless recall that, although massively challenged during the Gregorian Reform, it persisted strong and in various forms, with a legitimacy unquestioned by bishops and popes, at least until the French Revolution. Even Pius IX and his collaborators agonized over whether to invite the Catholic monarchs to Vatican Council I, 1870.[37] We must also recall that, despite what we generally read, the monarchs and lay magnates were often, though surely not always, more solicitous for the Church than their clerical counterparts.

The essential point for us, however, is to realize that the story of the mendicants is a story of ministry, and the story of mendicant ministry is inseparable from questions of church order. By the middle of the 13th century, and for some centuries thereafter, the most dynamic, visible, and articulate corps of ministers in the Church did not fall under the jurisdiction, for the most part, of the supervisors of ministry, the local bishops. The mendicants had their warrant from the bishop of Rome. Within that warrant they had a distinctive "order" of their own.

What was innovative here was not the *fact* that the bishops did not have supervision of religious, for that had never been consistently operative in the Middle Ages, or even antiquity. Nor did the innovation consist in exemption as a *juridical* reality, for that had ancient roots. It consisted rather in its being to a great extent an exemption for *ministry*. Local church order for ministry had to reckon with a more universal church order, which itself allowed for further diversities.

THE SIXTEENTH CENTURY

The later Middle Ages were dominated by the ministry of the mendicants—Dominicans and Franciscans, of course, but also Carmelites, Augustinians, and Servites. Although that ministry came under heavy criticism from influential persons like Erasmus and others, its achievements were considerable. It would continue to be, in renewed and somewhat different forms, an extremely powerful influence into the 16th and 17th centuries and well beyond.[38] Nonetheless, in the 16th century a number of important factors converged to effect further changes within Roman Catholicism. Two are especially important for our purposes: the Society of Jesus and the Council of Trent.

[36] See, e.g., *Handbook of Church History* 3, 566–70.

[37] See Roger Aubert, *Vatican I* (Paris: L'Orante, 1964) 50–51.

[38] See, e.g., John Patrick Donnelly, "Religious Orders of Men," in *Catholicism.*

If the Jesuits are to be placed in the history of ministry, they must be seen as fundamentally a continuation of the traditions that began with the mendicants and a powerful expansion of them. Nothing is more characteristic of Catholicism in the 16th century than the veritable explosion of ministerial initiatives. In this enterprise the Jesuits were only one force among many, but since they helped create and promote most of these initiatives, they can for our purposes be taken as emblematic.

Although surely not without its debit side, ministry in the Catholic Church in the 16th and 17th centuries was perhaps the most innovative and exciting in history. This well-kept secret began to be revealed only about 20 years ago and still cries for historians to do it justice. "Catholic Reform" of the 16th century was not, therefore, simply a "reform of morals," but a reform of pastoral practice and an immense expansion of its scope.

Perhaps the most striking aspect of 16th-century ministry was the energetic and hardheaded pragmatism that, in conformity with the medieval tradition, animated it. Whatever seemed to "produce fruit" in souls, whatever met a need, was pursued with creativity and method. Verifications for that generalization can be found in many sources, but perhaps nowhere more consistently than in the 12 volumes of correspondence of St. Ignatius himself.[39] This is all quite a contrast with the more "normative" approach to ministry that prevails today—and with the correlative lassitude of contemporary Catholicism and most mainline churches in many areas of the world.[40]

The dramatic baroque statue of St. Ignatius that stands in the basilica at Loyola, designed by Francisco Vergara in the middle of the 17th century, depicts him in a chasuble, holding a book on which are inscribed the words *Ad majorem Dei gloriam.* The book probably represents the Jesuit *Constitutions*, in which those very words occur so often, and the statue thereby fits Ignatius into the history of religious life. "From Pachomius to Ignatius"!

The chasuble, on the other hand, fits him into the tradition of priesthood. But depicting Ignatius as a priest does not automatically fit him into the history of ministry, which is where he just as deservedly belongs. While Ignatius surely found in the Mass a source of great personal devotion and relied heavily upon its power of impetration, he never

[39] *Monumenta Ignatiana: Epistolae et instructiones*, Monumenta Historica Societatis Jesu (12 vols. Madrid: G. Lopez del Horno, 1903–11). See also, e.g., André Ravier, *Ignatius of Loyola and the Founding of the Society of Jesus* (San Francisco: Ignatius, 1987) 359.

[40] See my "Tradition and Traditions: Historical Perspectives," *The Way* 27 (1987) 163–73.

considered it as such an instrument of ministry peculiar to his order. Not to exaggerate: there is an implicit co-ordination between priesthood and ministry, between word and sacrament, in early Jesuit sources. Nonetheless, one searches almost in vain in those sources for any mention of priesthood or ordination, whereas the word "ministry" occurs on practically every page. In fact, Vergara would have been even more faithful to the historical sources on Ignatius had he shown him in a pulpit holding a book inscribed *ministerium verbi Dei*. By the time Vergara labored, however, such a depiction would have seemed altogether too Protestant.

The fact is, nonetheless, that ministry of the word of God dominates the early Jesuit sources. It is the rubric under which we can gather Ignatius' many activities to be "of help to souls" for the 15 or so years between his conversion and his ordination.[41] It stands in first place in the so-called *Formula of the Institute*, the foundational document that constitutes the essential statement of what the order is all about.[42] Indeed, that phrase can be considered the genus under which almost all the other ministries listed in the *Formula* and in the Jesuit *Constitutions* can be gathered as species. In early Jesuit sources the "herald" model of the Church predominates over the model of the Church as sacrament, to use the well-known constructs of Avery Dulles.[43] (Dulles himself has correctly called attention to the discipleship model that is also operative, perhaps more radically, in those same sources.[44])

By ministry of the word of God the Jesuits of course meant preaching in the usual and conventional sense of the word. But, in continuation with the mendicant tradition, that preaching took place not only during Mass but also in church in the afternoons and other occasions—every day during Advent and Lent. It was also done in the street, hospitals, and other places. By the 17th century a number of new occasions had been created in which sermons played a major role—novenas, Forty Hours, Tre Ore. The presses were jammed with books by Jesuits and others with various "aids" to preachers, and the example and precepts of Cicero and the Fathers of the Church were carefully and sensitively scrutinized for whatever help they might give. For sheer quantity and effort, Catholicism in the late-16th and 17th centuries did not hold

[41] Ignatius' autobiography has several times been translated into English, most recently by Joseph N. Tylenda, *A Pilgrim's Journey* (Wilmington, Del.: Glazier, 1985).

[42] See *The Constitutions of the Society of Jesus*, tr. George E. Ganss (St. Louis: Institute of Jesuit Sources, 1970) 66 [3]. On the more general issue of priesthood and ministry in the Society of Jesus, see the commendable contribution by William J. Harmless, "Jesuits as Priests, Crisis and Charism," in "Priesthood Today and the Jesuit Vocation," *Studies in the Spirituality of Jesuits* 19, no. 3 (St. Louis: Seminar in Jesuit Spirituality, 1987) 1–47.

[43] *Models of the Church* (Garden City: Doubleday, 1978).

[44] "Imaging the Church" (n. 29 above).

second place to any Protestant tradition in preaching.[45]

For the Jesuits, however, ministry of the word of God extended beyond preaching. It included "sacred lectures" on the Bible and theological subjects, that is, series of instructions in church in the afternoons that were a clear forerunner of "adult education." It included catechetical instruction, a ministry that had practically disappeared in the Middle Ages but experienced a great upsurge in the 16th century. It included exhortations to religious communities and teaching local clergy about "cases of conscience." It even included "spiritual conversation" on the word of God among individuals and in small groups, on either a planned or spontaneous basis.

All these forms of the ministry of the word of God were integrated into one of the most important ministerial instruments that 16th-century Catholicism created: the "mission" to small villages and hamlets. The Middle Ages knew nothing like them, nor did the patristic era. These missions to the rural poor were excellently organized pastoral strategies, in which were combined preaching, catechesis, adult education, folk piety, and conversion to godly ways in the sacraments of Eucharist and especially of penance. The missionaries arrived at a locality in groups of two to eight, generally stayed for four to six weeks, and had clearly-formulated goals. By the 17th century the missions, these Catholic "revivals," had proved so successful that they also began to be directed to towns and cities. The new orders—especially the Jesuits, Capuchins, and Vincentians—took the lead.[46]

Few words are more familiar to us today than "mission," for even businesses sometimes profess to have one. Until the 16th century, however, it was practically restricted even in religious circles to describing realities of the Blessed Trinity. The Jesuits helped recover and popularize the word to describe how their ministries were to be made operative, in imitation of the "sending" of the apostles, and in early Jesuit literature "mission" is sometimes synonymous with "journey" and "pilgrimage."[47] Not by stable office but by mission, or by perception of need, did one undertake one's ministry. By the 17th century the word had been taken up by other religious groups and entered our common vocabulary.

[45] See my contribution "Preaching," to appear in the encyclopedia of Jesuit history now being compiled at the Jesuit Historical Institute, Rome. See also Peter Bayley, "Preaching," in *Catholicism.*

[46] See, e.g., my "Preaching," and Jean Delumeau, *Catholicism between Luther and Voltaire: A New View of the Counter-Reformation* (Philadelphia: Westminster, 1977) 189–94.

[47] See my "To Travel"; Mario Scaduto, "La strada e i primi Gesuiti," *Archivum historicum Societatis Jesu* 40 (1971) 323–90; and esp. F. Bourdeau, "Le vocabulaire de la mission," *Parole et mission* 3 (1960) 9–27.

The best publicized, though not necessarily the best studied, ministry of the Jesuits was the network of schools they established, which by the early-17th century numbered over 400 spread around the globe. Despite the role the Church played in medieval institutions of learning, i.e. the universities, neither antiquity nor the Middle Ages knew anything like the "church-related" schools created by the Jesuits and others in the 16th and 17th centuries. Even these astounding facts are not so impressive, for our purposes, as the change in mentality they indicate. For the first time in history, conducting schools and teaching in them had now become a form of ministry, formally considered such in the Jesuit documents and in those of other orders and congregations that shared with them in the general enthusiasm.[48] A 16th-century source captured that enthusiasm in a few words: *Institutio puerorum, renovatio mundi.*[49]

By formalizing and putting method into certain religious practices as old as Christianity itself, or older, the orders and congregations of the 16th century in effect created new ministries and instruments of ministry in the area we sometimes today dub "ministries of interiority." Outstanding among these was the retreat, which we can with a certain qualification say was created by the Spiritual Exercises and the practice that followed upon them. The practice of spiritual direction became so widespread among the devout and reflection upon it entered such a new phase that it is almost a different reality from what the Middle Ages knew. The printing press offered, of course, occasion to continue all the genres known in the Middle Ages, but the upsurge in quantity of books of "spiritual reading," as well as apologetics against the Protestants in certain areas of Europe, indicates a new ministry in the making. The principal agents of all these changes were the religious orders and congregations.[50]

The Jesuits, like others, were also active in "social" ministries, founding and promoting programs or houses to assist catechumens, reformed prostitutes, the poor and the ill, orphans and others. Of special note here is the concern to engage laymen and laywomen in these projects. These laypersons were often asked to finance them, but, in keeping with late-medieval traditions, they also were expected to engage personally in providing certain services on a daily basis. They not only collaborated in their management but were generally expected to bear primary respon-

[48] See, e.g., Paul Grendler, "Schools, Seminaries, and Catechetical Instruction," in *Catholicism.*

[49] Said by Juan Bonifacio, S.J., as quoted in John W. Donahue, *Jesuit Education: An Essay on the Foundation of Its Idea* (New York: Fordham Univ., 1963) 186.

[50] See my "Early Jesuit Spirituality: Spain and Italy," forthcoming in *Christian Spirituality* 3, ed. Louis Dupré (New York: Crossroad).

sibility for their ongoing operation.[51]

The list of new or almost new ministries that the 16th century brought into being could be extended further and refined, but it is even more important to point out a general feature of much of it that finds clear articulation in the Jesuit documents. This feature concerns the persons among whom religious priests exercised their ministry. The list given in the Jesuit *Formula* is authoritative: ". . . among the Turks or any other infidels, even those who live in the region called the Indies, or among any heretics whatever, or schismatics, or any of the faithful."[52] The "missions" to infidels outside Europe date back to the mendicants in the 13th century, with St. Francis himself preaching before El-Kamil, the Sultan of Egypt. These missions powerfully expanded in the "Age of Discovery" in the 16th century, when the mendicants were now joined by the Jesuits and others. Moreover, the Reformation created a situation that gave special urgency to ministry among "heretics and schismatics."

Jerónimo Nadal, the contemporary and best interpreter of St. Ignatius, reduced the Jesuit list in effect to *anybody* in *need*, especially those who are neglected and have nobody to minister to them.[53] Thus Nadal interprets the Jesuits' famous Fourth Vow. That vow to go anywhere in the world, if sent, in order to do ministry dramatizes the basic assumption that Jesuit ministry is perhaps as far removed from the pattern of stable and local *officium* as it was possible to get. It seems clear, in fact, that in the Jesuit documents the itinerant Paul is the implicit model for ministry.[54] "From *Paul* to Ignatius" would be the title of the appropriate book on the subject.

Peter also figures in the vow, in fact more explicitly. This vow about doing ministry anywhere in the world specifies the bishop of Rome as the one who would send the Jesuit on this mission. In Jesuit sources the formality under which the pope is viewed in this context is precisely his more universal responsibility and, presumably, vision. That is, he will see beyond the local Church—or even beyond the Church altogether, for he should be more aware of infidels, heretics, pagans, and schismatics. The superior general of the Society of Jesus for the same reasons has the same kind of authority to "send" any of his subjects anywhere.

The Fourth Vow serves another function important for our purposes. It provides a clear indication that religious profession was not a link

[51] See, e.g., Ravier, *Loyola* 359.

[52] *Constitutions* 68 [4].

[53] See my "To Travel."

[54] Nadal in fact states: "Petrus firmitatem et directionem, Paulus nobis ministerium in Societate nostra significat, et adiuvat uterque ut Ecclesiae Princeps" (*Orationis observationes*, ed. Miguel Nicolau [Rome: Institutum Historicum Societatis Jesu, 1964] 151 [41]).

simply with "Pachomius" but also with ministry—even though that latter link was often not explicitly expressed in the formula of the vows or, as with the Jesuits, not generally understood in that way. Ignatius once called that vow "the principle and principal foundation" of the Society.[55] He did not exaggerate. Other religious institutes, in the Middle Ages and of course in modern times, have in fact also had "special" vows that related in similarly direct fashion to ministry.[56]

If the Jesuits embody and symbolize one aspect of Catholic Reform in the 16th century, the Council of Trent does the same for another. In 1975 Hubert Jedin completed his massive, masterful history of the Council, the culmination of a lifetime of research and of training students in the history of every aspect of the "Tridentine era."[57] We are now better informed about the Council than we have ever been. Given the immense obstacles we now see the Council had to overcome during the 18 years over which it stretched, its achievements seem even more brilliant.

This research has also, however, made us more aware of the limitations of the Council and has not yet answered every question about its immediate impact upon the Church. In other words, now that we have so much solid information about Trent, we are faced even more squarely with questions about how to assess it.[58] In this task, especially as it pertains to our purposes, it is important to recall again the two stated aims of the Council, which in fact continued to guide it through its tumultuous course: (1) "to confirm doctrine" and (2) "to reform morals."[59] In actual fact, both of these aims admitted further specification. "To confirm doctrine" meant to deal not with all doctrines but only those attacked by the Protestants and, as things almost inevitably worked out, practically in the terms of the attack. "To reform morals" was taken as synonymous with the older phrase "reform of the Church," which had by 1545 become too dangerous and ambiguous. Trent undertook "to reform morals" through certain juridical changes. Masked therefore under "reform of morals" were issues of church order, little aware though we have been of their importance until recently.

All this means that in a period in which Roman Catholicism was

[55] See my "The Fourth Vow" and Burkhart Schneider, "Nuestro Principio y principal Fundamento: Zum historischen Verständnis des Papstgehorsamsgelübdes," *Archivum historicum Societatis Jesu* 25 (1956) 488–513.

[56] See, e.g., Johannes Günter Gerhartz, *"Insuper Promitto . . .": Die feierlichen Sondergelübde katholischen Orden* (Rome: Gregoriana, 1966).

[57] *Geschichte des Konzils von Trient* (4 vols. in 5. Freiburg i/Br.: Herder, 1950–75). Only the first two volumes have been translated into English: *A History of the Council of Trent* (London: Thomas Nelson, 1957–61).

[58] See, e.g., Giuseppe Alberigo, "The Council of Trent," in *Catholicism.*

[59] Sessio IV (April 8, 1546), COD 664.

experiencing an explosion of ministerial initiatives that in their intensity and creativity were for any given period almost unprecedented, Trent took little or no notice. Part of the explanation lies in the fact that many of these initiatives were happening contemporaneously with the Council and came fully into their own only after the Council ended. But the more fundamental reason is the agenda of the Council itself. Trent mandated a catechism, but has not a word to say about retreats, spiritual reading, spiritual direction, social ministries, "missions"—even about evangelization of the various "Indies" that had been under way for a half century and would eventually change the face of Catholicism. One catches in Trent only the slightest mention of schools and "adult education."[60] Trent took notice of the printing press in its concern about the Index of Forbidden Books (also a creation of the 16th century), but never proposed that the press might become an instrument of ministry.[61]

Jedin judges that the vision underlying Trent's many decrees on reform was to transform bishops "from feudatories into pastors."[62] That is, from exploiters of benefices into ministers. One would expect to find, therefore, a great deal in Trent about *ministries*, but, as I indicated above, one finds very little. Some of this blindness surely stems from certain assumptions about the unchanging character of the Church—and therefore of its ministries—that blinds one to changes actually taking place. It is not at all clear, indeed, that even the creators of the new ministries were fully aware of how innovative they actually were.

Preaching is one ministry that receives attention in Trent, although the amount of space actually devoted to it is small in comparison with the totality of the Council's decrees and canons. Trent's designation of preaching as the *praecipuum munus* of the bishop had great impact upon Carlo Borromeo and a few other reforming bishops, and hence contributed significantly to the general revival of this form of ministry of the word of God.[63] If we lacked this subsequent history about Borromeo and his likes, however, the lines from Trent on preaching could almost escape our notice. Moreover, Trent seemed to mean "preaching" in a most conventional sense and gives no hints as to how even this ministry might

[60] See Sessio V (June 17, 1546), ibid. 667–70. On this rather ineffective decree, see Jedin, *Trent* 2, 99–124.

[61] Sessio XVIII (Feb. 26, 1562), COD 723–24, and Sessio XXV (Dec. 3, 1563), ibid. 797.

[62] With Giuseppe Alberigo, *La figura ideale del vescovo secondo la Riforma cattolica* (2nd ed. Brescia: Paideia, 1985).

[63] Sessio XXIV (Nov. 11, 1563), canon 4, COD 763. On preaching see also Sessio V (June 17, 1546), ibid. 667–70. On Borromeo see my "Saint Charles Borromeo and the *Praecipuum episcoporum munus*: His Place in the History of Preaching," forthcoming in *San Carlo Borromeo: Catholic Reform and Ecclesiastical Politics in the Second Half of the Sixteenth Century*, ed. John Headley (Washington, D.C.: University Press of America).

be revived by new methods and techniques, subjects that in fact had already been greatly discussed "in the field" for decades.[64]

Since Trent felt obliged by the Protestant attack to deal with all the sacraments, it had occasion to deal with ministry when it considered the sacrament of orders.[65] In that decree, however, ministry is in effect not mentioned. For Trent the sacrament of orders relates to office and hierarchy, and it confers the power to administer the sacraments, most especially to confect the Eucharist.

Two features of the decree deserve comment. First, the correlation that we saw in Isidore among *officium*, ritual, and both major and minor orders had persisted up through Trent. In answering the Protestant challenge to the sacrament of orders, Trent in the process accepted, as it almost inevitably had to, older formulations and assumptions about the nature of priesthood. Secondly, the decree falls among the *doctrinal* decrees of Trent. Thus, what Trent is dealing with is the *idea* of what orders or priesthood is, without any attempt to correlate that idea with the living reality. This dichotomy between doctrine and practice manifests itself even in Trent, for in its *reform* decrees preaching and pastoral governance were taken into account.[66]

Although the correlation office-orders-ritual has even older roots, the specific identification of priesthood with the power to confect the Eucharist received a classic formulation with Saint Peter Damian, one of the Gregorian reformers of the 11th century.[67] Damian's identification is not surprising, since he lived in the monastic age that for all practical purposes knew no ministry, only liturgy. The model of the Church as sacrament never found fuller expression in social reality, for instance, than in the elaborate liturgies of Cluny.

[64] See, e.g., my "Content and Rhetorical Form in Sixteenth-Century Treatises on Preaching," in *Renaissance Eloquence*, ed. James J. Murphy (Berkeley: Univ. of California, 1983) 238–52, and now especially Debora Shuger, *Sacred Rhetoric: The Christian Grand Style in the English Renaissance* (Princeton: Princeton Univ., 1988).

[65] Sessio XXIII (July 15, 1563), COD 742–44.

[66] See Schillebeeckx, *Human Face* 197–201, and the perceptive article, with ample bibliography, by Severino Dianich, "La teologia del presbiterato al Concilio di Trento," *Scuola cattolica* 99 (1971) 331–58. See also Alexandre Ganoczy, "'Splendours and Miseries' of the Tridentine Doctrine of Ministries," in *Concilium* 80 (New York: Herder and Herder, 1972) 75–86.

[67] See his *Liber gratissimus*, c. 15 (PL 145, 118). See also Yves Congar, *L'Eglise: De s. Augustin à l'époque moderne* (Paris: Cerf, 1970) 170–71, and his "Modèle monastique et modèle sacerdotal en occident de Grégoire VII (1073–1085) à Innocent III (1198)," in his *Etudes d'ecclésiologie médiévale* (London: Variorum, 1983) IX. Congar's observation is apposite (158): "Il me semble que les XIIIe–XVe siècles aient été une époque essentiellement 'cléricale,' non au sens des problèmes politiques qui sont liés au cléricalisme, mais en ce sense qu'alors le Catholicisme est essentiellement religion du sacrement."

More surprising is that Aquinas' *Summa theologiae* two centuries later in effect repeats the identification—so strong is the force of tradition—when it speaks of the sacrament of orders. No correlation is made with Thomas' own priesthood as a member of a religious order whose priests by definition were "preachers."[68] It is significant that only when Thomas discusses religious life does he deal with ministries—in particular the ministries of preaching and hearing confessions, which he notes that both religious and "presbyteri curati" do.[69] When he treats of bishops, he recognizes in them an office grounded on the care of souls, but in effect he identifies this care more with *regimen* than with any direct ministry.[70] What is especially pertinent for us, however, is that Aquinas correlates ministry with certain forms of religious life rather than with the sacrament of orders per se.

The documents of the Council of Trent advert to the fact that religious were doing ministry, and tried to assure that this ministry be properly supervised. Nonetheless, the specific decree "Concerning Regulars and Nuns" deals practically exclusively with discipline internal to the orders and their houses, i.e. with matters pertaining ultimately to the personal holiness of the members, which betrays a mentality that will still view religious as essentially in the Pachomian tradition.[71]

At Lateran IV in the early 13th century the abbots far outnumbered the bishops. At Trent there were practically no abbots present, and for all practical purposes the only voting members were bishops. These simple facts already suggest that Trent would be a bishops' council, and, as I indicated earlier, a large number of reform decrees looked directly to the episcopacy—in an effort to "reform their morals" but also to enhance their authority. Trent knew no other way to accomplish these two goals than by creating and/or implementing certain juridical structures.

Were these goals for the episcopacy ever accomplished? In the long, long run there were surely some successes, and at least "on the books" episcopal authority in many areas was more fully postulated than ever before. As is well known, however, the authority that the Council in fact most strongly promoted, although only indirectly and beyond its intention, was that of the papacy.[72] Once again here we see how misleading official documents can be, for the authority of the papacy was never

[68] Suppl., qq. 34–40. Although the Supplement was not written by Thomas, it generally represents his thinking on a given issue, and even more surely that of his age; see, e.g., *Sum. theol.* 3, 82, 1.

[69] *Sum. theol.* 3, 188, 4; see also 2–2, 184, 6 and 8.

[70] Ibid. 2-2, 185. He does, however, implicitly recognize preaching, ibid., a. 6, ad 2.

[71] Sessio XXV (Dec. 3–4, 1563), COD 776–84.

[72] See, e.g., Alberigo, "Trent," and his "L'Episcopato nel cattolicismo post-tridentino," *Cristianesimo nella storia* 6 (1985) 71–91.

directly treated at Trent and, indeed, debate over the precise nature and extent of that authority came within a hair's breadth of utterly destroying the Council in 1563.[73]

As Trent treated of bishops and tried to strengthen their authority in their dioceses, it attempted to do the same for pastors and their parishes. These latter institutions were, after all, the articulation of the diocese. This aspect of the Council has generally received little notice, for to our contemporary way of thinking it seems to say little that is noteworthy, so generally has it been accepted. John Bossy has in recent years, however, repeatedly called attention to this phenomenon and has heavily criticized it for imposing on the Church a pattern of "parochial conformity." Such an effectively prescriptive pattern was unknown in the Middle Ages, when the pastoral machinery was more complex, variegated, and, according to Bossy, more integrated into the "natural" fabric of life.[74] Bossy sees the change as ultimately detrimental to religious practice.

Just when and why a pattern of "parochial conformity" took hold are questions that are not easy to answer; yet the answers must range beyond the legislation of Trent in order to be adequate. However, there can be no doubt, in my opinion, that by its decrees the Council set the Church on a long journey that by the 20th century meant that when people thought of "church" they thought of "parish," when they thought of "priest" they thought of "pastor." In the Middle Ages being enrolled in one's confraternity was sufficient to ensure Christian burial, just as that enrollment provided spiritual nourishment in the company of one's peers and professional "kin" during life. That is to say, from the sixth century even until long after the Council of Trent the parish church was only one element in a vast and lumbering array of other institutions like monasteries, priories, shrines, manor chapels, oratories, guilds, confraternities, third orders, sodalities, schools, and collegiate churches (to which list "retreat houses" would at a certain point be added) where in one way or another Christians satisfied their devotion. These institutions were, like the sect-type itself, "voluntary." Perhaps for that reason they were able to evoke engagement and thus help impart to medieval Christianity such vitality. The shift in church order that Trent legislated and promoted in this regard would obviously have immense impact, in time, on how and where persons would normatively—even obligatorily—be ministered unto and on what religious opportunities would generally be

[73] See Hubert Jedin, *Crisis and Closure of the Council of Trent* (London: Sheed and Ward, 1967).

[74] See esp. his "The Counter Reformation and the People of Catholic Europe," *Past and Present*, no. 47 (May 1970) 51–70. See also now the important article by Alberigo, "The Local Church."

open to them. The Code of Canon Law of 1917, and again of 1983, developed along the same lines.

VATICAN COUNCIL II

After Trent it was not until four centuries later that a council would once again deal with episcopacy, priesthood, and religious life. Vatican II believed itself to be in continuity with Trent on these issues, and to a considerable extent it surely was. In some ways, however, the differences are more striking than the similarities. The fathers of Vatican II spoke out of their experience of the Church of the 20th century, which, partly because of the long-range impact of Trent, was much different from the Church of the sixteenth. Moreover, the fathers of Vatican II, practically all of whom were bishops or their equivalent, had through their theologians perspectives, especially some historical perspectives, that Trent lacked. From these two frameworks of past and present they constructed models of episcopacy, priesthood, and religious life. These models or ideals they presented as such in clear, though often quite general, terms.

Precisely in the terms, or rhetoric, lies one of the great differences between Trent and Vatican II.[75] In its reform decrees Trent's language is invariably juridical. To discover the "ideal bishop" of the fathers at Trent, one must extract and reconstruct it from hundreds of juridical details. Vatican II, on the other hand, presented goals and idealized models. These goals and ideals were generally painted in the broadest possible terms, so as to include all. Two problems arise, however, from this approach. First, the ideal, general though it may be, does not always seem adequate to every situation. Secondly, these ideals sometimes imply or allow certain assumptions about church order or changes within it, but do not clearly state them. These two problems have sometimes been rendered more obvious by official documents issued after the Council than they were in the decrees of the Council itself, so these must also be given some consideration if we are to understand the present situation. For the sake of clarity and conciseness, however, I will gather what I have to say under the rubric of the documents of the Council that treat most directly of the issues that concern us.

Perfectae caritatis has provoked much discussion and even controversy over how to implement its injunction to religious to make changes in

[75] On the rhetoric of Vatican II, see my "Developments, Reforms, and Two Great Reformations: Towards a Historical Assessment of Vatican II," *TS* 44 (1983) 373–406.

their institutes while remaining faithful to their original charism.[76] The sources for the disagreements over how to interpret the decree in this regard are many and complex, but surely one of the most fundamental is the very framework in which the Council presents religious life. It is the framework of the three vows. It is the framework of the personal search for spiritual perfection (presumably enhanced in some cases with the additional adornment of ministry). It is the framework of from-Pa-chomius-to-Ignatius. Yet today we must ask: Does the traditional way of *interpreting* religious life fully correspond to the *tradition* of religious life?

Of the 25 sections of *Perfectae caritatis*, only two (nos. 8 and 20) are devoted to ministry.[77] Yet the Dominicans and the Jesuits—to name only some of the best-known and clearest examples—were founded precisely to do ministry. Indeed, to do ministry in quite special ways. But the framework in which *Perfectae caritatis* was conceived makes it impossible for it to take adequate account of this absolutely basic consideration. The postconciliar *Essentials of Religious Life* makes the problem even more manifest.[78] That document has been criticized for reducing religious life to a monastic model. The more general weakness, however, is that it implies that religious life, as we have generally known it since the 13th century, can be reduced to "the three vows." Absolutely constitutive though these vows are, they do not directly express the full reality.

Presbyterorum ordinis has not received much attention since the Council, but it is an important document.[79] Unlike Trent, it makes a clear correlation between priesthood and ministry. It also attempts, not altogether successfully, to break the identification of priesthood with confection of the Eucharist and states that "it is the first task of priests"

[76] For the history of the decree and commentaries, see *L'Adaptation et la rénovation de la vie religieuse: Décret "Perfectae Caritatis,"* ed. J. M. R. Tillard and Y. Congar (Paris: Cerf, 1967), and Friedrich Wulf, "Decree on the Appropriate Renewal of Religious Life," in *Commentary on the Documents of Vatican II*, ed. Herbert Vorgrimler (5 vols. New York: Herder and Herder, 1967–69) 2, 301–70. Two especially important treatments of the general problem are John M. Lozana, *Discipleship: Towards an Understanding of Religious Life* (Chicago: Claret Center, 1980), and Sandra M. Schneiders, *New Wineskins: Re-imaging Religious Life Today* (New York: Paulist, 1986).

[77] See the comments on these two sections by Wulf, *Commentary* 2, 352–53.

[78] The English text is in *Origins*, 13 (1983) 133–42, document dated May 31, 1983.

[79] For the history of the document and commentary, see *Les prêtres: Décrets "Presbyterorum ordinis" et "Optatam totius,"* ed. J. Frisque et Y. Congar (Paris: Cerf, 1968), and Friedrich Wulf et al., "Decree on the Ministry and Life of Priests," *Commentary* 4, 183–297. See also *Los presbíteros: A los diez años de "Presbyterorum ordinis,"* Teología del sacerdocio, no. 7 (Burgos: Ediciones Aldecoa, 1975), and Brian Charles Foley, "*De cura animarum*: A Voice for the Priesthood," in *Vatican II Revisited by Those Who Were There*, ed. Alberic Stacpoole (Minneapolis: Winston, 1986) 255–69.

to preach the gospel.[80] Moreover, while utilizing the triad priest-prophet-king to describe the function of "presbyters," it redefines those terms to integrate them into a more collaborative perspective than they directly indicate.[81]

Nonetheless, despite its many fine features and the good intentions that prompted it, religious must not be unmindful of the challenges it delivers to them. The document presents an ideal and a model of priesthood—a construct. This construct is based, first, on the analogue of the contemporary diocesan clergy. Secondly, the normative model that is operative, I suggest, is the patristic Church, as is somewhat indicated by the number of references to patristic documents.[82] The Church that Ambrose and Augustine knew was a close-knit community of clergy around their bishop, ministering by word and sacrament to a stable community of the faithful in the rather-well-defined world of the Christian emperors. That Church and world are, however, far different from anything we have known since at least the sixth century even, in my opinion, up to today. From what biblical scholars tell us, it also seems to be different in many respects from the Church, or churches, that we find in parts of the New Testament.

As I mentioned earlier, *Presbyterorum ordinis* makes three basic assumptions about the priest-minister.[83] The first concerns the place and structure of ministry. Although it is not always explicitly stated, the document presupposes as normative that the priest-minister will deal with a *stable* community, in which, moreover, a regular rhythm of liturgies of word and sacrament will be celebrated. The word "parish" is seldom mentioned, but the idea is omnipresent. At least by implication, the parish is normative for ministry.

The second assumption is almost a corollary. The stable community is composed of the *faithful*. Some notice is taken of what the Council elsewhere says about evangelization, ecumenism, and the manifold issues raised about "the Church in the modern world," but it is almost perfunctory.[84] The priest-minister of *Presbyterorum ordinis* will deal with the faithful, and his training as proposed in *Optatam totius* will be designed to prepare him precisely for that flock.

The third assumption relates to church order. The priest-minister is

[80] *PO*, no. 4. For a detailed comparison of *PO* with Trent, see *Les prêtres* 193–232.

[81] See *PO*, nos. 4–6. On the origins of the triad, see now Peter J. Drilling, "The Priest, Prophet and King Trilogy," to appear in *Eglise et théologie* (1988).

[82] See *Les prêtres* 376–77.

[83] These three assumptions also clearly undergird *Lumen gentium*, no. 28, which was foundational for *PO*. See *Les prêtres* 138.

[84] *PO*, no. 4, best indicates awareness of the necessity of evangelization.

in hierarchical communion with his bishop. The remote model from which this assumption derives seems, again, to be the patristic Church, and it suggests an appealing collaboration and co-ordination between the bishop and his clergy. But we must not miss how repeatedly this document, as well as others, returns to the relationship between bishop and priest, almost to the point of defining the priest-minister through that relationship. *Optatam totius* goes so far as to speak of the priest as participating in "the hierarchical priesthood of Christ," an intriguing notion.[85]

At this point it is hardly necessary to point out how difficult it is to reconcile these assumptions with the traditions of ministry in most of the religious orders. That ministry was not structured with an eye to a local and stable community, as symbolized by the parish, but transcended diocese and even nation—"to go anywhere in the world," as the Jesuit *Constitutions* say. Although all the orders ministered to the faithful, they had a special interest in heretics, schismatics, infidels. It was not without good grounding in tradition, for instance, that Pope John Paul II in his allocution opening the 33rd General Congregation of the Society of Jesus, September 2, 1983, especially commended to the Jesuits ministries like "ecumenism, the deeper study of relations with non-Christian religions, and the dialogue of the Church with cultures," and "the evangelizing action of the Church to promote justice, connected with world peace."[86]

Even among the faithful, religious orders and congregations have tended to have a special interest in those whom the ordinary ministry of the Church for one reason or another failed to reach: orphans, young vagrants, prostitutes, the "alienated"—or, on the other hand, those laity seeking to devote themselves to God and their neighbor in more challenging and unconventional ways. Moreover, their "instruments of ministry" showed an ingenuity that carried them beyond the rhythm of word and sacrament in the usual senses of those terms. Finally, the priests of the great orders had no hierarchical relationship with the ordinary of the place, but had a fraternal, or capitular, or "sect-type" relationship with their own ordinary.

This brings us to *Christus Dominus*, the decree on the pastoral office of bishops in the Church.[87] As adjusted to the bishops, the same three assumptions are operative as in *Presbyterorum ordinis*. The bishop

[85] *OT*, no. 2, "ad Christi Sacerdotium hierarchicum."

[86] This English version is found in *Documents of the 33rd General Congregation of the Society of Jesus* (St. Louis: Institute of Jesuit Sources, 1984) 77–84, esp. 81–82.

[87] For the history of the document and commentary, see W. Onclin et al., *La charge pastorale des évêques: Décret "Christus Dominus"* (Paris: Cerf, 1969), and Klaus Mörsdorf, "Decree on the Bishops' Pastoral Office in the Church," *Commentary* 2, 165–300.

presides over a local community, of the faithful, in hierarchical communion with the bishop of Rome. The convergence of these three elements manifests in a striking degree certain elements of the "church-type," for it projects a ministry based on office, on well-defined and normative functions, on authority that is clearly articulated and regulatory, and on the maintenance of faith and order. Although these elements have been traditionally associated with the office of bishop, they had never before been pulled together in precisely the same way and, of course, never before presented to the Church with the authority of a council. In comparison with these broad strokes in Vatican II, the "ideal bishop" of Trent seems lost in a myriad of juridical detail.

Nonetheless, underneath what often seem to be bland generalizations, *Christus Dominus* deals with church order in just as significant a way as the legislation of Trent. It projects a vision of church order that has raised a number of complex questions, as our newspapers seem to testify almost daily, but that in a number of instances seem fraught with special consequences for religious. The document states, for instance: "All priests, whether diocesan or religious, share and exercise with the bishop the one priesthood of Christ. They are thus constituted providential co-operators of this episcopal order."[88] The paragraph goes on to assert: "The diocesan clergy have, however, a [the] primary role in the care of souls because, being incardinated in or appointed to a particular church, they are wholly dedicated in its service to the care of a particular section of the Lord's flock, and accordingly form one priestly body and one family of which the bishop is father."[89] Pastors of parishes hold first place among the collaborators with the bishops in the care of souls.[90]

If "care of souls" (*cura animarum*) is taken in the technical and canonical sense, nothing new is being said here, for in that sense *cura animarum* refers to the office that has traditionally belonged to the diocesan clergy, especially pastors. Nonetheless, the groundwork seems to have been laid for a generalization made later about religious priests that relates priesthood as such to the episcopacy: "Religious priests, who have been raised to the priesthood to be prudent co-operators with the episcopal order, . . . may be said in a certain sense to belong to the clergy of the diocese inasmuch as they share in the care of souls and in the

[88] *CD*, no. 28. The second sentence is taken from the Preface of the ordination of priests. See the important qualifications by Mörsdorf, *Commentary* 2, 256.

[89] *CD*, no. 28. The Latin seems clearly to indicate the definite article for English, whereas the edition by Flannery (580) employs the indefinite: "In animarum autem cura procuranda primas partes habent sacerdotes diocesani . . . ."

[90] *CD*, no. 30: "Praecipua autem ratione Episcopi cooperatores sunt parochi, quibus, tamquam pastoribus propriis, animarum cura committitur in determinata dioecesis parte sub illius auctoritate."

practice of apostolic works under the authority of the bishop."[91] Just a few lines later a crucial and logical consequence is drawn for religious, and probably more directly for their superiors: "Furthermore, religious should comply promptly and faithfully with the requests or desires of bishops when they are asked to undertake a greater share in the ministry of salvation (*salutis humanae ministerium*)."[92] "Ministry of salvation" seems to have become here a synonym for "care of souls."

The following propositions, though crudely put, summarize this aspect of *Christus Dominus*. There is one priesthood, which cannot be defined apart from the "episcopal order." That priesthood is concerned with the "care of souls," which has meant and still seems to mean primarily the ministry of pastors of parishes under the bishop. Although religious orders of priests have in former times on occasion been forbidden such "care of souls," or, like the Jesuits, have themselves explicitly renounced it in favor of other ministries,[93] they now seem by virtue of their ordination almost to be destined for it. There seems to be, moreover, at least a suggestion that all "ministry of salvation" is reducible to "care of souls."

I would maintain, therefore, that for all their merit *Christus Dominus*, *Presyterorum ordinis*, and *Optatam totius* do not take into sufficient account the tradition of ministry and priesthood in the religious orders. The Council could not take this tradition properly into account because the history of it had not yet been done, or at least not done in a helpful way, for reflection on the nature of religious life was always encased in the from-Pachomius-to-Ignatius framework. This means that in effect the Council had little choice but to reduce religious life to the practice of certain forms of spirituality, some more "active" than others. When religious do ministry, they may enhance it with a special "spirit," but for all practical purposes they function as diocesan priests.

Confirmation of this interpretation can be seen in what the Council says about the exempt status of some religious. It asserts that the privilege of exemption from the jurisdiction of bishops "relates primarily to the internal organization of the institutes ... [so that] the perfection of religious life [is] promoted."[94] That was surely the sole purpose of the first exemptions of Cluny in the tenth century, but beginning with the 13th the most impressive privileges of the orders related directly to ministry. The great orders of mendicants, for instance, each had their

[91] *CD*, no. 34. The convoluted explanation that Mörsdorf gives of no. 34 indicates the complexity of the issues (*Commentary* 2, 266–68).

[92] *CD*, no. 35.

[93] *Constitutions*, nos. 324, 325, 588.

[94] *CD*, no. 35.

so-called *mare magnum*, their comprehensive grants of pastoral prerogatives. Moreover, even the "internal organization" of these and subsequent orders was directed to a large extent to ministry. The programs of study and formation themselves were not directed to "the love of learning and the desire for God" as in the monastic tradition, but towards more effective ministry.[95]

CONCLUSION

By this point I hope to have established at least that there are other possible ways of looking at the history of ministry and priesthood, of church order and reform, of spirituality and religious life itself. I would, moreover, contend that our more systematic reflection on these issues will be significantly hampered, even blocked, until we devise for them more adequate historical frameworks. Two items on this agenda are most urgent. First, we must try to achieve a better integration among themselves of all these aspects of church life which until now have to a large extent been treated separately and, in some cases, almost as if they had no relationship to one another. Such an integration would take special note of the millennium and a half between the end of the patristic period and the opening of Vatican II.

The second item would be to study all these aspects most diligently as they manifest themselves in the *life* of the Church. In other words, we must not look so exclusively to what the Church *said* about these issues as to how it has in fact *acted*. Besides its other merits, such a shift would bring scholarship into better conformity with what the Council itself implicitly enjoined with its profound statement in *Dei verbum*: "What was handed on by the apostles comprises everything that serves to make the People of God live their lives in holiness and increase their faith. In this way the Church in her doctrine, *life*, and worship perpetuates and transmits to every generation *all that she herself is*, all that she believes."[96]

We must, in any case, reckon that even religious geniuses like Dominic, Francis, and Ignatius may not have been fully capable of expressing what they were doing or hoped to do, so that that expression must confront their actions in the long context of the traditions in which they moved. For all their merits, to give another instance, the decrees of the Council of Trent do not tell us everything we need to know about ministry and priesthood in the 16th century. In fact, on these points the decrees are unwittingly but decidedly misleading.

[95] See my "The Houses of Study of Religious Orders and Congregations: An Historical Sketch," in Katarina Schuth's study of the future of Roman Catholic theologates, forthcoming (Wilmington, Del.: Glazier, 1988).

[96] No. 8, emphasis mine.

Studies along the lines I am proposing are not just an academic exercise. I believe that they have important repercussions not only on how "regular priests" think about themselves, and therefore are trained and pursue their ministries, but on other groups and on the Church at large. For all the confusion and complexity that encumber the issues treated in this article, confusion and complexity so profound that I have hardly been able to touch the surface, some rather specific conclusions have emerged.[97] In closing, the following considerations seem to me especially pertinent.

1. In the vast majority of orders and congregations founded since the 13th century, ministry has been at the center of their self-understanding. Definitions and descriptions of religious life that fail to take full account of this indisputable fact are, no matter what their other merits, misleading and harmful.

2. There have been at least since that time two quite distinct traditions of ministry that have given shape to the reality of priesthood in the Church. Both can claim legitimacy in the New Testament and in the long history of the Church. Both have served people's spiritual (and sometimes material) needs. Although different spiritualities have certainly animated them, these two traditions cannot be reduced simply to differences in spirituality. Moreover, while tensions have always existed between them and have sometimes erupted into ugly and disedifying battles, the genius of Catholicism up to the present has been its ability to contain them both within itself and not settle for neat resolutions or a single church order for ministry.

3. Although there has been considerable and healthy overlap, a sort of "division of labor" has in fact prevailed between diocesan and regular clergy over the course of the centuries. The "local" or diocesan clergy has ministered primarily to the faithful according to time-honored rhythms of word and especially sacrament. Religious, when they ministered to the faithful, did so in these ways but also particularly in others that were more appropriate to special groups and circumstances: through schools or soup kitchens, through retreats or running houses for reformed prostitutes, through books and journals, or through street preaching and "revivals." This division of labor has taken the religious even further afield, away from the "faithful," in order to minister in some fashion or other to heretics, schismatics, infidels, pagans, and public sinners.

[97] What I have proposed in this article both clarifies and obscures, e.g., conclusions reached in documents like *The Ministry in the Church*, Roman Catholic/Lutheran Joint Commission (Geneva: Lutheran World Federation, 1982), and "Ministry and Ordination" (1973), in *The Final Report*, Anglican-Roman Catholic International Commission (Washington, D.C.: U.S. Catholic Conference, 1982) 29–39.

4. The division of labor is not an accident of history. It reflects the two traditions that over the course of the centuries have manifested themselves with uneven beat but with considerable consistency in ways that can only be suggested here. The vocabulary, for instance, is different. On the one hand, words like "office" and "parish" recur, while on the other we find "need" and "mission." "Hierarchy" predominates in one, whereas "fraternity" or its equivalent is found in the other. For the one, "apostolic" indicates a conduit of authority; for the other, it suggests a style of life and ministry. For the first, ministry seems modeled on the Pastoral Epistles, the letters of Ignatius of Antioch, and the examples of Ambrose and Augustine. For the second, it seems modeled on Jesus and his disciples in the Synoptics, the itinerant Paul of his letters and Acts, and the example of the charismatic layman (later deacon) Francis. In the one instance, the model of the Church as sacrament seems especially operative; in the other, the Church as herald. The former relates more easily to "priest"—celebrant for the community and its public servant; the latter more easily to "prophet"—spokesperson and agent for special points of view. The first generally corresponds to the "church-type," the second to the "sect-type."

5. With the bishops and the diocesan clergy the force of that first tradition is today as strong as ever, perhaps stronger. Even more than ever is it being taken as normative and in some cases, indeed, as the tradition that admits no alternative. Its central concern is still, and by the very nature of the case seems destined to remain, ministry to a *stable* community of the *faithful.* The *parish* is thus the locus of ministry par excellence.

6. It can reasonably be argued that, if such a tradition and viewpoint should utterly prevail, it would lead not to an enrichment but to an improverishment of the Church and its larger mission. "Special" ministries, which religious can by reason of tradition and interest rightly claim as peculiarly their own, seem more needed today than ever. They will, of course, take different forms than in the past in many cases, and they require more imagination and daring than seem commonly to be expended upon them. But even among the faithful, many persons seem to be falling through the cracks of "normative" ministry, at least in Western Europe and North America. Here lies the challenge for religious today.

7. Again: if such a tradition and viewpoint should utterly prevail, it would in time deprive the vast majority of religious of the center and meaning of their lives. Ministry is not something one adds to one's vocation as a Franciscan or Jesuit upon ordination to the priesthood, but something that was central and intrinsic from one's very first moment in the order, no matter how imperfectly this might be expressed by the

ceremony of the vows.

8. Does not the teaching of Vatican II on the sensitive subjects with which this article has dealt need to be reviewed and enlarged? A subtle and implicit historiographical grid that seems to be widely operative in the Church today suggests that the Council has, after centuries of confusion, finally said the last word on all subjects, including these. But is this not a prideful bias towards the present that ignores the richness of the past and the potential of the future? Is it not far even from the intent of the Council itself?

9. Do we not need, therefore, especially to recover the pragmatic approach to ministry that current historiography is showing happily characterized our past, but that today seems to be ever more effectively smothered by the "normative" or by some idealized model? The abstract ideal can deliver death as well as life. In the mainline Churches—Protestant and Catholic—ennui, respectability, and dull liturgies and ministries hold sway in all too many places. It is not our "fidelity" that today needs testing, but our creativity.

10. The future of ministry in the Church is hidden in the mind of God—perhaps hidden more effectively than it has ever been. How do the laity figure into this future, how do women religious? Does religious life itself have a future? These are questions none of us can answer with any certainty. But we can try to think more adequately, and then act more appropriately, in relationship to priesthood, ministry, church order, and religious life as we actually have these institutions today.

INDEX